AF538908

SALES PROMOTION MANAGEMENT

Sales Promotion Management

Bir Singh

ANMOL PUBLICATIONS PVT. LTD.
NEW DELHI - 110 002 (INDIA)

ANMOL PUBLICATIONS PVT. LTD.
H.O.: 4374/4B, Ansari Road, Darya Ganj,
New Delhi-110 002 (India)
Ph.: 23278000, 23261597

B.O.: No. 1015, Ist Main Road, BSK IIIrd Stage
IIIrd Phase, IIIrd Block,
Bangalore - 560 085 (India)
Visit us at: www.anmolpublications.com

Sales Promotion Management

© Reserved

First Published, 2006

[Responsibility for the facts stated, opinions expressed, conclusions reached and plagiarism, if any, in this book is entirely that of the Author. The Publishers bear no responsibility for them, whatsoever.]

PRINTED IN INDIA

Printed at Mehra Offset Press, Delhi.

Contents

Preface

"Sales Promotion Management" as a paper is being taught at M.Com., M.B.A. and Other Management Courses at various universities and institutions. This book is designed as an introductory text to the above paper, encompassing vital information on all pertinent aspects. Thus the material presented here would be of interest as well as of great use to the students, teachers and professionals of Management Courses. This book will provide complete knowledge of sales promotion, personnel selling, consumer behaviour, deal prone consumer research, sales planning, evaluation and apraisal of sales personnel, product decision in sales promotion, secrets of sales performance, retailer and wholesaler promotion process, trade dealings, etc. to the students.

The major topics dealt in this book are—Sales Promotion; Promotional Mix and Personnel Selling; Consumer Behaviour and Sales Promotion; Deal Prone Consumer Research; Strategy of Sales Planning; Performance Evaluation and Apraisal; Effective Sales Personnel; Evaluation of Sales Promotion Experiment; Product Decision in Sales Promotion; Secrets of Sales Performance; Retailer and Wholesaler Promotion Process; Strategic Issues in Promotional Strategies; Substantive Findings in Trade Dealings etc.

It is hoped that all those will benefit from the contents of this book for whom it is meant. The author will feel amply rewarded, if motive is achieved.

Editor

1

Sales Promotion

A simpler way of viewing sales promotion is to say that it means special offers. Special in the sense that they are extra as well as because they are specific in time or place: *offers* in the sense that they are direct propositions, the acceptance of which forms a deal. As in most aspects of marketing, the rationale of sales promotion is to provide a direct stimulus to produce a desired response by customers. It is not clear, however, what the distinctions are between sales promotion and advertising, personal selling, and publicity.

Promotional advertising is the communication of ideas about a firm and its products through the standard commercial media. Some of the content of advertising messages may well be sales promotion in character. Public relations involves the installation and maintenance of mutual understanding between a firm and all who are likely to come into contact with it. Very little of the make-up of public relations concerns sales promotions, although it can spread the news of a successful scheme by insuring that it gets editorial mention, for instance. Quite often, however, as in the case of fairs and house journals, the borderline between sales promotion and public relations becomes obscure. Another area where the boundary is not so clear is that of involving product and pricing tactics. Suppose that Nestle decides to tape three packs of their Maggie Noodles canned biscuits together and sells them for a price slightly cheaper than three sold individually. Is this a banded multipack special offer and therefore promotional? In order or is it just an example of a *giantsized* economy pack and therefore a product or packaging tactic? In order to sort out which it is, the question has to be asked "Is it intended to be a permanent feature of the manufacturer's product policy to have the family pack as a component of the product?" If it is not, it is a sales promotion scheme.

The same sort of problem comes up when studying strategies run by firms in service industries. If a hotel offers cut-price accommodations at off peak-times of the year, is it a feature of the hotel management's pricing policy or is it a promotional tactic? If the hotel management provides price reductions on tickets to local theatres for their guests, is it part of the product or is it a device to attract customers for a limited period only? Again, the answer can only be given once the question about permanence is asked. Although industries such as food, drink tobacco, car, soap and detergent, pharmaceutical, domestic appliance, and oil are the best-known users of sales promotion, they are by no means the only ones. The aircraft manufacturing, ship-building, engineering, chemical, and retailing industries are also great sales promoters, even though they may not all be great advertisers. Sales promotion is not just confined to consumer goods, although it appears to be more widely used with consumer goods as the casual observer seldom comes into contact with capital goods firms and so tends to think that these techniques are confined to firms making goods sold to the ultimate consumer. There is little doubt that a growth of sales promotion has been quite substantial during recent years. On an average 20-30 per cent of typical company's promotional budget give towards sales promotion.

There are several possible factors that may have contributed to this dramatic growth.

1. There is a greater acceptance by top management of sales promotion as a sales-generating device.
2. Product managers have learned to implement sales promotion as part of their overall product strategy.

4. Inflation and other economic factors have made the appeals of sales promotion more attractive to the average consumer.

3. There is increased pressure on management to show a faster return on the promotional investment, which sales promotion can do.

5. These same factors have brought greater pressure from middle agents for sales promotion deals.

6. The increased competitive situation has forced companies to look for new advantages in the form of sales promotion.

As will become apparent later, many forms of sales promotion exist. Consequently, it is virtually impossible to establish a standardized set of reasons or objectives that apply to all sales promotion. While the intent of running a Rupees-off coupon in a local newspaper is intended to stimulate product purchase, free marketing research provided to a wholesaler may have an entirely different purpose. Suffice it to say that the ultimate objective to all sales promotion is to positively influence sales either directly or indirectly.

Yet there is a benefit in delineating the advantages sales promotion can offer the marketing manager. Perhaps the greatest strength of sales promotion is that it can be effectively, employed by businesses of all sizes. Because sales promotion devices can be relatively inexpensive and easily customized, sales promotion can be used by the smallest of marketers. For example, a small gift shop can easily employ gift vouchers, free samples, special offers, or double-stamp days if they see fit. Businesses is their creative skills in designing an appropriate sales promotion vehicle.

A second advantage in using sales promotion is its effectiveness in highly competitive market situations. Today, there are extensive choices available to each buyer, not only between brands of the same type of product, but between different types of products providing the same sort of satisfaction. Competition works itself out in the market place and particularly at the point of sales where the final deals are made and the act of exchange takes place. It is at the point of sale that a homemaker may actually made her decision on which toilet paper to buy, or a managing director decides whether to accept the terms and conditions of sale of a multi thousand-pound deal involving capital equipment that will be consumed over many years.

The third advantage for sales promotion is closely aligned with the tremendous increase in capital investment found in most industries. Because so many companies are capital intensive today, it is critical that economies of scale be reached in production as soon as possible. As a result, very high levels of production have to be maintained throughout the life of the product. Unfortunately, with increased competition and saturated markets, it is much more difficult to find outlets for these products.

Sales promotion has provided a partial solution to this dilemma in two ways. First, it has increased product turnover rates, thus improving the cash flow problem. Second, it has opened new outlets for these surplus products. For example, companies such as Titan and Phillips have found brand new markets for their products by offering them to companies as part of their employee incentive programs. As a result, thousands of watches and music systems have been offered as rewards for exceptional service or as prizes for sales contests.

A fourth justification for sales promotion is when an oligopolistic market situation exists. In this situation, just a few companies exist in the market, but competition is very intense between them. In the developed countries, conditions of oligopoly apply in industries such as oil, motor vehicles, aerospace, electrical and chemical products, processed foods, and toiletries, and also in the brewing industry banking, retailing and transportation. In all these industries, there is widespread use of sales promotion techniques. In the oil industry, there are the multitude of schemes offered through service stations, special contract terms negotiated with large users industry of fuel oil, free map and guide services, and so on. In the car industry, trade-in allowances on secondhand cars are customary as is plenty of discounting activity just before the introduction of new models. On the computer side, promotion takes the form of special rental arrangements and the provision of tailor-made software. Banking has become active in sales promotion through techniques such as free advice to customers, competition in deposit rates, money market rates, bank charges, and the provision of special offers to students, working women, and the elderly.

Why is sales promotion so prevalent in industries that are oligopolistic? The reason is not merely because of the size of each firm, but for this other good reason as well: no firm operating under these conditions likes to compete on price. If price competition arises, every firm is adversely affected because all other firms in the industry have roughly the same costs and are forced to match the price reduction to maintain their market share.

One major competitor determining when price changes are to occur-price leadership is normal practice, even if there is no formal price conspiracy in operation. Thus if they believe they have some fairly permanent advantage over their rivals that would make it difficult for them to follow.

Instead of price competition, rivalry takes the form of trying to increase business by expanding the share of market by better distribution, service, salesmanship and promotion. This is particularly true of industries where the total market is more or less static and saturated. It is when the battle is joined for replacement or repeat sales, as well as for competitors' customers, that the sales promotion war really heats up. This also effectively prevents newcomers from breaking into the market easily on a large scale because they cannot afford the selling costs.

As there are only a few firms in an oligopolistic industry for each participant to study, once a competitor's weaknesses become known its rivals are able to exploit them by skilful promotional methods. Then, the promotional battle tends to escalate automatically, especially when budgets are set using competitor's expenditures as a base which must be exceeded.

Promotional campaigns can be specifically aimed at competitor's weaknesses, and with much greater effectiveness if an industry consists of only a few firms. A fifth justification for sales promotion revolves around the perceived high risk the customer associates with committing resources in the purchase of a product. Although there is little evidence that sales promotion can change attitudes, there is evidence that most consumers see individual sales promotional schemes as quite distinct phenomena from the products with which such schemes are associated. That is to say, brand image is affected neither positively nor negatively by the value of a scheme to the buyer. It is simply an extra inducement to buy-its function is to change behaviour by providing a stimulus to buy.

Risk felt by potential customers is most likely to be present in the buying situation when:

1. The product is new and untried.

   Sales promotional remedy—sampling, de-monstration, trial run, guarantee of benefit, free trips for customer to visit the factory or other users.

2. Benefits will not be felt or completed for some time.

   Sales promotional remedy—delayed invoicing, premium offers, linked services.

3. The product on its own is not quite perceived to be adequate value-for-money.

   Sales promotional remedy—premium offers, couponing, collection schemes, and contests.

4. The buyer is afraid that new products will be launched thus rendering the one bought obsolete before it is fully depreciated.

   Sales promotional remedy—leasing agreement with discounts for trading-up, guaranteed buy-back arrangements.

5. The product will not be compatible with the buyer's consumption system.

   Sales promotional remedy—tailor-made package deal, training facilities, container premiums.

The final advantage in sales promotion is the existence of a large number of marginal customers. Marginal customers are those buyers who are almost at the point of purchase but not quite. Every other element of the proposition put to them has been assembled and still the deal has not quite been completed, just an extra push will do it. Sales promotion schemes provide a lastminute and specific inducement that is possible to introduce without disturbing any other element of the deal.

To summarize, sales promotion is no longer viewed as just a supplement to advertising and personal selling. In many instances, sales promotion is the major thrust of the promotional effort. Thus much of sales promotion is aimed directly at influencing behaviour. It does so by providing a last-minute stimulus to act in one way rather than another. It does not work upon a customer's felt need for a product in itself, neither does it attempt to argue a case; instead, it offers a direct inducement to act by providing extra worth over and above that represented by the permanent bundle of values built into the product at its normal price. It is essentially part of the deal because, by definition, these temporary inducements are offered at the time and place the buying decision is made.

They are therefore the last set of influences brought to bear upon that decision, having left behind not only advertising, but also personal sales techniques and packaging as major factors in the decision. This means that promotional inducements are powerful simply because they are the most recent of all influences; they do not need to be remembered; they are direct in their appeal and in the proposition that they make; and above all they seek a favourable response by demanding it.

The average consumer is always looking for a deal. This is true in respect to all phases of our lives, including jobs, products, and relationships. Sales promotion is effective in attaining that something-for-nothing benefit we are constantly seeking.

It appears that sales promotions tend to be most effective when they are offered as a temporary inducement. Even the most naive consumer becomes skeptical when a retail outlet runs a year-long sale. Thus sales promotions should be offered sparingly and for short durations of time. The following discussion deals with the various types of consumer sales promotion devices.

THE TOOLS OF SALES PROMOTION

The reader has already been introduced to most of the elements of the sales promotion mix, but to put them into proper perspective we shall list and describe them here in terms of the specific functions they perform. The tools of sales promotion are employed primarily by two of the principals of marketing: the manufacturer and the retailer. Although a few of the elements are used in common by each, for the most part the needs of the retailer differ from those of the manufacturer. Basically, manufacturers are interested in selling the specific products they manufacture to the wholesaler, to the retailer, and through them, to the ultimate consumer. The retailer and the wholesaler, on the other hand, want to sell any product they carry, and they don't care which manufacturer produced it—unless they, as resellers, are offered inducements by particular manufacturers.

To accomplish these ends, a manufacturer usually engages in three different sales promotion campaigns. One is aimed at inducing the consumer to buy the manufacturer's merchandise at any retail outlet. A second campaign is used to motivate its own salespeople to sell more and to induce wholesalers and retailers to sell its merchandise in preference to the products of other manufacturers. A third effort might be directed at other manufacturers or businesses that are potential users of its products. In order to influence consumers, manufacturers offer premiums, cents-off coupons, rebates, refunds, samples, sweeps takes, contests, games, point-of-purchase advertising, exhibits, displays, and demonstrations. Campaigns to motivate their own saies forces and those of wholesalers and retailers could include a sales contest based on sales beyond a specified percentage of the previous year's figures, for which the manufacturer would provide incentives in the form of cash, merchandise, or travel.

In addition, to woo wholesalers and retailers, manufacturers can offer dealer loaders, trade allowances, business gifts, and push money, and they can display their wares at trade shows. Retailers' main concerns are to attract consumers to their stores and to encourage them to buy. To this end, like manufacturers, they employ premiums, cents-off coupons, sweepstakes, contests, games, point-of-purchase advertising and advertising specialities.

In addition, retailers can distribute trading stamps. It should be pointed out that the retailer does not use such sales promotion items as premiums, sweepstakes, contests, and games to encourage the purchase of specific brands of products, as the manufacturer does, but rather to encourage overall purchases. For example, a customer may receive a premium from a retailer for total purchases of Rs 500 or more.

Sales promotion which is employed by manufacturers to encourage the movement of products to wholesalers and retailers is called internal sales promotion; that which is used to move products from the retailer to the ultimate consumer is known as external sales promotion. Internal sales promotion is said to push merchandise through the channels of distribution, while external sales promotion pulls it through. As defined, the job of sales promotion has two major functions: *(1)* to stimulate, encourage, motivate, persuade, and induce people to buy goods and services; and *(2)* to motivate sales personnel to sell. Each of t ese functions can be further subdivided to fit a number of diverse, yet specific, needs of the individual retailer, wholesaler, or manufacturer, with each function contributing to the overall objective.

1. To increase consumer sales:
   (a) To increase the frequency of use by present customers
   (b) To increase units of purchase
   (c) To extend the buying season or use period
   (d) To build continuity
   (e) To add new customers in the present territory
   (f) To add new customers by extending the present territory
   (g) To find new uses for a product
2. To foster goodwill
3. To introduce a new brand or product

4. To announce an improvement or change in an established product or its package
5. To counter the sales promotion and marketing activities of a competitor.
   (a) To meet price competition
6. To determine the effectiveness of consumer advertising
   (a) To test the effectiveness of consumer media
7. To increase the effectiveness of consumer advertising
   (a) To increase consumers' readership of advertising
   (b) To attract consumers attention.

1. To increase sales
   (a) To increase the inventories of wholesalers and retailers
   (b) To reduce dealer inventories to make room for a new or improved product or package
   (c) To discourage substitution by retailers and wholesalers
   (d) To gain the cooperation of retailers and wholesalers, sales personnel
   (e) To add impetus to a sales drive
   (f) To boost sales of a slow-moving item
   (g) To boost off-season sales
   (h) To increase sales in slow areas
   (i) To inform retailers and wholesalers' sales forces of marketing and promotional activities

(j) To facilitate the securing of shelf devices and point-of-purchase advertising space from retailers.

(k) To add interest to a product that is similar to a competitor's product.

2. To train retailers' and wholesalers', sales forces
3. To foster goodwill
4. To introduce a new product
5. To announce an improvement or change in an established product or its package
6. To counter the sales promotion and marketing activities of a competitor
   (a) To meet price competition
7. To determine the effectiveness of trade advertising
   (a) To test the effectiveness of trade media
8. To obtain a list of potential retail and wholesale customers
9. To increase the effectiveness of trade advertising and sales efforts
   (a) To increase retailers and wholesalers' readership of advertising
   (b) To attract retailers' and wholesalers' attention

Sales promotion techniques and personal selling efforts complement and reinforce advertising. The blend of these three activities constitutes the promotion mix. In this chapter we look at the ingredients of sales promotion: displays, packaging, sales incentives such as trading stamps and games, and their effectiveness. The latter part of the chapter is devoted to personal selling-its importance, its challenges, and its place in the promotion mix and then we look at the role of sales management. Sales promotion covers a wide range of techniques, such as demonstrations and exhibitions, samples, premiums, coupons and cents-off deals, games and contests, trading stamps, displays, store and window signs, and packages and package inserts.

One common example of sales promotion is use of premiums in cereal boxes. With young children, one wonder whether brand, taste, or nutritional value of the cereal is nearly important as the particular premium inside the box: the ring the toy, or the baseball card. In recent years, sales promotion strategies have proliferated. Trading stamps and games have waxed and waned. Reflecting the growth of self-service, packaging and point-or-purchase displays have become important as "silent salesmen." Increased emphasis the sales promotion is partly due to changes in marketing strategy, but it also hints at the sobering conclusion that advertising alone is not able to do the job.

Sales promotion has been called the "plus" ingredient in the marketing mix. This suggests that it is helpful but optional. At one time it was perhaps true that the absence of sales promotion might have no visible effects. This is no longer the case today. The use of trading stamps, coupons, and premiums virtually forces competition to come up with something similar; otherwise, business shifts to those firms offering extras and more excitement. And in the impersonality of the supermarket shelf, the attractive display and package become powerful selling tools. With the trend in retail stores to self-service, advertisers must depend on displays to remind consumers of the advertising they have seen.

An effective display for a product can boost sales. We know that the actual decision to buy in the some hinges on the consumer's attitude toward the brand (and, of course any prior experience in using the product), with advertising helping to mold attitudes. But in many instances the consumer does not feel strongly about any particular brand. This being the case, an attractive and striking package, good shelf position, and any point of purchase display may be the final influences and sales generate the brand that makes the last impression-at the point of purchase-makes the sale. Any kind of display that can be used either in a retailer's dow or inside his store is point-of-purchase advertising. The vary ranges from banners and easel-back cards to mannequins, merchandise stands or racks, to turntables or expensive mobile display in-store demonstrations. A display should be designed to meet needs of the retailer who will use it, while at the same time arising the best image of the product and brand. The bigger product however, is enticing the retailer to use the display material even though it is furnished free by the manufacturer. All advertising is susceptible to waste, but display materials are particularly so. Many signs and displays are buried in stockrooms and never used, or used ineffectively in poorly located windows, or not for the intended purpose.

Moreover, usually the smaller dealers-those who generate the least sales volume-are the most willing to use manufacturer-supplied display material. The major retailers are often more discriminating. Therefore, the manufacturer frequently finds that, even when his material is being used, the potential sales volume is not worth the cost. The container or wrapper for a product, the package, is generally regarded by consumers as part of the product. The package can add greatly to the appeal of the product, or it can detract from it.

Marketers have discovered that a well-designed package, one with certain convenience features, can prop up demand for a mediocre product, or can provide an element of differentiation which might not be possible otherwise. But more than this, good packaging can be a significant part of the promotional strategy and the point-of-purchase efforts. For products distributed through self service outlets, such as supermarkets where products must compete with as many as 7,000 other items, the role of the package assumes greater importance. It can enhance the image and present subtle selling appeals at that most decisive moment of choice. Even after the sale, the package can continue the selling job. The cigarette package, in particular, is displayed to other people each time the smoker extracts one of its twenty cigarettes; the package design then needs to be distinctive, and even prestigious:

> With television denied the tobacco companies, they are turning to catchy packaging to help market their new brands. For example, Lorillard Corporation's Zack has a package that looks like blue denim; Brown & Williamson's Tramps carries Charlie Chaplin's "Little Tramp" image; Liggett & Myers' St. Moritz is billed as the "first gold band, luxury length, filter cigarette."

Then there is the example of a manufacturer of frosting mix for cakes who thought he had improved the package by changing the illustration, only to find that the brand's market share was cut in half.

OBJECTIVE AND IMPORTANCE OF SALES PROMOTION

As we have discussed, Sales Promotion includes all activities which promote sales of the company's product and servites. These activities are called promotional activities and serve the following purposes:

(1) Providing Information. Promotion is an exercise in information, persuassion and influence. Thus, its major role is persuassive communication. The producer through promotional means provides information regarding the quality, different uses and the price of the produd or service to the consumers. The promotional means may be salesmen, dealers, press, and other supplementary activities.

(2) Increase' Sales Volume. The main purpose of all Promotional activities is to increase the sales of the product or products of the company. Promotional activities increase or help increase the sale by making effective upward change in the elasticity of demand of the product or service through various techniques *i.e.,* by distributing samples, free gifts, purchase premium, discounts etc. Such activities make the product popular and are complementary to press and'other media of advertising and personal selling.

(3) To keep the Memory Alive. One of the objectives of the sales promotion is to keep the memory of the product alive in the minds of the present customers. This work is done mainly by advertisement but other promotional activities help achieve this objective.

(4) To Arrest Seasonal Decline. In slack season, the promotional activities help in maintaining the sales of the product. Middleman (Distributors and retailers) and consumers offered attractive discounts and free gifts to lure them to purchase more and more. In this way, the producer arrests the seasonal decline in the demand of his product.

(5) To Induce Middlemen. The middlemen-wholesalers and retailers are induced to purchase more stock of company's product by offering more facilities such as credit facilities, higher cash and trade discounts, free gifts etc.

(6) To Face Competition Effectively. Promotional activities help the producer or seller to meet the competitive situations in the market. The competition may be from manufacturers or sellers of similar products or of substitutes. Competition in similar products may be quality competition or price competition. Promotional activities such as advertising giving information regarding price and quality of the product as compared to other similar products existing in the market or offering various facilities to middlemen with a view to sell company's goods in preference to other goods or offering gifts and discounts to customers, help arrest competition. In case of competition from substitutes having superior technology, promotional activities cannot help much. The only remedy of such type of competition is to improve the quality of the product through research and innovation.

PROMOTIONAL ACTIVITIES

Nothing happens until something is sold. The Sale Promotion activities help in promoting the sales of the product of the company very effectively. More and more promotional activities are required to induce customers to purchase and middlemen to sell more and more items of the product. In this way, promotional activities produce demand of the product in the market. In today's competitive world, these activities play an important role which can be judged from the following facts:

1. For Selling goods in Imperfect Markets. Every market is imper fect market where the product cannot be sold easily only on the basis of price differentiation. It is promotional activities that provide information abput the differences, characteristics and multitudes of the products of various competitors in the market. The customer is attracted to purchase the goods on the basis of such information. The middlemen also can vass the company's product on the basis of such points of differentiation. Thus, Promotional activities are necessary for selling the product successfully in the market.

2. Intense Competition. Intense competition has necessitated the promotional activities. When one manufacturer increases his promotional 'spending and adopts aggressive promotional strategy in creating brand image, others have to follow the sign. This leads virtually a promotion war. In such a situation, improving the product through research and innovative activities, is advisable.

3. For shortening the Distance between Producers and Consumers. There is no direct communication between the producer and the consumer. The distance between them has so widened in present days, that mass selling is not possible without getting them acquainted with the product and its distinctive qualities. Promotional activities, therefore, are necessary to narrow down this distance.

4. Increased Standard of Living and Employment Opportunities. Large scale production is the theme of the day and promotional activities are necessary for mass selling and large production. Sales promotion is the result of large scale production. The objective of large scale production can be achieved only through appropriate methods of large scale selling. Large scale selling is very difficult without promotional activities In large scale, production and selling, quality of goods is improved and prices are lowered down. It, thus, improves the standard of living of them assesby providing them better quality goods at lover prcees.

5. Effective Sales Support. Basic sales promotion policies supplement the efforts of direct (personal selling) and indirect selling (advertising). It is found that sales promotion activities support the salesmen's and make their efforts more productive. These activities reduce their canvassing time and also the turndowns.

6. Increased Trade Pressures. To shorten the distance between the producer and the consumer, a number of producers have preferred to sell the goods defect to consumers by cutting the chain of middlemen short. They have opened retail, outlets known as chain stores. Other large scale retailers such as departmental stores, super bazaar etc., have also come into existence. These retailers are successful in exerting great pressure on manufacturers to allow them discounts and other facilities. As they are largescale purchasers, and in a bid to support them due to great trade pressure, many manufacturers have resorted to sales promotion activities.

METHODS OF SALES PROMOTION

The various sales promotion devices (other than advertising, personal selling and publicity) are numerous and may be grouped as follows:

(A) Consumer Promotions

Sales promotion devices directed at consumers are aimed at increasing the demand of th company's product among existing consumers, or to attract new consumers to the company's product. Such devices may be used to rotaliate the Competitors' Sales Promotion or other promotional efforts. Such promotional devices may include:

1. **Samples.** At the time of introducing a new product in the market, the company istributes samples (Some quantity of the same product) free of cost of the purchaser of the product. Samples are distributed with aview to allow the customer to test the quality of the product so that he may' recommend the use of the product to others. The samples may be distributed door to door, offered in a retail store, or to professional for recommendation. The method is quite useful for promoting brand loyalty among consumers. It is a good method of demand creation because the user comes to know the result as soon as he uses the sample and buy the brand. Samples may be distributed before purchase or along with the purchase.

   Offering samples is quite expensive because it has cost and its distribution cost is also high. It may create a problem if product does not resemble with the quality of the sample offered.

2. **Coupons.** A coupon is a chit of stated value mostly kept inside the package, is given direct to the consumer at the time of purchase. It entitles the

consumer to a specified saving in the form of price reduction at the time of next' purchase. Sometimes, coupons are encashed by the retailers on behalf of the manufacturer. The 'retailers are reimbursed the value of coupons by the manufacturers. Since coupons are directly tied with the purchase of the product, it provides short term stimulus to the sale of the product.

What is important is that coupon does not affect the stated price of the product nor does it impair the dealer's margin.

3. **Premium or Bonus Offer.** It is an offer of certain amount of product (whether produced by the same manufacturer or not) to consumer free of cost along with the purchase of the company's product of a stated value or a special pack thereof. There are various forms of premium' or bonus offer:

   (a) **Coupons** are supplied for effecting price reduction.

   (b) **Factory in-pack Premium.** Such premium item is generally packed by the company in the box or package itself. It is very popular in case of baby food and tin food items. Spoons, cups, measuring glass etc., are generally packed with the product inside the container itself. Tooth paste companies offer a free tooth brush inside the tooth paste pack.

   (c) **Self-liquidating Premiums.** Under this type of premium, the cost of premium is collected from tbe customers though it is considerably low. Such premium items are offered along with the purchase of company's goods. This becomes possible because the manufacturer purchases these items in bulk.

4. **Money Refundoffer.** This offer is generally stated on the package itself or in the media advertising that the manufacturer will return the price of the product, if it not upto to sat is faction of the consumer, This offer is valid only for a stated period. For example Bull-worker exerciser is promoted this way.

5. **Price-off or Bargain offer Price or Temporary Price Reduction.** The customer is offered a price reduction over the printed or list price on purchases made during a fixed period. This is done to attract consumers of other brands to this brand or when a new product or brand enters the market.

   This method is supposed to be a weaker and less desirable method of sales promotion. It is because some retailers do not pass the price reduction benefit on to the consumer. This method is not conductive is building up brand loyalty because consumers temporarily shift their loyalty until the producer offers this scheme.

6. **Contests or Sweepstakes.** At times, consists are arranged with a view to attract new users to the company's product. Entry forms to contest are available with the purchase of the goods or carton flaps are tagged with the entry forms. An opportunity under this device is given to consumer to contest with a chance to cash prizes, or articles or free air trips. It is an indirect manner of introducing a new product or stimulating sales of an existing product.

7. **Bonus Stamps.** A premium in the form of stamps is given by the seller to consumers. The value of stamps received by the purchaser depends upon the value of purchase. The consumer goes, an tollecting stamps unless he has sufficient quantity of to obtain a desired

merchandise in exchange for the stamps from the stamp redemption centers.

8. **Demonstration.** This a method of promoting a new brand or article in the market. The product is demonstrated in producer's or sellers' stores, at fairs and exhibitions, temple festivals or even on door to door basis depending upon the size and value of the product. This method is most often employed for household appliances and new beverages. Tea in India was introduced in the market through demonstrations. Demonstrators are employed by the producers for this purpose.

9. **Buy-back Allowance.** This is an allowance following a previous trade deal and offers a certain amount of money for new purchases based on the quantity of purchase made on the first trade deal. The retailer on behalf of the producer collects empty cartons, bottles, flaps, tubes etc., from the consumers of a certain brand and encash them at a fixed price if they purchase the company's brand afresh. It extends the life of the trade deal and helps to prevent past deal sales decline. It greatly strengthens the buyer's motivation to cooperation the fIrst trade deal.

(B) Trade or Middlemen or Dealers' Promotion

When products are sold through middlemen (wholesalers and retailers or both), certain incentives are'offered to those middlemen so that they may store the company's product in large quantity. Such promotions or incentives are:

(1) **Buying Allowance or Discount.** A discount on purchases is red to the dealers to induce them to purchase company's product. Such discount may be either deducted on invoice price or on cash paid. Such allowance or discount may be given at a fixed percentage of total purchases above the minimum

fixed made during a fixed period of time or an extra purchases over a minin!um at every purchase. It increases the profit of the dealer/and sales to manufacturer.

(2) **Buy-back Allowance.** This method of promotion is practised to prevent a post deal sales decline. Under this method, the manufacturer offers a certain amount of money for additional new purchases based on the quantity of purchases made on the fIrst trade deal.

(3) **Store Demonstration.** Demonstrations for company's product are arrange in the premises of wholesalers and retailers. These demonstrations are arranged by the producer's sales force. For store demonstrations dealers are paid. It is good mode of advertising company's product especially new product. A good demonstrations will attract new customers. Customers may ask questions from the demonstrators to clear their doubts. Demonstrations can explain peculiarities of the. product to the prospecting consumers.

(4) **Display and advertising Allowance.** In this method, dealers display the company's product and they are paid advertising allowance by the company. The advertising allowance is paid on the .basis of space provided to display the manufacturer's product in the shop. In this way, company shares its advertising budget with the dealers.

(5) **Special Contests.** This is an indirect way of promoting sales. It is to stimulate and motivate distributors, dealers, and their sales staff and arranged by the manufacturer. Such contests may take the form of window display, internal store display etc., or sales volume contests. Çash prizes are offered to those who win the contest or make

the highest sales' during a fixed period of time. This certainly involves financial commitments. In view of the winning chances, sellers participate in the contests.

(6) **Advertising Materials.** Certain companies provide advertising materials such as store signs, neon-sign boards, shelf sign boards etc. With the dealer's name for advertising purposes. Other free goods like calenders, diaries and other publicity materials with the dealers' name and address are also provided. This type of promotion performs the twin functions of consumer education and convincing of retailers in the need for cooperation in the promotion.

(7) **Dealer Premium.** The dealer is offered a gift at the time of every purchase if the dealer purchases over a fixed quantity of the product. Such gifts are sometimes encashed at a fixed price.

(C) Sales Force Promotion

Personal selling by far is the most important method of Sales Promotion. To make it highly effective, sales force promotion schemes are felt necessary. The tools for Sales Force Promotion are:

(1) **Bonus to Sales Force.** A sale quota is fixed for each salesman during a fixed stated period on company's terms. Bonus is allowed to salesmen on sales in excess of the quota fixed. The salesman try to sell maximum possible quantities of product in a thrust to earn more bonus.

(2) **Sales Force Contest.** Sales force contests are announced by the company for the salesman. The top performer is offered cash prize in the form of cash or in some other forms (suth as promoting a person showing good performance etc.,). The sales man take interest and make efforts to redouble the company's sales.

(3) **Sales Meetings.** Conventions and Conferences. These are conducted by the manufactures for the purpose of educating, inspiring and rewarding the salesmen. New products and new selling techniques are discussed in such meetings.

The various devices discussed above may also be shown with the help of the following chart:

Tools or Devices of Sales Promotion

Consumer Promotions	Trade Promotions	Sales Force
1. Samples	1. Buying allowance	1. Bonus
2. Coupons	2. Buy-backAllow wance	2. Contests
3. Premium or bonus offer	3. Store Demons-strations	3. Meetings, Conventions, and Conferences
4. Money Refund Offer	4. Display and advertising Allowance	
5. Price off offer	5. Advertising materials	
6. Contests or sweepstakes	6. Special contests	
7. Bonus stamps	7. Dealer Premium	
8. Buy-back allow-ance		
9. Demonstration		

❐

2

Promotional Mix and Personnel Selling

The concept of promotional mix assumes that there is a variety of means for communicating with consumers. The term promotional mix refers to the combination of various types and amounts of various forms of promotion used by a marketer. The final selection of them depends upon the jobs assigned to promotion and the environment in which they are performed. The concept further assumes that there are different types of promotion and each are has its advantages and disadvantages over other forms. All types of promotions are not suited to all types of business. Certain promotion types are better suited for some tasks than others. All promotional types are compatible and interchangeable.

Mc Neal has asserted five constituents in the promotional mix *viz.*:

(i) advertising,

(ii) packaging,

(iii) personal selling,

(iv) publicity, and

(v) sales promotion. While Stanton has emphasised only three elements:

(i) advertising,

(ii) personal selling, and

(iii) sales promotion

Advertising is a paid form of non-personal presentation and promotion of ideas, goods and services by an identified sponsor. Personal selling is a direct method of selling goods and services through persons known as salesmen. It is a most effective way of presenting things to customers.

Packaging is another element in the mix. It carries messages through packages, its design and colour etc., to customers. Sales promotion is another way of attracting customers through various other means except advertising, personal selling packaging etc., such as discounts, free gifts, presents etc.

The determination of the various elements in the promotional mix depends upon a number of factors that influence the manager decisions.

These factors can be summed up as:

(1) the amount of money available for promotion purpose;

(2) the nature of market *i.e.,* whether local, regional, national or international;

(3) the nature of the product *viz.,* consumer or industrial, durable or non-durable or perishable;

(4) the stage in the product life cycle *i.e.* introduction, growth, maturity or decline.

Advertising, personal selling and sales promotion are genenilly employed on the basis of the promotional strategies and the nature of the market. Generally, speaking a promotion manager employees a combination of different forms of promotion because anyone cannot satisfy the need of the company. A good combination of advertising, personal selling and other promotion methods may increase the sales enormously at a most reasonable low price. Dependence on anyone form of promotion element is seldom effective.

Promotional Strategy

A good combination of various promotional elements is necessary for augmenting the sales of the company. Deciding about the various elements of promotion may be known as Promotional Strategy. Promotional strategy related to the marketing efforts to make the product actually flow through the marketing channels and to the target markets. Promotion involves the marketer's activities in communicating both with the members of the product target market and the middlemen to increase the chances that the planned sequence of sales or ownership transfers actually may take place.

The promotional strategy is always a part and parcel of the marketing strategy. An overall marketing strategy combines three main strategies *i.e.,* distribution strategy, promotional strategy and pricing strategy and promotional strategy is a combination of promotion elements *i.e.,* advertising, salesmanship and other promotional methods. Promotional strategy is thus a part of overall marketing strategy.

The following figure shows the relation of marketing strategy and Promotion Strategy with the Promotion Mix.

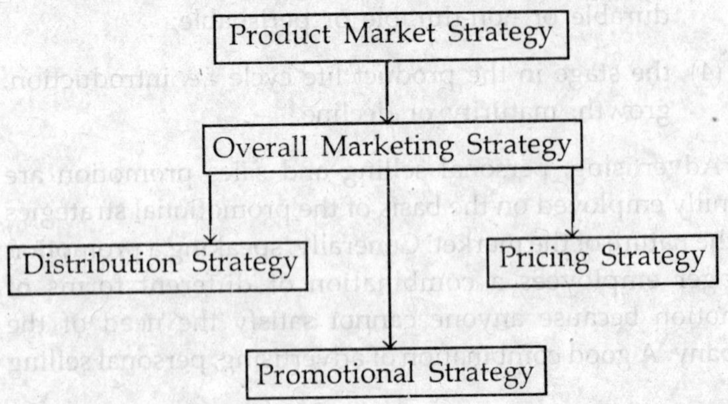

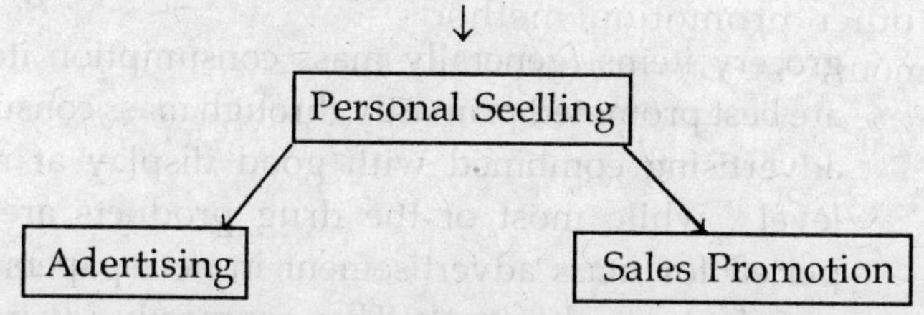

Fig. 1. Relationship of Marketing Strategy, Promotional Strategy and Promotional Mix.

Thus, Promotional Strategy as is determined by the management may take different types and amounts of personal, 'selling, advertisement and other forms of promotion. Management sets objectives determines policies and formulate strategies for each component of the Promotional mix. These individual strategies combindly are known as Promotional Strategy of the company. The promotional strategy should be closely associated with the overall marketing strategy and product market strategies while distribution and pricing strategies are closely associated with the overall marketing strategy. Thus, it is the management that decides the forms most effective for achieving the promotional objectives and optimise the expenditure on each promotional method. There is no ideal mix which may be suitable for all marketing situations. Every management has to develop its own promotional strategy keeping in view the market. The marketing conditions of the product, and the relative costs of different forms of promotion.

Determination of Promotional Mix

Promotional mix includes an ideal proportion of each element of promotion *i.e.*, advertising, personal selling and direct promotional activities. In determining, an ideal promotional mix, the following factors must be considered:

(1) **The Nature of the Product.** The nature of the product influences the decision of the promotion manager with regard to the selection of promotion mix. Many

grocery items (generally mass consumption items) are best promoted primarily through mass consumer advertising combined with good display at retail level ; while most of the drug products are not placed for mass advertisement in newspapers and popular general journals. They are mostly advertised in medical journals and personally promoted be medical representatives or salesmen pharmacists. They contact the physicians and surgeons who are the best agent for promoting a drug product. Similarly, convenience items like gift packs are promoted through personal selling combined with window display, while many of industrial products most of high unit value require a quite different mix.

(2) **Broad Differentiation.** It is another variable in determining Promotion mix. It shows the degree to which a marketer's brand usually affects the Promotional mix. Products having not much differentiation, say Modern bread or Britannia bread, personal selling will be the best way of promotion emphasising to get the product stocked in as many retail outlets as possible and to secure maximum and effective shelf space display. But in case of products having much differentiation like cosmetics, advertisement shall occupy a prominent position in the promotional mix.

(3) **Product Complexity.** Product complexity is another determinant of Promotional mix. If a product is of complex nature, highly traiped and expertised salesmen are required to contact the concerned consumers. Demonstration of the working may be the another way of promotional activity. If the product is not of complex nature, the firm concentrates much attention on mass advertising media.

(4) **Purchase Frequency.** It shows how frequently the final buyer buys the product. If a product is frequently purchased by the end-consumers. The marketer may depend upon mass advertising media to develop brand recognition among consumers, which creates a favourable disposition towards the product. But in case of products rarely or not frequently purchased by the consumers, heav expenditure on advertisement cannot be justified. In such cases, personal selling may be the best promotional device, persuading the proper outlets to stock the product and to push it over competitive branch when final buyers come to buy. Thus, purchase frequency has a decisive role in the determination of promotion mix.

(5) **Stage in the Product Life Cycle.** Different promotional mix will be required in different phases of the product life Cycle. At introduction stage, personal selling method is preferred because the innovator wants to study more about the product and its features in relation to other similar products in the market, consumers' behaviours. Advertisement may also be undertaken at this stage as it has its informative value. But during maturity stage of the Product Life Cycle, demonstration effect works well and the consumers follow the crowd.

(6) **Nature of Market.** Promotional strategy and promotional mix change from market to market. The distinction is very conspicuous. in the case of industrial buyers' and consumer buyers' market. In industrial buyers' market, advertising and personal selling both play important roles. Advertising play more of an informative role where as personal selling plays more of a persuasive role. But in consumer buyers' market, advertisement plays informative as

well as persuassive roles. Similarly, other variables like sex, fashion, age, education religion, place of residence etc., are worth consideration whereas these variables have no meaning for industrial buyers. For industrial buyers, certain other variables like relative size, bargaining power, buying responsibility etc., influence the promotional mix decision.

(7) **Changes of Various Elements.** Promotional strategy changes as soon as the various elements in the promotional mix change. The promotion for a matured product, generally aims at reminding the existing customers of its nature and value, whereas the promotion for a radically different new product aims at providing the early buyers with the information, they need to make buying decisions. Various promotion mixes may differ in their effectiveness in attaining these two different aims under various conditions. Hence, Promotional Strategy changes from time to time.

In a nutshell, one can asset that promotion is a key element in overall marketing strategy. Various promotional forms are communication devices which convey the producer's messages to consumers, but quite in different ways and effects. These elements thus play various roles in overall marketing strategy and if the management that has to decide a suitable promotional mix to suit the needs of the concern.

The main aim of all production activities is to sell the product and make profits. Manufacturer makes, all efforts to sell maximum amount of his product and in his efforts, he uses or tries to use an ideal promotional mix so that the main objective of the business to sell maximum amount of his product and earn profit. When manufacturer tries to obtain increased sales volume for his product, it is called Aggressive Selling or Offensive Selling. In this efforts, the manufacturer uses all his resources to get the objective of a higher sales volume by expanding the market for the product.

Aggressive selling answers the question—how much does the firm gain (in terms of sales volume with profit) by employing the various resources? It has an express objective of getting higher sales. Higher sales can be obtained from both or any of the following two ways:

(a) by adding more customers, loyal to the product. It is possible when market of the product is expanding.

(b) by capturing larger share of the total market demand. This can be done by persuing the users to switch over to company's product. In this situation, we assume that the market of the product is state (or the total demand of all the brands of the product in the market is static) one can increase one's sales only by snatching the market from ones competitors.

In the words of Whitehead. "In case of an expanding market an the firms may stand to gain by following the methods of Aggressive Selling. But, if the market is static manufacturer of a new product will have to be much more aggressive to capture the established market of competitors".

Defensive Selling

In contrast to Aggressive Selling, defensive selling is a ethod where the manufacturer makes various sales efforts to retain his customers. In other words, the manufacturer is much concerned about his well established market and tries to his level best to protect it from his competitors. Defensive selling emphasises the consideration as to how much the firm loses if it does not resort to efforts protecting its market. This situation arise as soon as the product reaches in declining stage of Product Life' Cycle Under this situation, the main point of consideration is how to survive in the market.

When Aggressive Selling is Resorted?

Usually, a manufacturer has to resort to the Aggressive Selling in the following circumstances:

(a) when the product has been qualitatively improved;

(b) when the manufacturer's product is superior in quality to that of the established competitor;

(e) when the aggregate demand of the product (or the market) is expanding fast;

(d) where the share of manufacturer in the market is very small;

(e) If the manufacturer has unutilised plant capacity with heavy investment, he will like to develop the market for his product rapidly so that demand of his product is equal to the optimum production capacity of his plant;

(f) when primary demand for a product is to be created, a provision must be made in the channel of distribution to educate consumers regarding the new product and its use.

Promotional Methods for Aggressive Selling

Sales promotion efforts used for Aggressive Selling may be divided in two classes—*(i)* Trade promotion, and *(ii)* Consumer promotion.

(1) Trade Promotion Methods

These methods offer special incentives to traders or dealers to buy and make efforts to sell company's product. Such incentives may take one of the following forins:

(a) **Trade Discount.** A special trade discount is offered, if the dealer purchases a'specified quantity or more of the firm's product.

(b) **Gifts.** Sometimes dealers are offered gifts or presents along with the purchase of a specified quantity. Presents are normally in the form of articles produced by other manufacturers. Sometimes cash is awarded in lieu of presents.

(c) **Extra Product.** Sometimes, the firm offers a fixed quantity of similar product free of charge, if the dealer purchases specified quantity or more of the product. In other-words, prices are charged for less quantity against purchasing a specified quantity. For example, a box containing 25 cakes of soap may be offered to the dealer for a price of only 20 cakes.

(2) Consumer Promotion Methods

Under these methods, consumers are lured to purchase the product of the firm and are given incentive for that. Prominent among such incentives are:

(a) **Coupons.** A coupon of a given value is given to the consumer against which he can purchase a particular product of the firm at a reduced price. (Price is reduced equal to the value of coupon). The retailer sells the product at a reduced price under an agreement with the producer to reimburse the value of coupons collected.

(b) **Self-Liquidating Offers.** Under this method, the ftrm offers an article at an attractive price if the consumer sends a given sum of money accompanied by a given number of box top from the packages of a particular product.

(c) **Bonus Offer.** Under bonus offer, manufacturer offers another product either manufactured by him or by some other manufacturer free of charge if the purchaser buys a stated amount of a product or a special pack thereof. Sometimes premium item is offered at a reduced price. The method is effective in a competitive market and is very popular now-adays.

(d) **Sampling.** It involves free distribution of a small quantity of the same product along with the purchase of the product or without any purchase of the product with the hope that consumer will be favourably impressed by its actual use and will eventually become a regular purchaser of the company brand. Samples may be distributed door to door or offered in a retail store, to professionals to onward recommendation. This method is useful when the firm introduces a new or improved consumer non-durable item. Also a firm whose market is held by competitors fmds free sampling method quite inexpensive.

(e) **Price Reduction Method.** This involves an offer to consumers of a certain amount of money off the regular price of the product. This is doJle to attract customers of other brands and is vcry effective in a competitive market.

The above mentioned methods of Aggressive Selling may be reinforced by combining all or any of the following methods:

(i) Direct method of selling (Personal Selling) through the use of door to door selling to make the product popular.

(ii) Offer of liberal credit facilities but without involving a risk.

(iii) Hire purchase and instalment payment methods of selling, and

(iv) Forming combinations.

Other Methods of Aggressive Selling

Some other Promotional methods may be combined for Aggressive Selling which are:

(i) Employment of missionary salesmen also known as promotional salesman who promote the sales of the product by callingupon the retailers.

(ii) In the chain of distribution, wholesalers may be eliminated. Instead, the fum may employ its own sales force to call directly or retailers.

(iii) The firm employs agents in different markets at attractive commission for the sale of firm's product aggressively and intensively.

(iv) New territories may be exploited and various promotion methods may be adopted.

(v) Individual letters may be posted to dealers and customers. This method is specifically useful if the number of customers is small.

(vi) Various incentives may be given to company's salesmen such as promotions and additional increment if one attained sales quota or if he makes the highest sales, increments or promotion, in this way, may be linked with the volume of sales.

In fact, an ingenious Sales Manager may devise a number of incentive scheme for Promoting Sales.

PROMOTIONAL MIX

Promotion is an important part of the marketing mix of a business enterprise. It is the spark plug of the marketing mix. It is a process of communiation involving information, persuation, and influence. It includes all types of personal or impersonal communication with customers as well as middlemen in distribution. The purpose of promotion is to inform, persuade and influence the propsective customers. Personal selling, advertising publicity and sales promotion are widely used to inform the people about the availability of products and create among them the desire to buy the products. Non business enterprise can market its products unless it undertakes promotional activities effectively. The prospective customers have to be informed about the product its features, utility and availability. The need for promotional activities has increased because of stiff competition, widening of market and rapid changes in technology and tastes of the customers.

The term 'promotional mix' is used to refer to the combination of different kinds of promotional tools used by a firm to advertise and sell its products. The main promotional tools or activities which make up promotion mix are personal selling, advertising, publicity and sales promotion. These are also known as elements of promotion mix.

In the modern business world, big business firms cannot depend upon a single promotional tool. They have to make use of all the promotional tools in different degrees depending upon the nature of produce, nature of competition and kinds of customers. The marketing manager is supposed to decide about the use of various promotional activities and allocate budget for them. while taking a decison about promotion mix, two factors need adequate consideration. Firstly, a combination of promotional activities are to be used because any promotional tool, used alone, may not prove fully effective.

Secondly, all promotional tools are not of equal importance and their importance may change with the change in business environment.

There is no tailor-promotional mix for a firm. Every firm has to design its own promotional mix, *i.e.*, to determine, the various promotional tools to be used for promoting the sale of its products. The most striking feature of the promotional tools is their cross-substitutability. They represent alternative ways to influence buyers. This substitutability calls for treating various promotional tool in a joint decision framework. Promotional strategy is determined by the product market strategy and over-all marketing strategy. Various combinations, types and degrees of personal selling, advertising and other promotional tools are brought together into a promotional mix to develop the promotional strategy. For each component of the promotional mix, management has to set objectives, determine policies and formu'ate strategies.

Scope of Promotion Mix

Promotion encompasses all the tools in the marketing mix whose major role is persuasive communication. Two best known form of promotion are personal selling and advertising. They are also the most important forms in terms of cost and market impact. Most of the firms use personal selling as an important part of promotional programme and it is commonly supported by advertising. Other forms of promotional tools are publicity and sales promotion. The four components, namely, personal selling, advertising, publicity and sales promotion, make up the promotion mix of a firm. A brief discussion of these components is given below:

1. **Advertisng.** Advertising is an imporant from of promotion. It involves transmiting standard message to a large number of intended receivers. Advertising is any paid form of non-personal presentation and promotion of ideas, goods or services of identified sponsor. The message which is disseminated is known as advertisement. Advertisement is a paid form of communication which is resorted to by an identified sponsor.
2. **Publicity.** Publicity is any non-paid mention of an organition of its products in the news media. It is non-personal stimulation of demand for a product by planning commercially significant news about it in a published medium or obtaining favourable presentation of it upon radio, television or stage that is non-paid for by the sponsor.

3. **Personal Selling.** Personal selling is the process of assisting and persuading a prospective buyer to buy a commodity in a face to face situation. It involves direct and personal contact between the seller or his representative with the prospective buyer. Personal selling is by far the major promotional method used to increase profitable sales by offering want satisfying products to the people.

4. **Sales Promotion.** Sales promotion includes all those activities, other than the three discussed above, they stimulate consumer purchasing and dealer effectiveness. The examples of sales promotion are: distribution of samples, coupons, premium on sale, trading stamps, displays, shows and exhibitions, holding contests, increasing public relations, etc. sales promotion techniques are designed to supplement and co-ordinate personal selling and advertising efforts:

   (1) To Spread Information. The main purpose of promotional activities is to inform the prospective customer about the availability, characteristics and use of a particular product.

   (2) To Stimulate Demand. Promotional activities create awaraness and build people interest in new products and new technology.

   (3) To Differentiate the Product. Promotion helps in differentiating a particualr product of the firm from the competing products of their firms. A business firm can supply data revealing how its product compares with other products.

   (4) To Highlight the Utility of Product. Promotion helps in letting the people know the utility of the new product. It also tells them how the concerned products will be helpful in satisfying their certain demand.

(5) ***To Stabilise Sales.*** In the modern age of competition, it is an important purpose of promotional activities to help in stabilising sales volume by reassuring the customers about the quality and price of the product. It is very much possible that a customer using a particular brand of a product may buy another one next time because the other brand is advertised so heavily.

DETERMINANTS OF PROMOTIONAL MIX

The managerial decision about the promotional mix of a firm is influenced by the following factors:

1. **Stage of Product's Life.** The stage of a products' life cycle is an important determinant of promotion mix. During the introduction stage, the customers are to be informed about the availability of the product and educated about its benefits and uses. That is why, most of the firm made use of all kinds of promotional activities to launch their products successfully. After the product has been launched, advertisement and publicity are more important to create continued patronage of the customers, to create a good image of the product and its manufacturer and to meet competition in the market. But during the last stage of the product when its sales are declining, it may be decided to make drastic cuts as pormotional efforts.

2. **Availability of Funds.** The allocation of funds by the top management for the promotional activities must be kept in mind by the marketing manager while determining the promotional mix of a firm. A firm with huge promotional budget can spend as all promotional activities. But a firm with financial constraints will be selective in the use of promotional activities. Personal selling is cheaper and more

effective in the short-run. Advertisement in reputed magzines and journals is very costly, but can attract the status conscious customers toward the product of the firm.

3. **Nature of Market.** Nature of market and customers determine, to a great extent, the promotional mix of a firm. For instance, if the customers are concentrated in a particular locality, personal selling is likely to be more effective. But if they are scattered widely in different parts of the country, advertising publicity, sales promotion and personal selling—all are necessary to push up a product. Advertisement and publicity are also important to attract the status-conscious customers.

4. **Nature of Product.** The type of promotional mix will differ depending upon the nature of the product. In case of sale of consumer's goods, advertisng, publicity and sales promotion are necessary in addition to personal selling. But in order to push up industrial goods, personal selling is much more effective because its market is easily identifiable, products are often made to specifications and a great deal of pre-sale and after-sale services are required to sell and install the product.

OBJECTIVES OF PROMOTIONS

There are three specific objectives of promotion:

(a) To Communicate,

(b) To Convince, and

(c) To Compete.

It has been pointed out that communication is the basis of all marketing effort. In fact, it involves much in addition to the stimulation of sales. Moreover, most marketing communications are promotional.

It is not enough merely to communicate. Ideas must be convincing so that action (purchase) would follow. In other words, distribution of information should be capable of producing marketing results.

A good product, an efficient channel, and appropriate price are not enough by themseleves. Communicaton and convincing elements should supplement to offer contrasts to the efforts of competitors. It may even be stated that the competitive characteristics of promotion defines its vital role in marketing strategy.

Communication is a necessary element in everyday and in every walk of life. People communicate for many reasons. A dynamic society cannot be there without sufficient modes of communication. Members of the society seek amusement, ask help, give help, provide information, all through some form of communication developed over centuries.

Promotion is the mode of communication adopted by business community for achieveing certain specific objectives. From the point of view of a seller such communications may become necessary to modify consumer behaviour and thoughts and/or to reinforce existing behaviour of consumers.

Thus, the objectives of promotion are as under:

(i) to provide information to prospective customers about the availability, features and uses of products.

(ii) to stimulate demand by creating awareness and interest among customers,

(iii) to differentiate a product from competitive products by creating brand loyalty,

(iv) to stabilise sales by highlighting the utility of the product.

Promotion has often been the target of criticism. Some opine that "promotion contributes nothing to society", and for some others "promotion forces consumers to buy products they cannot afford and do not need", and so on. It may be true that promotion can certainly be criticised on many of its aggressive and compelling factors. But it should also be recognised that it plays a crucial role in modern soceity, particularly in business, economic and social spheres of influence.

The objectives of promotion are illustrated in the following chart:

Hierarchy of effects	*General behavioural objectives*	*Specific behavioural objectives*	*Selected promotional mix elements*
Awareness ↓ Knowledge	Provide information	Obtain consumer recognition, gain consumer knowledge of product atrributes	Advertising, Publicity, Point of Purchase and Window displays
↓ Linking ↓ Preferences	Develop positive attitudes and feelings	Obtain favourable Attitudes, gain preference for brand	All media advertising, publicity and personal selling
↓ Conviction ↓ Purchase	Stimulus and retain desires	Sustain strong consumers preference, maintain continued purchase	P.O.P. displays, special offers, direct mail, personal selling

KINDS OF PROMOTION

1. Information Promotion. All promotions, essentially, are designed to inform the target market about the firm's offerings. Informative promotion is more prevalent during early stages of product life cycle. It is a necessary ingredient for creating primary demand. Such type of promotion is needed as the consumers make their purchases only if they are convinced about the product benefits. This could be done only with the help of communications and such communications are usually information-oriented and not sales-oriented, Naturally, this will help the consumer in this intelligent buying.

2. Buyer Behaviour Modifications. The effect of promotion is measured through the modification in consumer beahviour. The repeated advertisements and constant personal selling methods are designed to achieve this goal.

3. Persuasive Promotion. The basic purpose of promotion is to persuade people to buy. But many do not accept this goal, as it would involve high-pressure selling but essence of all promotion is persuasion. It is designed to stimulate purchase and to create a positive image in order to influence long-term buyer behaviour. Except on certain occassions promotion is not intended to create immediate response. Moreover, when the product enters growth stage persuasion becomes the primary goal of any kinds of promotion.

4. Reminder Promotion. This goal is adopted when the product reaches maturity stage. Insisting and emphasising brand names and product features in competitive terms is the central aim of reminder promotion. It simply serves as a "memory jogger".

PROMOTIONAL ACTIVITIES

After the product has been planned, the channels of distribution and physical distribution of the product decided, and the price structure evolved; the next step is to decide upon the promotional activities that the firm may follow. It has rightly been said that "nothing happens until somebody sells something." This gives in a nutshell the philosophy of promotional activities. The promotional activities are concerned with : *(a)* informing the people about products' distinctive want-satisfying characteristics and its availability;

(b) reminding people periodically about the product and its role; and *(c)* persuading the people/prospective buyers that make people to do what they might not otherwise do what they don't really want to do.

Promotion may be defined as "the coordination of all seller initiated effort to set up channels of information and persuasion to facilitate the sale of a good or service or the acceptance of an idea". In other words promotion refers to activities and processes designed to change or reinforce behaviour and/or ideas through communication. Promotion is telling and selling.

Selling, Promotion and Sales Promotion

Promotion is an exercise in information, persuasion and influence. These three are inter-related in the sense that to "inform is to persuade" and if "a person is persuaded he is informed," "Selling and promotion" are often used synonymously. Selling has been defined as "the personal or impersonal process of assisting and/or persuading a prospective customer to buy a commodity or a service or to act favourably upon an idea, that has commercial significance to the seller." On the other hand, "promoton" is the all inclusive term representing the broad field-advertising, personal selling, and sales promotion. "The promotional mix, therefore, deals with coordination of the sales force acitivities, the advertising programmes, and other promotional efforts, which may include packaging, branding, direct mail solicitation, point of purchased display, premiums, holding trade shows and exhibitions, use of samples of gifts."

It may be noted that "promotion" and "sales promotion" are different. Promotion is a very wide term including, advertising, personal selling. sales promotion and other promotional tools that can be devised to reach the goals of the sales programme. On the other hand, "sales promotion" is only a part of it. Sales promotion has been defined as activities other than personal selling, advertising and publicity, that stimulate consumer purchasing and dealer effectiveness, such as displays, shows and expositions, demonstrations, tension of each trade. Under instalment payment seller is to take overhead risks of bad debts and in order to minimise these higher prices are charged. Instalment system is limited to persons of good reputation and various non-recurrent selling efforts not in the ordinary routine." In retailing sales promotion is interpreted to cover "all methods of stimulating customer purchasing including personal selling, advertising and publicity. The important function of sales promotion is to serve as a bridge between advertising and personal selling to supplement and co-ordinate efforts in these two areas. The main purpose of promotion is to attract customers, awaken their dormant demand and stimulate them to act in the desired manner. Thus, establishing and maintaining communications with large market segments are the main tasks of promotional activities.

Objectives of Promotional Activities

The need for promotional activities has been recognised by the marketer for more than one reason. First, the physical separation of the consumers and producers, and an increase in the number of potential customers, have been significant to communication system.

Second, improvements in physical distribution facilities have expanded the area limits of the markets with which establishment of communication system becomes a necessity.

Third, a large number of wholesalers and retailing middlemen have developed between the producers and the users, which has necessitated that not only the consumers be informed about the benefits of the product, but also the middlemen need be informed about products. These middlemen, in turn, should also communicate with the retailers and consumers.

Fourth, when sale begins to decline, either due to preference for a new product brought out by the competitor, or a total dislike for it, promotion works as a stimulant to restore the demand for the existing product. It is needed to maintain the high material standard of living and the high level of employment.

Histya and Will put the objectives of promotion under three heads.

(1) Demand objectives, the idea of which is to influence, stimulate, maintain and create demand for a product.

(2) Communication objectives which aim at creating awareness, providing information to the customer and retailers about product features where products can be obtained, and what the products are capable of doing or achieving brand preferences.

(3) Specific objectives *i.e.* performance objectives which provide specific information about a product and which influence the decision of purchasing by the customer.

PROMOTIONAL PLANNING PROCESS

A crucial element from the cost point of view is promotion expenses. Not only huge amounts are to be spent on promotion, its controlling aspect is difficult. Hence, planning is essential in of promotion. The logical stages of promotional planning processes are as follows:

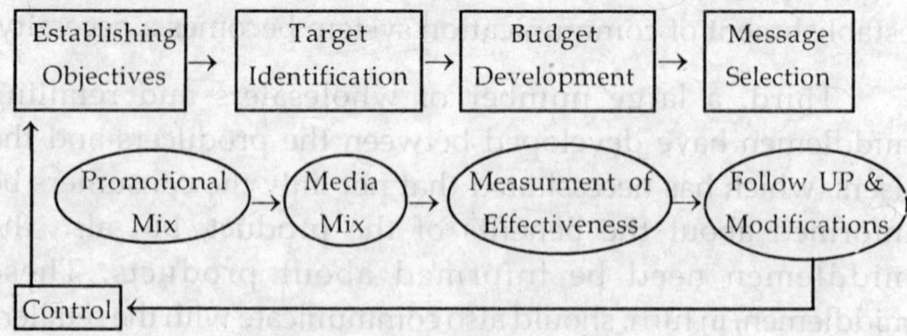

Fig. Promotional Planning Process

A separate and independent promotion plan has no place in a marketing-oriented company. Within the marketing plan for a particular product, there will be objectives that can best be achieved through promotion. But it much depends on how the resources could be used between different variables. For instance, there are different tools such as 'advertising, personal selling, sales promotion, etc. Usually five basic steps are followed in planning promotional activities:

1. Problem definition,
2. Definition of detailed objective,
3. Design of promotion mix,
4. Detailed planning, and
5. Monitoring and evaluation.

Promotional mix for the sake of discussion could be divided into three categories: Personal selling, Advertising and Sales promotion activities.

Factors Affecting Promotion Mix

While determining the promotion mix of a business firm, the following factors should be considered:

(i) **Nature of Product.** Different products require different tools of promotion. In case of industrial goods (like plant, machinery, equipment, etc.) personal selling is most effective because a great deal of presale and after sale services are required to sell and install the product. Such products are often made to specifications and the market is well identified. On the other hand, advertising and publicity are more important in case of consumer goods, particularly low priced convenience goods for daily use. In case of these goods the buying decisions are generally made at the point of purchasing and no installation is required.

(ii) **Stage of the Product's Life.** During the introduction stage the main aim or promotion is to create primary demand by emphasising the product's features, utility, etc. Therefore, a combination of advertising and publicity is required. During the maturity stage, advertising and personal selling are needed to ensure continued patronage of customers and to meet competition. During the decline stage, drastic cuts have to be made in the promotional efforts and sales promotion can be used to push up sagging sales.

(iii) **Nature of Market.** Number of location of customers exercise considerable influence on promotion mix. If the number of potential buyers is small and the customers are concentrated in a particular locality, personal selling is likely to be more effective. Where the members of customers is large and they are scattered widely in different parts of the country, advertising, personal selling and sales promotion all are required to sell the product. Type of customers also influences managerial decisions on promotion mix. Educated, urban and institutional customers require different types of promotion as compared to illiterate rural and household customers.

(iv) **Availability of Funds.** The promotional budget of the firm is an important determinant of promotion mix. If the funds available for promotional activities are large, a combination of all promotional methods can be used. But in case of financial constraints the firm has to be selective in use of promotional tools. Personal selling is cheaper and more effective in the short run. Advertising is costly but can attract a large number of customers.

(v) **Readiness of Buyer.** Different tools of promotion are effective at different stages of buyer readiness. At the awareness stage, advertising and publicity are more effective. At the comprehension stage advertising and personal selling play a greater role. During the conviction stage, personal selling is most effective. Personal selling and sales promotion are effective at closing the sale stage. Thus, advertising and publicity are more effective during the early stages of the buying decision process whereas personal selling and sales promotion are more effective during the later stages.

(vi) **Nature of the Technique.** Each technique of promotion has its unique features which must be understood before deciding the promotion mix. Advertising is an impersonal and mass method of promotion. It is a pervasive medium and colour and sound can be used to amplify the expression. Therefore, advertising can be used for both building a long term image of the product and for generating quick sales. Personal selling involves face to face presentation and is, therefore, more effective in cultivating relationships and building buyers' preference. Sales promotion offers incentives and induces buyers to buy now. It can create a quick response and boost sagging sales. Public relation enjoys high credibility and can be used to supplement the other tools of promotion.

(vii) **Promotional Strategy.** Promotion mix depends to a great extent on whether a company chooses a push or pull strategy to create sales. In a push strategy, the manufacturer includes his dealers to carry the product and promote it to consumers. Personal selling and trade promotion are more suitable to this strategy. On the other hand, a pull strategy involves inducing consumers to ask dealers to carry the product. Advertising and consumer promotion are more appropriate for full strategy.

PERSONAL SELLING

Personal Selling means the performance of actual selling acitivity. Personal selling is quite direct and personal. Personal selling involves oral conversation between seller and buyer for the purpose of making sales. Ultimate purpose of personal selling is to sell the goods to their ultimate buyers by bringing right goods and services into contact with the right customers. Therefore, personal selling is said to be the 'Back-bone of Marketing'. The term 'Personal Selling' has been defined as under :

Richard Buskirk, "Personal selling consists of contacting prospective buyers of products personally."

William J. Stanton, "Personal selling consists in individual personal communication, in contrast to mass relatively impersonal communication of advertising, sales promotion and other promotional tools."

Amercian Marketing Association, "Oral presentation is a conversation with one or more prospective purchasers for the purchase of making sales."

On the basis of analytical study of above definitions, it can be concluded that personal selling involves oral conversation between seller and buyer (when they come in contact with one another). The seller wants to convince the buyer of the goods and services which he wants to sell. When the buyer is convinced, he purchases these goods and services.

Thus, it is clear that personal selling is the most important of all the marketing efforts of an enterprise because through personal selling the consumers are encouraged to buy the product.

PROCESS OF PERSONAL SELLING

The activities involved in the selling process vary from salesman to salesman and also with selling situations. No one method is used by the two salesmen. Generally, the following process is utilised in selling a product:

(1) **Prospecting and Evaluating.** Prospecting consists in developing a list of potential customers. The first step in the sales process is to discover the names of prospects from several sources such as the company's sales records, consumer's information requests from advertisements, other customers newspaper announcements, public records, telephone and trade directories, who's who, yearbooks, and trade association list.

After developing the prospect list, a salesman evaluates each prospect to determine whether the prospect is able, willing, and authorized to buy the product. On the basis of this evaluation, names of some prospects may be deleted, while others are deemed acceptable and may be ranked in relation to their desirabilty or potential.

(2) **Approaching the Consumer.** This is most critical step because the prospect's first impression of the salesman may be a lasting impression that has long-run consequences. One type of approach is based on referrals; the salesman approaches the prospects and explains that an acquitance as associate, or a relative has suggested the call. The 'cold courses' is an approach in which the salesman calls or potential customers without their prior consent. 'Repeat contact' is another common approach, when making the contact, the salesman mentions a prior meeting. What type of approach would be suitable, depends upon the salesman's preferences, the product being sold, the firm's resources, and the characteristics of the prospect.

(3) **Preparing for the Sale.** This step consists in finding and analysing information regarding prospects's

specific product needs, current brands being used; feelings about other available brands and personal characteristics. This information is used in selecting an approach and in creating a sales presentation. The more information about a prospect that a salesman has, the better able he is to develop an approach and presentation that precisely communicates with the prospect.

(4) **Making the Presentation.** During the sales presentation, the salesman must attract and hold attention of the prospect in order to stimulate interest and convince and arouse desire for the product.

To attract such attention, the salesman should talk to the prospect briefly about the product either by asking a question that interests him or by display of some material, such as a sample, or by allowing the prospect touch, hold, or actually use the product. Demonstration may also be given about the product so that the prospect gets more involved.

(5) **Overcoming the Objections.** There are certain objections which can be anticipated and their answers formulated before the sales interview takes place. There are other objections which cannot be anticipated because they are usually related to the procedures of a particular business. For these objections, the following methods may be used:

1. Direct denial method (also called the "head-on or contradiction" method), under which the salesman should never contradict the buyers' observation. In such method, the salesman should keep in mind these guidelines; *(a)* He should not be offensive, rather he should smile; *(b)* The retail sales clerk should not attempt this method because he is seldom in a position to keep the

customers; *(c)* The type of customer must be kept in mind so that his feelings may not be hurt; *(d)* It should not be used if the objection has any 'ego' involvement in it.

2. The Boomerang method (also called the translation method), is so called because the object raised by the prospect often comes back at him as a valid reason for buying the product. This method is useful in meeting excuses that are not strongly backed by facts. It is effective only when the salesman is skilled in applying this technique.

3. Indirect-dential method (also known as "yes but method or 'sidestepping the question method), is most widely used method. It is a method of compromise because both salesman and prospects "bend" a little. They admit to each other that they both are right, but there is the other side of the problem to consider also.

4. Compensation method, which merely acknowledges the validity of an objection, but points out some advantage that is supposed to compensate for the objection, such as lower price, or special care of the product.

5. The Pass-up method, is one where the salesman smiles and tries to passover the objection especially when the objection is of trivial nature that it does not deserve a careful or thoughtful answer.

6. The question method, under which the salesman asks questions regarding objections, so that further analysis be made. The "reason objections" are answered with the word why because why reopens the discussion and the possibility of making a sale.

The salesman, while using any of these methods of handing objections, must be sure that he is applying the right method in such particular situation.

6. **Closing the Sale.** This step is the climax of the selling process in which the salesman asks the prospect to buy the product or products. "He who wins the last battle wins the war" is truly applicable to a salesman foreclosing in the test of every salesman. Inadequate preparation, poor impression, failure in meeting objections or wrong approach on the part of the salesman may come in his way. Buyer's fears and the salesman's attitude are two important obstacles of closing the sale. The sale must be closed only when the salesman knows hat the customer is prepared for it. The close of the sale depends upon the conditions, personality for the parties and the nature of the goods.

   Some of the effective ways of closing the sale are: *(i)* to take it for granted, *(ii)* offer some inducements, *(iii)* telling business stories how others have benefitted by the purchase of the products, *(iv)* fear of loss, *(v)* stressing minor but interesting details, and *(vi)* marketing a straight request for an order.

   The salesman may employ a "trial close" by asking questions that assume the prospect will buy the product, *e.g.* he might ask the potential customer questions about financial terms, desired colours, or sizes, delivery arrangements, or the quantity to be purchased. The prospects reactions to such questions usually indicate how close the prospect indirectly respond that they will buy the product without having to state those sometimes difficult words "I'll like it". A salesman should try to close at several points during the presentation, because the prospect may be ready to buy.

7. **Following up.** After a sale is closed,, it should be properly followed. The salesman should ensure that the delivery instructions given by the customer are properly followed. The salesman must visit the customer often to learn what problems or questions have arisen regarding the product "After sales service" should be punctual, quick and satisfactory.

Characteristics of Personal Selling

On the basis of above definitions of personal selling, following characteristics of personal selling may be enumerated—*(i)* Seller and buyers come in direct contact with one another. *(ii)* It involves oral conversation between seller and buyers regarding quality, price, characteristics, use etc., of the product. *(iii)* In personal selling, seller wants to convince the buyers about the goods and services which he want to sell. *(iv)* It involves the sale of goods and services personally. *(v)* It is most effective tool in increasing the sales. *(vi)* It helps in providing many important information to the enterprise regarding market. *(vii)* It is oldest method of sale of goods and services.

Functions of Personal Selling

Some of the important functions of personal selling may be summed up as under:

(i) To sell the goods to new and old customers;

(ii) To demonstrate the goods before customers;

(iii) To remove the doubts and confusions of customers about products;

(iv) To provide after-sale-services to the customers;

(v) To instruct the customers for the use of product;

(vi) To advise the customers on certain matters;

(vii) To maintain the record of sales;

(viii) To prepare long-term and short-term marketing programmes;

(ix) To train new salesman;

(x) To slove the problems of selling force.

MERITS OR ADVANTAGES OF PERSONAL SELLING

Some of the important merits or advantages of personal selling are as under:

1. **Helpful in Getting New Customers.** Personal selling helps in discovering and getting new customers. In personal selling, salesmen concentrate upon attracting the attention of new customers and encouraging them to buy the goods.
2. **Helpful in Removing the Doubts and Confusions of Customers.** Personal selling is the only tool of all the marketing efforts of an enterprise through which doubts and confusion of customers may be removed because buyers and sellers come into personal contact in personal selling.
3. **Helpful in the Demonstration of Products.** Personal selling demonstrates the products before customers. It provides an apportunity to the customers to see the practical use of the product and to understand it thoroughly.
4. **Helpful of Communication.** Personal selling is the most effective tool of communication between buyers and sellers. It communicates new products and their new uses to the customers. It also communicates the problems, doubts and grievances of customers to the management.

5. **Helpful in the Improvement of Product Specifications and Services.** As personal selling is the tool through which selllers come to know about the problems and grievances of customers, it provides an opportunity to them to know the defects of the products, and thus, it provides an opprotunity to impove product specifications and services.

6. **Helpful in Real Sale.** Advertisement and sales promotion are the tools which encourage consumers to buy a particular product while personal selling is the tool which actually sells the product to them.

7. **Helpful in Non-selling Activities.** Personal selling is helpful not only in the sale of goods and services but also in many non-selling activities, like— marketing research, sales forecasting, after-sale-services to the consumers and removal of the problems and grievances of consumers etc.

8. **It Provides Social Inspiraction.** Personal selling brings seller and buyer close to each other. They become friend to each other. Salesman behaves not only as a salesman but also as a friend, and guide with the customers believe upon the advice of salesman.

DEMERITS OR LIMITATIONS OF PERSONAL SELLING

Personal selling, though very useful in selling the goods and services of the enterprise, cannot be said to be free from limitations. Some of the important demerits and limitations of personal selling are as under:

(1) **Increase in the Cost of Sales.** Enterprise has to spend heavy amount on travelling allowances, commission and salaries of its salesmen. It increases the cost of sales which is added to the price of products.

(2) **Difficulty of Reporting at Right Time.** Personal selling can be effective only when the salesman reports at the time when the buyer is in a position to purchase, it is very difficult to know this time correctly and to report at this time. Thus, it has been the experience that the proper time of selling becomes a question.

(3) **Lack of Efficient Salesmen.** Success of personal selling depends exclusively upon the ability, capability and experience of salesmen. Qualified, trained and experienced salesmen are not available in required number or are available at very high cost. Thus, availability of trained and experienced salesmen is another important limitation of personal selling.

ADVERTISING

Advertising consists of those activities by which usual and oral messages are addressed to selected public for the purpose of informing and influencing them to by the products or services or to act or to be inclined favourably towards ideas, persons, trademarks or institutions featured. As contrasted with publicity and other forms of propaganda, advertising messages are identified with the advertiser either the signature or oral statement, further advertising is a commercial transaction involving pay to publishers, broadcasters on others whose media employed.

"Advertising is paid, non-personal communicating various media by business organisations, non-profit organisations and individual who are in some way identified in advertising message."

Clearly advertisement includes the following forms of messages. The out-door boards, our street cards, bus and train cards and in circular of all kinds whether distributed by mail, by person, through tradesmen or by inserts in packages, dealer help materials and efforts, store signs, house organs where picture used by advertising messages or signature of the advertiser.

Labels, toys and other literature accompanying merchandise are also deemed advertising, because they may reasonably be said to fall within the definition of advertising given above. Writers sometime includes these items.

In the foregoing paragraph, the informative aspect of advertising has been stressed. Though the basic purpose of advertising is to bring the advertised product as well as its features and uses to the notice of consumers, it has begun to be used for a number of other allied purposes now:

1. In the existence of intense competition has given rise to what may be described as competitive advertising. In other words, advertising is undertaken these days not only to inform people about of product, but is used also to maintain the demand for an existing product and to add to existing demand by weaning people away from rival products in the market. To take a concrete case, when the bottlers of Coca-Cola found a strong rival in Pepsi cola, they changed the tone and emphasis of their advertisements and began to emphasise that only 'it is real'.
2. Large-scale advertising is often undertaken with the objective of creating or enhancing the goodwill of advertising company. Thus, in turn, increases the market receptiveness of the company's product and help the salesman to win customers easily.
3. Advertising is used as a means to demand creation. Many needs of the people are the creations of advertising. Actually advertising seeks to channelise

the surplus incomes of the people towards those products which are not included among the basic necessities of life. In this process, it makes people conscous of the need not something without which they had been living so far. This consciousness is turned into desire, and an ardent desire, when the advertisevement continues to rub in the need for a product.

4. It follows from the above that advertising may be used with a view to preparing ground from a new product that is proposed to be introduced in the market. Most of the cinema advertisements are designed to serve this purpose. By the time a film starts its run at a theatre, the poeple are already prepared to receive it. That explains the gate-crashing and the heavy rush at the box office right on the opening day of picture. The readers would recall how ground is prepared for the opening and how enthusiastically the people rush to see it in the first week of its run.

FUNCTIONS OF ADVERTISING

Advertising has become an essential marketing activity in the modern era of large-scale production and severe competition in the market. It performs the following functions:

(1) It promotes the sale of goods and services by informing and persuading the people to buy them. A good advertising campaign helps in winning the new customers both in the national as well as the international market.

(2) It helps in the introduction of new products in the market. A business enterprise can introduce itself and its products to the public through advertsiing. No new enterprise can make an impact over the

prospective customers without the help of advertising. Advertising enables quick publicity in the market.

(3) Advertising facilitates large-scale production. Advertising encourages production of goods on mass because the business firm knows that it will be able to sell on a large-scale with the help of advertising. Mass production reduces the cost of production per unit by making possible the economical use of various factory of production.

(4) It stimulates research and development activities. Advertising has become a competitive marketing activity. Every firm tries to differentiate its product from the substitutes available in the market through advertising. This compels business firm to do more and more research to find new products and their new uses. If a firm does not engage in research and development activities, it will be out of the market in the near future.

(5) Advertising educates the people about new products and their uses. Advertising message about the utility of a product enables the people to widen their knowledge. It is advertising which has helped people in adopting new ways of life and giving up old habits. It has contributed a lot towards the betterment of the standard of living of the society.

(6) It sustains press. Advertising provides an important source of revenue to the publishers of newspapers and magazines. It enables to increase the circulation of their publications by selling them at lower rates. People are also benefited because they get new publications at cheaper rates.

(7) It buildes up the reputation of the advertiser. Advertising enables a business firm to communicate

its achievements and its efforts to satisfy the cusotmer's need to the public. This increases the goodwill and reputation of the firm which is necessary to fight comptition in the market.

OBJECTIVES OF ADVERTISING

A crucial step in any management effort is the establishment of operational objectives. In order to determine criteria for decision-making and measurement standards for evaluating the advertising effort, management must first establish advertising objectives. But, there is a wrong feeling that the effect of advertising could be measured in terms of product sales. Reaching the sales goal alone is not an indication of advertising effectiveness. Because, many other factors influence product sales including product availability, price, etc.

It is the this connection that the principle of DAGMAR becomes relevant. The DAGMAR—Defining Advertising Goals for Measured Advertising Results—approach defines an advertising goal not as a sales quota but as a specific effect on a target audience. In terms of the effect produced, an advertisement can either make the consumer aware of the existence of a product, provide the consumer with information about it, convince the consumer of the product's advantages over competitive offerings, or actually encourage the consumer to purchase the product.

As pointed out earlier, the purpose of advertising is nothing but to sell something—a product, a service or an idea. The real objective of advertising is effective communication between producers and consumers. In other words, the ultimate purpose underlying all advertising is 'increased awareness'. In marketing. The specific objectives of advertising are as follows:

(i) To make an immediate sale.

(ii) To increase market share.

(iii) To modify existing product appeals and buying motives.

(iv) To inform about new product's availability or features or price.

(v) To increase the frequency of use of a product.

(vi) To build primary demand.

(vii) To introduce a price deal.

(viii) To inform about a product availability.

(ix) To build brand recognition or brand insistence.

(x) To help salesmen by building an awareness of a product among retailers.

(xi) To create a reputation for service, reliability or research strength.

(xii) To increase the number or quality of retail outlets.

(xiii) To build overall company image.

(xiv) To effect immediate buying action.

(xv) To reach new areas or new segments of population within existing areas.

(xvi) To develop the overseas market.

As pointed out earlier, effective advertising management requires the establishment of goals as the first step. These goals will provide a basis for planning and evaluating advertising efforts. The objectives can either be communciation goals or sales goals. In a way, both are complementary. A communication goal would be to convey information or to maintain 'top of the mind awareness'. This is done by informing, persuading and reminding the potential customers.

KINDS OF ADVERTISING

Advertising may be classified into the following categories:

1. **Product Advertising.** Normal characteristic of advertising is to create primary demand for a product category rather than for a specific brand. It is wrongly believed that product advertising must stress on brand name. This is based on the feeling that a good image often enhances the effectiveness of product advertising. Naturally, the stress is laid on the brand. However, in practice, most companies were successful in marketing the product image by using the brand names (*e.g.,* Dalda, Dettol, Horlicks). In short, where the company tries to sell its product or services through advertising it may be referred to as product advertising.
2. **Selective or Competitive Advrtising.** When a product enters growth stage of the life cycle and when competition begins, advertising becomes competitive or selective. Here, the goal of advertising is to influence demand for a specific product or service. Often, promotion becomes less information and more emotional during this phase. Advertising may begin to stress subtle differences in brands, with heavy emphasis on 'brand name recall'. Pricing also will be use as a key promotional weapon as products become very similar.
3. **Institutional Advertising.** Where the objective of advertising is to project the image of a compnay or its services, it takes the form of an institutional advertising. These advertisements are not always directed only to consumers. Instead, it may be aimed at many of the various sets of public (shareholders, creditors, etc.). It is not at all product-oriented, but is designed to enhance the image of the company.

4. **Primary Demand Advertising.** It is intended to stimulate primary demand for a new product or product category. It is heavily utilised during the introduction stage of the product life cycle.

5. **Comparative Advertising.** This is a highly controversial trend in competitive markets that is recently noted. Such types of advertising stress on comparative features of two or more specific brands in terms of product/service attributes. This method is adopted in the maturity stage when similar products fastly appearing the market constitute a stiff competition. Comparative advertising delivers information not previously available to consumers". When comparative advertising appears it reveals the intensity of competition in the market.

6. **Shortage Advertising.** When shortage in the supply of products occurs, advertising often disappears into the background. A concrete example is found in the case of petroleum products that since the oil crisis in 1974, virtually advertising for these products ceased. But the intelligent marketers have found that advertising is still a viable marketing tool during times of shortage. This is what is termed as sortage advertising. In such kinds of advertising new promotional objective may be incorporated such as:

   (a) educating the user of more efficient means of utilising the product, thus reducing the demand;

   (b) to reduce customer pressure on the sales force;

   (c) improving goodwill; and

   (d) making appeal to save resources.

7. **Co-operative Advertising.** When manufacturers, wholesalers and/or retailers jointly sponsor and

share the expenditure on advertising, it takes the form of co-operative advertising. Such advertising would carry the names of all the parties involved. From the point of view of the customers this is beneficial as they could get the articles directly from the authorised outlets. For example, the manufacturers of cars undertake this type of advertising.

8. **Non-Commercial Advertising.** These are usually published by charitable institutions preferably to solicit general and financial help (*e.g.*, collection of donations or sale of tickets.)

9. **Direct Action Advertising.** Advertising that stresses and persuades immediate buying of the product is known as direct action advertising. Direct mail advertising is capable of achieving immediate action to a large extent.

10. **Commercial Advertising.** It is also termed as business advertising. As the name suggests such advertising is solely meant for effecting increase in sales. Usually the following forms of commercial advertising are recognised:

    (a) Industrial advertising—this is exclusively used for selling industrial products.

    (b) Trade advertising—advertising relating to a trade.

    (c) Professional advertising—undertaken by professional people such as doctors, accountants, etc.

    (d) Farm advertising—exclusively used for selling farm products such as fertilisers, insecticides, farm implements, etc.

Some kind of specialisation is found in all the above forms of advertising. Hence all these forms could be commonly called selective advertising.

MAIN MEDIA OF ADVERTISEMENT

Advertising media are the means to transmit the message from the advertiser to the particular class of people. A manufacturer can select any one or more of the following media of adverstisement to promote his sales:

1. Newspaper. A newspaper is generally a daily publication containing news and opinions about current events and feature articles. The improtance of newspaper is obvious from the fact that newspaper reading is a common habit of most educated people these days. Besides daily newspapers, there are bi-weekly and weekly newspapers also. Newspapers reach almost every place and are read by all kinds of people. Therefore, newspaper can be used as a medium of advertisement with great advantages. While selecting a newspaper for this purpose, an advertiser has to take into consideration the strength of circulation, the class of readers it serves, the geographical region over which it is popular and the cost of space. Newspaper advertising has many advantages. Firstly, a newspaper has large circulation and a single advertisement in a newspaper can reach a large number of people. Secondly, continuous advertisement is possible because a newspaper is published daily. An advertiser can repeat his advertisement either daily or weekly. Thirdly, newspapers provide flexibility in advertising in the sense that advertisement campaign can be initiated and stopped quickly. One day's notice is sufficient for this purpose.

Newspaper advertising has certain limitations also. Firstly, the life of a newspaper advertisement is very short. Moreover, people devoted only an insignficant part of their day's time in reading the newspaper. Thus, advertisements are likely to draw the reader's attention only casually.

Secondly, newspaper advertisement is successful only when the people to be communicated are educated. Thirdly, newspapers cannot be used for coloured advertisements since they are printed in black and white. Because of this, they may fail to help the customers in identifying the product at the point of purchase.

2. Outdoor Advertising. Outdoor advertising includes the use of poster displays, bill board displays and electrical displays. Posters are fixed or pasted on walls at important public places so that they may intercept the people on their way to work and back home. Painted or bill board displays involve the advertisements directly painted on the boards meant for that purpose. They are quite big in size and are fixed at outstanding locations like busy markets and crossings. Painted displays take the form of painted walls when the message is painted on the walls. Electrical display involves the use of electrical lights or neon tubes to attract the attention of people particularly during night. Generally, a short message is illuminated in tubes of different colours so that it is conspicuous and attractive. Electrical displays are fixed at heavy traffic centres.

Outdoor advertising is highly flexible and low cost medium. It is very useful for advertising consumer products because advertising can be displayed at various crowded crossings. Outdoor advertisement attracts the attention quickly and requires less time and efforts on the part of the readers. Moreover, a complete picture of the product can be advertised through outdoor displays. Business concern also use bill boards near the actual side of the business. The recent trend in outdoor advertisement is the use of public transport vehicles for advertising purposes.

3. Direct Mail Advertising. Direct mail is probably the most personal and selective of all the advertising media. Direct mail is used to send the message directly to the customers. For this prupose, the advertiser has to maintain a mailing list and the mailing list can be expanded or contacted by adding or removing names from the list. But a limitation is posed by the difficulty of getting and maintaining a good mailing list.

Advertisements that are sent by direct mail may be in the form of circular letters, leaflects folders, calenders, booklets and catalogues. Circular letters, folders, calendars, books catalogues. Circular letters are sent to the prospective customers to inform them about the merit of the product and to create their interest in the product. Booklets and catalogues contain the information about the products advertised. Information about the terms of sale and price of diffrent varieties of the product is given to the prospective customers through catalogues. Mail advertising has a personal appeal since it is addressed to a particular person. The message can be changed whenever the need arises. It also maintains secrecy in advertising. The competitors do not get the information about the advertised material. The main drawback of mail advertisement is that it is not suitable for all types of products and it has a limited coverage.

4. Film Advertisement. Films are also an important medium of advertisement. Business concerns usually get a short motion picture prepared and distribute it to different cinema houses for displaying it before the commencement of the regular shows or during the period of intermission. Such films are accompanied by running commentary to explain the features, uses and superiority of the product. But film advertisement can be adopted only by the well established firms. Since it involves high cost, small business firms can get cinema slides prepared for display in the cinema halls. Film advertisement is very effective since it combines spoken worlds and visual presentation of pictures. It also helps in selective advertisement. A trade can advertise his product only in a particular locality if he wants to attract the local customers only. The major drawback of film advertisement is that it is usually ignored by the people. Only a few persons are present in the hall before the start of the film and during the interval, and they too are busy in talking.

5. Television. Television is the latest and fastly growing medium of advertisement. It makes its appeal through both eye and ear. Products can be demonstrated as well as explained as in film advertisement. Television is a very costly medium of advertisement and can be made use of by the well established companies only. Another limitation of television advertisements is that once it is presented, its back reference is not possible as in the case of radio advertisement.

6. Magazine. Magazines or periodicals are an excellent medium of advertisement when a high quality of printing and colour is desired in an advertisement. Magazine advertisements can be directed towards a particular class of people and thus they avoid wasteful expenditure on advertising. Many specialised magazines or journals are published which can be used for transmitting the message to the particular class of customers. Magazine advertisements attract greater attention of the people since they are read more carefully and at greater leisure. The life of the magazine advertisements is longer. Magazines are preserved for a long period of time and are read time and again. Since advertisement copy presented in a coloured form, it creates and better image of the product advertised. Exact picture can be portrayed to enable the customer to identify the product at the point of purchase.

Magazine advertisements have certain less favourable characteristics also. Magazine advertisements are to be prepared and sent for publication well in advance. It is not possible to make the last minute change in the advertisement copy. Magazine advertisements are costlier than the newspaper advertisements since their circulation is small. Small circulation is also another drawback of magazine advertising.

7. Radio. Radio advertisements are gaining greater popularity these days. advertisements are broadcast from the transmitting stations of the commercial service of All India Radio and picked up by the receiving sets owned by the public. Radio advertisements are normally broadcast along with popular programmes of music. Even the sponsored programmes of interviews and plays can be broadcast over the radio.

Radio advertisements carry an effective appeal and cover numerous listeners of different tastes. People can listen to them even when they are busy in other activities. Radio advertisement also reach the illiterate people who cannot read newspapers and magazine advertisements. Radio also provides selectivity to some extent because advertisements can be included in different programmes meant for different types of people. In short, radio advertisements are very much suitable for the promotion of mass scale consumer goods. But demerit of radio advertisement is that it is non-visual. Sometimes, the message is not understood properly by the listeners. Moreover, the message may be missed by many listeners. In order to remove this drawback, many big advertisers give the same advertisement daily in different programmes.

8. Speciality Advertising. Many business firms offer speciality articles to the persent and prospective customers. These articles may be diaries, pen holders, desk trays, key chains, purses, paper weights, çigarette case and calendars. The name and address of the advertiser is printed in or inscribed on the sepciality items. They also bear the brand name of the firm. Since these articles are of daily use, they have greater capacity to remind their users about the brand name of the firm offering such articles.

9. Window Display. Windows display is an on-sight method of advertising. Goods can be exhibited in artistically laid out windows at the shop fronts or at important busy centres like railway stations and bus stops. Large show rooms are organised by the big manufacturers and wholesalers in the main market to advertise their products and attend to the queries of the prospective customers. The retailers also organise attractive display of certain goods in the windows of their shops. Window displays are very popular with the retailers since they help in informing the customers the types of goods available with them.

The main objectives of windows display is to draw the attention of the public and arouse their interest in the products displayed. Almost all the manufacturers insist that their products should be displayed at the retail shops. If a product is displayed properly at the point of purchase by the customers, it can make many customers to buy it. Many people having no preference for a particular brand may discover a particular brand quite appealing and attractive and may purchase it. Thus, window display creates the demand for the product. Windows display acts as a silent salesman. In order to achieve the purpose of windows display, cleanliness and a well furnished appearance for the window are essential. Articles should be arranged in a systematic way and, if possible, price tags should also be attached with the articles. It is also better if window displays are changed regularly to make the customers look at the displays every time they visit the shop.

CONCEPT OF SALESMANSHIP

The salesmanship has been expressed as an art of satisfying the customers' needs by I.J. Shapiro. According to him. "It is the art of successful persuading prospects or customers to buy products or services from which they can derive suitable benefits, thereby increasing their total satisfaction." The whole emphasis, at one time was on persuation of customers, but today the emphasis has shifted to the 'benefits attractive to prospects and customers, satisfying their needs.

Schiff has emphasised the behavioural aspect of salesmanship. Sales people are very often subjected to various unforeseen events with which they cannot cope. Sometimes, they have to call on such customers whom they do not like to approach but still they meet them with talent and tactfulness. In this way, salesmanship is the handling of unforeseen situations very tactfully and cautiously and thus achieving something from some unexpected corners.

However, good salesmanship also consists of helping buyers. Sales man, under this concept are not only interested in finding out the product what buyers wish to buy but also to educate them how a particular product or service can satisfy their needs. Hansen observes, "good salesmanship conisists of belping buyers solve their problems". Sales planning should therefore, 'aim at helping the buyers for which three basic steps are necessary *i.e.*, *(i)* establishing the objectives, *(ii)* gathering necessary information, and *(iii)* selecting appropriate tactics. The salesman, thus, first studies the buyers' problems, discover their actual needs and demonstrates how his product will help in meeting these needs. Good salesmanship is the result of careful analysis of the buyers' problems and their educate the buyers how the seller can solve their problems.

Stroh has, therefore, defined the term. salesmanship as "a direct, face-to-face, seller to buyer influence which can communicate the facts necessary for making a buying decision; or It can utinse the psychology of persuasion to encourage the formation of a buying decision."

Salesmanship, then, is seller-initiated effort that provides prospective buyers with information and other benefits, motivating or persuading them to make buying decisions in favour of seller's product or service. The sales persons have to interact customers and prospective in many different ways. Salespeople, in addition to knowing about the product thoroughly, have to be psychologist with some prospects, human computers with others, counsellor or advisors with still others and personal friends with others. Effective sales personnel adjust their personality on every call, making sure that what they say and do, is compatible with each prospects personality. Thus, salesmanship is an art of persuading customers and prospective to buy seller's product or service by educating them how certain goois can satisfy their needs. For this purpose, sales personnel study the needs' and problems of prospects and customers and find out their solutions.

Nature of Salesmanship

Salesmanship is one of elements of promotional mix like advertising, personal selling, packaging. Personal selling and salesmanship are most often used interchangeably but they are entirely different. Personal selling, along with other key elements of marketing such as pricing, advertising, product development and research, marketing channels and physical distribution, is a means for implementing marketing programmes. Perssonal selling is a broader concept and salesmanship is a part thereof. Thus, the main purpose of personal selling is to bring the right products into the hands of right customers and to make certain that transfer of ownership takes place wheteas the purpose of salesmanship is to pursue the customers and prospective to buy sellers goods and services.

Salesmanship is an art of selling goods and services of the seller to buyers. It is therefore, represents a seller-buyer interaction through salespersonnel. The salesmanship need not confine merely to personal selling alone. Salesmanship (art of selling goods) is used in advertising also. Advertising, therefore, sometimes called, 'salesmanship in print' or 'printed salesmanship'.

Personal selling and advertising are two means which the marketers use to inform or motivate customers and buyers to buy. Both means make use of salesmanship techniques. Salesmanship in advertising utilises non-personal presentation. Salesmanship in personal selling means a direct representation of salespersonal to persuade buyers to buy the sellers product or service, Non-personal presentation of salesmanship (through advertising) is less flexible that. personal presentation (face-to-face presentation) in personal selling. A unique advantage in personal selling is that the salesperson can usually identify differences among buyers and patterns his or her presentation according to their individual peculiarities.

The nature of salesmanship of consumer goods largely differs from that of industrial goods. The size of manufacturing units has considerably increased now-a-days and the decision-making has been decentralised in most of the establishments. Such companies often have detailed procurement practices through which no salesman could "take his way." Moreover, decentralised decision-making has become more complicated in multi-plant operations in different locations. To the salesman of industrial product, the problem is, however, more serious. The growth and decentralisation have posed new and greater problems in locating those who influence or make buying decisions. Even when the salesman locates the users,influencers, and decider , the problem is still not solved as the make-up of these groups keep changing due to promotions, transfers, retirement etc., of the concern persons.

Salesmanship for urban buyers is quite different from that of rural buyers. In urban areas, people are educated are aware of the products which may best suit their wants, through advertisement in different communication media. Hence, advertising is the best form of salesmanship in urban areas. Here, the job of salesman is not educate the buyers about their needs and therefore he is the least concerned with the 'demand creation. His main job is limited to problem solving. Hansen's remark is relevant in this case. "The results of various studies of personal selling, however, suggest that today needs are often discovered by buyers without the assistance of salesman. In these cases, the salesman's job is to solve the problem rather than to find it." The nature of salesmanship is entirely different as far as rural market is concerned. Buyers in rural areas are mostly uneducated (as it is in India) and therefore, they are aware of their needs. The salesman's job is to educate and enlighten them and this is the join of demand creation. So want-creating is the main task of salesman in rural areas. Role of personal selling here is limited.

Whether salesmanship is an art or a. science is a controversial subject. Some is of the opinion that it is an art whereas some argue that it is a science. It has been established that it is more an art rather than a science. However, certain theories have been developed recently but they are based only an experiences of the propounders. These theories emphasise the 'what to do' and 'how to do' rather than explaining why to do'. However, recently certain theories such as buying formula Theory or 'behavioural equation' theory has made an attempt to present the salesmanship as a science.

Scope of Salesmanship

The above analysis reveals the scope of good salesmanship. It helps to persuade the buyers to buy the goods hand educate them regarding the various commodities available in the market to satisfy their needs. Salesmanship is generally used to create demand of the product mainly in rural areas where the consumers are not aware of the products available that can satisfy their needs. Salesmanship create their needs and educates them how to satisfy. The salesmanship encourages salesmen to encounter a wide variety of unexpected situations experienced during day to day working and forces them to develop great competence and fitness to handle these situations. As a result, they have courage to bear whatever comes along. Salesmen recognise the great value of intelligent planning. They discipline themselves to think through each call in advance carefully and, therefore, are ore often in control of the sales situations in which they are involved.

Many salesmen try to set the objectives before making a call. In setting he objectives, they strike a balance between the realities of the situation and a full use of their talents. In setting the objectives, they should take cognizance of the fact that they have to change the behaviour of some other individuals. According to Reed, successful salesmanship ensure positive principles, beliefs and motives.

The salesmanship has a considerable impact on the business, as a whole. The interpersonal communication channel developed by the salesmanship creates a corporate image.

During their sales calls, salesmen generally encounter objections or statements by the buyers. The skilled salesman is not discouraged by such objections or statements. Such objections or statements provide feedback. The salesm should listen the objections very patiently because such listening may reveal factual information or attitudes which can be of great use to the salesman. Listening is not only hearing, it is something more. Listening involves hearing, plus observing the manner in which they are expressed: Salesmanship does not only provide feedback for the company to adjust, it also shapes good salesman. It is success of the salesmanship if he gets orders from the existing as well prospective customers.

THEORIES OF SELLING

The process of influencing others to buy may be viewed from four different angles on the, basis of different theories. The first two theories based on the experiences of sales persons or advertising professionals. These theories may be known as salesperson or seller-oriented theories. The third, the buying formula theory of selling is buyer-oriented. And the fourth 'The beavioural equation' emphasises as the buyer's decision process, but takes the salesperson's influence process into account.

First Theory: AIDAS Theory of Selling

The theory, (the AIDAS Theory) after the initials of five words representing five successive mental states of the prospects. ese states are : *(1)* attention, *(2)* interest, *(3)* desire, *(4)* action, *(5)* satisfaction. Credit mainly goes to Strong Jr. for propounding this theory which is based on the experimental knowledge prevailed in 1898. The theory presumes that a prospect who takes a decision to buy passes through five stages consciously. So, the salesperson's presentation must lead the prospect through them in the right sequence that will result in concrete sales.

The salesman should interview the prospect in a well planned and systematic manner so that the prospect is brought to all these five stage one by one systematically. These five stages are:

(1) Attention. This is first phase and the salesperson while interviewing the prospect, must put the prospect into a receptive state of mind or in other words, the salesperson, first should draw the 'attention' of the 'prospect' within a few minutes of the interview. The sales person has to have a reason or an excuse for conducting the interview. If the salesperson has madea previous appointment with the prospect, this phase presents no problem. But still without making an appointment, the sales person must possess, considerable mental alertness and tactful to begin with the prospect and draw his attention. The favourable first impression is assured by, among other things,proper attire, neatness, friendliness and a genuine smile.

(2) Interest. The second stage is gaining interest of the prospect. The salesperson should, therefore, intensify the prospect's attention so that it evolves a state of strong interest. Many techniques are used to gain interest. Some salespeople develop a keen interest in the prospect about the product during conversation. Another technique is to let the product handle the product or a sample. If the product is bulky or technical, sales, portfolios, flepcharts, or other visual aids serve the purpose. During the interest phase, salesperson should search out the selling appeal that is most likely to be effective. If prospect drops certain hints which the salespeople should use in selecting the appeal. Some salesperson should draw out the prospect by asking questions designed to clarify prospect's attitude and feelings towards the product. In addition prospects' interest are affected by basic motivation closeness of the interview subject to current problems, its timeliness, and their mood-receptive, skeptical, or hostile, and the salesperson must take all these factors into consideration in selecting an appeal to emphasize.

(3). **Action.** The desire for the product generated in the mind of the prospect would prompt the prospect to take action *i.e.,* to buy. However, the salesman is responsible for inducing action. An experienced salesperson rarely try to close unless the prospect convinced of the merit of the proposition. Thus, it is necessary for the salesperson to sense when the, time is right. Such tests like trail close or trick close should be used to feel the reaction of the prospect. The salesperson should straight forwardly ask the prospect for an order and get definite 'yes' or 'no'.

(4) **Desire.** The third phase of the selling process is to kindle the prospect's desire to the ready to buy point. The salesperson must continue the conversation along the main line towards the sale. During this phase, many factors disrupt the talks among which are development of sales obstacles, the prospect's objections, external interruptions, and digressive remarks. The obstacles should be faced tactfully and ways to be found to get round them. Objections raised by the prospect during the course of interview should be answered properly to the satisfaction of the prospect. If objections are anticipated

and answered before they are raised, the chance of making a sale is improved. External interruptions cause break in conversation. A good salespeople should summarize what has been said earlier as soon as conversation is resumed. Digressive remarks should be handled tactfully, with fineness but sometimes distracting digression should be handled bluntly.

(5) Satisfaction. After the customer has given the order the sales person should reassure the prospect that the decision was correct. The customer should be leftwith the impression that the salesman merely helped him in making decision. Building satisfaction means thanking the customer for an order and prompt him to reduce the order to black and white. The salesperson should also keep him promises, if made during interview.

Second Theory: 'Right Set of Circumstances' Theory of Selling

'The right set of circumstances theory' is also known as 'situation response' theory and it has its origin to psychological experiments with animals. The theory holds that the particular circumstances prevailing in a given selling situation cause the prospect to respond in a predictable manner. If the salesperson succeeds in securing the attention and gaining the interest in the prospect, and if salesperson presents the proper stimuli or appeals, the desired response would always be a sale. The theory also assets 'the more highly skilled the salesperson is in handling the total set of circumstances, the more predictable will be the response of the prospect? The salesperson, as the theory suggests, should try to control the relevant set of circumstances that may be external and internal to the prospect. For example, if salesperson asks the prospect. 'Let us go out for a cup of coffee'. The salesperson and the remak percent external factors. But at least four factors internal to the prospect affect the response: *(i)* to have a cup of coffee, *(ii)* to have it now, *(iii)* to go, out, and *(iv)* to go out with the salesperson.

Proponents of this theory over stress the external factors and ignore internal factors. They seek selling appeals that evoke desired responses. The salesperson who apply the theory feel difficulties traceable to internal factors, that is, prospects ingrained habits and instinctive behaviour. External factors are easy to contro but internal factors do no readily lend, themselves to manipulation. It is, therefore, a seller oriented theory and over stress the importance of salesperson controlling the situation. He does not handle the factors internal to the prospect carefully and fails to assign appropriate weight to response side of the situation response interaction.

Third Theory: Buying Formula Theory of Selling

We have discussed the two theories which are Seller-oriented. This theory is buyer oriented and takes sign of the buyer. In this theory, buyer's needs or problems get attention and the salesperson's role is simply to help the buyer find solutions. This theory purports to answer the question 'what thinking process goes on in the mind of the prospect that causes the decision: to buy or not to buy? The buying formula itself is a schematic representation of a group of responses, arranged in psychological sequence. This theory, therefore emphasises the internal factors if the prospects and de-emphasises the external factors on the assumption that 'the sales person is conscious of such factors which he will not ignore at all.

The origin of the theory is obscure but its recognisable versions appear in a umber of early books on advertising and selling. Several psychologists advanced explanations substantially. Similar to that contained in 'buying formula'. The name 'buying formula' is given to this theory by E.K. Strong Jr. and the following is the step to step explanation is given by him:

Reduced to their simplest elements, the mental processes involved in a purchase are:

Need (or problem)→ Solution→ Purchase

As one purchase leads to others hence continuing relations develop between buyer and seller. But it is possible only when the buyer is satisfied with the earlier purchases. Hence, fourth element is added: The four elements, then of purchases are:

Need (or problem)→ solution→ purchase→ Satisfaction.

Whenever a need is felt or a problem recognised, the buyer feels a discomfort. It means buyer is conscious of deficiency of satisfaction. In the world of buying and selling, the solution will always be a product or service or both and they belong to a potential seller. In purchasing, then, the solution has two parts: *(i)* product and/or service, and *(ii)* trade name (or naine of the manufacturer or company or salesperson). The formula, thus, will include these two elements in place of the 'solution'. The formula will be:

Need (or problem)→Product or service→trade name→ purchase→ satisfaction or dissatisfaction.

To ensure purchase, the product or service and the trade name must be considered adequate and the buyer must experience a pleasant feeling of anticipated satisfaction when thinking of the product/service or trade name. In a number of cases, an item may be viewed as adequate and also liked, and vice versa. Sometimes products/services are adequate but,not liked. Somethings are liked and bought and are admittedly not as good as competing items. Similar reasoning applies to trade name. Some sources of supply are adequate and liked others are adequate but not liked; still others are liked but patronised even though they are inadequate as compared to other sources.

Adding adequacy and pleasant feelings, the buying formula becomes

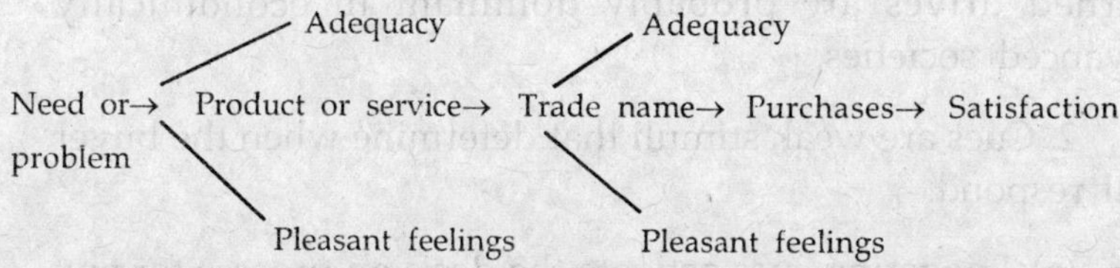

When a buying habit is being established, the buyer must know way the product or service is an adequate solution and why the trade name is the best one to buy. It is also necessary that the buyer must have a pleasant feeling towards the product or service and the trade name in order to maintain a buyer-seller relationship. If buyer's selection challenged, he must be ready to defend his action.

Fourth Theory: 'Behavioural Equation' Theory

This theory uses the stimulus-response model ('The right set of circumstances' theory) and incorporate numerous findings from behavioural research. In this way, it is a sophisticated version of 'the right set of circumstances' theory. J.A. Howard holds that the customer expresses his buying behaviour in terms of his purchasing decision process, viewed as phases of learning process.

Four essential elements of the learning process included in the stimulus: response theory are - drive, cue, response and reinforcement, described as follows:

1. Drives are internal strong stimuli that impel the buyer's response. There are two kinds of drives:

(a) **Innate Drives.** Are physiological needs such as hunger, thirst, pain, sex etc.

(b) **Learned Drives.** Such as striving for status, or social approval, are acquired when paired with the satisfying of innate drives, aud represent elaborations of the innate drives;

serving as a facade behind which the functioning of tile innate drives is hidden. In so far as marketing is concerned, the learned drives are probably dominant in economically advanced societies.

2. Cues are weak stimuli that determine when the buyer will respond.

(a) Triggering cues activate the decision process for any given purchase.

(b) Non-triggering cues influence but not activate the decision process and may operate at any time even through buyer is not contemplating a purchase. These are of two kinds:

(i) Product cues received directly from the product and are external stimuli such as package colour, weight or price etc.

(ii) Informational cues provide information of a symbolic nature about the product. These are also external stimuli and come from advertising, conversation with other people (including sales personnel) and so on.

(c) Specific product and information cues may sometimes work also as triggering cues. This may happen when price triggers the buyers decision.

3. Response is what the buyer does.

4. Reinforcement is any event that strengthens the buyer's tendency to make a particular response.

Howard has put all these four elements into a behavioural equation as follows:

B = P X D X K X V

Where B = Behaviour which is equivalent to response, the act of purchasing a brand or patronising a supplier.

P = Predisposition or the inward response tendency; which is the strength of the habit.

D = Drive level (amount of motiation)

K = Incentive potential which is the value of the product or its potential satisfaction to the buyer.

V = Intensity of all cues—Triggering, product or informational.

The relation among these variables, according to *Howard,* is multiplicative and additive. It simply means that if the value of any independent variable is zero, the value of will also be zero and there is no response at all. For example, if the individual is totally unmotivated (D = O), there will be no response.

Each time, there is a response (a purchase) in which satisfaction (K) received is sufficient to yields a reward, predisposition will increase in value. It means when satisfaction received yields a reward, reinforcement occur. What is reinforced is the tendency to make a response in the future to the cue that immediately precedes the rewarded response. After reinforcement, the probability increases that the buyer will buy the product or patronise the supplier in the future, the cue appears—in other words, the buyer has learned.

Buyer Seller Dejad and Reinforcement

In the interactions of a buyer and a salesperson, each can display a behaviour that is rewarding to each other, it is reinforcing. The salesperson provides the buyer, the product and the necessary information about the product and its uses that the buyer needs. Satisfaction of needs is the, reward to the buyer, who in turn, can reward the seller by buying the product. Each can also reward the other by another type of behaviour, that of providing social approval. The salesperson gives social approval to a buyer by displaying high regard with friendly greetings, warm conversation, praise and the like. In understanding, the salesperson – client relation, if we separate the aspects from social features *i.e.*, buying and selling. Each participant also places a value and cost upon the strictly social features. Behaviour concerning these features of the relationship consists of sentiments or expression of different degrees of liking of social approval. Salespersons attempt to get more or less valuable reward (rein forcement) either in sentiment or economic activity by changing his own behaviour or getting buyers to change his behaviour.

Salesperson's Influence Process. The process by which the salesperson influence the buyer can be explained in terms of the behaviour equation (B = P X D X K X V). The salesperson influences P (predisposition) dIrectly, for example, through interacting with the buyer in ways rewarding the buyer. The greatest effect on P, however, is though to comfrom using the product. The sales person exerts influence through D (amount of motivation). Such influence being especially strong when the buyer seeks information primarily in terms of informational cues. If the ends to be served through satisfying a drive or a need are not clearly defined, by helping to clarify these, the buyer's goals, the salesperson again exerts influencing through D. When the buyer has stopped learning—when the buyer's buying behaviour consists solely of automatic responses—the salesperson influences D by providing triggering cues. When the buyer narrows down the choices to a few sellers from whom to make the purchases, the sales person, by communicating the merits of company's brand, can cause it to appear relatively better, and thus affect K (its potential satisfaction for the buyer). Finally, the salesperson can vary the intensity of his effort, so making the difference in V (the intensity of all cues.)

Salesperson's Role in Reducing Buyer Dissonance

According to *Festinger's* theory of cognitive dissonance, when individual choses between two or more alternatives, anxiety or dissonance will almost always occur because the decision has certain attractive as well as unattractive features. After making decision, people always tead to expose themselves to information that they perceive as likely to support their choice, and to avoid information which support rejected alternatives. This theory applies to post decision's anxiety according to *Festinger*, but it seems reasonable to apply this theory to pre-decision decisions anxiety. *Hauk* for instance, writes that a buyer may panic on reaching the point of decision, and rush into the purchase as an escape from the problem or put it off because of the difficulty of deciding among, alternatives. It would appear, then, that a buyer may experience either predecision or post decision anxiety or dissonance or both.

According to *Howard*, reducing pre or post decision anxiety or dissonance is an important function of salesperson. *Howard* has considered four types of cases involving the salesperson's role in dissonance, function:

1. *An established Product—an going salesperson—client relation*—unless market is unstable, buyer tends toward automatic response behaviour, in which no learning is involved, and thus experiences little, if any, dissonance; but in so far as it occurs, the salesperson would be effective because the. buyer trusts the salesperson.

2. *An established product—a new salesperson—client relation* -The salesperson, being new, would be less effective in reducing dis-sonance.

3. *A new product—an ongoing salesperson—client relation*—Unless the buyer generalises heavily from personal experience with an established similar product, the buyer would experience dissonance especially, if it were an important product. Because of the established relationship with the buyer, the salesperson would be capable of reducing—dissonance.

4. *A new product – an salesperson – client relation* – The buyer would need dissonance reduction, and the salesperson would be less capable of providing it.

PERSONAL SELLING

Personal Selling is one of the forms of Sales Promotion. It is flexible and, a very effective method of communication. Unlike, other promotional technique, it develops a two way communication or mutual communication. Salesman communicates the message regarding the characteristics of the product and the producer to the customers or prospectives and receives communications from the customer in respect or their feelings, behaviour and learnings about the product and the producer. Inspite of its favourable characteristics, personal selling cannot be said to be the unique method of promoting sales, even though it is found effective in many industries. *Taylor Jr. and Robb Remark* – "however, like advertising, its degree of use in the promotiorial mix is variable and. depends on such factors as the nature of the product and its market. One national distributor of tobacco products, for example, uses no personal selling but relies mostly on direct mail advertising to sell its products. At other extreme, a producer of heavy manufacturing machinery spends more than 98 percent of its promotional budget on personal selling."

Often Personal selling and salesmanship are two terms which are used without any distinction. However, there are vital differences between these two terms. Personal Selling is a broader concept and involves oral presontation 41 conversation with one or more prospective buyers for the purpose of making sales. The main purpose of personal selling is to bring the product in the knowledge of the prospective buyers and convince them with the quality of the product and maky certain that ownership transfers take place. Salesmanship on the other, hand, is an art of using skill in selling the product. It may or may not form part of the personal selling. Salesmanship may be employed both in personal selling and in advertisement (impersonal selling). It is, therefore, sometimes, advertisement is called 'salesmanship in prin .' We are here using these two terms' (Personal Selling and salesmanship) synonymous to each other.

The American Marketing Association has defined the term Personal Selling as "oral presentation in conversation with one or more prospective purchaser for the purpose of making sales". *Richard Buskirk* has deemed the term as "personal selling consists of contracting prospective buyers of a product personally." Thus, Personal selling means contacting. prospective buyers for the purpose of making sales. The distinctive qualities of Personal selling are:

(i) Personal Contact. The salesman comes into contact with the prospective buyers and thus each party is able to observe at close quarters to each other and make immediate adjustments and thus make the encounter successful.

(ii) Cultivation of Relationship. Personal selling may lead to all kinds of relationship ranging from selling relationship to a deep personal relationship.

(iii) Immediate Response. Personal selling usually makes the prospeets feel a sort of peculiar obligation for having listened to the sales talks.

Importance of Personal Selling

Personal selling plays a pivotal role in the field of distribution of goods and services. A salesman is a guide and a friend of the consumer and a supporter and an aid to the producer. He helps the consumer, producer and the society alike in the following manner:

(a) Services to Consumers. A salesman helps the consumers in the following ways:

It is the salesman who introduces the product in the market and informs the customers about the new product and also about the producer. He also suggests them how to use the product and how the product can satisfy their needs. He removes every doubt from the minds of the purchasers and convince them about the quality of the goods and credibility of the producer. In this way, he helps converting wants into needs. The purchaser thinks himself honourable, in whom the producer is interesteed.

(b) Services to Producers. Personal selling also serves the producer in the following ways:

(i) He sells goods to the wholesalers and retailers in the channel of distribution and also to the consumer at company's terms.

(ii) He makes search for the new customers and convince them' about the use of the product.

(iii) Salesman induces the customers and new customers to purchase goods.

(iv) He cultivates newer markets and tries to sell more of the company's product.

(v) He helps in interpreting the sentiments of the market because he serves as a communicating link between producer and the consumer. He diagnoses the market and suggests the prescription to remove the marketing ills.

(c) Service to the Society. Personal selling also serves the society. The main purpose of personal selling is to increase the volume of sales. The sales go up with the serious efforts of the sales force. It results in large scale production and reduction of costs and prices. In this ways, society may get better quality goods at cheaper rates. Rate of employment also goes high. The standard of living of the society goes up in view of the large scale production.

Thus, Personal selling has made the large scale production and sales possible.

There are two types of Personal Selling Objectives *viz.*, qualitative and quantitative. The objectives may also be short term and long term objectives. Long term personal selling objectives are broad and general and there is very little change over time. Such objectives are always in conformity with the company' overall objectives. The short term objectives are more specific and mainly in conformity with the role assigned to the Personal selling as a part of the Promotional mix. These objectives change very frequently as soon as there is a change in the Promotional mix. Like Promotional mix short term Personal selling objectives may differ from market to market and from product to product.

According to *Cundiff, Still and Govani*, the Personal selling objectives are:

(1) to do the entire selling job (when there are no other element in the promotional mix);

(2) to 'service' existing accounts (*i.e.*, to maintain communications with present customers and taking orders from them etc.);

(3) to make a search for the new customers;

(4) to secure and maintain effective co-operation with the customers in stocking and promoting the product line;

(5) to keep customers informed on the changes in the product line and other aspects of marketing strategy;

(6) to assist customers in selling the product line (a through 'missionary selling');

(7) to provide technical assistance and advice to customers where the products are complicated and where products are designed strictly according to buyers' specifications;

(8) to assist with (or handle) the training of middlemen's sales personnel;

(9) to provide advice and assistance to middlemen on various management problems;

(10) to collect market information of interest to the company and report to the company management.

In addition to the above objectives as narrated by *Cundiff, Still* and *Govani*, there are certain other quantitative objectives.

(1) to obtain a certain sales volume as fixed by the company management;

(2) to obtain sales volume in ways that contribute to profit objectives, *e.g.*, by selling the proper mix of the products;

(3) to keep personal selling expense within a controllable limit; and

(4) to secure and retain a certain share of the market.

Short term personal selling objectives are usually quantitative objectives. Such objectives are to be attained within the Promotional period.

Qualitative personal selling objectives are usually long term objectives which do not change very often and are carried over from one promotional period to another promotional period. A change in personal selling objective can be effected only if the nature of sales job as well as the size and the quantity of sales force is changed.

In order to reach both quantitative as well as qualitative personal selling objectives, the management sets sales policies which serve as the guidelines for sales people. Such policies are framed by the company in advance, according to the Personal Selling Strategy of the company. Such policies provide general guidance on what to sell (product policies), whom to sell (distribution policies) and the terms of sales (pricing policies). Decisions on 'what to sell' and 'whom to sell' are to shape the fundamental nature of a company and are important determinants of two basic components of Personal Selling Strategy *i.e.,* kind of sales personal needed and the number of sales personnel needed. The sales related marketing policies vary with the Competitive selling.

Personal Selling Objectives and Personal Selling Strategy

The personal selling objectives of the company influence the personal selling strategy and the sales policies. In ordinary circumstances, personal selling strategies are designed on the basis of sales policies. While sales policies provide general guidelines for making personal selling decisions. Personal selling strategy determines the two important questions *e.g.,* the nature of sales job and the size of the sales force. While the personal selling objectives and sales policies both influence these two factors *i.e.,* nature of sales job and the kind of the sales force. The nature of sales positions varies from company to company according to the nature of the product. It may be possible that nature of sales job may vary even though the duties and responsibilities of salesmen in two different companies are similar. For example, the task of a Brooke Bond travelling salesman is entirely different from that of salesman of a product of a technical nature. In the first case, he is to get orders and supply the goods whereas in the latter situation, the salesman has to find out and convince the customer and aggressively seeks orders. The salesman in the first situation is demand satisfier whereas in the second situation, he is demand creater. Naturally, Personal selling strategy would substantially differ in each case.

Complexity of the product or product line also influences the Personal Selling Strategy. Sales policies and the nature of sales job. Product of highly technical nature and that of simple product may require different sales jobs. Consequently

Personal selling efforts and strategy differ. Similarly, sales jobs for different types of salesmen may also differ from each other. A trade salesman establishes long term relations with the customers whereas technical salesman assists the customers by providing technical assistance and advice which helps the company's sales to go up. Thus, personal selling and sales strategy differ from time to time, place to place and from company to company.

Similarly, type of customer not only affects the personal selling objectives and sales strategy but also influences substantially the nature of the sales job. The industrial user of the company's product will be required to be dealt with in a different way than the middleman buying the product for resale. Difference in salesman's role and tasks call for difference in sales job descriptions. Nevertheless, sales jobs may be categorised into limited number of groups *i.e.*, trade selling, missionary selling, technical selling and new business selling.

Thus, Personal selling, a very important element in the promotional mix, is greatly influenced by a number of factors. However, its success largely depends upon the salesman and his potentialities. Many companies compliment personal selling activities with advertisement and other sales promotion activities which work very well his promoting the sales of the company's product.

DETERMINING THE KIND OF SELLING PERSONNEL

One key decision on person selling strategy is that on the kind of sales personnel to employ. It requires consideration of the company's qualitative personal selling objectives *i.e.*, what contribution should be expected from those performing selling jobs towards the company's long term overall objectives? What should be their duties and responsibilities of such individuals? How should their job performance be evaluated? The management must squarely face up to these problems when it decides the kind of Sales Personnel to employ.

It is clear and beyond doubt that each company's individual requirements as to the kind of sales personnel are different because the qualitative personnel selling objectives of each company have some degree of distinctiveness. In addition, each company deals with a unique set of marketing factors, such as the strength and weaknesses of its products, the motivations and buying practices of its customers and prospects, its pricing strategy, the competitive setting (pure competition, monopolistic competition, Oligopolistic competition, etc.,) and the relative strengths and weaknesses of the competitors. Moreover, different selling jobs require different levels of selling and non-selling abilities, training and technical and other knowledge.

In determining the kind of sales personnel best fitted to serve the company's marketing needs, we must understand what we expect from them *i.e.,* the job objectives, the duties and responsibilities, and performance measures. Each salesperson has different job even in the same company. Knowing the salesperson's job means knowing the particular job for particular sales person. Knowing the particular job helps the management to fit the person to the job and job to the person.

Factors Determining the kind of Selling Personnel

The following factors are considered when making a decision on the kind of Selling personnel to employ. Such factors are: *(a)* Product market analysis; *(b)* Analysis of salesperson's role in securing orders; *(c)* Choice of basic selling style.

(a) Product-Market Analysis

No person is capable of selling all kinds of products to all kinds of customers. At one extreme, a salesperson sells single product to many kinds of customers. At the other extreme, a salesperson sells a wide line of products to a single kind of customers. Most ,salespeople sell some products to some kinds of customers. The selling job differs for each salesperson. The selling jobs may be categorized as *(i)* Product specialists, *(ii)* Market specialist, and *(iii)* Combinations of product and Market specialization.

A critical step in sales job analysis is to derfine the product market interaction with the help of product market grid as shown in the following figure 2.

Type of Market

Campus Bookstores | **Book Wholesalers** | **Retailers** | **Government Buyers**

Fig. 2. Product—Market grid tor a Book Publishing Company.

The grid demand a through analysis and classification of both of markets and products. The boxes in the above fegure indicate the different customers who might be sold different products. As the management decides which products should be sold to which customers. The blacked in boxes indicate the management decision on which products should be sold to which customers. The result helps answer the question, should over salespersons be product specialist, market specialists or both.

Product specialization is needed when the product is highly technical and needs advice of the sales personnel on its uses and implications. Market specialization is called for when the product is non-technical but different kinds of customers have unique buying problems, require special sales approaches or need special service. But in majority of cases, the sales personnel must have considerable knowledge of more than a single company product line and also in dealing with more than one kind of customers.

Determining the type and amount of specialization requires consideration of both the interdependence dimension and the expertise dimension. The four possible combinations of these two dimensions results in four different kinds of selling roles.

If the dominant interdependence is between customers (rather than between products), sales personnel should be specialists. They should be product specialists when the needed dominant expertise is in product technologies. They should be customer specialists when the needed dominant expertise is in customers' applications. Customer specialist need the support of market managers' who provide the necessary prospect expertise through their specialisation in applications in particular industries.

If the dominant interdependence is between products (rather than between customers), the selling organisation needs staffing by full live sales persons. If product technologies require the most expertise, sales persons sell, the full live to all kinds of prospects and supported by product managers who provide the needed product expertise. If customers' applications require the most expertise, salesperson sell the full live to particular kind of prospects.

In addition to product market interactions, other elements in a company's market situation affect the caliber of salesperson required. The size of customers or the geographical locations has bearing on the type of sales persons. Different talents for instance, are required in case, the most customers are large than if most customers are small. Similarly geographi- locations also have bearing on the type of salesperson needed. fn such or similar cases, appropriate grids assist in the analysis.

(b) Analysis of Salesperson's Role in Securing Orders

The second major factor in deterrnining the kind of salespersonnel is the analysis of role or roles in securing orders. The main objective of all salespeople is to seek orders. All salespeople seek orders aggressively in some situatio'ns but in others they take order coming their way, the relative emphasis or order taking and order getting varying in different selling environment. The salesperson for a product which is popular in the market, is simply a order take because the product is presold in the market whereas a salesperson trying to sell a product in the market and has to call on householders and customers most often function as order-getter, since getting orders is his main goal.

The salesperson's role in securing orders also vary with the Promotional strategy relied upon. Depending on the Promotional strategy Personal selling or Advertising – sales people may be either active or passive forces in security orders. If the promotional strategy of the manufacturer is to rely heavily on advertising to attract business and build demand, marketing channels include several layers of middlemen and the role of salesperson is only passive and he acts only as order take and order getter only incidentally. In the opposite situation where advertising is used only and mainly to back up personal selling, the sales person's role is active and the salesperson's role is that of order getter.

There are certain cases both in consumer goods and industrial goods marketing in which the salespeople play only a minor and indirect role in securing orders, the salesperson's major role being concerned with certain other matters. In consumer goods marketing, the missionary salesperson's major role is to assist middlemen in making sales to their customers. Orders from customers, then, will come *via* middlemen *i.e.,* indirectly rather than directly. In industrial goods marketing, such sales person (The sales engineer), plays two major roles: *(i)* Advising middlemen and the customers on technical product features and its applications, and *(ii)* providing design consultancy to middlemen and customers on installation or processes incorporating the manufacturer's products. The salesperson, then, gets order indirectly through middlemen.

(c) Choice of Basic Selling Style

The third important factor in determining the kind of Selling personnel is the basic selling style as is being practised by the company. Actually, each company has differences in marketing factors and therefore, it requires a different kind of salespersonnel that suits the company and can play a unique role even related to similar companies employing similar kind of sales personnel. There are four basic selling styles generally in use *i.e.,* Trade Selling, Missionary selling, Technical selling and New business selling.

1. **Trade Selling.** The trade salesperson develops and maintains long term relations with a stable group of customers. This is low-key selling having little or no pressure and the job is rather dull and of routine nature. This selling style is generally used for product having well established markets and the role of salesperson is only to take orders. In such cases, advertising and other forms of promotion are used as overall marketing strategy than is Personal selling. One important responsibility of the salesperson in this selling style is to help customers build up their volume through providing Promotional assistance. A trade salesperson most often devotes his time to promotional work with retailers and wholesalers.

2. Missionary Selling. The missionary salesperson do not sell to the end consumers. Their main obobjective is to increase the company's sales volume by assisting customers (generally wholesalers or sole selling agents) with their selling efforts. Missionary salesperson do not often get direct. orders, since the orders obtained result from the missionary's primary public relations and promotional efforts with customers of customers (indirect customers). Thus, their main job is to persuade the company's indirect customers to purchase goods from the direct customers. For example, a missionary salesperson of a drug manufacturing concern calls on retail druggists to acquaint them with the new product and to urge them to purchase the product with the company's direct customers (*i.e.,* wholesalers or sole selling agents) and to stock it. In some cases, missionary sales staff members call on individuals and institutions who do not buy the product themselves but influence its purchase by others. For example, a representative from a drug manufacturer may call on doctors and hospitals to acquaint them with the new product in a thrust to get the product recommended to patients who will buy it from retailers (indirect customers). Missionary selling like trade selling is a low key selling and requires no technical knowledge.

3. Technical Selling. Technical salesperson is a technical hand and his main job objective is to increase company's sales volume by providing technical assistance and advice to company's established accounts. His main function is to advise just like missionary salesperson but, in addition, sells direct to industrial users and other buyers. The technical salesperson devotes most of his time to acquainting industrial users with technical product features and its applications and to helping them design installation or processes that incorporates the company's product. In this selling style, ability to identify, analyse and solve problems is important.

Technical salesperson often specilize either by products or by markets. In selling large made-to-order installations, such as, stream turbine or electric generators, they have to work with other technical personnel having specialisation in different items in the product line.

4. New Business Selling. The new business salesperson's main job is to find out new customers or convert prospects into customers. Such salesperson are generally creative and ingenious and possess a high degree of resourcefulness. Few companies, have salesperson whose mainjob is to get new business whereas in some other companies, regular trade salesperson are expected to perform the job of new business salesperson also. However, these are two different jobs requiring, different talents and therefore, they generally ignore new business selling in favour of servicing their established accounts due to several reasons.

The company therefore, must choose the Selling style which suits its Selling Objectives.

Thus, the three basic factors as discussed above must be considered by a company when determined to consider the kind of Selling Personnel.

ROLE OF PERSONAL SELLING IN MARKETING STRATEGY

Marketing research assumes the responsibility of identifying customers needs and problems, while firm marketing mix provides the solutions. Marketing mix is a set of different strategies that a company utilises to implement its marketing plan and pursue its marketing objectives. It is composed of four major strategies *i.e.*, Product strategy, Price strategy, Distribution strategy and Promotion strategy. Personal selling plays important roles in different strategies.

Role of Personal Selling in Product Strategy

A fIrm's product is a bundle of benefits offered to the customers. This benefit bundle contains both tangible and intangible components. There are two types of benefits attached to the product-core or primary benefits and peripheral benefit. The core benefit provided by the company is typically the same as offered by other competitors. However, the peripheral benefits attached to the product act as a differentiating device that can create competitive edge. These are peripheral benefits which induce a customer to favour a particular product and personal selling plays a dominant role in it.

The management makes the decision about the features and benefits to be incorporated in the product and the compensation of the product mix. The product can be described in terms of its two dimensions. The number of product lines included (width) and the number of products within each line. (depth).

The Sales management generally does not take any part in making decisions regarding product design and product mix. But under marketing concept, Sales managers help specify desirable product features and benefits provide guidance during the product development phase. The participate in product testing and test marketing (testing the product in one segment of the market). They offer their valuable advice in making decisions of product mix because they are familiar with the market place. Sales management can also advise with respect to product sourcing *i.e.,* pointing out the source from where the product can be obtained by the company without its production in its own plants.

Role of Personal Selling in Pricing Strategy

The sales managers' role in Pricing. The product is gaining importance. Price is a value that the seller asks for his product or it is the amount of money for which the seller is willing to transfer the title of his product or service. A price is of little consequence unless it coincides with the value conceptions of prospective buyers *i.e.,* at what price the buyer is willing to purchase the product. The value conception determines the demand. According to the law of demand, the demand of product increases if price of that product goes down and *vice versa*. Elasticity of demand (level of change in demand in consequence of the change in the level of price) is another factor that decides the price of a product. Thus company can increase its sales volume by reducing the price but the level of price change depends upon the elasticity of demand.

But companies may have another option to increase its sales volume besides price manipulation. That option is non-price competition *i.e.*, selling the product at higher price but by creating a difference in the minds of prospective buyers about the company's product in relation to competitors' products. This permits, the seller to gain pricing flexibility and get a premium over the current marketing rate. Various techniques of non-price comptition may be innovative product and package design, distinctive positionting, selecting and aggressively promoting a brand name, offering superior service capability in case of durable consumer goods, providing widespread distribution network ete., which can create product differentiation.

By creating a meaningful difference in the minds of buyers, the company avails of certain freedom in pricing, the product and the Sales management can assist the management in a number of ways : *(i)* it can ascertain competitors' pricing strategies and gauge market reactions to alternative price levels, *(ii)* it can advise senior management in pricing decisions, or *(iii)* it can be granted discretion in adjusting the prices according to market conditions. In making individual product pricing decisions. One of the two approaches are followed: *(1)* Cost based methods; and *(2)* Market oriented pricing method. In cost-based methods price of the product is fixed by adding something for the profit to the cost. The sales managers are involved not only in setting prices by advising the senior management but also in keeping selling costs under control so that the mark-up not put the product at a price disadvantage.

Market oriented pricing, by contrast relies on the market response to alternative price levels. Market oriented pricing may be demand oriented and competition oriented. Demand oriented pricing basically means 'charge what the traffic can bear.' *i.e.,* on the basis of elasticity of demand. Sales managers play a major role in making assessment of consumers' response because they are familiar with the consumers response as well as competitive pricing behaviour. If the firm chooses to adopt competitive oriented strategy; The sales persons provide the information of competitive pricing behaviour. The knowledge assists in fixing the price of the product at, above below the competitive prices.

Role of Personal Selling in Distribution Strategy

Distribution is another component of marketing mix, which is concerned with the channel of distribution through which the product passes on to the ultimate consumers. The ownership of the product can be transferred in two ways — direct or indirect. In case of direct distribution, the ultimate buyer acquires the title direct from the producer whereas in indirect distribution, the transfer takes place through various middlemen in the distribution channel. In direct selling the organisation has full control over the distribution whereas in indirect selling, the producer has less control over the marketing process.

In both instances—direct and indirect distribution, sales management plays significant role in the distribution process. The sales management would be responsible for maintaining the supply line and making the goods readily available to the consumers otherwise production and selling efforts (mainly advertisement) might prove meaningless. In direct selling, the sales force has to contact the consumers of the product to convince them to buy the product. In case of indirect distribution, the sales management has to secure the support of Trade-jargon used to describe dealings with middlemen. Selling to the trade also requires a great deal of work with distributor's customers and prospects.

Role of Personal Selling in Promotional strategy

The final element of the marketing mix is the promotion that means the presentation of the persuassive message to the firm's target market in an attempt to stimulate sales. Personal selling is important in this task and plays significant role in conjunction with advertising and sales promotion. Advertisement is a long term tool designed to create awareness among the prospective buyers about the company's product and their major benefits. It creates positive attitude or interest among the message recipients. Sales promotion techniques support the other aspect of Promotional Strategy.

Advertisement and sales promotion activities are irrelevant unless order-getting function is not under taken by the sales force of the company. They pave the way for personal selling. Unless sales management procures the orders, other functions in the organisation are irrelevant. Sales management is a part of the team effort and must act in concert not only with the other components of the marketing mix but also with the various other non-marketing units.

Thus, sales management or personal selling plays significant role in the marketing mix.

COMPETITIVE SETIINGS AND PERSONAL SELLING SFRATEGY

Element of competition—the struggle among various fUms for their market share—is a fundamental aspect of a free economy. Individual companies operate in different competitive settings. Differences exist from company to company with respect to the maturity of the industry and the number of competitors. These differences result in different types of Competitive Settings. Economists have identified four types of competitive settings *i.e., (1)* Pure competition, *(2)* Monopolistics competition, *(3)* Oligopolistic competition, and *(4)* Monopoly or no direct competition.

Marketing strategy and consequently the personal selling strategy differ in different Competitive Settings.

Personal Selling in Pure Competition

Pure competition, as defined by economists is a market situation where there are a large number of buyers and sellers in the market place and none of them is too powerful to control or influence the prevailing market price. This situation is based on certain assumptions that:

(1) no single buyer saller is so large relative to the market that can influence the product's total demand or supply;

(2) the products of all sellers in the market are identical, so buyers are indifferent to which seller they buy. There is no product differentation.

(3) there is no artificial restraint on prices exist. (no administering of prices or control on prices by trade association, labour unions, or companies etc.)

(4) all buyers are fully informed about all sellers' prices. As there is no product differentiation, the buyers shall purchase from the seller who sells at lower prices;

Under this competitive setting, no market strategy is required because all products are identical and prevailing price in the market is the same for all sellers hence buyer has no preference of any seller over others. No seller can cut the price to gain business at the cost of others and if does so, he would immediately match the cut. No seller would push the sale of the product through advertising or personal selling because all buyers buy the goods on price basis that is the same in all cases and moreover they are fully informed about the prices. The sellers are not worried about the channels of distribution or physical distribution.

This type Competitive Setting is hypothetical and not present in any part of the—world. Consequently, it requires no marketing or personal selling strategy.

Personal Selling in Monopolistic Competition

In monopolistic competitive situation, same or all of the assumptions of pure competition do not hold good. Under monopolistic competition, there is a large number of sellers of a generic kind of product but product of each seller is relatively heterogeneous to consumers. Each seller's brand is in someway differentiated from every other seller's brand. They all are competitors and new competitors are not refrained from entering the market. Each seller wants to gain the market share through a combination of price and non-price factors. Every seller's brand is different in the minds of the buyers from competting brands. The consumer is convinced that all brands of the product though identical are not alike atleast in buyers' mind. By influencing brand preferences of buyers, every selles wants to gain market. Most of the buyers are not fully informed of the products or brands, of the same product offered by various sellers. Sellers of different brand (of the same product) differentiate their offerings through individualizing one or several components of overall marketing strategy. Unique packaging, an unusual distribution method (such as house to house distribution), pricing gimmicks (such as bargain offer may differentiate the product pricing.

However, in growth and maturity stages of product life cycle, sellers of the products differentiate them promotional strategy. Advertising is extensively used to differentiate the brand in the minds of buyers and to stimulate selective demand. Personal selling tries to maintain and strengthen the supply line and sees to it that desired distribution intensity is secured and maintained and that middlemen provide the needed push.

Monopolistic competition setting provides a new look to the overall marketing strategy. This type of setting provides marketing opportunities and requires skill in planning and implementing overall marketing strategy. The key element in planning the overall marketing strategy is to differentiate the product even if ever so slightly in some way. Appropriate promotion (usually some blend of advertising and personal selling) is the critical element in implementing the such an overall marketing strategy. The role of advertising in such type of setting, is communicating, the message to final buyers and the role of personal selling is servicing the distribution network and stimulating Promotional efforts by the middlemen'.

Personal Selling in Oligopolistic Competition

Under Oligopolistic competition, the number of marketers is small but each one is large enough to dominate the market. They are individually identified and known to each other and it is difficult for a new competitor to enter the market. Each competitor owns a large organisation and occupy a large market. Any change in overall, marketing strategy of one seller has repercussion on the others. Each one must weigh the possible reactions of other marketing strategy while planning its own overall marketing strategy.

Under this type of competition, a stiff competition exists in the market. If one acts in a particular way to dominate the market, others follow the suit. If one introduces an improved product, others will possibly lose the market share unless they respond appropriately and immediately. For this reason, each competitor watches closely, the changes brought about by other competitors in their products and such changes are either matched or countered. One's action towards increasing ones market share is initiated, improved upon, or otherwise countered by other competitors as rapidly as possible. Similarly, price cut of his product by one competitor, may result industry-wide price adjustments so quickly that they appear to result from collusion.

Personal selling plays very important roles in building and maintaining dealers co-operation, in servicing the distribution network and in gathering information about the competitors' actions. On the basis of information so gathered, counter offensives can be planned and implemented within no time just to safeguard company's own interests Under Oligopolistic situation, advertising and personal selling play very critical roles in communicating the message to the prospective buyers to influence their minds in favour of product brand. It is even more important to counter competitors move through advertising. Both Advertising and Personal selling help in implementing the overall marketing strategy.

Personal Selling in Monopoly Setting or No Direct Competition Setting

Monopoly is a market situation where only one firm dominates the market and there is no close substitute for the product. Prices are fixed by the firm on the basis of what the traffic can bear': Barring a few public utility concerns, such firms are very rare in our economy. Some other companies which are not actually monopolist but are innovators of a new product, sell their product in monopoly like conditions and they have directly no competition at all.

Both monopolist and innovating marketer must initiate and stimulate primary demand *i.e.,* demand for the product category through promotional (Personal selling and advertising) strategies aimed at influencing the final buyers and middlemen. Both (monopolist and innovating marketer) need distribution strategies providing for marketing channels, middlemen's cooperation, and the product's physical distribution, and putting into effect of these distribution strategies requires the effective implementation of personal selling strategy in terms of both kind and number of Sales personnel. Both require a pricing strategy. The Monopolist is free to charge any price on the basis of 'what the traffic will bear' to maximise his profits. The innovating marketer chooses between either a price skimming or a penetration pricing strategy, depending mainly upon how soon he expects direct competition to enter the market. Putting into effect the chosen pricing strategy calls for the effective implementation of Personal selling strategy by sales executives and sales personnel. Both seek to integrate their product, distribution, promotion (including personal selling and advertisement) and pricing strategies into overall marketing strategies consistent with their long term goals.

Thus, Personal Selling Strategy differs in different competitive situation.

❐

3

Consumer Behaviour and Sales Promotion

It is important for a marketer to understand all these variables so as to know as to why a consumer, behaves in the manner he/she does and how his/her mind is conditioned and influenced. One of the best way to get an explanation of this behaviour is to study the various factors and theories of consumer behaviour as derived from the behavioural sciences, namely, economics, psychology and sociology. Some of these have been discussed here:

Economic Determinants

Economists were the first to advance formal explanations of buyer behaviour. In addition, their studies of income and personal consumption and the concept of discretionary income help us to understand buyer behaviour. Generally, economists visualize the market as being made up of homogenous segements of supply and homogenous segments of demand. Economic theory describes humans as rational buyers who have perfect information about the market and use it to obtain optimum value for their buying effort and money. Price is regarded as their strongest motivation. They compare all competing sellers' offerings and, since all are alike in every respect, they buy the one with the lowest price. Above all, the economic person's behaviour is rational. Under these circumstances his or her buying choices are predictable and yield maximum value.

In some situations this model of the economic person helps us to understand and even predict consumer buying behaviour. It explains why a consumer may select the food store with the most or best "weekend specials" for his or her Friday shopping trip. It explains why a special on brand X may attract customer who normally buys brand Y. It also explains why a consumer, having decided to buy a new Ford station wagon, visits several Ford dealerships to get the best trade in the price. However, for the most part, decison making by individuals is far too compelx to reduce to the simplistic model of economic person. Although this model may explain, for example, why a buyer chooses one.

In striving for a realistic explanation of buyer behaviour, we must discard one assumption that pervades the concept of economic person—that markets are homogenous. Heterogeneity, not homogeneity, characterizes markets. The entire notion of market segmentation is based on the realization that not all buyers are alike—that they differ in numerous and distinctive ways. Further more, this heterogenity is evident on both the supply (sellers') and demand (buyers') sides of every market. Essentially, then, the overal marketing problem of the total economy is to match heterogenous segments of supply with heterogenous segments of demand.

This idea is consistent with those economic theories that explain competition among sellers by emphasizing innovative competition, product differentiation, and differential advantage. The position occupied by every firm engaged in marketing is in some respects unique. Each is differentiated from all other by the characterisics of its products, its services, its geographic location, or its particular combination of these features. Therefore, each firm's survival requires that it presents, to some group of buyers, a differential advantage over other suppliers. Any marketing organisation makes sales to a core market composed of buyers who prefer this source and to a fringe market made up of buyers who find the source acceptable, at least for occasional purchase. A firm's hard-core market is that segment composed of brand loyal buyers. The farther one goes from the core, out to the fringes, the less brand loyalty is shown by buyers, to the point where brand name is of little importance. The core market concept has special meaning for the firm that wants to increase its market share, since this normally means that it must concentrate its markting efforts in areas where its fringe overlaps that of another firm's. The key point is that, for a firm to increase its market share, it must expand at the fringes.

Numerous economic factors influence consumers in the ways in which they spend their incomes for personal consumption. In this section we examine a few of the more important uncontrollable economic factors, that is, those that individual firms cannot influence to any significant extent:

(a) **Disposable Personal Income.** Goods and services are produced for purposes of consumption; purchasing power is used to convert production into consumption and disposable personal income (*i.e.,* what people have to spend or save after they have paid their taxes) represents potential purchasing power in the hands of consumers. In most years, however, people do not spend all their income. Disposable personal income is used both for personal consumption spending and for saving.

Personal consumption spending tends both to rise and fall at a slower rate than does disposable personal income. But in inflationary periods, such as throughout most of the 1960s and 1970s, and well into the 1980s, spending sometimes rises faster than income. Generally however, in years of higher income, a lower proportion is spent and higher proportion is saved. In years of lower income, the proportion spent tends to increase while that saved declines.

(b) **Size of Family and Family Income.** Size of family and size of family income affect spending and saving patterns, but infortunately, little research has been reported on these relationships, and what studies have been done are relatively old. Two studies are cited here to illustrate the type of research that can provide useful information concerning spending behaviour as it relates to size of family and family income. The Wharton study disclosed that in urban families with lower incomes, average personal consumption spending exceeded income. it also showed that the average propensity to consume declined rather rapidly as income rose above the poverty level.

Findings of Researchers imply that significant changes occur in a family's spending and saving pattern as it moves from one income bracket to another. They also indicate that changes in the distribution of all the families in a population, relative to income brackets, may bring about significant changes in marginal propensities to consume and to save.

(c) **Consumer Credit.** Availability of consumer credit influences the pattern of consumer spending. Through credit, which allows one to buy now and pay later, a consumer commands more purchasing power than that represented by his or her current income. Availability of credit has been a key factor in the rapid growth of the markets for mobile homes, boats, camping trailers, and the like.

(d) **Consumers' Income Expectations.** The incomes that consumers expect to receive in the future have some bearing on their present spending patterns. In particular, spending for automobiles, furniture, major appliances, and other expensive items tends to be influenced by consumer's optimism or pessimism about future income.

(E) **Consumer's Liquid Assets.** Consumer buying plans are influenced, especially those for "big-ticket" items, by the size of their holdings of liquid assets—that is, cash and other assets readily convertible into cash, for example balances in checking and savings accounts, shares in savings and loan associations, deposits in credit unions, and holdings of government bonds and readily marketable stocks and bonds. Even though a consumer may buy with current income, the freedom with which he or she spends is influenced by his or her accumulation of liquid assets. Retired and unemployed individuals may use liquid assets to buy everyday necessities. Other consumers may use liquid assets to meet major medical bills and other emergencies.

(f) **Discretionary Income.** A family with money left over after buying such necessities as food, clothing, shelter, and transportation has discretionary income.

Even small fluctuations in income cause sharp repercussions in consumer's purchases of durables. This traces partly to the fact that consumers can postopone or speed up their purchase of such durables as automobiles, furniture, and major applicances. If a family is temporarily short of income, it can use the old refrigerator for another year or so. Or, if it finds itself suddenly with more discretionary income, it may replace the refrigerator this year instead of next. The quick response of durable goods expenditures to income changes traces also to the wide use of instalment credit in financing such purchases. Consumers are willing to increase instalment debt when income is rising and are reluctant to incur additional indebtedness when income is declining. Lenders are also more agreable to debt creation in prosperous times. Purchases of nondurables and services which are much less postponable than purchases of durables, react less violently to changes in income.

Sociological Determinants

Sociologists view marketing as involving the activities of groups of people motivated by group pressures as well as by individual desires. Their studies of sociological influences have emphasized the signficance of reference groups, the individual's concept of social role, the diffusion process, and social class as influences on hunan behaviour. These studies have demonstrated the importance of social factors in analyzing and influencing consumer behaviour.

(a) **Reference Groups.** The people with whom an individual regualrly associates exert strong influences on his or her beahviour. He or she must conform at least partially to their standards of beahviour to gain group acceptance. An individual's behaviour is also influenced by groups with whom he or she has little regular contact but with whom he or she identifies closely. Both types of groups are called reference groups, which include family and peer groups, social groups, and others, such as religious fraternal organisations.

(i) *Primary Groups.* These groups, fundamental in determining the social nature of the individual, are groups of people engaged in intimate, face to-face contact and cooperation. The most pervasive and traditionally the most influential primary group is the family, but with the emergence of the modern small, two-generation family, much of this influence has passed to other primary groups, particularly peer groups.

Peer groups are composed of individuals who spend considerable time together and are of fairly common age and social background. Among children, these are often play groups; among adults, they include neighbourhood and community groups. Other groups with varying degrees of socializing influence are religious, educational, and political institutions and work groups.

Each individual may hold membership in several different primary groups. At work one may be a part of a close-knit, friendly group of co-workers. As a Church member, one may or may not have close personal contacts with other members. As a member of social or fraternal organisations, one may be a part of still other primary groups. Any of these groups is classified as a peer groups if it is sufficiently homogeneous. Purely social groups are most likely to qualify. Some peer groups transfered national boundaries; scientists and professional people often identify strongly with counterparts in other nations. The peer groups has the greatest influence on the individual as a consumer because the group's general interests and mode of life are most nearly like his or her own.

(ii) ***Individual's Concept of Social Role in Groups.*** The way in which a person sees his or her role in the social groups in which he or she holds membership is important in explaining the person's motivation, A "rugged individualist" may enjoy establishing a reputation as one who set his or her own patterns of behaviour within existing group norms of acceptable conduct. Individualism was once a common mode of beahviour in the united States and is still important in some nations. Group behaviour has since evolved and become more important in the United States. The newer mode of behaviour requires close conformity to group norms. The group-oriented individual is anxious to fit into the behaviour patterns of his or her peers. What they do, the individual must do. This does imply, however, that the individual's pattern of behaviour is rigidly frozen. Groups norms may change, and the individual adjusts his or her behaviour accordingy. The group-oriented individual is seldom motivated by the traditional appeal of "being an innovator" or "leading the pack." To be motivated to action, one must first be persuaded that the suggested action is accepted by one's peers as the proper thing to do.

(iii) ***Significance of Reference Groups to Marketing.*** Knowledge of reference group and their influences makes it easier to explain why consumers behave in particular ways and-more important to marketers-to predict their behaviour. It explains, for example, why two groups of young people in the same community-one, high school seniors, and the other, college freshmen—adopt different styles of dress or other behaviour even though they are nearly the same age and come from similar family backgrounds. Even within a college freshman group, different reference groups dictate wide variations in dres and behaviour. Even the same individual behaviour differently at different times as he or she identifies with different reference groups. A young executive, for example, may dress and act conservatively when on the job and in other contact with businesss associates, but off the job he or she may be a sportscar racing buff and behave and dress very differently.

(iv) ***Influentials.*** An influential is a person who serves as an opinion leader of a group. Such opinion leaders are not confined to a single social class; they are found at all levels of society. Outwardly, influentials and those they influence (*i.e.,* others in the same social groups) are very much alike—they have similar incomes, occupations, family backgrounds, and so on. According to one sociologist, an individual's influence is related to; *(1)* who one is, *(2)* what one knows, and *(3)* whom one knows. For example, an unmarried girl may be a fashion leader because of who she is; and older woman her group's cooking expert because of what she knows; and a man his group's political leader because of whom he knows, not only in the group but also outside it.

Influentials play key roles in marketing. If an influential tries or uses a product, his or her followers are prone to do the same. Marketers, therefore, often target their promotional efforts to reach influentials and, through them, reach their followers by word of mouth or other subtle influences exterted by the influentials.

(b) **The Diffusion Process.** The social process of spreading information about new products or services to persuade consumers to accept them is known as diffusion. Studies of the diffusion process reveal that most users do not adopt an innovation simultaneously. The first groups to adopt an innovation is made up of a small number of "innovators." They are soon copied by another groups, who, although not venturesome enough to try first, want to be among the early users. Gradually, members of other groups adopt the innovation until it finally reaches market saturation. For a dramatically new product, such as television, the entire process may take ten years or more.

Fig. 'B'. The diffusion process is visualized as curve approching a normal distribution, with 16 per cent of the consumers in the combined innovator and early adopter groups, 34 per cent each in the early and late majority groups, and 16 per cent in the laggard group. It is important to identify target market segments at each stage in the diffusion process. In the intial phases of market introduction, for instance, effort and money may be wasted if the marketer tries to cultivate the entire market all at once.

The various adopter groups exhibit marked differences. The innovators are usually the youngest and have the highest social status and wealth; they are frequently cosmopolites and have professional, business, and personal contacts outside their own immediate social circles. Those in the early adopter groups are generally influentials but their contacts are restricted largely to their own local group, they enjoy high status within their own social groups, and they are usually younger than those in the groups followings. Those in the early majority group are the most deliberate; they will not consider buying a new product until a number of their peers (innovators and early adopters) have done so. Those in the late majority have below-average income and social prestige and are older than members of earlier groups. Laggards have still lower incomes and social status; by the time they buy a new product, the earlier groups are often already trying something newer.

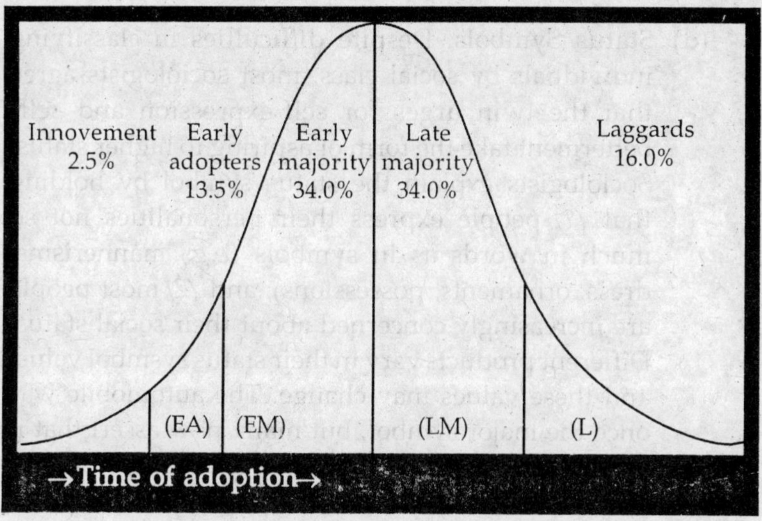

Fig. 'B' Classification of Adopter Groups

(c) **Social Classes.** Every society classfies its members according to some social hierarchy. All have people who occupy positions of relatively higher status and power. Most sociologists divide American society into three broad, roughly defined classes; the upper, middle, and lower classes. W. Lloyd Warner, on the basis of studies in three American towns, set up a hierarchy of six social classes; upper upper, lower upper, upper middle, lower middle, upper lower, and lower lower. Under Warner's system the class status of each person is ascertained by asking his or her equals, superiors, and inferiors to rank the person. This dependence on the ratings of others has been the main criticism of the Warner system. The ordinary citizen does not think in terms of this complex hierarchy and, when asked to classify his or her fellow citizens into the six groups, he or she shows little agreement with other who are asked to do the same thing.

(d) **Status Symbols.** Despite difficulties in classifying individuals by social class, most sociologists agree that the twin urges for self-expression and self-betterment take the form of aspiring to higher status. Sociologists explain the status symbol by holding that *(1)* people express their personalities not so much in words as in symbols (*e.g.,* mannerisms, dress, ornaments, possessions), and *(2)* most people are increasingly concerned about their social status. Different products vary in their status sysmbol value, and these values may change. The automobile was once the major symbol, but many now assert that it has been replaced by the house and its furnishings. The status symbol concept is a valuable one, for when the marketer recognizes that it is selling a symbol as well as a product, it views its product more completely. The marketer should understand not only how the product satisfies certain needs but how it fits into modern culture, because social classses exhibit differences in life-style."

Cultural Anthropological Determinants

Every culture evolves unique patterns of social conduct. Analysis of these patterns help in explaining the buying behaviour of individuals. Thus, the Japanese culture provides for certain patterns of eating, of dress, and social interaction; the Arbain culture provides for different patterns and both are different from those prevalent in the United States. Many aspects of American culture and subcultures within the United States are unique, including the roles of ethnic groups, religion, women in society, leisure time, and fashion as well as the population composition itself.

(a) **Religions.** Whereas the predominant religions of some nations stress passive acceptance of life, the Christian and Jewish religions, which comprise the basic religious heritage of American society, emphasize the perfectibility of people and their environment and, hence, encourage them to improve themselves and their way of life. Therefore, the production and consumption of goods are acceptable activities because they contribute to these goals. Within the American Judeo-Christian religious pattern, however, there are many individual sect and creeds. And although they share similar feeling about the overall social roles of production and consumption, consumption patterns of selected foods, beverages, and apparel very considerably among them. In other nations, religion has a different impact. Hinduism, for example, with its passive acceptance of one's role, affects consumption patterns in India.

(b) **The Role of Women.** Roughly one-half of adult American women work and have incomes of their own; labour-saving appliances provide the other half with more time free of domestic responsibilities and, hence, more time for shopping. American women has either sole or major responsibility for making many kinds of purchases and exert increasing influence on all buying decisions. As the women's movement has gathered strength, increasing numbers of women take active rather than passive roles in society—this trend has great signficance to marketing, especially in the choice of advertising themes. Throughout the world, women's role varies from a very small but growing place of women in Arab countries to the place of near equality in Scandinavia.

(c) **Ethinic Groups.** The United States is a melting pot of cultures and peoples, but this blending has not been complete. An identifiable American national culture has emerged, but it has not equally permeated all portions of society or all geographic regions. There is, for example, an African influence not only in the Deep South but wherever black people have moved in large numbers, a Mexican influence in the Southwest, a Scandinavian influence in Minnesota and the Pacific Northwest, and a Cuban and Puerto Rican influence in many cities, including Miami, Chicago, Washington, D.C., New York, and Philadelphia. Although ethnic differences tend to decrease with each generation in the United States, their continuing existence helps to explain differences in consumer motivation and behaviour that would not exist in a country with a population of common cultural heritage. Yet there are also nations which have multiple cultural heritages that remain distinct for generations, as, for example, Switzerland. In such nations, marketing plans must take into account variations in the different cultures.

(d) **Fashion.** The role of fashion in American society has been growing in importance. With widespread ownership of television sets, not to mention rising circulations of magzines and newspapers and the increasing mobility of consumers, fashion news is disseminated in minimum time. The time span covered by the appearance of a new fashion, its adoption by a few pacesetters, its rise to popularity, and its subsequent decline is becoming progressively shorter. At the same time, expansions in discretionary income permit consumers to spend more in their attempts to satisfy the desire for change. Since there are increasing numbers of group-oriented people and fewer individualists more importance has been placed on conforming to fashion changes.

(e) **Leisure Time.** Increasing number of people have greater amounts of leisure time, and this is reflected in changes in value and the way of life. Instead of buying an expensive car to impress friends, a consumer may buy an economy model in order to buy a boat, shop, or fishing equipment. New homes are planned to simplify participation in leisure-time activities. People have ceased being producers for much of their lives and have become active consumers for the products and services that go along with increasing leisure. The old Puritan dictum that "For Satan find some mischief still for idle hands to do" is being overthrown, but the Puritan influence still remains in the United States. People refer to "active" leisure rather than just to "leisure"—the active disassociating leisure from the guilt-loaded idea of 'loafing."

(f) **Population Composition.** Most of the population growth throughout the world is in metropolitan areas; but the United States, it is in the suburbs rather than in the cities themselves. This trend has marketing significance because the subordinate often represents a different market than the city dweller. The suburb retains much of the character of a small town—thus, neighbourhood and local social group strongly influence individual consumption patterns.

The population composition of the central core cities has been changing to a predominantly low-income and poverty-level group of consumers. At the same time, an increasing proportion of central-city residents are members of minority groups—from 1960 to1980, for instance, New York's black population more than doubled. Low-income and ghetto groups are often served by different marketing institutions than those serving others; recent studies have raised questions as to whether such groups are being served adequately. One counter trend should be mentioned: the "back-to-the-city movement," a social phenomenon evident in certain large cities that can be traced to the increased giving inconveniences resulting from the extreme sprawling of sub urban areas.

Psychological Determinants

There have been three major approaches to the development of a psychological theory of human behaviour: the experimental, the clinical, and the gestalt. Experimental psychology has concentrated upon physiological tensions or body needs as motivational forces and has experimented with both human beings and animals. In clinical psychology, the basic physiological drives are examined as they are modified by social forces. Gestalt psychology, often called social psychology, regards the individuals and his or her enviornments as an indivisible whole and considers individuals behaviour as being directed toward various goals. Each approach adds to our understanding of human behaviour, but thus far no single psychological theory of consumer motivation is completely adequate or satisfactory in explaining buyer behaviour. Consequently, marketing has borrowed those theoretical concepts that seem most applicable.

(a) **Attitudes and Learning.** Studies of learing and the related areas of recognition recall, and habitual response have furnished markets with several keys to understanding consumer behaviour. Concept borrowed from learning theory help in answering such questions as these; How do consumers learn about products offered for sale? How do they learn to recognize the recall these products? By what process do they develop buying and consuming habits?

The current trend in psychological thinking is to look at the total experience of the individual and to consider learning as a process in which total functions are altered and rearranged to make them more useful to the individual. Particualr external stimuli do not always activate predictable responses, because motives and other factors internal to the individual also affect responses. What does this mean for the marketer? Simply that the buyer is influenced not only by external stimuli—for example, the marketer's promotion—but also by internl factors.

(b) **Motiation—Various Explanations of Buyer Behaviour from Clinical Psychology.** Clinical psychology has evolved from the pioneering work of Signmund Freud. The principal motivation research techniques in marketing trace to concepts originally developed by clinical psychologists. Among the most important of these concepts are as follows:

1. *The Unconsicous.* This concept was championd by Signmund Freud, the founder of psychoanalysis. According to him, the mind contains ideas and urges—some conscious and some beneath the threshold of consciousness but all influencing behaviour. People are not consciously aware of all their motives and this explains why consumers are often unable to articulate their real reasons for buying or not buying. Recognizing the existence of the unconscious mind, motivation researchers use indirect approaches, such as depth interviewing. More conventional research approaches, such as direct questioning, have been unsuccessful in providing data sufficiently reliable to justify predictions of consumer behaviour. Practical marketers, of course, have long known that there are often wide discrepancies between what people say they will buy and what they actually do buy.

2. *Free Association.* The principle of free assoicaiton, which traces to Freud and is used extensively in psychoanalysis, has also been put to use by motivation researchers in their development of indirect research techniques. As Newman says, "The basic idea is that if a person gives up the usual logical controls he exercises over his thoughts and says whatever comes into his mind at the moment in the presence of a skilled listner, unconscious feelings and thoughts can be discovered." Thus, an application of the principle of free association is found in in-depth interviewing, many of the techniques of which take the form of word association tests, in which respondents are asked to give the first word that comes to mind for each of a list of unrelated words. Given the word rain, for example, the respondent might reply drop. Among the many marketing applications of word association tests are those of screening possible names for new products, measuring the penetration of advertising appeals, and approximating the market shares of different competitors.

3. *Rationalization.* This concept relates to the mental processs of finding reasons to justify an act or opinion that is actually based on other motives or grounds than those stated, although this may or may not be apparent to the rationalizer. In advertising, rationalization may often by capitalized upon by providing readers or listeners with a plausible, acceptale reason for buying in situations where they may be unwilling, consciously or unconsciously, to admit the real reasons. The prevalence of rationalization in our society explains why such

direct quesions as "why did not buy this?" or "What were your reasons for buying?" so often fail to uncover the real buying motives. Thus, when it is suspected that rationalizing is a factor in consumer behaviour, indirect research approaches, such as depth interviewing, are used.

4. *Projection.* This concept concerns the reaction that occurs when a person, seeing someone else facing a certain problem or situation, assumes that the other person's reactions would be the same as his or her own. In other words, he or she ascribes his or her own motives to the other person. Putting the projection concept to practical use, motivation researchers have designed projective techniques (*e.g.*, the stimulus picture) that provide a means for uncovering consumers' hidden or unconscious motives and attitudes.

Other Associated Concepts

It is true that the human mind working at the unconscious and subconscious levels is an important determining factor in consumer behaviour. Nevertheless, there are other important factors assoicated with the consumer personality which exert considerable influence on his purchasing decisions. These factors include the following:

(i) **Perception.** We have learnt that a person is motivated to act when an appropriate stimulus is offered. But there is an intervening factor in between stimulus and response. The response is dependent on the way the stimulus is interpreted by the person towards whom it is focussed. Kerby has described such interpreted stimuli as perception. He further says that a wide range of things that can happen to either stimuli, the observer or the situational elements, will cause two people receiving what appears to be precisely the same stimulus to interpret it differently. People behave in response to a need, but the specific response will be determined, in a large measure, by the individual's assessment of the benefits it will produce, which almost inevitably is an interpretational matter. Therefore, according to Britt "the various ways in which the consumer perceives products and services play a large part in his behaviour in the market place". A consumer may perceive satisfaction-delivering attributes in a product whereas an other may not. It may be so on account of the product's image in the market place notwithstanding technical superiority of the competing brands.

(ii) **Personality Traits.** While highlighting the personality in consumer behaviour, psyhologists with interest in marketing, have often referred to the contributions of personality traits. According to Britt, every one has a very personal and unique way of responding to his environment. In fact, our ways of behaving are usually sufficiently unique to enable other individuals to describe us fairly accurately as talkactive, shy, bold, timid or otherwise. When our friends use such adjectives in speaking about us they are referring to our behaviour traits. Personality traits have been defined as "those characteristics that account for difference among people and that are predictive of their behaviour". More specifically, a trait has been defined as "any distinguishable, relatively enduring way in which one individual differs from another". Thus, behaviour of every individual is different from another and can be identified in terms of certain unique characteristics called traits. These personality traits have been classified in a variety of ways depending upon the type of personality measurement techniques used.

(iii) **Attitude.** Like personality traits attitudes of consumer also influence the buying behaviour of people. A loook at the buying decisions process shown in Fig. makes it clear that the decision depends upon the pre-disposition of the consumer. The predisposition, whether positive or negative, towards a product may be explained with the help of his attitude towards that product or the company promoting it. Allport has defined attitude as " mental or neural state of readiness organized through experience, exerting a directive or dynamic influence upon the individual's response to all objects and situations, with which it is related. Simply stated, attitude may be described as a predisposition of a person to act or react in a certain manner towards an object or stimulus, say, a person or product. Psychologists have recognised two major components of attitude, namely, cognitive and affective. The cognitive component consists of knowledge or beliefs about an object while the affective component consist of the way a person feels towards an object. An attitude may be either cognitive or affective or both. When it is a combination of two, it is relatively more stable.

Nevertheless, conflict in a person's attitudes does exist at times. This makes prediction of behaviour difficult. Notwithstanding, an understanding of attitudes provides a useful guide to consumer behaviour. It is often said that atttidues, even if accurately known, do not provide an infallible guide to consumer beahviour. In this reagrd, Kerby has pertinently remarked that "a guide does not have to be infallible to be useful. Rather, the fact that behaviour does not invariably follow attitudes is a complication with which marketers must cope".

(iv) **Self-Concept.** Still another concept relevant to the study of consumer behaviour is that of self-concept or self-image. According to it, an individual's behaviour is conditioned by his own image as viewed by himeslf or the manner in which he wants others to see him. The view of Self inlcudes not only one's physical being but evaluations and definitions of Self in terms of strength, sophistication, fairness honesty, etc.

(v) **Gestalt Approach.** Gestalt psychologists believe that an individual perceives products and ideas as parts of the whole instead of isolated and segregated segments. It is based on the premise that the 'total is different from that sum of its parts'. The term gestalt means 'form' or 'configuration'. The Gestalt theory states that stimuli area perceived in relation to the ogranisation of one's experiences. Also, every person tends to organise parts of information and ideas into whole so as to respond to stimuli. It is so because perception based on parts differs from that based on the whole. Therefore, marketers should attempt to avoid action which by itself may not be negative but becomes so when combined with other parts of actions already initiated or likely to be initiated. It is so because consumer will not think of only one action of marketers but the totality of the actions. For example, a marketer has built up his image as the one who sells highly priced quality products through prestigious stores for high-income groups consumers. If this marketer goes in for periodic reduction sales then his consumers would add this information to other parts and organise another whole or gestalt which may not be compatible with their self-image. Thus, the marketer would not tend to lose his clientale on account of a mis-fitting part which by itself is not harmful but becomes so when combined with others.

(vi) **Cognitive Dissonance.** Largely based on the gestalt approach, the Theory of Cognitive Dissonance was propounded by Festinger. This theory is based on the premise that a person strives towards consistency (consonance, agreement, equilibrium) wihtin his cognitive structure (set of beliefs about products, people, events, and other objects) and attempt to reduce tension so as to make life comfortable'. Inconsistency (disharmony, frustration) which has been called dissonance by Festinger, is a state of psychological tension/anxiety which may result from any decision, say, purchase of a product. It has, therefore, been also called post-decision anxiety.

This theory centres around the idea that if a person knows various things that are not psychologically consistent with one another, he will, in a variety of ways, try to make them more consistent.

NEED SATISFACTION AND BUYER BEHAVIOUR

Psychological studies indicate that human activity, including buying behaviour, is directed toward satisfying certain needs. Not only individual acts in the same way in the effort to fulbill these needs; the actions of the each not only depend upon the nature of the needs themselves but are also modified by the individual's particular environmental and social background. The motivation for any specific action derives from the tensions built up to satisfy needs, needs that frequently lie beneath the threshold of consciousness. Whatever action the individual takes is directed toward reducing these tensions.

Although clinical psychologists have not agreed on a single list of needs.

The different lists available show more agreement than disagreement. In one list, illustrated in Figure above 'A', Maslow enumerates needs in their order of importance for

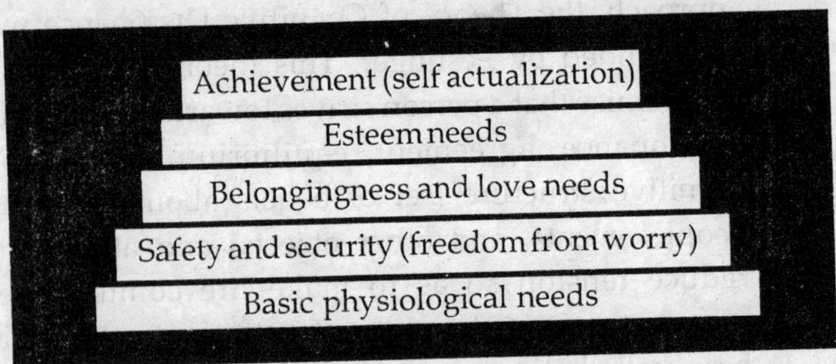

Fig. A Maslow's hierarchy of needs

most people with the most basic needs at the bottom of the figure. According to him, an individual normally tries to satisfy the most basic needs first and, satisfying these, he or she is then free to devote his or her efforts to the next one shown on the list. Each category of need on the Maslow list is described as follows.

(i) **Basic Needs.** The needs to satisfy hunger, thirst, sleep, and so forth. These are the most basic needs, and until they are satisfied, other needs are of no importance.

(ii) **Safety and Security Needs.** In modern society, these needs are more often for economic and social security rather than for physical safety.

(iii) **Belongingness and Love Needs.** The need for affectionate relations with individuals and a place in society is so important that its lack is a common cause of maladjustment.

(iv) **Esteem Needs.** People need both self-esteem, a high evaluation of self, and the esteem of others in our society. Fulfilment provides a feeling of self-confidence and usefulness; nonfulfilment produces feelings of inferiority and helplessness.

(v) **Achievement Need.** This is the desire to achieve the maximum of one's capabilities. Although it may be present in everyone, its fulfilment depends upon prior fulfilment of the more basic needs.

Often the marketing success of a brand depends on its ability to satisfy several needs at once; motivation research techniques are available to identify the strength or weakness of a product in terms of the needs it fulfills. The concepts of needs and the theory that individuals normally try to satisfy them in some order are specifically significant.

They buyers see both themselves and the products they buy in terms of images. These images are the formalized impressions residing, consciously or unconsciously, in the minds of individuals with regard to given subjects. Patterns of buying behaviour are influenced by the images that consumers have of different products, particular brands, companies, retail outlets, and of themselves, Because images affect consumer buying behaviour, marketers take them into account in drafting promotional plans and programmes. Differences among individuals, products, brands, and the like result in different images, and motivation research is used not only to identify the nature of images but also to detect the implications for marketing action:

(a) **Self-image.** The self-image is the picture that people have of them-seles-the kind of people they consider themselves to be and the kind of people that they imagine others consider them to be. Different people have different kinds of self-images, and this gives rise to market segmentation along psychological lines. For instance, the woman who sees herself primarily as a good housewife and mother exhibits a different total pattern of buying behaviour from that shown by the woman who sees herself as a social leader or professional careerist. It many buying situations an individual prefers to buy those products and brands whose images appear consistent with his or her self-image. However, the power of the self-image as a buying influence varies from individual to individual and even within the same individual as he or she makes different buying decisions at different times.

(b) **Brand Image.** The brand image, another stereotype, results from all the impressions consumers receive, from whatever sources, about a particular manufacturer's brand. In the minds of consumers familiar with a particular brand, there tends to be considerable consistency in the brand image or, as it is sometimes called, the brand personality. For competing brands there are in the minds of consumers distinctive images. Similarly, retail stores exhibit distinct images or personalities, as do corporations.

Consumers' appraisals of the distinctivness of a brand's physical attributes not only affect the brand image but also have important implications for marketing. When consumers believe that the brand is physically different from competing brands, the brand image centers on the brand as a specific version of the product.

TYPES OF BUYING BEHAVIOUR

Consumer decision making varies with the type of buying decision. There are great differences between buying toothpaste, a tennis racket, a personal computer, and a new car. Complex and expensive purchases are likely to involve more buyer deliberation and more participants. Assael distinguished four types of consumer buying behaviour based on the degree of buyer involvement and the degree of differences among brands.

(1) **Dissonance Reducing Buying Behaviour.** Sometimes the consumer is highly involved in purchase but sees little difference in the brands. The high involvement is again based on the fact that the purchase is expensive, infrequent, and risky. In this case, the buyer will shop around to learn what is available out will buy fairly quickly becase brand differences are not pronounced. The buyer may respond primarily to a good price or to purchase convenience. For example, carpet buying is a high-involvement decision because it is expensive and self-expressive; yet the buyer may consider most carpet brands in a given price range to be the same.

After the purchase, the consumer might experience dissonance that stems from noticing certain disquieting features of the carpet or hearing favourable things about other carpet. The consumer will be alert to information that might justify his or her decision. In this example, the consumer first acted, then acquired new beliefs, and ended up with a set of attitudes. Here marketing communications should aim to supply beliefs and evaluations that help the consumer feel good about his or her brand choice.

(2) **Complex Buying Bahaviour.** Consumers go through complex buying behaviour when they are highly involved in a purchase and aware of significant differences among brands. Consumers are highly involved when the product is expensive, bought infrequently, risky, and highly self-expressive. Typically the consumer does not know much about the product category and has much to learn. For example, a person buying a personal computer may not know that attributes to look for. Many of the product features carry no meaning : "16K memory", "disc storage", "screen resolution", and so on.

This buyer will pass through a learning process characterized by first developing beliefs about the product, then attitudes, and then making a thoughtful purchase choice. The marketer of a high-involvement product must understand and information-gathering and evaluation behaviour of high-involvement consumers. The marketer needs to develop strategies that assist the buyer in learning about the attributes of the product class, their relative importance, and the high standing of the company's brand on the more important attributes. The marketer needs to differentiate the brand's features, use mainly print media and long copy to describe the brand's benefits, and motivate store sales personnel and the buyer's acquaintances to influences the final brand choice.

(3) **Variety—Seeking Buying Behaviour.** Some buying situations are characterized by low consumer involvement but significant brand differences. Here consumers are often observed to do a lot of brand switching. An example occurs in purchasing cookies. The consumer has some beliefs, chooses a brand of cookies without much evaluation, and evaluates it during consumption. But next time, the consumer may reach for another brand out of boredom or a wish for a different taste. brand switching occurs for the sake of variety rather than dissatisfaction.

The marketing strategy is different for the market leader and the minor brands in this product category. The market leader will try to encourage habitual buying behaviour by dominating the self space, avoiding out-of-stock conditions, and sponsoring frequent reminder advertising. Challenger firms will encourage variety seeking by ofering lower prices, deals, coupons, free samples, and advertising that presents reasons for trying something new.

(4) **Habitual Buying Behaviour.** Many products are bought under conditions of low consumer involvement and the absence of significant brand differences. Consider the purchase of salt. Consumers have little involvement in this product category. They go to the store and reach for the brand. If they keep reaching for the same brand, it is out of habit, not strong brand loyalty. There is good evidence that consumers have low involvement with most lowcost, frequently purchased products.

Consumer behaviour in these cases does not pass through the normal belief/attitude/behaviour sequence. Consumers do not search extensively for information about the brands, evaluate their characteristics, and make a weighty decision on which brand to buy. Instead, they are passive recipients of information as they watch television or some print advertisements. Advertisement repetition creates brand familiarity rather than brand conviction. Consumers do not form a strong attitude toward a brand but select it because it is familiar. After purchase, they may not even evaluate the choice because they are not highly involved with the product. So the buying process is brand beliefs formed by passive learning, followed by purchase behaviour, which may be followed by evaluation.

Problems in Studying Buyer Behaviour

It has to be made clear at the outset that there is no unified, well defined, tested and universally established theory of buyer behaviour. What we have today are certain ideas propounded for describing buyer behaviour. In their approach and content these ideas vary widely from one another. Some of these ideas have taken their cue from economics, others from psychology, and yet others from several of the social sciences simultaneously. These concepts have been developed after extensive study and research. Individual firms have conducted studies; professional researchers have also studied the subject on their own. All these studies have contributed to a heavy assortment of information on buyer behaviour. But a universally accepted theory of buyer behaviour is yet to emerge. It is with an understanding of these limitations that we have to proceed further with the topic.

Buyers needs and desires are innumerable. And they vary from security needs to aesthetic needs. These needs and desires are often at different stages of emergence and actualization. Some are latent, some are manifest, some are dominant. The buyer has his own ways and plans of meeting these needs. Some of these needs are within his means. He can easily meet them. Some are too costly for him. He may keep postponing the purchase.

And this buyer is exposed today to a world of information—about new products, new services, new uses for existing products, new ideas and new styles. His attitudes towards this bombardment of information is also peculiar. He might ignore certain pieces of information, whereas he may actively seek out some other information. He may read a certain message, but may not disgest it. He may merely overhear some message about some product and it may get registered in his mind. In other words, he filters the information in a rather unconscious manner. His perception is partial, in the sense that he perceives and retains what he would normally like to perceive and retain. This selective perception is actually his defense mechanism against the information explosion to which he is constantly exposed.

And when he takes a buying decision, there is no rigid rule to bind him. Sometimes, the decision is taken on the spot. That does not necessarily means it is an irrational decision. Sometimes he may decide after making a long search, after evaluating the various alternatives available, and after reassuring himself with the experience of those who have already purchased the product. Still, he may find later that his purchase was impulsive or even foolish! He may go to a shop after having taken the decision to buy a product. Still he may not buy. For no apparent reason, he may postpone the purchase or even drop the very idea of purchasing.

The very essence of buyer behaviour study is the recognition of the fact that the buyer is a complex person, influenced by the social environment in which he lives, his family, his society, his neighbours, his friends, his job, his colleagues-everything leaving some imprint on him, influencing him in this day-to-day life. His purchases and consumption are carried out within the larger context of his day-to-day living. And his role as a buyer is not distinct from his role as a human being. Buyer behaviour, after all, is only a specific aspect of general human behaviour and is therefore as complex as general human behaviour.

SIGNIFICANCE OF CONSUMER BEHAVIOUR

When a person gets his pay-packet at the beginning of each month he sits down with his wife and prepares the family budget after carefully apportioning amounts to different items of expenditure. However, after a trip to the market with his family, he finds that the whole 'exercise in rationality' (budget) had been futile as the purchases made by him are not compatible with the budget items. On recapitulation and analysis, he finds that it was his wife, son, daughter and even he himself who were responsible for this deviation. All of them had made a contribution in making this budget upside down. The deviation was attributed to the arousal of new needs on account of new produts displayed, better packages, better credit facilities, charming saleswomen/menship and also beacause a nou-yeau riche neighbour was buying some particular article. While making purchases, the son had a friend's dress in his mind, the daughter had her class teachers' new lipstick in her mind, the wife was thinking of a particular sari she had seen at a party, and he himself was overawed by his neighbour's choices. This whole behaviour of a person (s) while making purchases may be termed as consumer behaviour. It has been defined as "the process whereby individuals decide whether, what, when, where, how and from whom to purchase goods and services'.

In this process, the consumer deliberates within himself before he finally makes a purchase move. This deliberatin relates to many variables and is aimed at solving consumption problems. Amongst these problems, the first and foremost is to decide whether to spend money or to save it. Once a decision is taken to spend money, the second problem is to decide what to buy because the needs are multiple and resources scarce. Therefore needs are to be ranked in terms of priority. The subsequent consumption problems relate to the place from where to buy, the mode of purchase—large/small quantities, cash/credit purchases and the like—and, last, the seller/shop from whom to buy.

This whole consumption behaviour consists of both physical and mental activities. The physical acitivities involve visiting a shop, examining product, selecting products or eating/drinking outside; that is, the actual act of consumption. Mental activities, on the other hand, involve deliberations within and forming of attitudes, perceiving communication material and learning to prefer a particular brand of product.

Consumer Behaviour and Consumption Behaviour

Consumer behaviour relates to an indiviudal person (micro behaviour), whereas consumption behaviour relates to the mass or aggregate of individuals (macro behaviour). "The study of consumer behaviour always focuses on the decision processes of the individual consumer or consuming unit, such as the family. It includes all the efforts to describe and explain one or more act of choice either at a given time or over a period of time. In contrast, the study of consumption behaviour is concerned with the description and explanation of the behaviour of aggregates of consumers or consuming units, again at a given time or over a period of time. The subject matter of consumption behaviour parallels at the aggregate level to that of consumer behaviour.

Consumer Behaviour and Buyer Behaviour

The area of consumer behaviour includes activities of both ultimate and industrial consumers. The former is the end-user of the product/service whereas the latter is only an intermediate user who adds further value to the product/service before it is consumed by the end-user. When behaviour of both the kinds of buyer is under reference, the term used to denote it is "buyer behaviour'. When the behaviour of only end-users is under reference, the term 'consumer behaviour' is used to denote it.

The relevance and importance of understanding consumer behaviour is rooted in the modern marketing concept. In order to operationalise this concept, management attempts to solve some consumption problems of consumers. However, no business can possibly help consumers solve their consumption problems unless he understands them and unless he makes an attempt to comprehend the buying process and the factors influencing it.

Consumer behaviour is dynamic. Therefore, it is necessary to continuously study, analyse and understand it and monitor this understanding to the marketing management so that effective decisions can be taken in respect of products, price, promotion and distribution. The profit position of a product hinges on the kind of predisposition-positive/negative—that a consumer has developed towards it. It is essential to study and analyse it in order to understand why he/she has developed such a predisposition? Besides, the Indian marketing conditions in particular the role of the Government and the steadily emerging consumer movement, necessitates that marketers in India must understand consumer behaviour—their needs, aspirations, expectations and problems. It will be extremely useful in exploiting marketing opportunities and in meeting the challenges that the Indian market offers.

Thus, in substance, it may be said that in the interest of effective marketing decisions, marketers must develop an understanding of their consumer's behaviour, the buying process and the factors influencing this process.

STAGES OF CONSUMER BUYING PROCESS

In order to understand consumer behaviour, it is first essential to understand the buying process. During the last two decades, numerous models of consumer behaviour depicting the buying process have developed. All these models treat the consumer as a decision-maker who comes to the market place to solve his consumption problems and to achieve the satisfaction of his needs. Amongst all these models the one given by Howard and Sheth is the most comprehensive and largely approved. However, as the Howard-Sheth model is a very sophisticated model.

A simple model is composed of three stages—'Input-Process-Output'. Input is a stimulus. It is provided by two sets of stimulus variables, namely, the firm marketing efforts and the social environment. The firm's marketing effects are designed to positively expose, inform and influence consumers. These efforts include product/service itself, advertising, price strategies, distribution network, and in fact all marketing functions. For example, when a company introduces a new brand of detergent powder or a television set, it may run a series of radio commercials with supporting press advertisements. The social environment serves as a non-commercial source of consumer information and influence which is not under the direct control of the firm. It includes reference groups and individuals, family members, social class and castes, culture, and the like. Both these stimulus variables influences consumer and the buying process.

Stages of Buying Process

The buying process is compared of a number of stages and is influenced by an individual's psychological framework composed for the individual's personality, motivations, perceptions and attitudes. The various stages of the buying process are described here:

(1) **Need Recognition.** Need recognition means awareness of a want, a desire or a consumption problem without whose satisfaction the consumer normally builds up tension. For example, a busy housewife may feel the need for a washing-aid on account of her desire to find more time to spend with her children. This recognition of the need for a washing-aid might activate her to search for some aid may be manual or mechanical-say, a washerman/woman of a washing machine. Nevertheless, it is possible that she might be already aware of some such product (aid) before she recognised its needs. In order to accept this possibility, the arrow head between need recognition and product awareness stages has been reversible and a path is included to indicate movement from the need-recognition stage directly to the interest stage.

(2) **Product Awareness.** In this stage, the consumer is exposed to the existence of a product that may satisfy a need. This awarness may be on account of the search carried out by the consumer himself/herself or because of a firm's communications through advertising or salesmanship or through social environment. This awareness may be neutral or active. When no need is currently recognised by a consumer the awareness is neutral because there is

no immediate interest in it. When a consumer is already aware of a product and subsequently recognises a need, then the product awareness is active, and immediately converted into interest. In our example of the housewife requiring a washing-aid there was already a need recognition for a washing-aid. When she was exposed to a press advertisement or radio commercial about a particular washing machine her interest in it was aroused.

(C) **Interest.** Interest may be viewed as a state of mind that exists when a consumer perceives a need and/or is aware of alternative products capable of satisfying that need. Consumer interest is indicated in the consumer's willingness to seek further information about a product. At this stage the consumer is actively involved in the buying process and pays attention to the product. However, if he loses interest during this involvement, his/her attention will be diverted and the buying decision process will break down. In our example of the housewife requiring a washing-aid, she may look for further information about these machines ones she became aware of such machines. The kind of information she may look for is about the alternative washing machines available in the market-place, their relative price, operational efficiency, warranty and service facilities.

(4) **Evaluation and Intention.** Once interest in a product (s) is aroused, a consumer enters the subsequent stage of evaluation and intention. The evaluation stage represents the stage of mental trial of the product. During this stage, the consumer assigns relative value-weights to different products/brands on the basis of the accumulated stock of product information and draws conclusions about their

relative satisfaction—giving potential. After this evaluation, the consumer develops the intention either to purchase or reject the product/brand. The final purchase will, however, depend on the strength of the positive intention—that is the intention to buy. In our example of the housewife, after arousal of her interest in washing machines, she will compare the stock of information she has accumulated for the different washing machines in the market and then evaluate the value of each one of them before she develops the intention to buy. However, if she feels that a washerman/woman would serve the need then she may altogether reject the idea of buying any washing machine.

(5) **Output.** Output is the end result of the inputs of consumer behaviour. It emerges after these inputs are duly processed by the consumer. Output is composed of purchase and post-purchase behaviour.

(6) **Purchase.** Purchase is a consumer commitment for a product. It is the terminal stage in the buying decision process that completes a transaction. It occurs either as a trial and/or adoption. If a consumer is buying something for the first time then from the behaviour viewpoint it may be regarded as a trial. This trial enables him to accumulate experience about the product purchased. If this experience is positive in terms of satisfaction derivation, then repeat purchases may occur otherwise not. For example, when a new brand of bathing soap is introduced in the market, the consumer may buy it for the first time as a trial. However, repeat purchases will occur only when he is satisfied with its performance. But the possibility of a trial-purchase is not available in all cases. In the case of consumer durables such as scooters, refrigerators and the like, a trial is not possible,

because once a product is purchased, it has to be adopted and repeatedly used. Adoption means a consumer decision to commit to a full or further use of the product. In our example of the housewife, the washing machine is not open for trial purchase; it will have to be adopted only.

(7) **Post-purchase Behaviour.** Post-purchase behaviour refers to the behaviour of a consumer after commitment to a product has been made. It originates out of consumer experience regarding the use of the product and is indicated in terms of satisfaction. This behaviour is reflected in repeat purchases or abstinence from further purchase. If product-use experience indicates satisfaction then repeat purchases will occur, otherwise not.

FACTORS AFFECTING THE CONSUMERS BUYING BEHAVIOUR

There are many factors which affect the behaviour of consumers. These factors may broadly be divided into two parts—(I) Economic Factors; and (II) Psychological Factors. The details in this regard are as follows:

(I) Economic Factors

Economic factors are the factors which affect financial conditions of a consumer. Some of the important economic factors affecting the behaviour of a consumer are as follows:

(1) **Personal Income.** Income of a consumer is the most important factor affecting his demand. A consumer has to fulfil his unlimited wants within his limited sources of income. If the income of the consumer is high, his demands will be more.

(2) **Consumer's Credit.** The increase or decrease in demand is also affected by the facility of credit available to the consumers. If the facility of credit is

available to the consumers, their demands will increase.

(3) **Family Income.** Family income of a consumer also effects his purchasing power. If the family of a consumer is living below the poverty line, his demands will be very limited. On the other hand, if the family of a consumer is happy and prosperous, his demands will be more.

(4) **Expectation of Income.** If a consumer expects an increase in his sources of income in future, his demands may be more. On the other hand, if a consumer expects a fall in his sources of income in future, his demands will be limited.

(5) **Discretionary Income.** Discretionary income means the income which is left after meeting all the necessities. Such income can be used by the consumers at their own discretion. This type of the income will increase the purchasing power of consumers.

(6) **Government Policies.** Goernment policy, particularly the rates of taxes in the country, affects consumer behaviour to a great extent. If the rates of income tax in the country are high, the purchasing power of the consumers will be low. Low rates of income tax can help in increasing the demand of consumers.

(II) Psychological Factors

(1) **Basic Needs.** Every Consumer has some basic needs which he wants to fulfil first of all. These needs may differ from person to person and from time to time. *Prof. A. H. Maslow* has described basic needs of a consumer as follows—*(i)* Physical; *(ii)* Safety; *(iii)* Love; *(iv)* Prestige; and (v) Self-ego. Prof. Maslow stated that a consumer wants to fulfil his needs in this order.

(2) Learning Theory. Learning theory is very important to study the behaviour of a consumer. With the help of this theory, the marketers may understand the motives for the satisfaction of which, a consumer purchases a product. According to this theory, following factors affect the behaviour of a consumer:

(i) Motivation. There are many buying motives which affect the behaviour of a consumer to a great extent. These motives may be categories as emotional, rational, natural and learnt.

(ii) Repetition. Continuous touch of a consumer with a product helps in increasing his knowledge about the product. For example, continuous advertisement of a product for a long time increases the knowledge of consumer about the product and the consumer are inspired to consume such product.

(iii) Group Influence. Group influence also affects the behaviour of a consumer. For example, if a prestigious person of the society or if a rich person starts to consume a particular product, many other persons will start to consume the same product.

(iv) Conditioning. The condition of a product also affects the behaviour of consumers. For example, if the packing of a product is very attractive, some new consumers may purchase the product for this reason also.

(3) Image. Image is the thinking of consumers about a particular product. This image affects their buying behaviour to a great extent. Image may be of many types such as self image, product image, brand image etc.

(4) **Clinical Psychology.** Clinical psychology includes following two factors:

*(i) **Rationalisation.*** Rationalisation means to study the reasons for which the consumers buy a product. Every consumer is a rational and makes rational purchasings, So, a marketer must study these reasons.

*(ii) **Unconsciousness.*** Unconsciousness is the stage of a consumer when he is not in a position to explain the reasons for which he buys a product. A marketer has to be much more vigil and careful about the study of behaviour of such consumers.

After making a study of the factors affecting the behaviour of consumers, a question arises as to which factor affects the behaviour of a consumer more. Some scholars are of the opinion that economic factors play more important role in determining the behaviour of consumers while some other scholars think that psychological factors play much more important role in this direction. The fact is that both the factors play equally important role in determining the behaviour of consumers. Therefore, a marketer must make a deep study of both the economic and psychological factors affecting the behaviour of consumer. Advertisement programme of an enterprise must include both the factors, as far as possible.

❐

4

Deal Prone Consumer Research

CONSUMER RESEARCH

The basis of Consumer Research lies in the fact that mass production and consumption have brought about a standardization in the habits and the tastes of the mass of the people. It has therefore, become possible to examine the habits of a whole market by conducting tests upon small samples.

The uninitiated may be sceptical. It is an affront to our dignity and our belief in our own individuality, to be informed that we are in fact, just one of a herd and that the habits by which we live our lives-and the urges which motivate them— are paralleled by those of the vast majority of our fellow citizens. Whether we like it or not, however, there is overwhelming evidence, not only in the United Kingdom, but throughout Western Europe and the United States of America, that this standardization of taste and living habits exists. It has been accentuated in the last decade or so by a blurring of the boundaries of what were once described as working- and middle-class incomes.

If he is to know his consumer, therefore, the Marketing Manager. must know about Consumer Research. He must understand the techniques employed in the selection of test-samples of the population, know how interrogations are carried out and how the mass of information derived from research interviews is coded, classified and pnally presented in the form of statistics. He must understand not only how these statistics are arrived at but how to interpret them and use them as a basis for his marketing decisions.

It is unfortunate that the credibility of the methods used in the conduct of mass surveys should have been put in question by the apparent failure of opinion polls to predict correctly the outcome of elections, both in the United States of America and in Britain. It must be realized, however, that opinion research differs considerably from consumer research. The opinion researcher will, for example, ask people their opinion on a topical controversial issue of the day. Direct questions seeking an opinion rather than a fact may not produce a truthful answer. Respondents may offer an opinion regardless of whether they hold it or not, rather than admit to not having any opinion at all. Similarly, when people are asked how they intend to vote, it is easy for a misleading set of answers to be obtained. There are those who will say that they intend voting for Mr A or Miss B, but when the time comes their opinions may have altered or they may not even trouble to vote at all.

The consumer researcher, however, is dealing not with opinions, but with behaviour. One of the factors which has been established by Market Research organizations over many years, both here and abroad, is the general honesty of ordinary people. When asked to provide facts about how and when and where they do their shopping and the uses to which they put the products which they buy, the great majority of people tell the truth to the best of their knowledge. The main hazard for the researcher is not, indeed, the deliberate lie but inaccuracies which can creep in due to mistakes caused by poor memory. Because this problem is recognized, however, steps are taken, in both the formulation of questions and in interviewing methods, to overcome the difficulty.

We can, therefore, forget the possible shortcomings of the opinion polls, recognizing the additional hazards under which they must work. Our purpose is to consider the credibility of the results of consumer surveys where people are, in the main, invited to respond to a series of questions regarding their buying habits and the uses to which, they put the various types of merchandise in which the survey is interested.

USES OF CONSUMER RESEARCH

Increasing sophistication of marketing methods generally has led to a more sophisticated approach to the question of consumer needs. Whereas Consumer Research was, at one time, solely concerned with establishing the how, the why and the when of the purchase of goods or services, it is now more interested in the use made of them by the ultimate consumer. Indeed, research now concentrates a people's composite activities as distinct from a single activity or process.

We have already referred to the importance of identifying new consumer needs in order to formulate new products and services to satisfy them. It is by a study of the behaviour patterns of people that their unrecognized needs may be established. Modern research endeavours to discover how people live and work in their homes, the times of day at which they take their meals and the particular meals at which they eat certain foodstuffs. Efforts are made to find out how kitchen equipment is used and the part it plays in the general activity of for example, the preparation of a meal or dealing with the family laundry. The finding of research of this nature is a guide not only to the future design of such equipment but also to their methods of promotion and presentation to the buying public.

Consumer Research seeks to establish the total number of potential consumers for a given product and then to subdivide them by sex, age group, marital status, occupation, social class and geographical location. Bearing in mind that a consumer is not necessarily the same as a customer, it is the function of Consumer Research to find out who actually buys the product in question and where it is bought: at the corner shop, or the co-operative store, at a chemist's or a grocer's or at a multiple store. Finally, it seeks to establish when the product is used and how it is used.

DISCOVERING HOW THE CONSUMER'S NEEDS CAN BE SATISFIED

Apart from identifying the consumer to whom we aim to sell our product, the findings of Consumer Research will indicate the kind of product which the consumer is more likely to buy because it will more exactly satisfy his need.

The types of domestic equipment which consumers possess will have an effect upon their use of products in their homes. The optimum size of food storage containers should relate to the size and shape of the storage area of the most popular sizes of domestic refrigerators: the market for humidifiers must relate to the number to homes in which central heating is installed; the market for bathroom fittings is dependent upon the number of dwellings which have bathrooms. Such examples seem self-evident. What may be less evident are those factors which determine the extent of a market. Can one assume that the market for tubular garden furniture is limited to the number of homes with gardens? What about the needs of caravan-owners, many of whom doubtless live in apartments without even a window-box. In assessing the optimum size for a motor-car, for example, there are many facets of the consumer's needs which must be studied. A model aimed at the middle-management executive in the £3,000-£5,000 per annum income bracket must be large enough to provide an adequate status symbol. It must also fit into his garage. He will probably live in a modern house in a modern suburb and have a garage of a standard size. If the car one hopes to sell to him is two inches too long and he cannot close the garage doors he may change his mind and order another make which is just the right size.

Consumer Research can indicate to the Marketing Manager the preference of consumers. Why is one brand of washing-up liquid preferred to another? Is it the quality of the product, its utility, the design of the package or its promotion—its brand image which evokes a favourable response?

It can also alert the manufacturer to possible changes in the market brought about by changes in consumers' needs. It must be remembered that no market ever remains static. It is constantly undergoing change. A product, popular and in great demand today, may be dead inside two years. Similarly, a market can decline and ultimately disappear as the fickle public whim changes. In today's trading conditions, when society, both at home and abroad, is undergoing major changes in its behaviour, its standards and its ambitions, the Marketing Manager must for ever be on the look-out for the advent of new consumer needs which conflict with the current demand for his particular product or service. Thus the popularity and comparative cheapness of foreign travel creates and satisfies a demand and in so doing tends to absorb some of the surplus purchasing power which might otherwise have been spent, for example, on new house furnishings.

Sometimes, Consumer Research can come up with surprises for the Marketing Manager. He may discover that his product is being used, by some consumers, for purposes for which it was not originally intended. Such knowledge may enable him to promote this new need and thus expand the size of his market. Consumer Research will also provide evidence of the consumer's views on competitive products and their performance. What is it about a particular competitive product that the housewife prefers?

The Marketing Manager must be careful in the inferences which he makes from Consumer Research. The wrong inferences will lead to the making of wrong decisions. The value of statistics prepared as the result of research surveys depends entirely on the interpretation put upon them and the use made of this additional knowledge. It is easy to misread a set of statistics. The researcher should ensure that the figures the produces are correctly defined; but the Marketing Manager would be well advised to take nothing at its face value. He should check the sources from which the figures have been obtained to make sure that the definitions used are correct.

METHODS OF CONSUMER RESEARCH

There are three main methods used in Consumer Research. These are: desk research; field research; motivation research. Each method has a part to play in providing the Marketing Manager with a picture of the men and women who will consume his product or use his service.

Desk Research

The starting point for any form of market research is that which can be done – as the name implies – seated at one's desk. There are masses of statistics prepared by government departments, trade associations and market research consultants readily available to the would – be researcher and which he can consult without stepping outside his own office. Before we consider these, however, let us take a look at information which is likely to be at the Marketing Manager's elbow; namely, the records kept by his own company. All trading organizations keep records of one form or another, such as customers' accounts, turnover figures, product sales totals, sales area turnover figures and salesmen's commission records.

(a) Company Statistics. All of this statistical information can provide useful guidance for the formulation of marketing decisions. It may require arranging and analysing. One may have to go back over a period of five years or so, and seek some relationship between products and product groups in

terms of volume and turnover. The company's sales figures should provide a barometer to indicate seasonal fluctuations. Indeed, any major fluctuations in turnover must have a cause and the discovery of that cause may well indicate some characteristic of fluctuating consumer needs or buying habits.

Customer Research in the industrial goods field can begin with a similar examination of company records. Since individual customers are identifiable, they can be categorized according to the products they use as well as the after processes to which the products are put. Existing information, rearranged in this manner, can tell one a great deal about the market in which one is operating as well as highlighting factors which hitherto may have been obscured.

(b) Trade Statistics. Statistics relating to the pattern of production and consumption in a particular trade or industry are usually available, in a classified form, from the appropriate trade association. Trade directories, year books, trade periodicals and the financial press are additional sources of market information.

In addition, there are in the United Kingdom, as in most other industrialized countries in Europe and North America, firms who specialize in the provision of trade and technical information. They can provide market research services and will under take to furnish to subscribers up-to-date information on market growth and trends.

(c) Government Statistics. The United Kingdom government provides, through Her Majesty's Stationery Office, a very considerable amount of statistical information of value to trade and industry.

Field Research

Although desk research will provide the Marketing Manager with a great deal of general information with regard to general economic trends, it is unlikely to provide him with any guidance on the consumer's reactions to his own specific range of products or to those of his immediate competitors. It is this kind of research which is vital if one is to pursue a fully consumer-orientated marketing policy.

(a) Consumer Sampling. The foundation of the sample method in consumer research relies on two factors. The first, to which we have already referred, is that the vast majority of people interviewed in a survey will give answers which are true to the best of their knowledge. The second is that it is usually possible to establish that the sample is, within fairly acceptable limits, representative of the whole.

It is important that one should understand the importance of this second factor. Upon the degree of probability which exists in any survey will depend the credibility of its findings. If there is reasonable doubt that !he sample which is being examined is not representative, then it will be better to abandon the project and start again; because a wrong sample will produce wrong results which could be disastrous for those who may decide to act upon them.

How certain can one be that any sample is truly representative of the whole?

Let us consider, for a moment, a typical example of sampling, frequently undertaken by businessmen when entertaining their more important clients. When they order a bottle of wine they will, in the first instance, be shown the bottle with its cork intact. This enables them to be assured that the description on the label coincides with the particular vintage which they have ordered. Subsequently, the wine waiter will uncork the bottle and pour a small sample of its contents into the host's glass for him to taste and test. Now, this conventional method of approving wine is based on the overwhelming probability that the sample which is taken is representative of the whole of the contents of the bottle.

Few consumer surveys are quite so undeniable! Indeed, in an effort to overcome this problem, market researchers have developed a number of methods all aimed to achieve the highest degree of representativeness compatible with reasonable economy.

We have already referred to the possibility that false statements made by individual respondents could have a detrimental effect upon the value of the survey. In practice, however, it has been found that a false statement in one direction is usually cancelled out by an equally false statement in the other. Where it is discovered, in a survey, that a high proportion of false answers have been given to a specific question, it is usually because that question has been badly phrased. Note that I say obviously false answers. When we come to consider the preparation of questionnaires it will be seen that the series of questions put to respondents can be designed in such a way that untruthful answers can be pinpointed without much difficulty.

The obvious advantage of the sampling technique compared with a total survey of the whole market is that the cost of the sample survey is much smaller. However, since the size of the survey will have a direct bearing on its cost, it will be dependent upon the budget which has been allocated. The ideal sample is a microcosm of the entire population. It should be noted that the words population or universe refer, in market research parlance, to the sub-section of the actual population which one is investigating. A universe, therefore, may be the total number of school teachers, or the total number of families with two cars.

It is the composition of the sample that is more important than its size. It should be remembered that the researcher is not trying to establish a large or a small sample upon which to carry out his survey but one of optimum size. If for example, one intends to survey a whole country, one would arrange about 2,000 interviews for the sample. This figure, however, would apply equally to countries with such divergent population sizes as, let us say, the United Kingdom, the United States of America, or Germany or Holland. Where the universe is uniform it is often possible to work with a smaller sample, but it must remain a true cross-section of the population.

Where the universe is not uniform, the researcher will probably divide it up into sections or strata which are uniform. It will be appreciated that when this occurs the size of the sample which is decided upon will depend upon the size of the smallest sub-section. This is because no sub-section can contain too few respondents. However, this could lead to the necessity of interviewing such a large number of respondents that the entire survey would be hopelessly uneconomic.

Let me explain this with an example. Let us say that we select a sample containing 2,000 interviews in order to study the buying habits of a universe of, say, 750,000 people. In order to represent adequately the views of the various categories of people which make up that universe, 50 persons have been included to represent those with an income in excess of £10,000 per annum. Now it must be obvious that 50 is too few to reflect adequately the variety of viewpoints, personal interests and buying habits of the highly paid section of the universe.

The problem is, that if we were to double the quantity of the £10,000-a-year people the whole sample would have to be doubled. That would be very expensive. The way round this problem is to double only the number of highly paid people and increase the sample to 2,050 interviews. A correction is made to the final results when the figures which relate to the answers given by the wealthy respondents are halved. Thus the proportions are maintained and the final results derived from the survey are not distorted. This device is known as weighting the results.

There are various methods of selecting samples for consumer surveys. Those most frequently employed are the probability, the random and the quota systems. In practice, researchers often use hybrid methods to suit the type of research in which they are engaged.

(b) The Probability System. Using the grobability system, the researcher prepares a list of the names and addresses of the entire universe which he proposes to survey. He discovers these names in city and trade directories, telephone directories or professional list. Copies of electoral rolls, obtainable from local authorities, are also used. Once his list is complete, the researcher sets out to select a representative sample in a uniform basis. Thus, if he intends to work with a sample of 5 per cent of the universe, he will select one name in twenty. He will not merely select 5 per cent of the list of names, because to do so would fail to ensure that the spread of names was even.

The researcher must be on his guard lest bias should enter into his sample. It has been found, for example, that people with the same initial letter to their names are not free from bias.

Since uniformity is the essence of this particular method, the interviewers employed to carry out the survey are not allowed to choose the people to be interviewed. Were they to do so, this could introduce bias because, naturally, each interviewer will be biased, to some extent, in the kind of person she selects.

There are a number of problems with the probability system of surveying, Researchers find difficulty in getting a list of all the names and addresses which make up the universe, which is not surprising. Electoral rolls and other published lists of names quickly become out of date. Also, the time spent in selecting respondents from these lists is expensive.

A further problem is that, to maintain the uniformity of the survey, a person whose name has been selected on the list must be interviewed. The pattern of uniformity will be broken if a neighbour is substituted. At first glance this may seem like pedantry carried to excess. On second thoughts, however, it will be seen that the way of life and, therefore, the buying habits of the woman who is frequently out and, therefore, difficult to get hold of, will be different from those of the woman next door who, on the contrary, is readily available simply because she is nearly always at home.

(c) The Random System. The Random System is a simplification of the above. It does not require a complete register of the population which is being surveyed. Small areas of the country are selected at random and in each of these districts one particular address is chosen, also at random, as the starting point of the interviewer's route. Calls are then made at every house in the street whose number ends in a randomly chosen unit. The interviewer then moves to the next street which has been chosen on a random basis and the process is repeated.

A modification of this method is to list, in the first instance, all the districts in the country, urban and rural, and then to select, on a random basis, a limited number of districts for the conduct of interviews. Within those districts houses will be selected at random. Thus the geographical scatter of the homes which have been selected for interviewing is reduced without causing any reduction to the representativeness of the sample.

(d) The Quota System. A further modification and the method most frequently used for consumer surveys is known as the Quota System. Here, the first stage is to decide upon the size of the sample which will be taken and then to stratify the universe. This stratification-or dividing into sections— will be carried out on the basis of age, sex, marital status, income group, occupation, and the size of the town, suburb or village in which the respondents live.

When this has been completed, the entire sample is divided by the total number of interviewing days which are considered necessary to complete the survey. For example, if we assume that an interviewer can complete twenty interviews in a day and that the total number of questionnaires to be: filled out numbers 2,000, the sample will be divided into 100 parts. Each interviewer is then given a quota, in this case twenty persons, whom she must find and interview. She is entrusted with the task of selecting her own respondents, but these must fit closely the various categories the researcher will stipulate, based on the stratification of the universe already carried out.

The Quota System is not considered to be as representative as the Probability or Random methods, but it is much cheaper to operate. The costly listing of the entire universe is eliminated and the interviewer does not have to make recalls to interview specific people not at home at the time of her first visit, as is the case in the other two methods.

(e) The Use of Consumer Panels. One of the major drawbacks to all the above methods of personal interview surveys is that they do not provide a means of supplying continuous information on the buying habits of the respondents.

The Marketing Manager needs, in addition to research reports on specific consumer reaction, some form of permanent consumer audit by means of which he can monitor the buying habits of the respondents, their degree of loyalty to any particular brand and when that loyalty comes to an end and they change to another brand. He also needs some means of gauging consumer reaction to advertising and promotion, not only of his own product, but of those of his competitors as reflected in possible changes to buying patterns.

To provide this continuous information, panels are set up of respondents, selected either randomly or by the quota method, and who are prepared to supply information on their shopping activities over a considerable period of time.

A housewife panel for consumer products would normally consist of about 2,000 respondents, representing as closely as possible a cross-section of the universe under scrutiny They would usually be recruited by personal interview and thereafter communicate with the market research organization by post. They are supplied with a diary in which they are asked to keep a record of all their purchases of certain branded goods. The information required is usually fairly simple, consisting of the name of the brand, the packet size (where this is applicable), the price paid and name of the shop where the product was purchased. At the end of each week (or month) the housewife returns her diary to the market researcher and receives a new one for the subsequent period.

Consumer panels are seldom maintained by single business organizations. The cost of setting them up and maintaining them is very high. They are usually run by market research organizations to provide research data for a group of product manufacturers.

Cost is not the only problem. Researchers have constant difficulty in maintaining a panel once it is set up. The number of housewives prepared to undertake this work is limited and many find it tedious. Too high a turnover of respondents, however, will reduce seriously the very continuity which is the whole purpose of the panel. Furthermore, some housewives find that the task of writing the simple details of their purchases in a diary is difficult. However, those with a low degree of literacy cannot be eliminated from the sample because the semi-literate members of the universe have to be represented.

Perhaps the greatest problem with regard to consumer panels is the danger of bias creeping in simply because the respondents, by undertaking panel membership, cease to be fully representative. They can no longer think and act in quite the same way as other housewives when they go shopping. The significance of their choice of purchases will introduce a degree of self-consciousness not experienced by the hundreds of thousands of other housewives whom they are intended to represent.

(f) Interviewing Methods. The basis for the sampling of respondents in a consumer research survey is to ask them to provide answers to a questionnaire. There are several different methods of approaching respondents, including the personal interview, group interviews, the use of postal questionnaires and telephone interviews.

1. *The Personal Interview.* It is not surprising that the personal interviewer, approaching respondents at their homes, in the street or at work, achieves a much greater response than any other survey method. The interviewer can by her presence, encourage the respondent to answer each question in the questionnaire and she can assist her by explaining the reasons for the survey and the importance which attaches to the respondent's contribution. Mistakes made in answering questions or misunderstanding of the meaning of questions can be dealt with at the time, thus reducing considerably the number of spoiled questionnaires which would have to be disregarded at the editing stage.

   A good interviewer can add considerably to the response she obtains from her interviews by the assessment she makes of the individual respondents. She is often provided with a special form in which she can enter comment of this nature.

   The drawback to the personal interviewer method is that it is expensive—Apart from remuneration there is the question of travelling costs, which can be considerable, particularly when a sampling method is being employed which may involve the interviewer in a number of recalls upon respondents. Even with the quota system, which avoids such recalls, the interviewer may have to devote considerable time to finding respondents who have the desired characteristics-age, sex, income bracket, occupation-to fit into her quota. The interviewers themselves must be carefully selected. Apart from all considerations of suitability one must take account of the fact that the interviewer is a personality who will have her own ideas and opinions which, however detached she may try to be, must create some bias.

2. *Group Discussions.* Some researchers select a small group of respondents representing a cross-section of the universe to be surveyed and invite them to attend a group discussion. Such gatherings are usually chaired by an experienced interviewer who, instead of conducting interviews, puts a number of points to the meeting to provoke discussion.

The resulting conversation can be recorded on tape for subsequent examination by the research team. They are concerned not only with what the respondents have to say but the way in which they say it. By such means the broad opinions of a representative group of housewives may be considered; but the information gathered has, of course, no statistical use.

3. *Postal Surveys.* The conduct of a postal survey which eliminates the need for trained interviewers is obviously much cheaper than systems requiring the employment of paid inter-viewers. There are, however, a number of problems.

The questionnaire sent out to respondents through the post cannot be as comprehensive as that used for a personal interview. Since there will be no interviewer at hand to explain the questions they must be put in an elementary manner and require as little writing as possible on the part of the respondent. The normal method is either to frame questions which require a simple 'yes' or 'no' answer, or to provide several alternative answers to each question and respondents are asked to put a mark against the one they consider applicable.

One of the main difficulties with the use of postal questionnaires is that only about one person in ten will take the trouble to respond. Furthermore, the fact that they have taken this trouble, whereas the other nine out of ten have not, suggests that they are probably not typical of the universe they are supposed to represent.

Various devices are employed to encourage respondents to respond. Sometimes a free gift is attached to the questionnaire and the researcher hopes that the respondent will feel obliged to complete and return the questionnaire.

Like all unsolicited direct mail approaches-of which this is but a specialized category – the accompanying letter of explanation must be concocted in such a manner that the respondent is urged to make the necessary effort to read and complete the questionnaire and post it back. This letter must explain the purpose of the survey in terms which the respondent will under – stand and, ideally, which will excite some interest on his part. It is sufficient to say her that postal surveys form an important part of mail order trading and are frequently used to gain market reaction to new products and new selling techniques as well as the creation of mailing lists.

4. *Telephone Surveys.* Having far less application than the postal survey, market research by telephone has been used to question consumers with regard to purchases of cars, domestic appliances and various types of household goods. It is a method used more widely in the United States where a far greater number of households possess a telephone than is the case in Britain.

   The method is comparatively cheap, immediate responses can be obtained and the interviewer can telephone a large number of respondents in a fraction of the time it would take to make personal visits to their homes.

   There are major drawbacks. Since the possession of a telephone is very far from being universal, respondents reached in this manner will not be typical for many types of surveys. The number of questions which can be put to respondents is, once again, extremely limited. Attempts to establish their age and occupation are likely to meet with an immediate rebuff. Generally speaking, people do not like being telephoned by complete strangers asking them questions and, more often than not, a semi-hostile response is likely to be encountered.

Motivation Research

In all the methods of consumer research which we have so far discussed, the researcher has been establishing ways and means of discovering how people behave in relation to certain products. The questions put to respondents in the probability, the random and the quota systems, and by means of the consumer panel, refer to the make of product they have purchased, the retail outlet from which the purchase has been made, the date and the time of the purchase and the quantity of the product which they have bought. Such information, reduced to statistical form, provides the Marketing Manager with important guidelines on the state of the market and its likely trends and also on the situation of his own product and the products or his competitors within that market.

In spite of this abundance of information, however, one essential question is still left in the air This question is: why does the consumer behave in the way he does?

Upon reflection, it will be apparent that none of the research methods so far discussed can answer this question adequately. We have seen that ordinary people will, on the whole, provide truthful answers with regard to their purchasing habits for a wide range of the goods and services which they buy. When it comes to the question of why they purchase particular products, from a particular retail outlet at a particular time, accurate answers are far more difficult to achieve. For one thing, the motives which prompt a considerable proportion of purchasing behaviour are entirely subjective and it might be difficult for the respondents themselves to offer any logical explanation. Secondly, people's motives for wanting to buy certain products or to use certain products in certain ways, their preferences for one brand as against another, for shopping in one type of store as against another, are rooted in habits or mental attitudes which, even if they were recognized by the respondents, they would often not wish to divulge to the research interviewer. If pressed to provide explanations for their actions, they would in all probability, take refuge, consciously or subconsciously, in evasion or falsehood.

It has therefore, long been recognized that research into the motives of consumers—or, as it has come to be called, motivation research—is a specialized field and demands specialized methods of approach on the part of the researcher.

Motivation Research originated in America. It was found that purchasing behaviour of consumers resulted from influences which could be divided into two groups. The first of these was external influences, such as the size of the family being catered for, the social class to which they belonged, the appeal of the product in its physical form—such as its size, shape, taste or smell—and its emotive appeal by means of advertising and promotions. The second group consisted of internal influences such as the consumer's personality characteristics, acquired knowledge, moral standards, superstitions and religious beliefs.

To tap this subterranean flow of motives the consumer researcher has turned to the field of clinical psychology and has adopted and adapted a number of its techniques. The methods used in Motivation Research are considerably more expensive than conventional methods of consumer research. Respondents are asked to submit themselves to various types of psychological tests such as word association, sentence completion and cartoon tests. These are all designed to establish subjective reactions to certain stimuli, as a result of which—it is claimed—the researcher can classify the pattern of their behaviour.

It is hardly surprising that a method of research intended for commercial purposes which relies upon methods still at the pioneering stage of medical research should not receive universal acceptance in the business world. Indeed, considerable scepticism exists as to the value of motivation research. Apart from doubts as to the validity of its methods, a major drawback is that, in general, it does not lend itself to statistical treatment.

Motivation Research is a complex subject. It is still very much in the stage of innovation and there can be little doubt that, as science delves deeper and deeper into man's mental and emotional processes, there will be greater opportunities for, and confidence in, the motivation methods of consumer research.

The Construction of Questionnaires

All forms of consumer sampling, with the exception of certain types of motivation research, have as their basis a list of questions which the respondent is invited to answer. The construction of a questionnaire is, therefore, a vital part of the research process. The success of a survey will depend as much upon the way in which the questionnaire has been prepared as upon all the other factors we have already considered.

The market researcher will, in the first instance, wish to know exactly what information the Marketing Manager requires and secondly, how he wishes that information to be presented to him. Armed with this knowledge, he will be able to prepare a series of questions for respondents to answer which will be strictly relevant to the purposes of the survey.

In drawing up his questionnaire, the researcher will take account of four main considerations:

1. The general subject of the survey
2. The classification of respondents
3. The provision of control questions
4. Questions designed to establish the information required.

When approached by an interviewer and asked to provide answers to a questionnaire, the majority of people will wish to know something about the survey before they accept. They are likely to ask for whom the survey is being conducted and what is its purpose. Although the respondent has a perfect right to request and to receive such information, disclosure of the name of the sponsor and the purpose for which the survey is being conducted, can, on occasion, be undesirable from the sponsor's point of view. If, for example, one is surveying a market in which one is not currently active, but into which it is intended to enter as part of a diversification programme, such information is obviously highly confidential. To disclose one's hand to competitors at such an early stage could have serious consequences.

There are other reasons why a manufacturer may not wish to have his name disclosed to respondents. If the men and women who are being interviewed are aware that the survey is being conducted on behalf of the manufacturers of a particular brand, this is likely to cause some bias to enter into the way in which they answer the questions. According to the make-up of the individual, there could be a tendency not only to over- or under-criticize the product in question, but also to read into the questions interpretations which do not apply.

To overcome these difficulties it is not uncommon for researchers to omit the name of the sponsor firm from the questionnaire. Alternatively, companies with unknown—and therefore, innocuous—names are founded specially so that their names can be shown on questionnaires and cited to respondents on demand.

Similar problems arise with the question of the title of the survey. Here again, in the interests of security, or to avoid introducing unnecessary bias into respondent's answers, it may be desirable to avoid an exact statement of purpose. This can be achieved by the use of a general rather than a specific title. In his efforts to avoid the disclosure of confidential information regarding his client, the researcher must be equally careful not to mislead the public by stating to respondents things which are not true.

To assist classification and to enable comparisons to be made from the answers of various sub-groups of respondents, it is normal for the first set of questions to establish facts about the person being interviewed, such as:

1. Sex.
2. Age.
3. Marital status.
4. Occupation.
5. Membership of professional organization/trade union, etc.
6. The occupation of the head of the household.
7. Does the family own the house it lives in?
8. Is it rented?
9. Is there a telephone?
10. At what age will the children in the household, if any, leave school?
11. What is the family income?

It will be seen that some of these questions intrude deeply into the respondent's personal and financial affairs and the problem of truthful or untruthful replies has to be faced. Sometimes researchers put such questions at the end of the questionnaire in the belief that by the time this stage has been reached the interviewer will have succeeded in establishing a friendly relationship with the respondent, thus reducing his or her natural suspicison or feeling of embarrassment.

Researchers are often divided on the controversial question of whether or not the name of the respondent should be recorded. There is a strongly held opinion that a guarantee of anonymity allows the respondent to relax and generally produces more truthful replies.

The researcher's next consideration, before he prepares his questions on the general subject-matter of the survey, is to decide upon the number and nature of the control questions which he will incorporate into his questionnaire. Control questions aim to check the accuracy of the respondent's answers to the standard questions. Where an answer to a control question is at variance with the answer given to a standard question, it is apparent to the researcher that incorrect replies have been recorded. When this occurs the entire questionnaire will be eliminated from the survey.

Care must be taken in the wording of the control question. If it merely repeats the original question it is likely to be answered in the same vein and no control will have been achieved. To be effective it must broach the same subject as the standard question but from a different point of view.

In deciding upon the wording of questions and their sequence in the questionnaire, the researcher must bear in mind the mental attitude of the respondent. He, or she, has been approached by the interviewer, who has explained what the survey is about, that they have been selected by pure chance and are; therefore, representative of public opinion and to invite their co-operation in providing answers to certain questions which will contribute to the success of the project. It is important that the confidence of the respondent should be established as quickly as possible as this will enable him to relax and to co-operate in the interview.

The work of the interviewer in achieving this desirable state of affairs will be assisted by the way in which questions are worded and the sequence in which they appear on the form. As soon as the introductory questions, which establish the respondent's characteristics, have been dealt with, it is important to move on to questions dealing with the substance of the survey and which are likely to engage the respondent's interest. One question should succeed another in a logical sequence because this enables the interest to be maintained and avoids the irritation which can occur when the respondent is asked to switch his mind from one topic to another to answer questions which may appear aimless in their intent.

One of the major problems of consumer surveys which are concerned with people's behaviour rather than their opinions, is their dependence upon the memory of respondents. We have said before that, generally speaking, the public is prepared to co-operate in research of this nature and wrong answers are seldom given intentionally. However, questions which relate to such mundane matters as the last time one purchased a certain brand of washing powder are hardly likely to stimulate the memories of most people, and the housewife must be forgiven if she cannot remember the price she paid for it or the shop where she bought it. Experience has shown that, for the best results, one should seek information about goods bought only the day before. Slightly less reliable results will be achieved from enquiries made into purchases of a week before. If one seeks to take the respondent back over a period of two weeks or more, answers of doubtful accuracy can be expected.

As to the type of questions to be used in questionnaires, these fall, generally, into three categories:

(a) Dichotomous Questions

(b) Multiple Choice Questions

(c) Open-ended Questions.

Questions which can only be answered by the words 'Yes' or 'No' are called dichotomous questions. Where these are used in a questionnaire; it is usual to state the alternatives and add spaces for 'Don't know' and 'No answer'. Researchers like dichotomous questions. They make the work of interviewing much easier and also simplify the counting of results. An example of a dichotomous question is 'Did you go abroad for your holiday last year?'

A multiple choice question is one which admits several alternative answers. When these are used in a survey, the alternative answers are provided and usually the respondent is invited to choose the answer with which he agrees. Again, statistical analysis is simplified. A multiple choice question will ask: 'If you went abroad for your holiday last year did you travel by *(1)* scheduled airline, *(2)* charter flight, *(3)* boat and rail, *(4)* boat and by car?'

The open-ended questions provide for much greater latitude on the part of the respondent. He is invited to answer the question in his own words and the interviewer enters that answer on the form. An open-ended question will ask: 'Why did you go abroad for your holiday?'

Care must be exercised in the use of words in questionnaires. They should be kept as simple as possible. It must be remembered that, in the majority of surveys, a cross-section of the population will be interviewed and this must, of necessity, include people of the lowest intelligence and education as well as the highest. Every word which is used should have a precise meaning, because if the respondent is in any doubt as to the meaning of the question which is put to him, he is liable to give a genuinely mistaken answer. Unfortunately, many of the words in the English language have more than one meaning or a different meaning in different parts of the country.

That enemy of the researcher, namely bias, can be introduced unwittingly to a survey by the use of ill-advised questions. If you ask a housewife: 'Do you give your children a cooked break-fast every morning?' she may well imagine that to answer in the negative would suggest that she was failing in her duty as a mother. A better approach would be to say: 'Some children like a cooked breakfast; others have no appetite first thing in the morning. Do your children like a cooked breakfast or do they not like a cooked breakfast?'

Once all the questionnaires in the sample have been completed, the researcher is faced with the task of processing the information he has obtained. The first step is to edit the questionnaires. Editors are appointed, whose job it is to check every questionnaire to make sure that correct answers have been given. This is achieved by means of the control questions which have been inserted for this very purpose. Researchers refer to the 'Triangle Clause' which consists of three related questions within a questionnaire each of which approaches the same subject from a slightly different angle. If it is found that one of the answers to these questions contradicts another, it can be assumed that the answer which has been given to the third question decides the issue.

Having ensured that the information which appears in the questionnaire is satisfactory, the editor applies code numbers to each answer. Where dichotomous and multiple choice questions are used throughout a questionnaire, these are usually coded in advance. The open-ended questions are rather more difficult to classify. They are often grouped and tabulated by hand and those answers which do not fall into any convenient group are placed under a miscellaneous heading.

Finally, the coded answers are tabulated, by hand, by means of punched cards or by use of a computer. From the figures thus produced, the market researcher prepares his statistical tables.

In this chapter, we have considered, in some detail, the methods employed by consumer research and, more particularly, the conduct of sample surveys. In the majority of small and medium-sized commercial firms it is unlikely that the Marketing Manager will become directly involved in the details of consumer research. It is specialized work and few companies have their own market research departments. Even where such departments do exist within the business organization, it is normal practice for the conduct of field research to be undertaken by outside agencies. These can be either independent firms or the market research departments of advertising agencies.

Independent organizations differ very considerably, according to their degree of experience and the nature of the work in which they specialize.

Market research departments of advertising agencies usually specialize in advertising research. There has been an increasing tendency, however, for the advertising agency to attempt to provide a complete marketing service to clients and this has involved them in various branches of consumer research. The general practice is to undertake the organization of a consumer survey, but to sub-contract to outside agencies the work of interviewing, editing and tabulating. The final report on the survey is then presented by the advertising agency's own market research, specialists.

❐

5

Strategy of Sales Planning

On hearing the term" strategic planning," most people tend to think of LRP and simultaneously position next year's operational planning as tactical. This confusion can be extremely costly in that next year's opportunities then are approached tactically, piece by piece, rather than strategically as a whole. Surprisingly to some, LRP and SMP are more alike than different. All the things a strategic planning group must have a command of the process itself, the phases and sequence involved, the steps to be taken, the tools that can be used, and the skills required are exactly the same. What differs is the people involved, their subject matter, the resulting document, and the kinds of work generated by the decisions made during the processes.

In the LRP process, presidents and senior executives probably staff analyze issues in the light of corporate strengths and weaknesses to develop a mission statement. Then macro goals are set, and strategies are developed to achieve them This process results in business plans which call or things such as research projects, acquisitions, new corporate structures, changed personnel requirements, and capital needs for the base business and new business over the next 2 to 5 years. While SMP takes its cue from the goals established during the LRP process, it usually involves line managers who make target market selections, establish next year's objectives, develop strategies, and then correlate tactical plans and a budget that will direct. and control next year's marketing activities.

Since nearly all direct marketing companies, other than the most entrepreneurial firms in their startup years, attempt to plan operations 6 to 9 months in advance there are two fundamental reasons why such planning should be strategic in nature. First, the operational planning must be done anyway. Second, operational plans that are rooted in effective strategic thinking not only catapult profit levels but also point out otherwise unseen disaster areas. It does not matter what size a direct marketer is SMP is an imperative for realizing the profit potentials that are inherent in the degree of change expected for the remainder of the 1980s and the 1990s—a degree of change that Alvin Toffler calls "the third wave"—which will make that of the 1970s seem small in retrospect.

Before addressing how you should structure and manage the planning process itself, let's examine what a strategic marketing plan is and is not. It is not summary notes from a series' of meetings a proposal, a set of recommendations, an agency, programme, or a project outline.

It is not a suggested course of action, a list of creative ideas or tactics, media or lists to be tested, or projects that may prove interesting to do. Your directresponse marketing plan should be the written, comprehensive product of direct marketing professionals, resulting from their creative analysis and problem solving, decision making, and specification of all the direct-response operations that will be implemented in the next marketing year. It includes what will be done, who will do each project, when the projects will be started and completed, how they will be done, what they will cost, and the priority of each project. It also states clearly how each project relates to all others and how much revenue and profit, both acquisition year and life cycle, is expected from them.

Once you had created a plan like the one described above, it has significant and various uses. Top management can use it to gain a more thorough understanding of why requested funding should be approved and how next year's operations relate to their long-range planning, and they can assess line performance more accurately. Line managers, departmental personnel, and vendors can use it to develop superior tactical work as well as to control implementation of project timing and costs and improve quality.

In sum, SMP delivers nine major benefits to a company, because it:

1. Forces three-dimensional thinking
2. Allows specialists to perceive interfunction relationships otherwise missed
3. Generates an extraordinary enthusiasm that improves tactical creativity
4. Allocates resources to have an impact on the most profitable potentials
5. Creates benchmarks in advance for future decisions
6. Improves staff quality control and deadline performance
7. Elicits improved vendor performance
8. Enables faster rollouts of successful programmes and faster shutoff of failures
9. Saves substantial top and middle management time and stress during the implementation stages.

Many strategic marketing plans have been produced by a planning department staffed with specialists trained to ;work with senior and line management inside the traditional corporate structure. Usually these staff personnel begin as honeybees gathering input from line managers and then massage the data into hypothetical possibilities that are presented to and discussed with management. The advantages of this approach are twofold. There is a constant overview perspective that sees the whole and relates each part to bottom-line impact, and the planners are experienced in using the tools available for incisive strategic decision making. What is really needed and wanted is a marriage of logical and quantitative factors with psychological and qualitative thinking that is three-dimensional as well as linear: perception that goes outside the lines without violating the principles of geometry. Just as art does not contradict science, marketing strategy need not violate the fundamental principles that govern direct marketing success.

A coregroup can function with as few as three members as long as the various essential perspectives are represented. Properly directed and interactive, the "composite eyes" of this group of direct marketing specialists can bring obstacles to the surface and create strategies that the best of planning experts by themselves generally could not. Here is what to look for when selecting each coregroup member who will become part of your creative network.

* The plan manager should be a direct marketing generalist who knows how to listen and has superior oral and written communications skills. Experience in pianning techniques and strategic development is quite helpful but not absolutely necessary. The plan manager will function as the group's job captain, responsible for scheduling meefings, start and stop tracking during meetings, recording and distributing coregroup decisions, and assigning between-meeting work projects to individual coregroup specialists.
* The marketing member should be a direct-response generalist with the deepest possible background in customer acquisition and life cycle marketing, a creative strategist rather than a tactical specialist.
* The media specialist cannot be wedded to lists or publications only but also must bring an informed

perspective on the relative strengths and weaknesses of all major response media: mail, magazine, newspaper, telephone, TV, adio, co-ops, syndication, and multimedia.

* The creative director should provide imaginative idea sparks, in contrast to the dimension of logical analysis provided by other group members. Experience in telephone and broadcast as well as direct mail and print space is desirable.

* The production manager must be conversant with all forms of direct-response production and costs, a tactical generalist whose major contribution will be to keep you in the world of the possible using state-of-the-art technology.

* The data processing specialist is needed for two primary reasons realistic knowledge of what your marketing data base can process and track, and the source of information regarding what can and cannot be done in the expanding world of word processing,

* Manufacturing or merchandising and fulfillment members are needed to ensure that your response programs do not outrun or short-circuit your fulfillment and customer service resources. This all too common eventuality will destroy the future profits from customers converted in next year's operations unless expert and well-informed represen tation expresses itself during strategic planning meetings.

If you set up a strategic planning coregroup in such a way that it effectively forms a network capable of challenging assumptions and using chance, you will find individual members seeing in new ways, recognizing patterns, and making connections that enable the group as a whole ro generate innovative and powerful strategic decisions. As a first step, select your coregroup members from those line personnel who currently are producing your direct-response programs. They can be in house, from your agency, freelancers, or consultants. Make sure that each function needed to engage in direct marketing is represented marketing creative media, financial production, data processing, manufacturing or merchandising, and fulfillment. If you're a smaller company in which single individuals wear many hats, that is fine.

If you do not have sufficient know-how on research, testing, yield analysis, or specialized industry knowledge as a part of your coregroup members' experience and skills, these resources should be brought in on an ad hoc basis, Whoever said that the whole is greater than the sum of its parts was right and your core group may well prove that observation. However, there is a danger in this kind of group approach, You must ensure that the coregroup will develop and maintain the overview that is absolutely necessary for successful strategic planning and that the group will not get bogged, down in detail by addressing pieces of your overall opportunity that are in actuality low-priority items in terms of bottom-line impact and significant growth. These pitfalls can be avoided if you use proven planning techniques and tools that eliminate tunnel vision and vested interests. You also must make certain that each coregroup member understands the basic planning ground rules and how the tools are supposed to be used, and you must allocate sufficient time for individuals in the planning network to accomplish their normal line functions while participating fully in the strategic planning process. The basic core group operating ground rules are simple to state but require a greater than average effort to make them work because they contradict much of what we have been taught as well as the conventional wisdom.

1. **Hierarchy**. During core group meetings, there is no pecking order whatsoever. Normal lines of authority

and reportability do not obtain and no individual has the authority to overrule any group decision.

2. **Subject Matter.** While all subjects are to be addressed and stressed on an informal, free-form basis, the phases of the planning process cannot be taken out of sequence. Tactics cannot be worked on until all strategy has been fully developed, objectives must be established before obstacles and advantages develop, and objectives cannot be created till all background material has been dissected and organized for the strategic planning process to begin.

3. **Perspective.** The predominant perspective is thatof the group as a whole. While each member can and should contribute from his or her area of expertise or specialization each must strive to approach decisions and value judgments from the standpoint of a direct marketing generalist assessing the relationship of any part to the whole.

4. **Decision Making.** Decision making is on a consensus basis only. Ideas, observations, opinions and individual judgments should flow freely, with dissent encouraged, However, all coregroup members must realize fhat their ideas must be presented in such a way as to obtain agreement of all other members before positions can be adopted and decisions can be considered to be made. Given the divergent perspective of each coregroup member, a great deal of heat will be generated on occasion. That is fine as long as the heat is transmuted into light by the group as a whole.

We have, found four tools to be particularly effective for developing direct-response strategy and plans. Two of these – the task method and fast-tracking-help maintain the needed overview. The other two-adversary analysis and brain-storming-help members of your network use chance, recognize patterns, and make connections. The task method is in essence zero-base marketing. It requires that each individual block out preconceptions about what is "always best" or what "cannot be done."

After relevant marketing information has been isolated from all the data assembled, coregroup members mentally block out all constraints and start to develop objectives, move on to identify and prioritize all obstacles and advantages, create strategy, and only then analyze available resources to apply constraints to the task decisions that have been made. After modifications or an approved increase in resources that can be made available, tactics are developed, and then the entire plan is subjected to risk-gain analysis.

Fast-tracking is an ideal process for strategic market planning in that it is complementary to the task method, forces overview thinking and decision making, and speeds up the entire planning process by a substantial margin. Developed in the construction industry during the 1960s in order to reduce design and building cost and lapse times, the technique was radical. But it was a successful departure from the traditional step-by-step architectural design process. Instead of architects working virtually alone to interpret the building owner's needs from initial concept to finished specifications, coordinating at various stages with the engineering firms involved, and finally turning completed plans and final specifications over to the general contractor, who then would develop bids from many subcontractor specialists, all major disciplines worked together from the beginning of the design process.

Architect, engineers, contractor, and key subcontractors were directed by a construction manager charged with keeping this interdisciplinary group on track. Ideas, observations, and judgments flowed freely, with disagreement encouraged in order to apply maximum feasibility stress to any proposition under evaluation.

No detail was allowed because major decisions were made in needed sequence. Parameter specifications were created and then checked for viability between meetings. They were reviewed at the next group meeting and then modified or finalized before the next set of needed decisions was addressed. Final details were implemented just before actual project work commenced. The results were significant and a bit startling. Costs were reduced substantially, building performance improved, and costly re-dos were eliminated. The same process can be used to improve the design and reduce the costs of direct response marketing programmes. The basic criteria governing the process are exactly the same:

1. All major disciplines are involved throughout.
2. Discussions are informal and intensely interactive.
3. Develop parameter specifications that allow final detail to be created later.
4. Major decisions only, no detail is allowed.
5. Fatigue-stress all proposals surfaced.
6. No skipping ahead; subject matter is addressed in rigid sequence.

The adversary system is essentially a series of freewheeling rap sessions rooted in conversational debate by the members of the planning network. Unlike brainstorming, in which negatives are not allowed as ideas surface, all ideas are attacked in the open as they evolve. While core group specialists should speak from the standpoint of personal expertise, ideas can and should come from anywhere on any topic.

Spontaneity and "top of the mind" reactions are essential, and network members must have the courage and maturity to see some of their ideas dismantled by the group as a whole. All decisions must be reached by a consensus of the entire group, and so it is necessary that votes for and against be taken on the basis of each member's overview rather than that member's specialty. While this ground rule may seem time-consuming on occasion, its importance cannot be overemphasized. Brainstorming is a creative technique that is useful when a network gets blocked or when an impasse in conversational debate is reached. This fantasy approach is simple, and the ground rules are few; it does not require extensive training or experience with the process to make it work.

First, you select one core group member as your brainstorming leader, who will be the only one in the group to maintain contact with reality. All others think outside the lines and free-associate within the following guidelines.

(a) No critical judgments on any ideas are expressed.

(b) Group menbers let go and simply react to ideas as they evolve.

(c) Each idea is developed till the leader stops discussion.

(d) The leader simplifies the meaning of each idea as it comes.

(e) The more free-form and fun, the better.

This kind of brainstorming is a three-step process: preparation, brainstorming and analysis. Define the problems to be addressed in writing at the outset. Set quotas for the number of ideas to be developed and then set a time limit. Since you will not be analyzing the ideas as they evolve, you will find that you are able to bring many to the surface in a relatively short time period. Make certain that each participant understands the ground rules before you begin. As soon as all are prepared, have at it. After the brainstorming session, use the adversary system to place a comparative value on each idea in terms of logic, reality, and usable resources.

Once you have chosen your method of planning and have assigned responsibility for strategic development, you are ready to begin work on the first of six phases that constitute the total planning process. In the first phase, coregroup members will turn raw data about potential markets into information that enables them to identify target markets on a qualitative and then a quantitative basis as well as evaluate the resources available to reach those markets. If the data available are not reduced to direct marketing essentials, coregroup members will be swamped by unrelated facts and almost certainly will miss relationships that are crucial for strategic decision making.

It is not an exaggeration to state that as much direct-response profit is lost in phase 1 as in any other phase of your work or for any other reason: mispositioned creative strategy, weak media analysis, anemic strategy development, inferior tactical development, deficient capabilities for response tracking,. etc. Recognize the difference between data and information. At the end of each trading day, stock exchange floors are strewn with pieces of paper recording the day's transactions. Imagine the most skilled investment analyst trying to make decisions based on the information buried in all those data. But the next morning, when the transaction data have been converted to information in newspaper financial sections, judgment can be applied toward making informed decisions. Turning marketing data into marketing information for your strategic planning coregroup's use is just as critical a process. Too often the assumption that everyone comprehends "enough" leads to too little time and thought being dedicated to organizing and boiling down data so that residual information can be seen in its true significance.

The first step is for the plan manager to gather and format all relevant information. Two resources must be made available for the plan manager to accomplish this: in-depth knowledge of direct marketing principles and librarian skills. If the manager has only the organizing component, the significant will not be separated from the incidental: if he or she has only the direct marketing insight, information will be assembled in formats that confuse rather than enlighten. Available data must be turned into relevant information in each of the following areas.

(a) Preliminary situation statement

(b) Industry maturity and business phase

(c) Direct marketing margins

(d) Product features

(e) Competition

(f) Sales Planning

(g) Needs and wants

(h) Benefits

(i) Customer profiles

(j) Profile summaries

(k) Market segments

(l) The buying process

(m) Perception of need

(n) Current resource levels

Each area should be addressed individually and in this order.

This should be written before any major effort is devoted to converting data into information. The purpose is to tell you and each coregroup member what you do not know as well as what you do know and what you think you know. The statement addresses each subject listed above in order and is comprehensive but not deep in detail; it is a precis rather than a fully documented narrative. Once completed, the written statement is distributed to each core group member as well as any other personnel who might be a source of marketing input. Each recipient should study this opening statement from two standpoints: to suggest any important ingredients that have not been included, and to determine what each recipient can input for amplification. The following checklist is helpful as a stimulator for coregroup members and as a control reference for the plan manager to ensure that all potential sources of critical information have been probed.

(a) Your house list

(b) Right-hand drawers of company veterans

(c) Previous research and analytical reports

(d) Competitive data

(e) Ex-customers

(f) Previous inquirers

(g) Complementary product in to

(h) Customers

(i) List brokers

(j) Media vendors

(k) Government reports and statistics

(l) Foundation research

(m) Production vendors

(n) Award case histories

(o) Association reports and statistics

(p) Industry consultants

(q) Media libraries

As you all do your homework and scan your memories, contacts, and references, you often will be astonished at how much significant information surfaces from the most mundane and unlikely places. Once relevant data have been collected by the plan manager, the data must be boiled down and organized into essential facts and relationships. Summary statements should be developed in each subject area in a sequence of most important to least important, and documentation should be included in the background appendix, classified and indexed for ready access. Insofar as possible, express all statistical data incrementally and comparatively as well as absolutely. Do not spend undue time at this stage initiating research or indulging in work projects to extend the information in hand. When key elements are missing, simply note them as critical yet "missing". You will address them in depth when you reach the phases dealing with objectives and obstacles. When this in-depth revision of the original preliminary situation statement is completed, it should be distributed to each coregroup member for study before the first network session. If the documentation is too bulky for distribution, simply include the classification and index for the supporting materials and distribute them to individual members on request. All documentation should be available, however, at all coregroup meetings.

Finally, do not be surprised if this phase of your work consumes as much as 50 per cent of the time needed for the whole process. Louis Nizer, the attorney, attributed his consistent courtroom brilliance to his three P's and commented that 95 per cent of his success was due to preparation and perspiration and 5 per cent to performance.

At the first meeting, the coregroup members should move on an adversary and evaluation basis through each of the background areas to satisfy themselves that the information at hand has been developed as much as possible before beginning the remaining phases of the planning process. Do not short-circuit this effort in your anxiety to move on to the next phase. Key elements that are overlooked or not perceived here will have a disproportionately negative impact on strategic development and profits.

The second part of your background organization identifies whether the industry in which you are going to compete is embryonic, growing, mature, or aging. Where your industry is will have a great deal to do with the kinds of objectives you develop and the types of obstacles and advantages you have. You should define your industry in terms of total dollar sales per year and number of units sold and then in terms of competition by annual sales dollar volume, size of customer base, and market share. Do not at this stage spend much time on in-depth analysis of each competitor and be careful not to include sales figures that include products or services that are not competitive with you. It is equally important to know the stage your business is in as well as your own sales statistics in terms of customer base growth, attrition, average dollar sales per year per customer, cost per inquiry, cost per order etc. Usually only one business is "fitstest with the mostest" in any given marketplace. If you are not that business, view your competitors as a strategic sources of crucial information not otherwise available to you then leverage that information to the maximum.

As competitors communicate in direct-response form, they are telling you continually what is and what is not working in your marketplace. Accurately analyzed, their offers, creative platforms, and media selections can focus customer profiles, needs, and wants related to benefits, price points, and size of markets. But you must work at organizing the signals they are sending you. Determine their media usage in terms of frequency and total expenditures, identifying primary and secondary media.

For new products or new markets, be certain to apply all manufacturing of merchandise supplier costs and all fulfillment costs to establish marketing margin ranges. Then use general media costs per thousand, as shown in the following table.

Media	Average CPM,$
Telephone	1,8000
Direct, mail	300
Newspaper inserts	27
Magazines	15
Newspaper Rap	9
Television	3

In addition to CPM, you must use conservatively estimated response rates based on your own previous experience or general industry response ranges. Now allocate overhead costs, and your coregroup members will have a working measurement of allowable cost per order, (CPO) cost per inquiry (CPI), and range of contribution to promotion and profit (CPP), Be certain that these parameter statistics include life cycle values for each customer acquired unless there is absolutely no potential for back-end sales and profits. To sum up, there are five steps involved in preplanning mathematics:

1. Identify conservatively estimated response rates.
2. Compute CPP.
3. Develop proforma profit and loss statements

4. Make a halt decision if your numbers don't make direct marketing sense in terms of risk-gain potential.

5. Factor customer life cycle values into your analysis.

Here you simply want to define what each product is and what it does. Written descriptions by each coregroup member should be lean and skeletal yet comprehensive. No special effort should be made at this stage to translate product features into customer benefits, although any natural "top of the mind" benefits statements need not be removed. Costs of manufacturing and fulfillment as well as the percentage of overhead to be applied should be included in the written descriptions. There should be no attempt at creative copy since the thrust now is toward clarity, brevity and inclusiveness.

Although the phrase "Needs and Wants analysis" sounds dull, it often induces dynamic coregroup sessions and is the springboard to benefits evaluation, customer profile identification, market segmentation, and strong creative platforms. No matter how self-evident needs or wants seem to be, the strategic planning coregroup should put them under a marketing microscope for closer inspection. They should be analyzed at two different stages in phase 1: from the standpoint of common sense, logic and general knowledge and again after each potential customer profiles perception of need has been established. In consumer programmes, it is useful for core group members to individually apply the basic 8 before discussing needs and wants. These are:

1. Making money

2. Saving money

3. Winning praise

4. Self-improvement

5. Impressing others

6. Helping children and family

7. Saving time or effort

8. Having fun

Then distinguish between a need and a want and decide which your product or service will be satisfying. The owner of on outdoor swimming pool may want a solar sun blanket to keep her pool water warm at less cost, but she needs a basic pool covering for winterizing if she lives in the snowbelt. Similar real distinctions exist in business and industrial markets. When the EPA mandated a large leap in minimum gas mileage per gallon.

Detroit needed to find a way to lighten their product by nearly 1000 pounds per car. Before that, product designers and management might have wanted to lighten cars by using lighter metals, but they did not need to. As the coregroup raps about needs versus wants and the type of satisfaction delivered, inevitably customer characteristics will be mentioned: age, income, sex, education, occupation, and marital status. Lifestyle characteristics such as athletics, politics, intellectual, and hobbies also will be discussed.

Capture these demographic and psychographic data as they evolve but do not at this point try to develop complete pictures of various customer potentials. Instead, coregroup members should start to be more specific in their descriptions of the kinds of needs or wants satisfied. How will the customer make more money? Or save it? Or impress others? As you refine the satisfactions, more profile characteristics will emerge. Capture these and start connecting the characteristics. When you've connected as many as possible, prioritize the satisfactions you've identified from most important to least important by coregroup vote. Stay at it till the network reaches consensus. Then apply the six basic drives to your priority list:

1. Self-preservation
2. Love
3. Duty
4. Gain
5. Pride
6. Self-indulgence

After you have done this, repeat the whole process. Once this is completed you will have a clear picture of which needs and wants can be satisfied by your products or services and some idea about the types of customers you should seek. These same criteria apply in business and industrial markets, but there you must overlay one pervasive motivation: 'recognition by business peers and management.

Benefits are what prospects think about and evaluate before buying and what suspects give little or no serious consideration. Consequently, your product's benefits not only govern creative strategy and tactics but also are a prime tool in determining who the best potential customers actually are. Benefits prioritization is often a critical tool in certain marketing situations, and it is always an important one. Here the core group starts by listing every possible benefits anyone can think of Translate all the product features described in step 2 into clear, tight benefits statements.

Now have the coregroup vote on the most important benefit and rap till consensus is reached. Do the same until all benefits have been prioritized. Do you have a unique selling proposition, the U.S.P. all direct marketers covet? Be brutally honest with yourselves about this, for the marketplace will be. If you truly have the competitive advantage of a USP, your ultimate strategy will be vastly different.

Customer profile analysis is crucial in directresponse marketing. direct marketer's most important resource is not the order but the orderer, not the response but the responder. Discovery, accumulation, retention, maintenance, and retrievability of profiles and response history are the cornerstone of profit in direct marketing.

Maximum profit is generated by defining customer profiles accurately, searching out segments of the total potential customer base with similar characteristics, and then soliciting and resoliciting them effectively to maximize sales during responder life cycles. When only a one-time sale is possible, identifying customer profiles in terms of best CPO through to breakeven profiles enables you to spend your direct-response dollars most cost effectively.

In short, the more precisely you define and rank your profiles, the less you will spend to obtain initial orders and the higher will be your response rates average order dollars and dollars per customer per year. Direct mail, the parent of direct-response marketing, has proved this time and again. This is why your best ZIP codes will pull 300 per cent better than your worst: there are more similar profiles within the best ZIPs. Profile similarity makes it possible for the various forms of regression analysis to identify markets on the basis of profitability. Consequently, the strategic planning coregroup should spend whatever time and effort are necessary at this stage to categorize and rank profiles as precisely and accurately as possible.

Five major tools can be used to isolate the profiles you must find: response graphics, demographics, psychographies, geographics, and special graphics. While sufficient information from only one of these can be enough for profitable direct marketing the more relevant information you have from each area the sooner you will reach maximum profits, both acquisition and life cycle. Therefore, each source must be examined in depth.

Response graphics are simply the historical actions taken by customers in response to specific types of products. The basic formula employed by the mail-order industry since the 1930s has been decency, frequency, and monetary value, but it is helpful to isolate variety also. Run this analysis against your house file first if applicable. It is axiomatic in direct-response marketing that previous responders will respond better than non responders. Most research supports the contention that roughly one-third of wage-earning Americans are not responders yet and may never be but that the remaining two-thirds are responders, with half of them responding on a regular basis and half on a sporadic basis. Some posit that 50 per cent of adults in the United States are mail order buyers and that the remainder are "see touch and feel" buyers at retail. Whatever the actual split, the difference between the two is critical in your profile analysis. However, keep in mind that large number of previous non responders have been converted to responders over the past 10 years and that magazine subscriptions responders are not mail-order buyers until proved otherwise. When you are entering a new market or selling a new product unlike those you have marketed before, your house file response information will not help much. Demographics refers to the factors of age, sex, and family status, education, income, occupation and shelter. At a minimum, accurately identifying demographic customer characteristics enables you to zero in on publications and specify micro segments of lists for mail and telephone efforts; sometimes this is a key analytical factor in determining your best broadcast markets for television response. These customer indicators can be computer-combined with responder files through listgrafting techniques or can be positively merge-purged against master computer data bases to identify where the best customers are.

In business and industrial markets, demographics relates to business entities rather than individual consumers but is no less useful or important. SICs isolate business by industry and type of business within an industry, and various list compilers further segment by annual dollar volume, number of employees, etc. Psychographics isolates potential customers in terms of their Lifestyle characteristics. Everything from antique collecting avid book reading, camping, fishing, and flying through political activism, stamp collecting, investing, tennis, and wine drinking is grist for the marketing analyst. By 1982, one fast-growing computer data base had 6 million consumers identified by any of 54 lifestyle characteristics crossed with age, sex, marital and family status, occupation, and type of shelter. Geographics tells one where the current customers reside and in certain instances where the best prospects are likely to be. For example, salt-polluted areas adjacent to the U.S. coastline are clearly targets for the sale of home water distillers, whereas municipal wells invaded by toxic chemicals are not necessarily adjacent to bodies of salt water. In the United States, isolation of target markets by geographic location is nearly unlimited in flexibility and reach.

Country	1
Census regions	9
States	52
ADIs	200
SMAs	265
Sectional centers	870
Counties	3,150
School districts	12,500
Census tr-+acts	34,600
ZIPs	36,000
Census blocks	287,000

Special graphics are any characteristics not included among the four first sources. For example, pool ownership could conceivably indicate a lifestyle characteristic, but it does not necessarily do so. Individuals with high blood pressure, who are prime targets for the sale of a water distiller, do not necessarily have any demographic, psychographies, geographic, or responder characteristics in common. Once the coregroup has gathered, organized, and preliminarily combined characteristics into discrete profiles, here is a process that can be used to further verify or refine customer profiles.

1. Coregroup members study individually each profile established thus far.
2. Each member jots down "top of mind" characteristics that relate to specific product purchase potentials.
3. Each member then compares the prime benefit with each profile. Is it the same? If not, match benefits to appropriate profiles or describe a profile that would relate to the prime benefit.
4. Depending on the consensus and confidence level of the coregroup as a whole, profiles then are identified as viable or as needing further verification in the objectives, obstacles, or strategy phases of the planning process.
5. Do the same for each benefit on the benefits list.
6. Coregroup adversary analyzes each member's benefits and profiles list, raps, and ranks agreed on profile and benefit combinations from best to least.

No matter what your market-consumer, business, or industrial—there are always steps before the buy-no buy decision is made. There are always buying actions and sometimes buying influences.

There are five steps, or buying actions:

1. Recognition of need
2. Evaluation of solutions
3. Recommendation of product type
4. Selection of brand
5. Approval of purchase decision

In consumer markets, very often one individual takes all the actions, sometimes in a matter of minutes in a very informal way. He or she recognizes the need, mentally or actually compares and evaluates types of products that could satisfy the need, makes a mental recommendation about brand, and then mentally approves the expenditures needed to acquire the product. In other instances, usually with more expensive products or products that will be used by more than the individual in question, there can be buying influences who can have an impact on the buying decision. The sale of water distillers is a case in point. Any family member may recognize the need for pure drinking water, but the mother of the house probably will want to compare makes, features, and benefits of various types of this kitchen appliance, and the father will have a voice in an expenditure of $250.

However, this type of multi-influence buying process is a prime characteristic of business and industrial markets, in which many individuals, often specialists, control the buying actions before a purchase decision can evolve. Professional analysis, specifications and requisitions, budgets, and approvals are par for the course. Be aware that the buying process is a gauntlet and that anyone of the buying influences has the power to negate the sale. Consequently, your creative strategy, the amount of versioning you do, the number of solicitations you make, and your entire marketing strategy may well depend on exactly what the buying process is: how many influences there are and the steps each influence must take in the process itself. Once you have discovered the process as it relates to your products, revisit your list of profiles and link any buying influences that exist to the related profile.

Never assume that actual needs are perceived needs. Often they are not the same, and your response will misfire to whatever degree your assumed perception of need was off target. Examples abound but one of the best is Monex International's direct marketing programme to sell Krugerrands shortly after Americans once again could buy and own gold. It was 1979, and Monex assumed that investors knew why they should invest in gold and understood the mechanics of making the purchase. They headlined their response ads in the financial press "Get 20 for the money and one for the show" and concentrated on convincing potential investors that gold coins were the best way to invest in gold as compared with bullion or gold stocks. The programme was not a bomb, but someone challenged the assumption that most investors knew much about gold at all, since 40 years had passed since Americans could legally own it. After research, their new ad approach was headlined

Gold – how to buy it, where to buy it...

and why you should.

The ad went on to give the history of gold's reemergence into America's financial investment opportunities and how simple it was to buy and sell gold. The results? The cost for an inquiry was reduced by an increment of 56 per cent, and the average order size grew by an increment of 20 per cent. The reason for this was a more accurate assessment of perception of need combined with creative execution as professional as on the first attempt. Take our home water distilling appliance. In areas where municipal aquifers have been salt-polluted, perception of need is acute, as evidenced by the fact that these areas consume 56 per cent of all bottled water in the United States, and in 1979 bottled water sales exceeded $550 million. Yet the actual need of residents in those areas was comparatively lower than that of residents in areas where the municipal wells had been invaded by toxic chemicals carded by groundwater checked, perception of need never would have helped you market a water distiller. Your core group now should evaluate each customer profile identified in terms of perception of need and then rerank profile priorities according to the perception factor.

While it is true in one sense that the medium is the market in direct response, do not limit your strategic analysis of target markets in terms of the existing media reach. Instead, start by identifying the quantity of customer potentials that exist within each one of the profile segments your core group has isolated and then start to work on where they are located and how to reach them cost-effectively. Do not start with any specific medium and explore laterally. Here is a sequence of steps that can be used to examine the total U.S. marketplace to ferret out those market segments which represent profitable marketing potentials for direct-response operations. Not all the steps apply to each product or marketing situation. Your coregroup members may find themselves moving through any given step simply by deciding that it is not applicable to this specific situation.

1. Start with your number one profile, complete your analysis of it, and then move on to the next profile until you have analyzed each profile on your potential customer list.

2. Define each profile segment geographically on the basis of any relevant distribution limits.

    a. for retail traffic building, apply store location parameters.

    b. For lead-getting programmes for localized sales people, supply sales office parameters. Keep in mind that all consumer segments are reachable by mail.

3. Reduce any geographic "wholes" by special graphics that are applicable snowbelt for pool covers, salt polluted areas for water distillers, entire country for new mothers, etc.

4. When your profiles contain key demographic characteristics, quantify each by applying national census summary statistics.

5. Merge-purge your own customer file segments against the quantities determined in step 5 and determine if geocoded census tract back-scanning can isolate and identify similar-profile tracts throughout the country. If not, cluster by ZIP code counts.

6. For each profile segment, apply maximum media reach quantities to your total universe in terms of each medium in the following order of priority:

   Responder lists

   Mail-order publications

   Listed telephone numbers

   Compiled lists and general publications

   TV, newspaper, and regional and local magazines against high-priority clusters.

7. Explore all list-grafting potentials.

8. Evaluate each medium in terms of response potential versus cost efficiency. Keep in mind that at this point, your coregroup is not but rather applying the relative strengths and weaknesses of each major response medium to the market segments you have

isolated and ranked in order of response profitability potential.

Now that the core group has determined target markets by size and by the types of customers within them as well as product benefits and media available to reach each segment, you are ready to analyze the resources you have at your disposal to address these market opportunities. If the strategies and plans you create produce sales that outrun your organization's fulfillment capabilities, consider your programme a failure rather than a success. One of the fundamental differences between selling and marketing is that the prime function of selling is to create an order, whereas the prime function of marketing is to create the most profitable customer. By definition marketing must go beyond selling to produce satisfied, enthusiastic customers who will want to buy again and recommend your products and company to others. This principle of marketing applies to all businesses but especially to mail-order and direct-response marketing because there is no person-to-person contact between buyer. and seller. Consequently, the strategic planning coregroup must be as diligent and creative in providing for your order fulfillment and customer service performance as they are in providing for customer solicitation and order generation. A few years ago, an industry veteran claimed that if we could deliver the product in 3 days, we'd own the world, and there is reason to believe he was right. Research clearly shows that repeat purchase and the lifetime value of a customer are directly related to the speed and accuracy with which initial orders are handled. As an integral part of the planning process, the following ten capabilities must be assessed in terms of handling current order levels and any growth that the strategic plan may call for:

1. Ordering forms and instructions

2. Receiving mail and telephone calls

3. Processing orders
4. Checking credit
5. Addressing and list maintenance
6. Controlling inventory
7. Reporting and controlling
8. Order filling and shipping
9. Billing
10. Handling complaints and adjustments.

You cannot achieve 100 per cent effectiveness in any of the ten areas because of three factors that are not ,under your complete control: customers, vendors, and carriers. But it is critical that you identify deficiencies in all operations that are under your complete control. Any that are discovered not to be controllable should be precisely identified for consideration in the objectives phase. While all these areas are important, reporting and controlling bears further investigation, for it is this "feed" to your marketing data base that enables you to track response, sales, and profits in terms of customer profiles. Any deficiency in this area of tracking and measuring response should be considered a major obstacle that must be corrected in the strategic planning process arid the allocation of resources that the plan will call for. The strength, weakness, and extent of your front-end resources also must be determined accurately in the planning process.

Be as brutally honest with yourselves on this point as you were in assessing your USP. Do you really have state-of-the-art knowledge and hands-on skills in all the recently developed areas of direct-response marketing? If your creative people are great in print, are they as effective in telephone, film, or multimedia? Are your list personnel skilled in the other response media that have emerged or are emerging rapidly? Of course, you must consider the financial resources available for use. This does not preclude the task method approach. It merely lets the core group know when additional financial resources must be requested if they are justified by risk-gain analysis in phase 6.

After each of the foregoing areas has been addressed and evaluated by the core group, the plan manager is ready to put together the final preplanning situation statement, which should be written in the same sequence in which subjects were addressed during the background analysis process. Now all relevant information in order of importance under each information category will definitively identify what is known and that which is not yet known or in hand. The completed document should be distributed to all coregroup members for in-depth study before the first core group meeting to establish objectives. Each core group member should bring his or her situation document to each meeting, and the plan manager is responsible for having all documentation available at each meeting.

Developing objectives that permit effective strategic decision making is as much an art as a science, but it is not magic. Your planning group's command of this skill will determine whether you aim the organization's time money, and talent at operations that in reality have a low priority or steer your direct response horsepower into channels of substantial growth that are somewhat selfrenewing. Objectives that are conceived too narrowly apply an enormously wasteful amount of direct marketing activity to profit potentials that represent only a small portion of the growth that is realizable. Recognize that objectives are rudders that pull your direct-response strategies toward the most important marketing opportunities. Realize that a 10 degree error here can turn into a 1000-mile "miss" of the major ports you are headed for, leaving you at sea rather than unloading cargo. Here is a step-by-step method that can help you create objectives that are reachable and worth realizing:

1. Have your coregroup free-associate a list of possible objectives for next year's operations, never losing sight of lifecycle implications.

2. Adversary analyze each potential objective on the list in terms of the following criteria:

   (a) Does it focus on results?

   (b) Is it measurable? If yes, how?

   Rate of return

   Ratio to sales

   Percentage of market

   Number of units

   Dollars to accomplish

   Time to accomplish

   Other

   (c) Does it contain a single theme?

   (d) Is it challenging? A strategic objective should stretch your existing capabilities but not break any corporate bones. Setting comfortable objectives is as damaging to profit production as tilting at windmills is to morale.

   (e) Is it realistic? Do you have, or can you obtain, the resources needed in time?

   (f) Does it contribute to higher goals, such as longrange goals, department-to-division goals, division-to-corporate goals, or corporate-to-parent goals?

If any objective evaluated cannot be developed to the point where it satisfies the first five criteria of adversary analysis remove it from your list of possible objectives. Only without meeting objective can you proceed without damage to your strategic plan. As a matter of business courtesy and practical judgment, it is best when ranking objectives to state why any objective has the priority assigned it even though it does not contribute to a higher goal.

3. Place any objectives that are totally financial in nature in a category separate from those which are not totally financial in nature.

4. Rank the financial objectives and then the other objectives on the basis of two factors only: next year's bottom line and life cycle contribution. Consider your numbers from two standpoints in each case: marketing margin and contribution to overhead and profit.

5. Examine the kinds of objectives you have developed and prioritized in the light of the industry's phase and the phase your own business is in.

6. Bring in a fresh set of eyes, either a direct marketing generalist or a group that has not been part of the planning process thus far. This devil'sadvocate can be from within your company or the outside. Background should be provided prior to the attempt to find 'any weakness or omissions in your statement of objectives. Finalization of the objectives phase occurs only after your coregroup has analyzed objectives in light of the devil's advocate's input.

Most treatments of strategic planning move directly from developing objectives to the creation of strategy. While that sequence obviously has producced a great deal of profitable strategy, the introduction of a step between objectives and strategy can yield uncommon results. It is a step that illuminates the mind and vitalizes the judgment. It simply involves addressing, evaluating, and "connecting" obstacles and advantages to the objectives you just completed working on. Of the two, obstacles are the most misunderstood and underutilized.

Obstacles that are clearly seen and assessed can lead to profits. When discovered, evaluated accurately, and linked to objectives, they can galvanize the coregroup's innovative insights unlike any other tool available. Considered from another angle, if only one major obstacle is overlooked or badly underestimated during the planning process, it can turn a profitable marketing programme into a total loser. Two examples will clarify this point. For our manufacturer of pool covers, product quality was as good as but no better than that of two larger competitors, price was the same and delivery was comparable. There was no realistic way to change those three factors. There was no competitive advantage. Clearly, a powerful strategy would have to be discovered and implemented if any significant gains were to be realized. For our manufacturer of water distillers, residents were drinking toxic chemicals in their tap water but had no knowledge of the danger, in contrast to residents in salt-polluted areas. This was a major obstacle that steered the strategy for marketing to them. Turning obstacles into profits during the planning process can be managed in much the same way that objectives were addressed, using the same basic-planning tools.

1. Free-associate any and all obstacles of whatever type that come to mind
2. Link each obstacle that surfaces to the specific objectives it impacts. Do not be concerned if a single obstacle blocks multiple objectives. List it under each one that is relevant, since it is likely that a different strategy may be needed to overcome it.

3. Rank the obstacles to each objective on the basis of the resources needed.

Throughout this process, significant clues as to how to allocate resources and also some hints as to "right-on" strategies will evolve. Do not pursue strategy development at this point. Once you have developed and assessed the obstacles to next year's direct marketing efforts, you are ready to work on competitive advantages. Use the same process and the same tools to discover, evaluate, and link your advantages to your objectives.

Trying to answer the question "How do you actually develop strategy?" is like trying to answer the question "How do you actually get an idea?" While both questions are rooted in logic and understanding, both go beyond mere logical analysis and linear thinking. Effective strategies, like creative ideas, emerge from" outside-the-lines" thinking that does not violate fundamental principles. "Eureka" moments— :those moments of illumination and insight when you know you have it cannot be produced on demand or in a production-line atmosphere. Harry Hepner's comment, quoted earlier in the chapter, "Creative thinkers continually waver between unimaginable fantasies and systematic attack" is relevant here. So it is of the utmost importance to establish an atmosphere in which the free play of the mind, and the free interplay of minds, can readily occur. Let's define strategy before going any further. It is an elusive concept used too often is confused with tactics. There is good reason for this confusion; as can be seen when one consults the dictionary for clarification. The standard dictionary defines strategy and tactics as follows:

Strategy: the art of-devising a plan toward a goal

Tactics: a device for accomplishing an end

Since these definitions do not shed much light on the distinction, our working will be as follows.

Strategy is the advantageous employment of various resources as an integrated whole to cause a planned effect.

Tactics involves actions of lesser magnitude than strategy and are carried out with a limited end in view.

With that distinction in mind, here are some guidelines for your strategy creating sessions.

1. Work on the strategy to achieve one objective at a time.
2. Review each objective and its associated obstacles and advantages before development activity begins.
3. Maximize the interaction between coregroup members during the strategy sessions.
4. Assess the viability of your strategies between working sessions.
5. Start with your highest-priority objective and work your way through to the last.
6. Give your devil's advocate maximum latitude when he or she attempts to destroy the rationale for your strategies.
7. Prioritize the strategies agreed on within each objective the strategies impact.

Keep in mind throughout the process that strategy can and does obtain in any activity related to direct-response marketing; production and fulfillment as well as creative and media, research and testing as well as financial and customer service, morale and administrations as well as marketing and sales. For the swimming-pool cover manufacturer with no unique selling proposition for its dealers in snowbelt areas, three strategies were developed and they resulted in an increase in sales volume of over 40 per cent with no decrease in profit level on sales. They were:

1. **A Dealer Push-pull Programme.** A customer information booklet comes from Centurv Products and the dealer who stocks Century pool covers. Pool owners will be offered the booklet "free from their dealer" through an ad in Pool News, which has a biennial circulation to 700,000 pool owners. Dealers are preinformed of this offer to their potential customers. Those who stock Century covers receive an inventory of the booklets free of charge.

2. An offer that adds a customer information value to the basic commodity being sold. The dealers sad that it takes pool owners 3 days to winterize the poll properly and that they often make mistakes that cause their pools to deteriorate, or cost them money for repair. So the cornerstone of the October to April direct-response programme is a small booklet entitled How to Winterize Your Pool. It gives complete and truly useful step-by-step information to pool owners.

3. Use of integrated multimedia to dramatize the first two items. Direct mail, print ads, and trade shows.

Tactics are as natural and integral to a marketing plan as children are to a family. No strategic marketing plan can be considered complete without them since no true assessment of the resources called for by the plan can be made without them. Plan tactics are the written parameter specifications that define the work projects needed to implement strategic plans and guide the people who actually will do the tactics during the upcoming marketing year. It is important that these parameter specifications control the work to be done without restricting the creativity of those who actually will perform the work.

This part of your written plan spells out exac!ly what projects will be worked on in the coming year, when they will start and finish, who will do each, approximately what they will cost, and how each project relates to all others called for by the plan. Tactics include but are not necessarily limited to the following:

Solicitation Packaging for all Media. Direct mail, magazine and newspaper RAP and insert ads, telephone scripts, TV and radio ads, collateral, and multimedia combination

Concept and themes

Copy platforms or story boards

Graphic approach

Component specifications

Media selections for all programmes, controls, in all media to be utilized.

Lists and specifications

Magazines and newspapers

Telephone, incoming and outgoing

TV and radio

Collateral outlets

Support media such as co-stuffers, and syndication

Research projects and test structures

Focus group

Intercept personal

Direct mail and telephone

Test cell specifications

Timing and rollout parameters

Fulfillment, customer service, and response tracking specifications

Schedules, quality control procedures, and costs for all projects

Remember, the planning process must go far enough into detail that there is absolutely no doubt in the minds of those who will implement the projects as to what is to be done and what results are expected from their efforts.

Now that you have completed the tactical elements of the marketing plan, six more steps are required before you "freeze" the plan for presentation management for approval and funding:

1. Predictive yield analysis
2. Writing the plan
3. Devil's advocacy
4. Final coregroup consensus
5. Implementation criteria
6. Formatting the presentation

This is the moment of truth in the planning process, the point at which you pull together all your cost factors, compare them with reasonable forecasts of response, and then relate those to your calculations on Breakeven, CTOP, and life cycle value. Use your own previous response rates, recision data, and attrition curves if they are applicable. If they are not, search out industry statistics and apply them conservatively. It is possible these calculations will send you back to the drawing board if the coregroup judges the amount of resources called for to be prohibitive in terms of risk-gain probabilities.

As agonizing as this is when it occurs, it is less agonizing than failure after implementation and much less costly.

The entire plan, including documentation, must be committed to written form. The sequence of information is exactly the sequence in which the planning process took place:

Background summary

Objectives

Obstacles and advantages

Strategy

Tactics

Yield analysis

Implementation criteria

While each coregroup specialist should provide factual and rationale input at the plan manager's request, they also may be asked to contribute copy. If so, it is still the plan manager's responsibility for final editing that ensures that the written plan will reflect the decisions made by the core group consensus during the plan development process. When the written plan is distributed to core group members before the final adversary review meeting give it also to a devil's advocate who previously has not been part of the planning process in any way and include that person or group in the final coregroup review meeting. The ground rules for adversary analysis and consensus approval also apply to this last meeting before presentation to management.

Clearly, the line personnel who actually will implement the plan's projects must have some flexibility when addressing. real-world problems that cannot be foreseen in any planning process. However, the plan's essential specifications cannot be changed arbitrarily without sacrificing the value and probably the intended performance of the projects undertaken. We recommend that you use the adversary system throughout implementation during your operational year. Any line personnel who interpret plan specifications differently creative, graphics, and data processing, for example must attempt to reach consensus on the best way to proceed. If they cannot reach consensus after a reasonable amount of time has been spent in discussion, the matter is taken to the next logical superior with oversight responsibility. All sides of the question at hand are presented with pros and cons, and then a decision is made. If the manager hearing the case is unable to decide, it goes up the line; in certain instances, the coregroup itself may have to be reconvened. Generally speaking.

> Essential changes such as offer, creative platform, media, price, product, etc., require coregroup analysis and approval.
>
> Important changes such as list substitutes, test structures, etc., require marketing director approval.
>
> Incidental changes such as paper stock, copywriter switches, etc., require only appropriate department head approval.

The criteria and guidelines you use should be spelled out in writing as part of the written plan itself, because after the plan has been approved, all departments will use their copy of the plan's rationale and specifications in much the same way that a building contractor uses architectural plans and specifications to erect a building.

The plan in final written form should be distributed to top managers for review and study at least one week before the formal presentation for approval. However, the sequence of the plan summary presented at that meeting should be different from the sequence in which the plan was written.

Financial analysis summary

Objectives

Obstacles and advantages Strategy

Summary of tactics

As these summary areas are presented and discussed the coregroup's knowledge, and the written plan itself can and should be used to respond to specific questions that arise, clarify positions taken, and explain decisions.

❐

6

Performance Evaluation and Appraisal

The top management determines the corporate objectives and goals and the departmental heads, including top sales executives derive departmental objectives out of them. Departmental objectives, therefore, must be within the framework of company's overall objectives. The sales department, like other departments, frames policies and plans in order to achieve such objectives. Then, Sales management group designs sales programmes and campaigns determines specific methods and procedures, and takes other needed actions, including those necessary for making changes in the sales organisation to execute, the policies and implement the plans. In performing these and other managerial activities like planning, organisation, directing, coordinating and controlling, the sales management also 'coordinates the department's activities with other related activities performed by other departments.

Management of sales force is an important task of sales managemerit and therefore, their performance must be evaluated from time to time in order to determine the performance of the sales management, and on which the success and failure of the organisation depends. In evaluating performance four major steps are necessary *i.e.*:

1. Establishing Performance Standards

This is the first step in the valuation process. Setting standards is necessary for evaluating the actual performance, but depends upon, the nature of selling job other words, sales job analysis is necessary in order to determine job objectives, duties and responsibilities and the like. These in tun depend upon the company's selling strategies. Setting performance standards for those 'selling personnel, who are engaged mainly in new business selling reguires the use of measures quite unlike those used for sales personnel engaged in trade selling. The performance standards should be designed to measure the quality of performance of activities that the company considers most important.

The other important consideration in setting performance standards is the recognition of true nature of selling job.

A considerable market knowledge is also required for selling performance standards. The sales management befere setting of standards, must be fully award of the total sales potential and the share of each territory capable of producing, evaluation of customers and prospects in terms of potential profitability for each class and sizer of account, competitors' strengths and weaknesses, practices and policies, and selling expenses in different territories.

Performance standards can be set either in quantitative terms or in qualitative terms against, which actual performance of individual salespersons can be measured. Qualitative analysis may include: *(i)* sales volume, *(ii)* number of orders secured, *(iii)* number of sales calls made, *(iv).* number of service calls made, *(v)* number of new accounts opened, *(vi)* expenses incurred, and (vii) territory contribution:-"to profit etc. The quatitative considerations may include: *(i)* degree of product knowledge, *(ii)* quality of sales presentation, (iii) personality traits rating such as initiative judgement, *(iv)* self organisation *i.e.,* managing time, handling of correspondence, reports etc. *(v)* customer relationship, *(vi)* knowledge and education, *(vii)* nature, behaviour, manners, and neatness etc. Quantitative factors are more specific andobjective whereas qualitative factors are subjective. The management must try to set standards to measure the performance of sales force taking quantitative and qualitative factors into consideration.

2. Recording Actual Performance

Having set the performance standards, the next task before the management is to record the actual performance of the sales force. In other words, it is gathering of information on performance. The management must derfine the necessity of information, determine the sources to obtain it and set methods in operation to collect it.

There are two basic sources of obtaining performance information: *(i)* Sales and expense records maintained chiefly for accoupt purposes, and *(ii)* reports of various sorts obtained primarily for the use of sales management. Such reports are from *(a)* Sales personnel (Field sales reports), *(b)* lower echelons of sales management, and *(c)* information contained in the sales forecasts.

Actually every company has a wealth of data in the internal sales and expense records, but such information cannot be used in its raw form. It requires reworking or reprocessing before making its use for sales control purposes. Such data contribute a lot to determination and measurement of actual performance.

3. Evaluating Actual Performance against Standards

The most difficult step in evaluation process to compare actual sales performance of sales force with the set standards. The task is difficult because it requites a decision on the basis of records gathered on the actual performance. In case the actual performance is equal to standard, the evaluation shall be equal to unity, if performance is less than standard, it is less than unity and incase the performance is above standard, it is more than unity in cases, where evaluation is greater than unity or less than unity, the standards should be reassessed and confirmed that they are realistic. If they are realistic, the performance greater than unity amd equal to unity, should be awarded and performance below unity should be set right taking remedial measures.

Purely mechanical and arbitrary comparison should be avoid because of three principal reasons: *(i)* The same standards are seldom applicable to all sales personnel because individual, their capabilities, capacities talents and skills vary from person to person and from environment to environment. Even different sales territories are different in potentials and contribution; *(ii)* evaluation requires the value judgement of the evaluators. It is something more than a mere comparison; and *(iii)* certain complications develop in relation with individual performances to standards. For example, when two or more sales persons work on the same account or when on account deals both with the salesperson and with the headquarter or home office.

The evaluation requires both quantitative and qualitative standards to compare the actual performance. A personnel with apparently poor, performance as gauged by quantitative standards needs both judgement of action and deep understanding of market conditions and other factors. A person, showing improvement over earlier performnace, but still not upto standard performance, should be encouraged, but if he continuously fails to attain standards, there may something wrong with the standard which should be reassessed. The management should be prepared to ignore one or two negative, but negligible points or corrective measure should be taken. In all the case, the performance should be evaluated on the basis of some concrete data or information.

4. Taking Appropriate Action

The actual performance of sales force hardly tallies exactly with set standards. But if performance of most of the salespersonnel continuosly or more often are below or above standards, it needs some action. There are three alternatives:

1. Adjust the performance to standards by increasing the degree of attinment of objectives through motivation;
2. Revise the policy/or plan or the strategies used for their implementation, to fit better the achievement of objectives; or
3. Lower or raise the objectives or standards and/or criteria used in measuring their degree of attainment to make them more realistic.;

The nature and effectiveness of the actions resulting from these decisions, in turn, are conditioned by the executive's judgement, his background and experience knowledge of the situation and skill as an administrator.

TYPES OF STANDARDS

Company use various standards to evaluate the performance of the salespeople. Standards facilitate the measurement of progress mode towards departmental objectives, bot specific and general. Specific objectives vary with the change in the company's marketing situations, profits, and growth, but they should be reconcilable with the general objectives of the department as well as of the company. First, general objective is to be established (say to achieve a sales volume of Rs. 10 lakh higher than the previous year's sales volume) and various plan, strategies programmes, and polices are developed to achieve the general objective. For this purpose, general sales volume objective is broken down and translated in specific objectives. Performance standards are then, established for the business as a whole and, ultimately, for each salesman.

Performance standards may be quantitative or qualitative depending upon various factors.

Quantitative Performance. Most companies use quantitative standards to meausre the performance of the company and of the sales-force. The particular combination of standards chosen varies with the company and its marketing situation. Quantitative standards, in effect define both the nature and desired levels of performance.

Quantitative Factors. The performance can be evaluated on quantitative basis, both input (efforts made to secure a certain fixed amount of sales volume), and output (actual results achieved) should be specifically ascertained and correlated for this purpose. Quantitative performance evaluation can therefore, be an effort benefit analysis in quantitative terms.

The productivity of salespeople should be evaluated by correlating the two variables, input and output. Input variables may include call rate, expenses incurred, non-selling activities, total time spent etc. and output variables may include orders booked, total sales volumes in terms of amount or quantity, gross margin net profit etc.

Quantitative standard must provide a clear description of, what management expects from salespeople in terms of accomplishment. Each individual member of the sales force should have specific definitions of various aspects of his or her prerformance, which are to be measured and also the unit of measurement *i.e.,* sales volume, expense ratio, order booked etc. It would help the salespeople to be effective in their mission and more purposeful in their activities; They will minimise the waste of time and efforts. Thus, the sales management In last develop some standards to gauge the performance of the salespeople.

Progressive companies generally, use a combination of standards to measure the performance of salespersons because they recognise that a single performance standard cannot provide around basis for appraising an individual's total performan. In the past, only sales volume was taken as the sole standard for performance evaluation, but today sales managers realise that a sales volume level can be attained without earning profits, that may not be correct base. Further, sales volume is affected by a number of factors over, which sales personnel (ever sales management) have no control such as strength of competition, promotional support etc. Thus, other performnace standards are used for evaluating the overall performance of salespeople.

Similar limitations are attached to other quantitative standards. In order to measure the achievements in terms of profits, for example, certain quantitative performance standard is essential. Other factors affecting profit margin shall also be taken into account such as selling expense, sale mixture, call frequency rate, the cost per call, the size of the order, frequency of the order etc. certain factors, in this regard, are uncontrollable. This limits the scope of a performance standard as a tool to measure the performance.

The following are certain output factors which every often used for performance evaluation:

1. Sales volume by products either in terms of amount or number of items sold;
2. Sales volume as a percentage of quota or territorial potential;
3. Gross margin by product line, customer group, and order size;
4. Orders:
   (a) number of orders,
   (b) average size of order (in terms of rupee volume),
   (c) Batting average (orders divided by calls).
5. Accounts:
   (a) Percentage of accounts sold to contacted,

(b) Number of new accounts added duriug the period,

(c) Number of lost accounts.

Some useful input factors are also used for evaluation purpose are:

1. Call rate (Calls per day),
2. Days worked,
3. Direct selling expenses, in total and as a percentage of sales volume or expense quota,
4. Noising activities:

(a) advetising displays set up,

(b) number of service calls made,

(c) number of meetings held with dealers and distributors.

It will be misle.ading if sales management evaluate the performance only on the basis of single standard. It should carefully use a combination of a number of performance standards side by side making necessary allowance for uncontrollable reasons.

Various Quantitative Performance Standards

Most companies use quantitative standards to evaluate the sales force performance, because they are measurable and very clearly defined and understood by both sales management and salespeople. Such standards, however, may differ from company to company. Some companies use combination of various quantitative standards and such combinations also differ from company to company. Once the quantitative standards or combination of quantitative standards for each sales person is set up by the management, they should be communicated to individual salespeople with clear description of what management expects from them, because quantitative standards are used almost as much for stimulating good performance as for measuring it. The actual performance would then be compared from standards set and evaluated in quantitative terms.

The various quantitative performance standards in use are discussed as follows:

1. Quotas. A quota is a quantitative objective expressed in absolute terms and assigned to a specific market unit (sales person or territory). The term may be expressed either in physical term (in quantity of sales) or in rupee term. It specifies desired performance levels for sales volume; for such budgeted items like gross margin, expenses, net profit and return on investment; for accomplishing selling and non-selling activities and combination of these and other similar items. Assigning quota for individual sales persons gives answer to the question, what management expects from them in aspecified period. Realistic quotas can be fixed only when the management has realistic objectives in realistic and specific market situations based on various information and market knowledge. Usually quota is fixed for individual salespeople and the marketing segments or territories, in certain cases, quotas for middlemen such as agents, dealers, wholesalers, retailers etc., are fixed. Sales quota is generally, fixed for a sales region or other marketing unit at higher organisation level and then broken down and re-assigned to lower level units, such as sates district, sales supervisors, sales territories; sales persons etc.

Sales quota is considered a device for proper administration to direct and control sales activities. But it can be more effective, if it is based on "detailed, but accurate market information and adequate value judgements and administrative skills. Quotas are closely linked with sales forecast and sales budget. However, actual relation between these three variables differs from company to company and also the procedure used in forecasting, budgeting and quota-setting.

2. Selling Expense Ratio. This is ratio of selling expense to sales volume. By this ratio, sales management seeks to control the selling expenses in relation to sales volume. Target selling expens ratio should be set individually for each sales person, because there are a number of factors which affect the selling expense ratio, some of them are controllable by the salespeople and some are not. It is, therefore, necessary to set such standards aft reconsiderable market study and anlysis of expense conditions and sales volume potentials in each territory.

An attractive feature of selling expense ratio is, that the salesperson can affect it both by controlling the selling expenses and by making higher sales volume. In both the cases, selling expense ratio will be lower. From the stand point of its use for control purposes, the selling expense ratio has several shortcomings: *(i)* It does not take into account variations in profitability of different products -so, a sales persons having favourable selling expense ratio, may be responsible, for disproportionately low profits. Indirectly, it means, the salesperson has over-economised on selling expenses and sales volume suffers. 'Thus, this rerformance standard may unnecessarily cause the salespersons to over economise selling expenses at the cost of sales volume. *(ii)* In times of declining general business, strict adherence of predetermined selling expense ratio may inhibit sales personnel from exerting efforts to bolster sales volume.

In computing, selling expense ratio, practice differs from company to company, as to expenses which are included in selling expenses. If such indirect expenses like national advertise home office sales department expenses, and branch managers' and supervisors salaries etc., are included in selling expenses over which sales personnel have no or little control. But some executives argue that sales personnel influence the selling expenses ratio to sales simply by putting forth the selling efforts, only those expenses should be included in selling expenses, which are the related to their direct selling efforts. Some companies, therefore, consider only such expenses to be included in selling expenses, which are directly incurred by sales personnel in their efforts to sell company's product and which are also controllable by them.

Selling expense ratio standards are more extensively used in industrial undertakings than by consumer-product industries. The reason being that industrial-product companies rely much to personal selling and entertainment of customers. Consequently, their sales personnel incur more selling expenses including higher costs for travel and subsistance.

3. **Territorial Net Profit or Gross-Margin Ratio.** It is also an important variable, generally used by the management for evaluating performance level of each sales territory and each sales person. Each sales territory is considered a separate unit for making assessment of the territorial contribution to company's net profit. Selling personnel can influence the net profit ratio either by reducing the selling expenses or by increasing sales volume or by both. They can also emphasise more profitable products and devote more time and effort to the accounts and prospects that are potentially the most profitable. The net profit ratio is a device to contrul sales volume and selling expenses, as well as net profits. The gross margin ratio provides a way to control sales volume and the relative profitability of the sales mix (*i.e.,* sales of different products to different customers), but it does not control the expenses of obtaining a filling orders.

The standard is subjected to certain shortcomings:

(i) Net profit or gross margin ratio when either of them is used as a performance standard, sales personnel may be tempted to 'high spot' their territories, neglecting the products haven't low profitability and over emphasizing the sale of those products which earn high profits. Similarly, the salespeople may neglect the solicitation of new accounts or marginal accounts and may concentrate only big accounts. Both these situations may not be in the interest of the company in the long run.

(ii) Similarly, both ratios are influenced by certain factors which are largely beyond control of salespeople. Such factors may be as pricing policy followed by management, delivery costs, etc. which are totally beyond salespeople's control. Such factor may vary from territory to territory, thus influencing the net profit or gross margin ratio differently indifferent territories.

The use of this technique cannot be invalidated only because it has certain weaknesses. Management may use other quantitative techniques to offset the weaknesses of this technique. It should also be noted that management should not make salespersons accountable for those factors which are beyond their control.

4. Territorial Market Share. Like quota system, it is also a control technique. It helps the management to evaluate the performance of its sales force on territory-by-territory basis. Management sets target market share percentage for each territory on the basis of data available. Sales personnel accept it as their personal objectives. Actual performance is, then, compared with the industry-performance on territory by territory basis and thus, management measures the effectiveness of sales personnel in obtaining market share. In order to have closer control over the individual salesperson's sales mix, management has to set target for each product in each territory as a percentage of total market share.

5. Average Order Size. Average order size may be used, as a standard for evaluating the performance of a salesperson. It seeks to control the frequency of calls on different accounts in a thrust to control the cost per call or order. It helps in allocating the time and efforts of a salesperson in a territory. The usual practice is, to set standards for different sizes and classes of customers. It virtually reduces the number of calls on some accounts and this increases the frequency of calls on smaller customers using most of their time getting orders from them.

6. Sales Coverage Effectiveness Index. This standard is intended to control the thoroughness with which a salesperson works the assigned territory. The index consists of the ratio of the number of customers to the total prospects in a territory. To apportion the salesperson's efforts more profitably among different classifications of prospects, individual standards for sales coverage effectiveness can be set up for each class and size of customer.

7. Average Cost per Call. To emphasise the importance of making profitable calls, a target for average cost per call is set. When there is considerable variation in costs of calling on different sizes or classes of accounts, standards are set for each category of account. Target average cost per standards also are used to reduce the frequency of calls on accounts responsible for small orders.

8. Call-Frequency Ratio. A call frequency ratio can be calculated by dividing the number of sales calls on a particular class of customers by the number of customers in that class. Management, thus, establishes different call frequency ratios for different classes of customers and concentrates itself on those accounts most likely to produce profitable orders. In setting call frequency ratio, management should assure that the interval between calls upon each customer class is proper neither too short to get unprofitably small orders nor too long to lose sales to competitors.

9. Non-selling Activities. Some companies use quantitative standards for their non-selling activities such as dealers' displays, co-operative advertising contracts, training distributors' personnel and goodwill call on distributors' customers, after sale services, entertaining and conducting hospitality receptions for prominent and anticipated customers etc. Such non-selling activities create goodwill and public image of the company. When the management considers any of such non-selling activities important it may set appropriate standards for such activities. Thus, on the basis of standards set, actual performnace may be evaluated. Such standards are usually expressed in absolute terms.

A company, thus, uses different types of quantitative standards for evalutfug the performance of its sales force. The company may use more than on standard for this purpose.

Qualitative Performance Criteria

Like quantitative standards, qualitative standards may be useful in evaluating the sales force performance. However, qualitative standards are subjective and cannot be used widely. Qualitative criteria are used for appraising the performance characteristics that affect sales results especially over the long run, Qualitative criteria defy exact defmition and, therefore must be described generally. Most executive, do not attempt to define the desired qualitative characteristics with any exactitude; instead they arrive at general and informal conclusions regarding the extent to which each sales person possesses them. In some of other cases, such criteria are set formally setting out a detailed check list of subjective factors.

Salespersons' qualitative constibutions help the management in attaining quantitative standards. Say, for example, skill and tactfulness of a salesperson to -deal with customers, generate and maintain good customer relations, ultimately increasing the sales volume of the company.

Executive value judgement plays the major role in the qualitative appraisal of personnel performance, but it depends on maturity and soundess of the executive, who evaluates. appraisal of personal qualities, therefore, is dependent on the sound policies of the executives which can be evaluated by an approval.

FIELD SALES REPORT

Performance evaluation of sales personnel can be undertaken only on the basis of information relating to the market and sales personnel.

There are mainly two sources of such bformation *i.e.,* *(i)* Sales and expense records as maintained by the company mainly for accounting purposes such as invoices, complaints received from customers from time to time, volume-cost-profit experience with kinds of promotions etc., and *(ii)* reports from sales people and other sources for the use of management making analytical evaluation.

Field Sales Reports

Perhaps the most widely used source of information for evaluation purposes is field sales reports (reports submitted by the salespeople themselves to the management for time to time). Such reports provided a good mutual communication system between those preparing reports and those receiving them. It rpovides a good interaction between salespeople and field sales management, and field sales management and headquarters.

Field sales reports provide headquarters' sales management with a basis for discussion with sales personnel and field sales management. Such reprots indicate the matters on which salespeople need assistance and encouragement. Sales management may conclude on the basis of such reports whether, sales people are calling on, and selling to the right people, and whether, they are making too few or too many calls. They also assist sales management in deermining, what more can be done to secure more and larger orders. Field sales reports, thus, provide the raw materials that sales management makes use of, for gaining insights, which provide background materials for evaluation purpose.

A good field sales report also assist the salespeople to make their own self improvement programmes. They become their own critics and control instruments. Self criticism is rather more valuable and more effective than that, emanating from headquarters. It provides an effective association with management.

Purposes of Field Sales Reports

The general purpose of all field sales report is to provide information needed for evaluating the performance of sales personnel. However, they contain certain additional information, which are generally used by the management for other administrative purposes. A list of purposes, served by field sales reports are as follows:

1. To Provide data for Evaluating Performance. Information required to evaluate the performance of sales persons are mainly contined in field sales reports such as details concernign accounts and prospects called upon, number of calls made, number of orders obtained, days worked, kilometres travelled, selling expensys incurred, displass erected, co-operative advertisements made, training of distributors personnel acomplished, missionery work performed and calls made with distributors sales personnel etc. The data may also be used for setting standards and formulating different sales policies;

2. To help Salesperson Plan his or Her work. On the basis of report submitted by a salesperson, he himself can evaluate his performance on the basis of set standards, and can plan his or her work accordingly. He can plan his itineraries and make sales approaches to use with specific accounts and prospects;

3. To Record Customer's Reactions. Reports contain customers' suggestions, complaints, reactions about new products, service policies, price changes, price policies, advertising compaigns etc. In the light of such suggestions and reactions, management may make necessary changes in its policies and practices;

4. To report changes in local business and economic conditions, may be due to or change in government policy or due to other social or economic factors;

5. To log Important Items of Territorial Information for possible later use in case sales personnel leave the company or are reassigned to other territories;

6. Information of Competitors Activities. One of the important purposes, the report serves, is together information on competitors' activities such as new products, market rates, promotion devices and changes in pricing and credit policies etc. The mangement may make necessary improvements or changes in its policies and products to meet the challenges of the market;

7. To Keep the Mailing list for Promotional and Catalogue Material Current; and

8. To Provide Information Requested by Research Personnel. For example, data on dealers' sales and inventories of company and competitive products.

Types of Field Sales Reports

Field sales reports can be classified into six general groups:

1. Progress or Call Report. Most companies make use of a call report or progress report. It is prepared individually by the salespersons either for each or cumulatively covering all calls made during a fixed', period, say every day or week. Progress report keep management aware of salespersons activities, provide first hand information about the standing of the company with individual accounts, and in different territories and also records the information, which may assist the salesperson on his, revisits to customers and prospects. Such especially designed for the purpose and cotains almost all information not only about sales or orders obtained, but also specific class of customer or prospect, competitive brands handled, strengths and activities of competitors, bets time to call on the accounts etc.

2. Expense Report. Mostly sales personnel are reimbursed for expenses they incur in performing their jobs and therefore, they submit detailed item-wise expense report for the purpose of general administrative control and also for income tax assessments. Such reports help the, management to control the nature and amount of salesperson's expenses and also the salespersons exercise their own control over expenses. Sales person's periodical expense reports remind them to be under moral obligation to keep their expense in line with their reported sales volumes. Such reports may be used by the management to cohtrol sales expenses line with sales volume and also to control their remuneration plans.

3. Sales Work Plans. In many companies a salesperson has to submit his future work plan for a specified future period say a week or a month containing such details as accounts and prospects to be called upon, products and other matters to be discussed, routes to be travelled and hotels and motels, etc. The main purposes of this report is to help salesperson in planning and scheduling activities and to keep the management informed of his or her whereabouts. For management control purposes, the report provides information needed for later comparison of salesperson's plans and their accomplishments. thus, the work plan provides a basis for evaluating sales person's ability to plan the work and to work the plan.

4. Lost Sales Report. The report contains information about the customers lost during a specified period. It provides information required for evaluating a salesperson's abilities to keep customers sold and to sell against competition. The report describes the reasons for the loss of business, and also salesperson's opinion. It guides the management to point the way to needed sales training, changes in customer service and product improvement. It also requires further investigation in respect of various reasons forwarded by the salesperson in the report.

5. **New Business or Potential New-business Report.** Such reports inform management of accounts recently obtained and prospects, who may become company's new sources of business. It provides data for evaluating the extent and effectiveness of development work carried on by salespersons. The other purpose of this report is to remind the sites person not to confine himself to old and well established accounts. He should contact the prospects to make them regular customers of company's product. The management on the basis of such reports, may evaluate the effectiveness of prospecting.

6. **Report of Complaint and/or Adjustment.** The report contains various complaints received and/or adjustments required about the company's products, selling policies and practices etc. The report provides information needed for analysing the nature and volume of complaints arising from an individual salesperson's work, the incidence of specific - complaints by class of customers, and cost of complaint adjustment. The information also assists management in detecting needed product improvements and changes of merchandising and service practices and policies. Such data are very helpful, when decisions are taken in respect of sales personnel training programme, selective selling and product changes.

In this way, salespersons submit a variety of reports containing variety of information on different market and business aspects. The management may form, change or amend its policies, practices and programmes on the basis of such reports. Reports assist in evaluating sales persons qualitatively and quantitatively.

PERFORMANCE APPRAISAL

Appraisal and evaluation both are used synonymously in most of the cases as the two, more or less, carry the same meaning. However, for the purpose of distinguishing and identifying, sales evaluation can be defined as measuring the performance effectiveness of sales people while performance appraisal is the measurement of effectiveness and potentialities of sales managers or executives. Like sales person, sales managers or sales executives are subject to periodic appraisal. Periodic appraisal of managerial personnel is an essential need especially in big corporations to design or redesign the management development programmes.

Performance evaluation of salespeople is conducted by the sales management, whereas the performance appraisal of sales managers or sales executives is done by top management in the organisation. Strauss and Sayles have asserted -"In the typical large company, every manager is subject to periodic appraisal of his performance". According to Flippo, there is no choice with the firm as to whether or not it should appraise its personnel and their performance. It is therfore, an essential function of the management to appraise its executives including sales executives quantitatively and qualitatively. Such appraisal may be made either by the top management or by the personnel management on behalf and under authority of top executive in large companies.

Managerial personnel appraisal is generally used at two occasion. One, initial appraisal made at the time of selecting the managerial personnel for training and the other, promotional appraisal or potential appraisal gerierally, carried out at the time of promotion at higher post. The main purpose of initial appraisal is to find out, if the individual has an aptitude for the job in which he is being trained. In companies, where there is no programme for management training before placing the personnel on the job, the worth of the new incumbent is appraised on the job during probation period. Promotional appraisal aims at locating and identifying personnel for promotion to higher job from within the organisation. Their performance on the present job and potential for higher job are appraised the they are finally selected for higher job.

Performance appraisal of sales executives has the following objectives:

(i) A well planned appraisal plan is necessary to locate and identify, personnel, who may be promoted to higher job from within the organisation. Individuals, who have potentials for promoting to, higher jobs selected are eligible for selection.

(ii) Talents and capabilities of the old and the new executives may be located for their future development.

(iii) The utility of the existing development programmes for executives may be evaluated and assessed, whether there is a need of modification in the programme.

(iv) The worth of each executive may also be evaluated taking into account the job requirements.

(v) Top executives may have a comparative view of the capabilities of the executives in the same cadre.

(vi) The performance appraisal of sales executives is useful not only to evaluate their overall performance, but also facilitates the management to form a rational transfer, policy in the best interest of the concern.

Performance appraisal of sales executives is virtually a control device in the hands of management, and also evaluates the sales department indirectly. Hence, performance appraisal is a must in the organisation as a control device.

Approaches to Performance Appraisal

Usually, there are three approaches to appraise the Sales managers and Executives: *(i)* A casual, unsystematics, and often haphazard appraisal, *(ii)* Traditional and highly systematic appraisal, and *(iii)* Mutual goal setting through Management by Objectives (MBO) programme. Casual or unsystematic approach is very common, but now trend has been cbanged and many rums prefer to used systematic method of appraisal. According to a study conducted by Varney Glenn H., 80 per cent of western companies (out of a sample of 1,000 companies) use formal appraisal system. But still small firms cannot follow this system. In India, apart from small firms, big firms do not use formal appraisal system extensively. However, in India, all firms, irrespective of their size, appraise the performance of their executives one way or the other.

(A) Informal Method or Appraisal

In small firms, (and in (same big firms, also) informal or casual methods are used. Such method of appraisal are quite unsystematic and unscientific performances are evaluated by the boss in a primitive way of informal rating system. The rating largely depends on the behaviour, humbleness,loyalty, Honesty and obedience in his performance. They (managers) accept the goals set by the boss though unrealistic and whether they are able to achieve them or not. However, they always strive had to achieve them. The result largely depends upon the value judgement of the boss and what the, boss thinks of the subordinates.

The system cannot be said to be rational on two counts: *(i)* the behaviour of the subordinate may be good towards his boss, whereas his general behaviour and attitude may be harsh towards his customers and colleagues and may be deterimental to the business as a whole; *(ii)* the boss need not be an expert in rating and evaluation, which affects his value judgement There may be occasions, when the subordinate does not obey his boss, but in the interest of the enterprise, he shall be regarded as dis obedient in the eyes of the boss, which may affect the appraisal a lot. Traditional boss wants implicit obedience of his colleagues which the modern manager does not accept the situation. This approach, therefore, never yield a good result. This is one of the reason, why many of the companies make use of the systematic appraisal mechanism one way or the other.

(B) Traditional, Formal and Systematic Appraisal

More and more large scale companies now use most modern appraisal techniques like MBO. But traditional formal and systematic methods are not absent. Systematic approach include various methods of performance appraisal for managerial personnel including sales managers. Pertinent among them are: *(i)* Ranking, *(ii)* Person to person comparison, *(iii)* Grading method, *(iv)* Graphic scales method, *(v)* Check lists method, *(vi)* Forced-choice description, *(vii)* Selection of critical incidents method, *(viii)* Descriptive evaluation method, *(ix)* Group appraisal method, and *(x)* Field review method.

Now, we shall discuss these systematic methods of appraisal in the following lines one by one:

(1) Ranking Method. It is one of the oldest and the simplest forms of formal systematic appraisal. Under this method, each person is compared with all others. Various personal attributes like personality traits, achievements, potentialities, and the confidence of top authorities are considered and compared. Man is compared as a whole and no attempt is mode to fractionize the rates or his performance. The appraisal is made either on the basis of written documents and records as maintained by the employer or on personal judgement of the boss. It is a simple process of ranking the executives from the highest to the lowest based on their overall perform on the job.

The method is the best provided the number of employees is very small and the work done is of quantitative nature otherwise, the evaluation on this basis is quite impossible in a big concern. In practice, it is very difficult rather undesirable to compare a man with all other executives in the organisation because human personality in itself is very complicated and no one can be compared with all others as a whole. Another difficulty with this system is that, it does not indicate the degree of difference between the first ranked and second ranked persons.

To overcome this problem, a simplified technique of ranking known as 'Paired Comparison,' techniques. Here, each man is compared with all others in pairs. Suppose, for instance, there are five officials in an organisation A,B,C,D, and E. A's performance is compared to B's and decision is made whose performan is better. Then A is tom pared with C, D and E in order. B,C;D and E shall also be compared likewise. Thus, the use of the paired comparison technique with these five officials would mean a total of ten decisions. Only two ,people being involved in each decision. The results of these decisions will be tabulated and rank is allotted from the number of times each person is considered to be superior.

(2) Person to Person Comparison or Factor Comparison Method. Under this method, certain factors are selected for the purpose of comparison such as leadership, initiative, dependability, reliability etc. Thereafter, a five point master scale is designed for each factor by the appraiser. A scale of man is also created for each factor putting the best at the top and the worst at the bottom, an average man in the middle and on below average and the other above average. Each executive then compared with the man in the scaled and certain points for each factor are awarded to him, thus, comparing each factor at a time instered of comparing the man as a whole.

The system has very limited use for personnel appraisal, because designing of master scale is a complicated task. This system of measurement now-a-days is used in jobs evaluation being known as 'factor comparison method.' Though, it is highly useful in measuring jobs; it has very limited use in measuring people.

(3) **Grading Method**. Under this method certain categories of worth (such as excellent, very good, good average, poor, very poor etc) are established in advance and defined carefully. The actual performance of each employee is then compared with the grade definitions and the person is allocated to the grade, which best describes his performance. The number of grade may differ from company to company.

The grading system is sometimes modified into 'forced-distribution system', in which, certain percentages are fixed for each grade, for example, 10% of total personnel must be in the top grade, 20% to the, second and so on. It also tests the rater's performance. However, this system is not useful in a small group.

(4) **Graphic Scales (or Rating Scales) Method.** It is an approach similar to person-to-person comparison, but with the difference that the degrees on the factor scale are represented by definitions rather than by key people. Various degrees are possible for each factor. For example, exceeded the quota consistently, achieved the quota consistently in all the five preceding years, quota exceeded in certain years and quota achieved in remaining years, achieved fixed quota in most of the years, achieved 75 to 99 per. cent quota etc. The selection of factors is the most important part of the system. There may be two types of factors: *(a)* executives characteristics, and *(b)* e. ecutives contributions. The characteristics denote the personal quality of the person on the job such as dependability, ability, initiative, leadership, cooperativeness etc., on the other hand, contribution denotes what the person produces such as quality or quantity of work, responsibilities assumed and specific job accomplished. The number of factors ordinarily used varies from nine to twelve.

Graphic scale system is very popular technique for appraising the performance and personal traits, though it imposes a heavy burden on the rater. One must report and evaluate the performance of subordinates on scales involving as many as five degrees on twelve different factors for perhaps twenty to thirty people.

(5) Check list Method or Questionnaire Method. All the above techniques and their effectiveness depends upon the value judgement of the appraiser. In order to, reduce this excessive dependence on appraiser, a checklist system is utilised. The appraiser does not evaluate executive's performance. He simply reports the performance. The evaluation of the reported behaviours is finalised by the personnel department. Under this system, a checklist or questionnaire is prepared in the form of a series of questions concerning the executive and his behaviour. Rater reads the question before the concerned executive and the executive answers the question in yes or no. The personnel department evaluates the executive on the basis of checklist completed by the rater.

The system is subject to bias or prejudice of the rater. Further, it is difficult to assemble, analyse and weigh a number of statements about the personal characteristics and contributions. The system is suitable only in the cases when the appraiser has complete knowledge of the job and the person concerned.

(6) Forced Choice Technique. One of the main objectives of this system is to reduce or eliminate the possibility of appraiser's bias by forcing a choice between descriptive statement of seemingly equal worth. Two or more questions are asked and the rates is expected to select any one of them. For example, the rater may ask, which of the two statement is more descriptive of the employee in question:

(i) Give good and clear instructions to his subordinates;

(ii) Can be depended upon to complete any job assignment.

The answer then may be compared with the secret scoring key which are determined in the basis of a study of the existing personnel. As the correct answer to such questions are not apparent it depends, to a large extent, on the rater's bias.

The system suffers from a number of weaknesses: *(i)* The system is very costly, lengthy and time consuming, *(ii)* In order to emphasise the employee development, this system provides only very limited scope; *(iii)* Raters often object to being-forced to make decisions, which they feel cannot or should not be made.

(7) Critical Incidents Methods. The theory on which this approach rests is that there are certain key acts of behaviour of the employee that make the difference between success or future on the job. The rater must record or check certain kinds of events that occur in the performance of the rater's job. These events are critical incidents. Such incidents may be : *(i)* supervising sales personnel, *(ii)* handling customers' complaint, *(iii)* Communicating information and diagnosing special problems. The incidents so collected are weighed and ranked in order of frequency and importance. This provides a basis for rating score.

There is much scope in this method of biased decision. It does not provide sufficient scope for rating all the factors needed since it gives extra emphasis to certain given incidents. it will be very difficult to rate the employee, in case the incident does not happen. It is also difficult for the superior to decide what is critical or exceptional.

(8) Descriptive Evaluation Metbod. Here the appraiser prepares a written descriptive report of the performance of the employee on the job, which includes the factual and concrete description of his personality of behaviour, quality and quantity of work performed by him and his work level. Such description gives complete account of what the appraiser thinks of the man's personality. Such system is recommended for a senior managerial position. The rater in this method should be more observant and qualitical.

The system is also not free from defects. It demands more time than average.

(9) Group Appraisal. Under this system, the performance is not evaluated bya single rater, but a group of appraisers sit together and evaluate the performance of the employees.The group consists of immediate boss and other similar ranked senior efficials having knowledge of the employee under review. The method is objective in appraisal and constructive in approach and does not allow the element of bias, but, the system is very much time consuming.

Thus, the above systematic methods of performance appraisal are used The appraisal would be more effective if it is undertaken by the immediate spperior. Some companies, however; follow this practice with the help of the personnel department. In certain companies, the appraisal is done by a committee considering of immediate boss and two or three more similar ranked managerial personnel. Rating can be made once or twice a year. It is equally important that rater should be trained.

(C) Management by Objective

Management by objective is far more than an appraisal process. It is rather a way of management. Organisations are composed of a multitude of people, performing various specialised activities contributing to basic organisational objectives.

The concept of management by objective is a process or a system in which the superior and the subordinate managers. of an organisation jointly identify the organisation's common goals, defming each individual's major areas of responsibility in terms of the results, what are expected of him. These goals serve as standards for operating the unit and also in assessing the contribution of its members. According to Odiorne – "Management by objective is essentially a system of incorporating to a more logical and effective pattern the thing many people are doing, albeit in a somewhat chaotic fashion, or in a way that obscures personal risk and responsibility": In this context, it can be asserted that the management by objective is a system or technique or management that defines individual executive responsibilities in terms of corporate objectives in order to execute the given programme so as to minimise the expenses and maximise the contribution and also social benefits.

The system is of recent origin. The system was traced to origin by Peter F. Drucker in 1954.

The Process of the System

The first and foremost step in the process is to formulate a strategic plan and define the corporate aims and objectives in short, medium and long term in the key areas of the business. The plan should include the cour of action and the resources required to meet these objectives.

Another important step in the process is to fix up the roles of individual managers and to fix up unit objectives. The desired output at each individual level should be agreed to improvement possibilities are identified and incorporated in individual and corporate achievement plans. After a given time, systematic review should be carried out to assess the result of the performance. In the structure of organisation, it is essential to allow complete freedom of action and flexibility to each manager. Proper motivation also plays a dominant role in the process of MBO.

There are a number of managers in each level *i.e.* fIrst line, middle line and lower line in an organisation. Each manager functionsmdependently and suggests the goal for himself in identification of the corporate goals as set by the top level manager. At each level, evaluation and review of objectives set and goals achieved are made every now and then.

In the beginning of the budget year, the top level manager and his subordinate managers agree on targets of performance which each of them should achieve for that year. Then, the managers individually set objectives and goals for their respective activity and work accordingly in order to achieve, what they have agreed to attain during the period. The process goes on to down level. The actual performance then evaluated with the set objectives.

Utility or the System

Thus, MBO involves all the managerial personnel in the organisation hierarchy. The system provides for orderly growth and development of the organisation by means of statements of, what is expected of everyone involved and measurement of what is actually achieved. Many chronic problems of managing managers are thus, solved automatically. It enhances, the possibility of obtaining coordinated effort and teamwork without eliminating personal risk taking. Major areas of responsibility for each person is set. One major importance of this system is that, it provides a means of determining each manager's span of control. It also helpful in developing the basic characteristics of managers. But, one thing should be noted here that, personality discussion should be avoided as fur as possible. The discussion should be concentrated on job, results, objectives, reasons, methods etc. ❐

7

Effective Sales Personnel

The sales manager and his firm have invested considerable money, time, and effort to recruit and select a new salesperson. The effectiveness with which the manager uses indoctrination and training does much to determine whether a good investment was made or whether money and effort were thrown down the drain. Frequently the manager assumes that he has hired a winner—a proven, experienced salesman, who needs only to be handed a sales kit and pointed in the direction of prospects—and that before long, the orders will begin to flow in. Such an assumption is one of the greatest misconceptions in sales management.

Salesmen are people, not counters or pawns with dollar signs on them. They may have considerable knowledge and selling skills, but being people first and producers second, they need security, acceptance, recognition, encouragement, and sometimes a kick in the pants.

They produce because they have a desire to work with and for their leaders, a confidence in their ability to do the work, a belief that management will help them, and a faith in their superiors that will carry them through inevitable disappointments and discouragements. These inner resources, without which no salesman can succeed are fostered largely by the sales manager and his staff. It is the sales manager who equips salesmen for success. The manager who thinks and acts in terms of what the can do for his salespeople normally finds that he more he gives, the more he gets.

The new salesman can be compared to a market opportunity that is ready to be tapped and cultivated. Both must be developed carefully before their possibilities become actualities. The sales recruit has been influenced by parents, teachers, and former employers. Management has not hired him because he has the knowledge, skills, experience, and desire to be successful on his own, but because it is confident of its ability to convert a newcomer with appropriate "can-do" and "will-do" characteristics into an effective producer for his new' company.

The initial step in this conversion programme is sales training—the process of imparting knowledge, developing skills, and shaping attitudes nd work habits for the purpose of maximizing the sales person's effectiveness.

Shaping Attitudes and Work Habits

The new salesman reports to work with stars in his eyes. He has been wooed by the recruiter. He has survived the successive hurdles of the selection process. He may have been wined and dined and given every attention during the hiring sequence. The recruit feels wanted, valued, and enthusiastic.

At this point, many sale managers are guilty of a glaring error. They ignore the newcomer, shifting their attention to other functions, such as putting out "fires," hiring other people, doing paper-work. A relocated employee may be left on his own to locate a new residence, find a school for his children, initiate family social contacts, meet his fellow workers, and generally establish himself and his family in a new and possibly strange community. As described by one authority:

It comes as a blow to the new worker to encounter such apparent disinterest, since during the previous period in which he was being interviewed for a job he was given the utmost care. Then suddenly the honeymoon is over; he now knows it was just sales talk. The administrator has forgotten that many people allow. their social and psychological needs to overrule their economic requirements.

Often the indoctrination process is limited to getting the new salesman souped-up enough to get out and knock on doors.

> You convince him there's nothing to it. Here's the presentation and there are the prospects. All you do is go out and show the product to the prospects and the money comes rolling in. Being a good salesman yourself, you can tell this story so persuasively that the new man is convinced.
>
> Of course, he hasn't learned anything, but you've got him wound up enough to go out and make contact with prospects. The law of averages will take care of him. If he hits enough doors, he'll find an order somewhere. May be h 'll make it and may be he won't. When he finally falls by the wayside, you can hire another poor slob to do the same thing. Hire enough people and you'll probably make your district quota.

Strangely, the foregoing procedure frequently follows a meticulous recruiting and selection sequence.

The new sales recruit may be lonely, uncertain of what he is getting into, a bit frightened, may be even desperate. He may be down on his luck or discouraged. The Horatio Alger dream may not be coming true. Perhaps he has experienced the taste of failure. Perhaps a new sales position is his gamble that it can be different and he is experiencing the feeling of a man putting his few remaining chips on this turn of the wheel. He needs to be encouraged and to feel a strong, sure, helping hand.

Indoctrination should build understanding and convictions that will last, not wear off the way a quick shot in the arm does. Indoctrination is a necessary preliminary functions, separate from training. Plunging headlong into training frequently results in instant terminations.

Indoctrination should be a positive processwelcoming the recruit to his new work environment, introducing him to fellow workers, informing him of job details and company philosophies, policies, and expectations, and generally preparing the recruit for his subsequent training and his subsequent life with the new company.

The Right Mental Attitude (RMA)

Many salesmen trend to resist training, especially if they are not convinced of its value to them. The trainee must respect the company, its products, its selling methods, and its policies toward solving customers' problems. Above all, the recruit must be convinced of his sales, manager's willingness and ability to tell him, show him, and teach him how to be productive. Trainees need more than a warm and friendly leader.

Research has shown that nice guys often make bum bosses. The power-driven manager has been found to be the most successful sales manager because of his basic desire. to influence and lead others by creating a good climate. His subordinates have both a sense of responsibility and a clear knowledge of the organization. They adhere to the work rules, not because they are hit over the head, but because they become loyal to the institution.

The power-driven manager will quickly convince the recruit that the RMA and solid work habits will develop the salesman's ability to manage himself, which is a prerequisite for managing prospects and closing sales. Such a manager will do what he requires his salesmen to do. His attitude will be "Let's go into the field together; when it rains on you, it will rain on me."

He will demonstrate that classroom-taught selling methods work in the field. Numerous cases have been cited where a sales trainee is trained in the classroom to use a given sales technique but when he is field-trained, the trainer uses an entirely different method. For example, the trainee is taught to use a semi-automated sales presentation but his field trainer uses a completely different, unstructured form during the initial field training.

What knowledge does a salesman need?

A salesperson comes to his firm with a certain level of education, experience, and knowledge. However, there is always a gap between what the trainee already knows and what he needs to know. The size of this gap depends on whether the recruit is new to his present firm, new to the product he will sell, or new to the occupation of selling. The sales trainee must first be made aware of his own role with respect to both prospective buyers and his own organization. He must clearly understand the functions he is to perform and the environment in which he is to perform them.

Knowledge needs will vary widely with the type of sales position. Usually, where the salesperson's primary function is in-store or route selling, the required knowledge is quite simple and can be obtained by reading descriptive literature and manuals, attending brief classroom sessions, and observing an experienced salesperson. The knowledge-gathering process may be considerably more complex and time consuming for many other sales-force members. For example, the aspiring salesperson in life insurance or real estate may be required to take in-house or outside courses, do considerable studying at home, or use programmed learning materials in order to prepare for license-granting examinations. Industrial selling will often require extensive exposure to formalized training media including audiovisual materials, literature, lectures, case histories and field trips. Because trainees have had different levels of preparation, some firms will divide the training program into segments so that a trainee can attend only the session which he requires.

In general, the salesperson must acquire knowledge about four broad areas of the company; its offerings, its environment, its history and policies, and its operations and procedures.

Offerings

It should be reassuring to even the most inexperienced sales-person that he knows more about the product than any prospect he will ever encounter. Thus, he should be intimately familiar with every feature of every product he sells and with how it is designed and manufactured. In addition, he must be aware of why the product incorporates these features and of what benefits the features give to the ultimate purchaser. He must be prepared to discuss limitations in usage as well as causes and frequency of failures. He must understand the foundation of his firm's pricing programmes, discount prices, and advertising allowances.

Environment

The salesman should be familiar with his competitors, their relative sales and profit volume, and their methods of operation. He must understand the advantages and disadvantages of his competitors' products, prices, and selling programmes, as compared with his own. Moreover, he must be aware of the extent to which competitive offering are being accepted by the marketplace.

He should be able to determine customer needs and whether or not these needs are currently being satisfied. He should understand the dynamic influences in the general environment, including changing life styles, social pressures, technological advances, regulatory activities, and business trends, as they affect present and emerging new markets. Finally, he must attempt to understand why his customers, and his customers' customer , do or do not buy.

Company History and Policies

The salesman should understand why his company uses its current channel structure and distribution methods. He should understand and be able to support his company; policies concerning returns, allowances, billings, cancellations, and markup-granting policies. He must also know the company's history, philosophy, objectives, and standing in the trade. He must be aware of policies concerning personnel and compensation. He should be familiar with the background of the firm's executives.

Company Operations and Procedures

The salesperson should, be able to discuss his company's plan of organization and the relationship of the sales function to other functional areas. He should be particularly familiar with the areas of the company which closely support the selling operation. He should have a through understanding of the company's sales-control techniques and systems, including the format and need for call reports, sales meetings and clinics, quota systems, and profit-sharing plans.

He should be well versed in the principles behind the company's selling techniques as they apply to stimulating purchases, solving customer problems, and upholding the highest standards of ethical selling practice.

Developing Selling Skills

After a sales "trainee has obtained the required knowledge, he must acquire the necessary skills to use that knowledge effectively and productively. In contrast to the acquisition of knowledge, developing skills require practice, either in front of prospects or under conditions that closely simulate such situations.

The mastery of selling, not unlike the mastery of gold, require continuous practice of the fundamental techniques, under the watchful eye of the sales manager, the selling pro. However, the golfer including the weekend duffer, views golf as a pleasurable recreational activity, an opportunity to enjoy himself with his friends, an athletic function which has no major impact on his financial resources or family happiness (unless he's a heavy better or his wife is a gold window). Thus, he can enjoy the game despite his inability to developing golfing skills.

Needed Skills

In broad terms, the successful sales trainee must learn to apply the principles of the company's selling techniques. Applied to the basic promotional functions introduced, he must learn how to find prospects, call on them, stimulate desire for possession, close orders, and, retain customers.

He must develop an instinct in selling situations for perceiving and diagnosing prospects' problems and needs, for probing and finding clues which will enable him to uncover latent desires, and for providing a desirable remedy at the right moment. Especially vital in developing communications skills is learning how to listen, absorb, and react when prospects, managers, and peers are expressing their needs. Salesmen must learn how to plan and use their time systematically and how to analyze their successes and failures so that each experience serves as a building block for future self-confidence and success.

Skill-training Methods

The trainer must foster instinctiveness in communication by compelling the trainee to actuaily perform selling activities. Reading, hearing, and thinking, as previously indicated, are not enough. Skill training calls for more than telling the new person what to do and how to do it. It calls for showing and teaching him how, and then reviewing and critically analyzing the trainee's performance.

Skills can be developed in the training classroom through role playing, relevant sales case work, analysis of salesmen's call reports, business games, and other methods.

A unique skill-development methods was devised by the Seminar Film Company, which customizes "film that talk back" for larger firms. This method employs movies showing typical company prospects in various situations, and calls for instinctive sales responses. For example, the movie might show a protective receptionist being approached by a salesman and saying, "Yes,. may I help you?" immediately a vanishing white line appears on the screen and the sales trainee must learn to respond before the line disappears. Mter the trainee has delivered his response, the receptionist might say, "I don't believe Mr. Big will have time to see you today."

Field Training

Despite the helpfulness of şimulated situations, true interaction with prospects can only take place in the field. Ideally, as the trainee observes the field trainer in action, he will be convinced that what he was taught really works. The trainee observes the field trainer's selling plan, prospecting, setting of appointments, approaches in business offices and at residential doors, sales presentations, doses, use of rebuttals—all the consecutive detailed steps of selling under live conditions.

The astute trainer will confer with the trainee after each call or series of calls to answer questions, to associate what happened with material covered in classroom training session, to highlight critical 'incidents that took place during the call, to explicitly recall the reason for the success or failure of the call, and to allow the trainee to take notes where needed.

After field observation by the trainee has shown him how, the trainee does it himself while the field trainer observes. Often the trainer and trainee will alternate in making calls and also have "curbstone conferences" between calls. The trainer can use a prepared checklist to quickly locate a trainee's weak points. The alternate calling system is particularly. useful when the trainer uses his own presentation to demonstrate the method of correcting weaknesses in the trainee's presentation. The trainee's next presentation should include the improvements that have been recommended by the trainer.

Any system that requires a sales manager or experienced salesman to observe the trainee is costly since the trainer's personal production will normally be reduced. Moreover, a trainee is often reluctant to perform in front of experienced salesmen or managers for fear he may do poorly and be subjected to considerable negative criticism. Therefore, if the curbstone conference or endof-the-day critique is to be welcome by and constructive to the trainee, the trainer must focus on showing the newcomer how to improve his strengths rather than on emphasizing his weaknesses. Many firms will compensate trainees by, paying them full or partial commissions on sales made by the trainer. These earnings are deserved when the trainee has been active in setting up prospects for the trainer.

Training Sequence

As mentioned earlier, the realities of the firm's specific selling situation may not be obvious to the trainee until he has observed in the field. If prospects are hostile, if his trainer meets with many rejections, if the work locks too demanding, the trainee may become disenchanted and either leave at once or continue his training with tongue in cheek.

For this reason, some sales managers schedule field observation as the first item on the training agenda even before indoctrination and inside training. Of course, this may not be necessary if field observation is part of the selection process. Although etirly field trips may be effective in separating the men from the boys and saving the time and costs of training those who disqualify themselves, it may prematurely expose an unconditioned trainee to complex salesman-prospect interactions which would be better understood following detailed classroom training.

The primary objective of field observation is to demonstrate the application of company selling techniques and methods. If preliminary field observation is to be used at all, it should be in addition to not instead of, the field sessions that follow inside training. Obviously the costs of additional field training and the risk of confusing the unprepared newcomer are related to the nature of the specific selling task.

Standardisation and Discipline in Training

Sales training is a planning process in that it establishes the specific courses and methods of action that management desires the new salesman to follow. Supervision involves directing and controlling the activities of the salesperson to be sure he does not wander too far from the prescribed course of action. Any plan must be subject to a certain amount of standardization and the people who implement the plan must be disciplined to some degree. Properly applied, standardization and indiscipline are more for the benefit of the salesman than for his managers and company. Standardization prescribes a tracks for the salesman to run on while discipline keeps him on the track.

Many salespeople are narcissistic exhibitionists at heart, and are never happier than when in front of prospects making a pitch. They love to be the center of attention and find that an audience aspires them to surprising heights of artistry.

Yet, it has been found that even better salespeople do not have the raw creativity to develop original selling techniques.

Sales Presentations

It was indicated earlier that sales presentations with high amounts of company input were perceived by sales executives as most effective in facilitating the training of sales-force members: Yet the memorized presentation was rated as least effective. Despite the apparent ease of training a person to plug in a projector of flip the pages of an easel, flip chart, or read-off binder, this training procedure is not completely without challenge. The trainee must still be taught to gain an audience, neutralize, and prime the prospect for a captive session. One well-known, direct-selling company delivers the sales presentation by use of three- ringed binder containing more than twenty laminated pages which the sales representative turns and reads to Mr. And Mrs. Prospect. The placement of the husband and wife is quite critical and the salesperson must memorize the following lines in order to set up the presentation:

> In order to give you the information you've requested without omitting anything, or without being too wordy, the company has prepared a rather colourful open letter which they have asked me to cover with you. So that you can see it all right, Mr. Prospect, could you sit on the sofa on my right with your wife on your right?.

Sales trainees often find it difficult to memorize lengthy presentations. Therefore, training consists of pounding the material into the salesman's brain by use of repetitive drills and role-playing sessions. This process demands much of the trainer's time, patience, and energy. Moreover, salespeople often resent being servile to considerable structure in terms of what to say and how to say it.

Yet, salesmen are best compared to actors who must be fed their lines. They may be articulate, but they are not necessary good extemporaneous speakers. For example, when they are thrown off stride by some incident or interruption, many salesmen tend to return to the beginning of a sales presentation section.

A. number of training procedures can develop skills in extemporaneous speaking, delivering lines, and reading with feeling, enthusiasm, and sparkle. One trainer holds impromptus speaking sessions where trainees are required to deliver spur-of-the-moment three minute speeches on such far-out subjects as baby carriages; grandfather clocks, and mirrors. In another organization trainees are drilled in reading brief arbitrarily selected newspaper articles aloud in a sparkling arid scintillating way.

Rebuttals

Even the veteran salesman often has difficulty in coping with a new objeftion or new form of sales resistance. When salesmen get together at sales meetings, conventions, social events, or over a cup of coffee, they exchange ideas or phrases which have worked in the past. The newcomer has not had these opportunities and is concerned with his ability to handle objections such as "I'am happy with my present supplier" or "how to I know it will sell" or "the price is too high "or "I've used up my open-to-buy." As mentioned earlier, many firms prepare a booklet of standard rebuttals and verbal-proof stories which respond to recurrent objections. Classroom drill sessions help the trainee build a reservoir of answers to meet nearly every contingency. Some trainers recommend ways that the salesman can use his rebuttal folder in the presence of the prospective customer in case of memory lapse.

Input by the Fledgling Salesperson

It would seem that the new salesman would be delighted to be guided by a structured, proven selling plan that has been designed by specialists. This is quite true during the early training stages.

But the person in selling is pften quite impatient. If the company selling plan does not result in instant results, the greenest recruit may not hesitate to figure out a better way. This amateurish reconstruction is, more often than not, so ill-conceived and remote from the company plan that the product could not be given away much less sold.

Even the intelligent trainee who experiences early successes by using his learned routine with few modifications is likely to try to improve the system. This person may want to do his own thinking and use his own knowledge. He absorbs the company method, evaluates it, masters it, and then comes to his own conclusions. Certain adjustments in the sales presentation may come quickly, but the major changes may involve matching the presentation with the salesman's personality. In due time, he is still using a structured presentation but the structure is a result of input by both the company and the salesman.

Organising for Training Effectiveness

In larger organizations, the sales-training function may be a team effort. Home-office personnel may design the programme, the district manager may supervise the training programme, staff instructors may conduct classroom sessions, while experienced salesmen, unit field managers, branch managers, or the district manager himself may conduct the field-training activities.

When the inside training programme is divided into discrete sessions or courses, outside training specialists or consultants may be called upon to conduct various segments. For example, several sales consulting firms are specialists in lead-getting or telephone selling, or servicing department stores.

In smaller firms and in the local operations of some larger firms, a single sales manager may personally perform all the training functions listed in the first paragraph of this section. In considering such a possibility, one reopens the argument of whether the sales managers should be actively involved in personal selling and field-related activities.

In some companies, trainees are sent to universities or special school for part of their training. Occasionally sales trainees join other newly hired people in indoctrination sessions conducted by the firm's personnel department. The lineup of training personnel will depend on the size and the unique demands of a given firm. One useful guideline is to delegate the field training to the same 'individual who will later be responsible for supervising the trainee. This is particularly effective when the supervising manager receives permanent overrides on the trainee's production. Money is a major motivating force for convincing field managers to develop skilful trainees.

Duration of Training Programms

Some training programmes can be completed in a few, hours; others last for two or more years. If the trainee is salaried, it will be to the firm's advantage to prepare him as quickly as possible for field productivity so as to avoid undue delays in generating a profit on the firm's investment in training and compensation costs. New salesmen who are compensated on a commission basis, are anxious to go out in the field as soon as possible. If there is neither money nor the promise of a paycheck in time to pay the grocery bill' the new salesman may be persuaded to search the want ads for a salaried job.

The speed of of training a given individual will receive depends on the number and complexity of the knowledge, skill, and attitude requirements, the number of trainees being trained simultaneously, the availability of trainers, whether training is done individually or in classes, where the training takes place, the steps in the training process, the design of the training programme, the teaching ability of the trainers, and the learning capacity of the trainees. When replacement trainees are readily recruitable, trainers may have limited patience with" trainees who catch on slowly.

When one speaks of the speed of training, the question arises as to when a new salesman is no longer considered to be a trainee. However, one approach suggests that the salesperson moves through a salesman's career cycle (SCC) consisting of the four stages or preparation, development, maturity, and decline. This model suggests that the preparation stages is concluded when the salesman competes his initial training and is permitted to call on prospects without being accompanied by a field manager. To determine whether a given sales trainee should be advanced to the development phase, management might require an affirmative answer to each of the following questions:

1. Is he aware of his specific job requirements?
2. Does he have favourable attitudes toward the learning process?
3. Does he perceive direct and purposive relationships between customer needs, company goals, and his own behaviour?
4. Has he developed an understanding of personal interaction and the barriers to making it successful?
5. Has he developed the skills to put his knowledge into action?
6. Does he appear willing and able to acquire new capacities?

Training Locals

In practice, field training takes place in the prospects office and residences, on curbstones, in restaurants, and enroute to and from sales calls. In large firms, inside training may either be decentralized, and allocated to local district or branch offices, or centralized in the company's home office.

Decentralization has a number of advantages in that the trainee is trained by the same people who will ultimately supervise him and benefit from his productivity on a regular basis. Moreover, he will be indoctrinated in the same regional environment that he will have to "live with" when he advances to the development stage of his career cycle. The disadvantage is that training personnel in the local office may be part-time trainers who may not offer the trainee the required intense attention because of other managerial demands such as administrarive duties, hiring, supervision, and personal selling.

In a centralized framework, a full-time staff of teachers is usually available. Indeed, there are advantages, from a learning viewpoint, in being removed from the distractions and temptations of one's daily routine. Yet there is little doubt that centralized training is costly in terms of financing trainees' travel and hotel expenses and supporting large scale training facilities and personnel.

In a number of firms part of the initial training takes place at national or regional headquarters and part in a local setting. Normally, the visit to central headquarters will come first. Promising recruits are introduced to members of top management, taken on a detailed tour of the central office, and provided with a basic introduction to company policies and philosophies and fundamental selling techniques. The detailed nitty-gritty skill-development exercises take place in the local office, where they can be reinforced by training in the field.

The Meaning of Supervision

The overriding importance of supervision is accepted by most sales executives. Yet, there is limited agreement as to the precise meaning of supervision in a selling framework. Some view supervision as synonomous with management, that is, the act of getting things done through people. Such a viewpoint includes almost all the subject areas covered in previous chapters including planning, coordinating, directing, and inspecting activities.

In a somewhat narrower context, supervision has been looked upon as a process whereby sales managers influence salespeople in much the same way as salesmen influence prospective customers. In this sense, the purpose of the supervisory relationship is to guide the behaviour of sales-force members in a direction that is compatible with the goals of the firm. One weakness of this approach is that the employee is seen as a passive object being manipulated to carry out mandates of others rather than as an active seeker of goals. This is analogous to a seller who fails to reconcile his own interests with those of the prospective customer.

A Personalised Technique

Therefore, this chapter treats supervision as a one-on-one technique to guide and motivate the individual salesman and to provide him or her with continued help in planning activities, utilizing time and efforts more effectively, and developing the instinctive skills to deal with unique situations. Effective supervisions improves the salesman's can-do and will do characteristics, with emphasis upon the latter.

Ideally, the salesmen's initiative should come from within. Management's job is to help salespeople develop their self-motivation, realize their growth potential, increase their capacity for assuming responsibility, and achieve a readiness to direct behaviour toward the goals of the organization. Yet, it has been found that even in an ideal organization climate, many salesmen when left to their own devices do only the minimum which they believe will be acceptable. Even money, the well-known silent supervisor, will not inspire all salespeople. It is the sales manager who determines what his salesmen will accomplish.

Supervision Purposes

Supervision takes place in the field and is oriented to the salesman's daily activities in front of prospects. Supervising sales-force members is aimed toward *(1)* improving the salesman's morale; *(2)* uncovering selling deficiencies; *(3)* providing additional training; *(4)* enforcing company needs; and *(5)* stimulating improved performance.

An examination of these aims reinforces the notion, that supervision involves directing and controlling the activities of the salesperson to be sure he does not wander too far from the plan of action that was prescribed in the training programme. The larger portion that was prescribed in the supervisory activities required to achieve these aims.

Neglect of the Supervision Programme

There is little doubt that one-on-one supervision of sales personnel is a neglected function in many organizations. Five reasons are offered for this neglect: it's not needed, it's too costly, too time consuming; too difficult, and resented by salesmen.

There is tendency on the part of some sales managers to dichotomize sales-force members into two groups—those who have it and those who don't. The first group consists of the self-starters who require little supervision; the second group is made up of the helpless and hopeless weak sisters who could not make the grade even with supervision twenty-four hours a day. This sink or-swim approach neglects the fact that the largest group of people on any salesforce are neither topflight nor weak. Most salespeople are in the development phase of, the salesman's career cycle (SCC) and may be required to make many sacrifices, work long and possibly odd working hours, and sustain numerous refusals and substantial chastisement. They have the capacity to learn and the willingness to endure negative situations, but they have a periodic need of tender care by management.

One cannot dispute the fact that it is costly and time consuming to supervise the individual salesman. The reader is surely aware that the field sales manager wears many hats. He is frequently engaged in admini;trative functions and in recruiting, training, and acquiring personal sales. He often writes the house organ, conducts local sales meetings, and designs and administers contests. In terms of profitability, he often questions the wisdom of working in the field with a salesman or paying a field supervisor to perform this function.

Sales-force members are frequently so scattered geographically that it is difficult for the supervisor to spend much time with each subordinate. In addition, due to the unpredictability of human beings, every demand upon the supervisor is unique. The active field supervisor may spend time with a different salesman each day. Each salesperson may face a different problem and react in a different way. The supervisor is under pressure to uncover the deficiencies and re-commend an instant solution. He has a new audience every day, somewhat like the baseball star who is expected by every new group of spectators to hit a home run.

Often, it is the salesmen who need help the most that are least receptive to supervision. They are convinced that the supervisor is there to appraise, evaluate, spy, and criticize rather than to assist. They become salesmen to enjoy freedom from close supervision and control. They may employ questionable selling techniques which they do not want management to discover. Finally, they may not be sold on the supervisor's ability to be helpful and may regard his visit as destructive and wasteful in terms of preventing the salesman from making his planned number of customer contacts.

The Salesman's Morale

For every salesperson who is helpless and hopeless, there are many who can be developed into outstanding performers if their weaknesses are spotted and corrected in time. This is particularly true of inexperienced salesmen who have yet to accustom themselves to the rejections and disappointments that are a part of selling. In the absence of proper supervision, they may resort to flight tactics, fight tactics, or other "coping devices."

Outward manifestations of emotional flight by the salesperson can be recognized in behaviour such as the following:

1. He avoids prospecting for new customers.
2. He avoids contact with difficult customers.
3. He is willing to spend considerable time in waiting rooms or driving in his car in order to avoid customer contact.
4. Instead of asking for orders, he develops a sizeable group of people who want to think it over, thus creating a list of imaginary future buyers.
5. His apathy towards prospects turns to sympathy.

Under stress conditions the salesman may become so nervous that he may remove himself from the field and resort to such coping devices as sleep, drugs, alcohol sex, golf, movies, and so on.

Fight Tactics

In contrast to those who attempt to escape from the tensions of the sale job, there are those who display fight reactions. For example, a salesperson may behave as follows:

1. He finds fault with his company and with its products, promotional methods, prices, service, methods, etc.
2. He complains to and about sales supervisors, exaggerating and falsifying to strengthen his attack.
3. He may speak against the company when dealing with customers or prospects, criticizing products, services, prices, methods, management, and policies.
4. He may display hostility in dealing with customers or prospects.
5. He may not get along with people and this may, result in disputes, violence, and dismissal.

Reasons for Low Morale

When the salesperson's work assignments provoke intolerable anxieties in him, it may be the result of the inherent disappointments of selling, described earlier by the selling pendulum. There are also more specific reasons. The salespersons may have been assigned to duties beneath his capabilities, with resultant routinization and boredom. On the other hand, he may have been placed in a job that is clearly over his head, in terms of his ability to function and to engage in the required personal relationships. For example, a salesman may be quite successful when he is supplied with qualified prospects by his employer, but he may find it difficult to create leads by his own efforts, that is, by telephone solicitation, cold canvassing, and other creative prospecting methods.

The company may fail to provide a strong, compatible supervisor. Instead, the latter may be weak, incompetent, vindictive, punitive, unreliable, and/or authoritarian. Management may fail to structure and define the salesman's duties, goals, responsibilities, and scope of authority. He does not know what his job is, how well he is doing, or where he is going.

The salesperson may be placed in a work environment where he is not accepted, either covertly or overtly, and where his past history or present inadequacies may be sources of rejection or conflict. Even when the salesperson is not subjected to open attack, he can be deprived by the in-group of support, membership, and acceptance and can become, in essence, an outcast.

In addition, salesmen fear slumps, layoffs, and discharges when the general outlook for the health of a company or an industry is not favourable.

Low morale is fostered by the absence of a shoulder to lean on someone in the firm to answer the salesman's job-related questions and also help in solving his personal problems.

Counselling

Consider the case of the salesman who complains of a sales slump that has persisted for two weeks. Such a salesman requires understanding and support by his sales manager. The manager should listen carefully to the salesman's account of his experiences and encourage the salesman to disclose why he feels the slump has occurred. The manager should not attempt to judge the salesman or to offer unsolicited advice. The aim of counseling is to render the salesperson independent so that he will be able to solve similar future problems by himself. Thus, the competent sales counsellor will help the salesman to help himself.

Presume that in this case the sales supervisor uncovers no serious flaws in the salesman's work habits or sales techniques. He should seek to build confidence in his subordinate by showing him that the slump is the result of nothing more than the "law of averages" in action. The following is one way a supervisor could convey these thoughts:

> John, suppose I were to toss a coin in the air a thousand times and record the result of each toss on a sheet of paper. No doubt the final tally would work out to somewhere near five hundred heads and five hundred tails, right? However, if I examined the results very carefully, I would likely discover certain streaks of ten heads in a row or eight tails in a row. These streaks are quite normal as is the steak of "no sates" that you are now encountering. In other words, there is absolutely no pattern to occurrences of heads and tails or sales, and nonsales. All we know with certainty is that, in the long run, about half of the tosses will result in heads. Similarly, in your own case, about 25 per cent of your sales presentations over the past three years have resulted in sales and, as you continue to improve your skills, your conversion rate will also improve over time.

The important thing to remember is that the "head" on the coin does not become upset when "tails" comes up ten times in a row. Similarly, you have little to worry about when you run into a negative streak. Think of yourself as a coin that accepts nos as well as yeses in a sequence that is impossible to predict.

As shown in the above example, counseling may be the ideal solution for an imagined sales problem. Often, however, the concern is quite real and the salesman has truly developed certain bad habits or weaknesses that must be spotted and corrected.

Many sales managers are of the mistaken impression that coaching in the field means that the sales manager should pick up a sales kit and take the slumping salesman out on a few calls to show him how easy it is to make a sale. This may prove that the firm's product can be sold, but it will not prove that the salesman can sell it. Therefore, it must be repeated that it is insufficient to just tell or show the salesperson how to do it. He must be taught how, and this calls for the supervisor to alternate calls with the salesperson and observe him until he masters the techniques bring taught. Only then will the supervision process bring about self-development.

Activity Reports

Despite the acknowledge importance and effectiveness of field supervision, it is quite costly in terms of demands upon the sales manager's time and energy. Moreover, selling deficiencies can often be uncovered in the office with equal effectiveness. In fact, there are certain continuous inside methods of supervision that may be more effective than field supervision, which is necessarily occasional.

One such technique is the proper use of activity reports or call reports. Unfortunately, the literature has stressed the use of these reports for evaluation and for assisting management rather than as tools for uncovering the salesman's deficiencies and improving his performance.

This author prefers to call them activity reports rather than call reports since the report, properly designed, develops more data when it includes all the activities and not just the results of sales calls on prospects or customers. This need is properly emphasized when one remembers that selling is more than what happens in front of the prospect.

Consider the following sample report of the past week's activities prepared by a salesman who obtains all his prospects by use of the telephone:

Number of the telephone calls 110

Number of telephone contacts with prospects 73

Number of appointments made by telephone 26

Number of sales presentations completed 4

Number of sales 1

The salesman earned only $90 in weekly commissions even though his sales conversion rate, one sale in four presentations, was approximately equivalent to the company average. The problems is that only four sales presentations were delivered despite twenty-six appointments.

There are two possible explanations for this performance: either the salesman did not bother to keep most of his appointments or the appointments were so poorly set up that the prospects were unwilling to keep them. A detailed review of each appointment would covered, counselling may be called for. Otherwise, coaching in the technique of making solid appointments by telephone may be required. In either case, there is little need for the sales manager to accompany the salesman on field calls, at least until the results of the present counselling and coaching have been studies.

Providing Additional Training

The salesman's activity report and its subsequent analysis may pinpoint the need for improving the salesman's sales presentation or his closing techniques. He may require additional training in technical aspects of the product, in preparing proposals, or in analyzing customer requirements.

He may be referred to various books or technical manuals, asked to reread material published by the company, enrolled in company refresher programmes. Some firms supply sales-force members with programmed learning materials to be studied or played at home. In all cases, a plan of action must be developed to offer direction to the salesman. An important part of this plan is the follow-up procedure, which makes sure that the additional training results in improved performance.

Stressing Company Needs

Supervision is much more than altruistically serving the needs of sales-force members. This and the previous chapter have focused on improving the company's selling effectiveness by developing a thorough knowledge of the salesman's needs and behaviour. However, the achievement of company goals is the sought-after reward for the skilful development of happy salespeople.

In most cases, the company plan requires that the salesman be disciplined to do the company job the company way. The salesman's needs must necessarily be servile to those of the company. Accordingly, management is often willing to tolerate such negative situations as high turnover of salespeople, low sales-force morale, and numerous customer complaints if such conditions are required for the achievement of company objectives. Happy salesmen and a low turnover rate are of little comfort to a company in distress.

The pattern of supervision should be adjusted to the needs of the firm. Frequently, salesmen's priorities must be reordered to generate a prescribed product or customer mix. Management may compel salesmen to concentrate on slower-moving items in the product line or to focus on larger rather than smaller customers. Sometimes salesmen are required to submit detailed expense accounts or the company places a limit on travel and entertainment expenses.

The company might also impose certain credit restrictions or adjust its minimum down-payment requirements, advertising allowances, or billing terms. These techniques can be considered to be "automatic supervisors" in that they control the salesman's actions and exert constant pressure on him to conform to the overall sales plan set forth by management.

It may also be in the company's best interest to control the content of the sales message to prevent inaccurate or unethical statements by sales-force members. The memorized or otherwise structured sales presentation is a highly effective method of accomplishing this objective. This type of sales message also assists the sales supervisor in trouble shooting the poor producer. Many firms that depend on standardized or canned sales presentations argue, that supervision boils down to seeing that the scilesman does not deviate form "the standard pitch".

The demands of consumerism have persuaded may sales managers to step up the intensity of monitoring the sales calls of new of questionable salespeople. A number of firms, especially those who sell directly to consumers, have initiated a postsale system of verifying the sales transaction with the new customer for the purpose of uncovering misunder standings, complaints, or buyer's remorse. The order is not processed until all customer grievances have been settled. One firm, which sought to control sales misrepresentations and irregularities, supplied salesmen under surveillance with the names of bogus prospects in whose premises tape recorders has been planted. The latter plan was costly in that those who assisted in the detective work were well compensated for their cooperation. It was, however quite effective since several unethical salespeople were caught red-handed and either were reprimanded or terminated.

Stimulating Improved Performance

Some readers may question the need for this section in the chapter on supervision. They may say, "If the salesman's morale is, improved, if his selling deficiencies are uncovered, if the appropriate additional training has been provided, and if the company needs have been stressed, improved performance by the salesman will be an automatic result.

Perhaps the salesman shouldn't have been hired in the first place. Perhaps he was oversold in the job interview, accepted the job as a temporary stopgap, recognized early that the job did not suit him, and is floundering because he never did have his heart in it.

Perhaps the salesman was inadequately trained for his particular job assignment.

On the other hand presume that the selection and training functions were performed properly. The salesperson may still flounder or fail for two major reasons: *(1)* incompatibility with management, and *(2)* a lack of positive and constructive leadership. Personality conflicts are often difficult to resolve. Extreme sensitivity, as well as a string sense of self-righteousness, often lead to incompatibility and friction. Early exposure and a frank discussion of differences are usually quite helpful. But what is meant by that intangible something called "leadership"? Of the thousands of definitions that have been advanced over time, the most meaningful one is a sales management context is "that ingredient of personality which causes people to follow."

Leadership

Burton, Bigelow once described the sales manager's leadership as "a priceless ingredient that turns the effort of ordinary salespeople into extraordinary results." These ordinary people are characterized by similar attitudes and motives which the sales supervisor must understand and know how to deal with. According to Bigelow, mediocre people prefer to avoid making decisions;

are lukewarm and uncertain in their enthusiasm;

lack faith in themselves and have little native confidence in others'

are afraid of responsibility and inhospitable to any suggestion that they accept it'

are undecided as to where they are going-even as to where they want to go.

If one is mindful of the old Chinese proverb which says "knowledge, like water, takes the form of the vessel into which it's poured," one will no doubt argue that the sales leader who can transform mediocre people into productive producers is a rare genius. Alexander Hamilton rejected the notion that the expert leader is a genius when he observed:

Men give me credit for some genius. All the genius I have lies sin this When I have a subject in hand, I study it profoundly. Day and night is before me. I explore it in all its bearings. My mind becomes pervaded with it. Then the effort which I have made is what people are pleased to call the fruit of genius. It is instead the fruit of labour and thought.

Sales leadership is the process of shaping a human being, molding him, as if he were clay, into what the leader wants him to be, until he is capable of performing as the leader wishes him to perform. Fortunately, what a sales leader does is considerably more tangible than what a leader is. Past experience and current practice indicate a number of guidelines, of varying degrees of importance, for the effective leadership of sales personnel:

1. Keep salesmen excited.
2. Expect enough-not too little-not too much.
3. Establish clear-cut objectives.
4. Set up a step-by-step programme to reach sales subjectives.
5. Sell the programme enthusiastically.
6. Plan ahead for yourself and your sales force.
7. Coach salespeople in the how as well as the what.
8. Continually inspect and promptly correct.
9. Sell the sales force on the importance of the job.
10. Challenge the fighters-bolster the timed.

11. Tell salespeople how they stand.
12. Use the power of incentives.
13. Bestow praise when earned.
14. Be the boss through thick and thin.
15. Set the pace.
16. Encourage and assist salespeople, one at a time.
17. Display wisdom, fairness, and human understanding.

The above list was succinctly summarized at Willy Loman's funeral in the play "Death of a Salesman".

The job of the sales manager is to help the salesman to keep the smile and the shoe-shine, to avoid the earthquake, to keep the spots off his hat, to make the salesman dream the right dreams, and then help to make these dreams come true. "Many salesman can outsell me but none can outtry me."

Supervisory Techniques

The above statement, made by a salesman of construction equipment, is a tribute both to the man who made it and to his supervisors who provided the spark that started the motivational process within him. Such an attitude is indicative of collaboration and interdependence between the salesperson and management through the development of mutual target setting. How does such mutuality come about?

One way of promoting greater sales efficiency, raising salesforce morale, and blending the goals of the organization and the individual so that the achievement is mutual is management by objectives (MBO). This process features management's use of input from the salesman in every phase of the selling job. The specific goals of the salesman and the firm are discussed openly so as to establish common targets and agree, upon strategies for reaching these targets. This will be achieved only if the planning sessions are of the give and take variety. The salesman can benefit from management's broad experience in dealing with other salesmen. Conversely, management often has much to gain by granting the employee equal time to inject his intimate knowledge of the marketplace into the discussion.

In MBO, criteria are agreed upon for the appraisal of sales results. This opens the door for supervision because the sales manager can focus his supervisory efforts on areas where the salesman is failing to meet mutual objectives. In turn the sales-force member will expect and receive help in the form of advice, reprimands, retraining, etc., when needed. Deviations from the planned selling results provide automatic feedback which, in turn, serves as meaningful input for the planning of future goals, srateygies, methods of appraisal, and rewards for both parties.

The give-and-take exchange between management and the sales-force member becomes more fruitful and acceptable to the salesman when at least a portion of the input from management is objective and based on hard data. For example, one author describes the computerbased system used by an industrial marketing firm to help he salesman use field time more effectively. In this system, the salesman feeds the computer data on each of his accounts, such as number of calls made in the current three-month period, number of expected calls in the upcoming quarter, average time per call, expected annual sales, expected sales for each account, and the sales adjustment factor. based on the account's impact on profitability due to purchased product or commissions. With such data, the computer is then programmed to fit sales-response curves through expected sales volumes of different call frequencies. It then prints optimum call policies designed to maximize sales, profits, and commissions. This approach relieves the salesperson of arduous calculation chores while helping to coordinate cost control and time management factors.

In essence, the MBO approach compels the sales manager to study each salesperson and customize the goal-setting and supervision package to satisfy each employee's unique set of needs and expectations. Instead, management may discover that the sales force can be subdivided into a few group of employees who have common needs and goals. This alternative method of "sales-force segmentations" calls for applying different motivation, communication, administrative, goal-setting, and supervisory principles to each group in order to achieve maximum performance from each.

Mossien and Fram suggest several bases for salesforce segmentation. First, salesmen can he segmented by job title so that a person would be classified as a trainee, salesman, senior salesman, or master salesman, depending upon his level of productivity. In segmentation by financial recognition, some salespeople would be on salary plans, others on commission programmes, and still others on mixed plans. Commission and bonus rates and salary levels would be geared to the needs and productivity of each group.

Other bases for segmentation are by peripheral benefits and personal recognition. For example, company cars would be available to certain groups and not to others and there would be separate sales contests, award incentives, national sales meetings, and retraining sessions. Segmentation by communication differences is based on the belief that it is inappropriate to address the top professional in the same manner as one addresses the neophyte. Accordingly, it not far-fetched to consider the preparation of separate house organs, newsletters, and local sales clinics for each of the sales-force segments.

The underlying value of this motivating method is that it provides a system by which career salespeople can grow in status, financial remuneration, and level of communication with management. The differing needs and motivational requirements of various salesforce members are recognized without the need for the extensive customization that is demanded in the MBO process.

One authority has stated that education may be one of the greatest forces for motivating sales-force members. No salesman will ever live long enough to learn all he needs to know about selling through his personal experiences alone. That's why salesmen read books, watch other salesmen, and exchange ideas by participating in meeting and seminars. Knowledge drives out fear. The absence of fear creates confidence. Confidence is based on understanding which must be assiduously cultivated if it is to bear good fruit.

The best way to motivate a customer to place reorders is to sell him a product that produces favourable results. Similarly, the best way to motivate a salesman to learn is to offer him instruction and guidance that is convertible into productive sales results.

Every salesman must be handled differently. The "can't" salesman needs a boot. The "won't" salesman needs a needle. The wounded salesman needs a band-aid. Finally, the producing salesman needs a blue ribbon which may prevent him from becoming ill at a later date.

The diagnosis or troubleshooting process can take place in the office, in the car, on the curbstone; on the golf course, in the lunchroom, or any place that the salesman and his supervisor can meet on a one-on-one basis. A useful troubleshooting tool is the checklist or a "why I didn't get the order" form. The checklist should consist of a lengthy list of items covering every facet of the selling programme, from prospecting to closing. The checklist is a sequential inventory of techniques or characteristics which are necessarily possessed by the "ideal" salesman. By periodically discussing and observing the items on the list, the supervisor is in a position to note a salesman's points of strength and weakness relative to a given selling situation or over a period of time. The salesperson may also use the checklist as a selfimprovement tool by evaluating his own strong and weak points.

Too often selling errors are not permanently corrected by the sales supervisor. One sales researcher suggests the use of "dialogue analysis" as a method of reorienting experienced salesmen. In this approach, transcriptions of conversations between salesman and prospects are analyzed. The dialogues recreate real situations involving communications between people. These conversations are analyzed for proper use or misuse of techniques, ideas, concepts, and strategies in selling. Although the best method of collecting dialogues is by use of concealed tape recorders, some managers, salesmen, and prospects may find this method objectionable and even unethical. An imperfect but useful alternative is dialogue material contributed by salesmen or sales managers as a result of their recall of selling experiences. Dialogues illustrating specific points are easily remembered by salesmen and are, therefore, more beneficial than most methods in developing an understanding of the important principles of good selling.

❒

8

Evaluation of Sales Promotion Experiment

Evaluation implies a process of systematically uncovering deviations between goals and accomplishments. When weaknesses are identified, the firm will devise and implement. corrective methods through supervision and other control devices. When strengths are indicated, by the discovery of deviations in a favourable direction; management will use this information as a valuable aid in the anticipating and dealing with problems in future periods. This may take the form of revising performance standards and generally reappraising present policies, procedures, marketing communication methods, and potential opportunities for the firm. Thus, the evaluation process aims at "both prognosis and diagnosis and is considered to be a preventive and curative marketing device."

In summarizing the sales-management process, significant steps can be identified: *(1)* establishing standards of performance; *(2)* assembling and preparing resources for performance; *(3)* directing sales performance; *(4)* measuring actual performance results; *(5)* comparing these results with established standards; and *(6)* taking appropriate action in response to measured deviations, The reader will observe that step 5 is in essence, the evaluation step and step 6 is management's attempt to react to the observed gap between expectations and actual results.

It will also be noted that previously discussed processes of stimulating and supervising the sales force are important parts of step in that they are designed to maintain and improve sales-force performance. This chapter will fill in the missing links in steps 5 and 6 and will concentrate on the methods for measuring sales-force performance and minimizing dysfunctional activities.

Appraising Overall Performance

The company audit is the summation of the audits of each of the firm's functional areas, that is, marketing, engineering, manufacturing, etc. Similarly, the marketing audit is an after-the-fact analysis of each element in the marketing mix, that is, selling, advertising, pricing, distribution, product policy, packaging, etc., and also of the linkages among these elements. Obviously, conducting company or marketing audits is such a sizeable task that few firms schedule them regularly.

The sales audit is a bit more manageable and considerably more popular. Basically, it consists of analysis of sales volume and costs expended to achieve that volume. If advertising, product planning, and other audits in the marketing area are conducted simultaneously, the resultant coordination of findings is often quite useful in pinpointing conflicting goals and strategies and costs that should be corrected.

Sales Analysis

Since sales analysis is the process of comparing actual sales with some established sales standard, it would seem that the analyst should do nothing more than see whether the company has met its forecast. In many firms, this is exactly what happens. If the analysis takes place at an interim period in the fiscal year, deviations between forecast and actual sales will dictate either a revision of the forecast or a revision of sales policies, strategies, or tactics.

Ordinarily the analysis will be considerably more complex. For example, actual sales volume may be compared simultaneously to forecasted sales, sales potential, last year's sales at the same date, average sales or some other criterion. Sales may be defined in terms of orders received, cash receipts, or shipments. As Sales may be measured in dollars, units, as a percentage of the year's sales, or in relative terms. Sales volume may be broken down by product categories, customer types, territories, salesmen, order sizes, etc.

Obviously, the most readily available company sales figure is the combined sales of all products in all territories to all customers. However, this figure may be of limited value in that it does not disclose relevant weaknesses among products, territories sale-force members, or customer types.

The United States territory is found to be right on forecast with negative deviations appearing in the reference books and children's books divisions. The Orient territory is the weakest in the firm except for outstanding performance in the reference books division. Management must ascertain whether the deficiencies in the Orient territory stem from exclusive concentration on reference books and musical records or whether consumers in the territory are not receptive to the other products. Also, since the United States operation is the only division that performs well in marketing children's records it may be that the product design is not appealing to European and Oriental consumers.

Cost Analysis

It was indicated that sales production and. cost control mechanisms operate in union to achieve the firm's hierarchy of selling goals. There is little purpose in achieving sales goals in the absence of profitability. Therefore, a meaningful sales audit may have the ultimate purpose of detecting deviations between forecast and actual profit figures within the same segments studied by the sales analyst.

Historically, sales managers are not cost oriented. This is not to say that they do not recognize the need for profitable sales volume. However, they often make the mistake of treating volume development and cost control as two totally disassociated, separate entities. Some sales leaders are so otivated to generate sales that they give little thought to the costs of obtaining those sales. Others are myopic with regard to cost/volume relationships.

For example, consider the sales manager who regards the straight-commission plan as least costly to the firm, since the firm incurs no compensation costs unless sales are produced. This view-point disregards the direct costs of excessive recruiting, hiring, training, and the intangible costs of lost sales. Sales managers, in pursuit of sales, are often reluctant to delete unprofitable products, drop unprofitable customers, or eliminate unprofitable territories.

Whereas sales managers may be receptive to reports or computer printouts from the financial department that deal with cost elements of the sales audit, cost analysis is rarely initiated by sales management. They presume, often correctly, that the preparation of cost and profit analyses is a broader marketing function and, in fact, an area of concern to all functional areas of the firm. As such, the sales manager is willing to delegate the duty to financial and accounting people. The sales manager is typically concerned solely with costs over which he has control such as recruiting, selection, training, supervision and compensation expenses.

Product sales managers in multiproduct companies are sensitive to company methods of allocating various distribution costs to specific product areas. Many of these costs are common rather than separable as in the case of rents, office equipment, advertising, computer services, administrative salaries, and physical distribution resources. Moreover, within the sales department, the sales manager finds it difficult to divide common fixed costs among products, territories, customer types, and sales-force members. Thus, in contrast to sales analysis, cost analysis is complex, time consuming, and often disturbing.

Apprasing Individual Performance

Management gathers information on the individual salesperson's performance for three major reasons-to reward him, to punish him, or to improve him.

Obviously the good performer should be properly recognized in the form of increased compensation, promotion, or awards. Similarly, the poor producer should be denied-these forms of recognition and, when necessary, he should be dismissed. However, the ideal purpose of the performance evaluation is to uncover the areas where corrective measures will serve to improve the sales-force member's future results.

Evaluation Bases

The frustration of attempting to evaluate a group of salesforce members on the basis of field results was demonstrated in an article by Richard I. Levin. Five hypothetical company salesmen were ranked by using, alternatively, gross sales, margin dollars, margin per cent, controllable profits, net profits, new accounts, and percentage of sales potential. Each salesman was rated first and last at least once, indicating that a salesperson can look good or bad depending on the base used by management to evaluate him.

Quantitative evaluation standards can be based on the sales-man's results or his efforts. Several result-oriented factors were given in the previous paragraph. There are others, including sales volume as a percentage of quota; conversion rate; and number of orders cancelled, returns, misrepresentations, or claimed irregularities. Evaluation based on effort rather than results is justified on the grounds that favourable output is a function of favourable input. Among the input factors used in appraising sales personnel are number of sales contracts, number of sales presentations, amounts of time spent with existing customers, and contributions at sales meetings and clinics.

A salesman may be appraised qualitatively in terms of his attitudes toward and concern for company relations, such as:

1. Awareness of job requirements.
2. Attitudes toward the learning process.
3. Perceptions of customer-company-salesman relationships.
4. Understanding of personal relationships.
5. Coordination with other functional areas.
6. Activities as pacesetter, coach, field trainer.
7. Willingness and ability to acquire new capacities.
8. Willingness and ability to recognize problems and provide needed feedback such as information on competitive activities.
9. Product-line concentration.

A salesman's relations with customers may also be judged on the basis of such skills as problem solving, general availability and proficiency in providing service and assistance. An all-encompassing evaluation criterion is the representative's knowledge about his job as it relates to results. This includes such areas as his understanding of product features and applications, markets, customers, and competitive strategies; his prospecting talents; his ability to overcome objections; and his skills in delivering the sales presentation.

Numerous sales supervisors use a list of difficult-to-measure personal characteristics to intuitively discriminate successful from unsuccessful salespeople:

Appearance	patience	empathy
verbal ability	dependability	ego drive
initiative	stability	enthusiasm
imagination	aggressiveness	willingness to listen
ambition	flexibility	judgement

The reader should be cautioned against thinking that all successful salespeople possess all or most of the above qualities. In many selling situations, several of these characteristics are unnecessary and even detrimental.

The appropriate combination of appraisal criteria depends on the specific selling framework and on the broad corporate, marketing, and selling objectives. In establishing goals for individual salesmen, management must take care to avoid the condition of suboptimization. For example, it is not uncommon for the result-oriented high producer to be indifferent to company and customer needs, including ethical considerations and posttransactional requirements of regular customers.

Information Sources

Supervision and evaluation are interdependent and continuous processes. The field sales manager cannot work closely with a subordinate without being aware of his strengths and weaknesses. Salesmen discuss each other with members of management. Customers and prospective customers praise and complain about sales personnel. A certain amount of informal, subjective appraisal of selling activity is both inevitable and desirable. However, a major step toward the improvement of the evaluation method occurs when judging becomes systematic. A systematic procedure is. one in which a framework is supplied to ensure that the evaluation is complete, free of personal bias, consistent over time, and comparable in scope for all those being assessed.

The final rating of a salesman's performance should be a composite of information received from many sources, with each source appropriately weighted. The obvious source of quantitative information is the record kept by the firm, that is, the "bottom line". How did salesman Kelly do in terms of number of orders, sales volume, gross margin, and selling costs? Such information about "how much" is supplemented by information about "why" provided by other sources. The field sales manager is in a position to discuss the quality of Kelly's sales presentation, his work habits, his rapport with prospects, his devotion to his work, his mental attitude, etc.

Activity reports turned in by the salesman provide valuable information about effort such as prospecting methods, number and frequency of calls, number of presentations, time spent in entertaining clients, etc. These reports are especially useful when combined with informal comments and solicited remarks from prospects or customers. In this age of consumerism, input from buyers is easily obtained during order-verification phone calls or through frequently used mail questionnaires which seek information for improving the offerings and services of sellers.

The Salesman's Career Cycle

It has recently been suggested that evaluation standards and supervisory measures should be related to the position of the salesforce member in his career cycle. Analogous to the product life cycle, the career cycle has been suggested as a continuum that ranges from the recruitment of a new salesman to his termination. Unlike with a product, however, a salesman's termination can be voluntary as well as being an action of management; a salesman can become tired, bored, disgruntled, or deceased at the peak of his productivity.

The salesman's career cycle, (SSG) moves through the stages of preparation, development, maturity, and decline, and he can repeat any stage or the entire cycle any number of times. The time interval of each phase is determined by a complex interaction of variables based on personal, management, buyer, and environmental factors.

Training is the essential ingredient in the preparation phase. The experienced salesman who has just shifted to a new product or a new company will, in most cases, require less preparation in terms of indoctrination and initial training than the novice who is in his first selling job. If the trainee is new to the company, it is management's responsibility at this early stage to integrate the company's requirements with the salesman's own needs and abilities as an autonomous agent.

The salesman who has survived the preparation phase must now convert his training into productive results. The salesman's productivity rises slowly in the development phase. Predominant management responsibilities consist of identifying and correcting evolving field problems and undesirable behaviour patterns. Depending upon the size and dispersion of the sales force and the sales manager's span of control, sales performance data will be obtained by written, telephone, or face-to-face communication with the salesman, or discussions with prospects and customers. When sales problems cannot be identified and corrected in the office, the sales manager must accompany the salesman in actual field selling situations, where on-the-spot coaching and curbstone conferences may take place. Supervision, field control, and retraining of the salesman must be carefully planned, staffed, activated, and controlled in order to close gaps between desired results and present performance.

The first sign that a salesman has reached the, maturity stage is a levelling off of his productivity. Some salespeople seem to reach a 'rated capacity' beyond which they are unable or unwilling to go. These salesmen may be content with their present sales volume and income, such that unusual efforts and sacrifices may not be perceived as worthwhile.

The dynamics of society call for a new level of management of establis ed sales-force members. Retraining should be aimed at widening the perspectives of proven producers. Less paperwork may be required, and these salesmen may be given greater freedom in allocating their time and negotiating prices and other relationships with customers. In addition to the normal financial rewards and trophies, recognition, praise, a!ld intense management involvement should be used to stimulate effort and productivity.

Mature salesmen can be used as pacesetters, teachers, and field trainers. Even the most successful sales representative has a tendency not to want to be a sales man all his life. Thus, top producers are logical targets for proselytism by rival firms who offer new challenges, more security, and prestige in the form of new and more exciting product and market opportunities, more or different compensation, and offers to enter management.

As salesmen enter the decline stage, management may take frenzied steps to inject belated doses of retraining and motivation. Yet there are few instances where management is able to help a rapidly declining salesman overcome the negative attitudes that limit his effectiveness. Resistance by prospects, low occupational status, inadequate intrafirm communication, neglected training, and poor earnings are difficult to reverse and usually result in a severely demotivated employee and, in some cases, impairment of health, alcoholism, and eventual termination. Recruitment of an energetic replacement retriggers the cycle.

The Evaluation Sequence

The discussion that follows outlines the steps for implementing the SCC model while summarizing one suggested series of evaluation steps. Of significant importance is the method of combining the information from various evaluation sources.

The first step is to itemize and carefully define the criteria to be used in evaluating sales-force members. A given company may use all or some of these items or may substitute those which fit unique company objectives.

Appropriate evaluation instruments are sent to selected raters after they have become thoroughly familiar with the relevant criteria and their intended use. If customers are used as a source of appraisal information, the questionnaire or rating form must be designed with unusual care in order to elicit the desired qualitative data in a constructively way. Company records supply quantitative information, while supervisory personnel, peers, and the salesman himself can provide both quantitative and qualitative data.

Once the evaluation data have been returned to the controlling office, information derived from the various sources should be compared to uncover rating biases and inconsistencies in the salesperson's behaviour, skill, and production pattern. The controlling office will' then convert the stream of appraisal information into a composite or overall score that reflects the weighting of the subjective and objective criteria employed. There are many methods for converting a number of selected performance measures into an overall rating or index. One is to compare the measure on every evaluation item for each salesperson with ail "ideal" measure for that item, so that an "index of deviation from perfection" may be computed.

The final step is to compare the current evaluation with those of previous periods. The direction and intensity of a given salesman's rating will govern his proper placement in the SCC.

Using Evaluative Information

It was indicated earlier in this chapter that a salesman. may be evduated in comparison. with established standards in comparison with his own prior performance, and in comparison with other salesmen. In each case, the sales supervisor should recognize individual differences among sales-force members. Some of the best salesmen are slow learners. The fastest learners sometimes lack the instinctiveness to react to unique selling situations. If the evaluation process is to serve as a means for motivation and direction of selling efforts, the supervisor will be required to compare his findings over time and to use these findings constructively and in keeping with the selling goals of the firm and the potential of each individual sales force member. The astute sales manager will use each salesperson's skills where they will both do the most good and prevent individual weaknesses from causing destructive effects. Where possible, this will call for the matching of products, territories, and customer types with salespeople who are capable of handling the respective assignments.

Transmitting Evaluation Information

There is nothing more motivational to a successful salesperson than earned praise from his boss. Recognition sets into motion new urges and often new and better accomplishments.

Conversely, even the poor or marginal salesperson should be promptly informed of his progress, standing, and need for improvement. Sales managers are often hesitant to dismiss an ineffective producer. A cautious approach while gathering information is commendable, but once it is determined that a salesman is unlikely to improve, termination should be prompt and efforts, should be redirected to more likely candidate. There are numerous examples of sales managers who are reluctant to fire a man because he was a highly touted recruit or because the firm has already invested a sizeable sum of money in training and compensating him. The necessity for eliminating salespeople with little chance of success was emphasized by the sales manager who, when congratulated upon his excellent sales staff, replied: "I had to hire and fire thirty-seven people over the past three years in order to build my present team of twelve fine salespeople."

It was indicated earlier that a salesman's weakness in performing a single basic sales task can overwhelm his strength in performing all other selling tasks. Thus, the salesman's value to the firm is signified by the totality of his effectiveness in performing his entire job rather than by a weighting or mathematical averaging of the various individual tasks. Accordingly, the skilful evaluator is not unlike the researcher who, in keeping with selling objectives, objectively analyzes and synthesizes each unit of information from each data source.

❑

9

Product Decision in Sales Promotion

The product policy of a firm is one of the most important aspect of its operation. It is concerned with establishing objectives and guidelines which determine the nature and extent of the goods and services that the firm decides to market to its target customers. It covers existing as well as new goods and services. For the success of a firm, it is of utmost importance to plain its product, product mix. Successful marketing operations are built around two essential elements—Product and Markets. In other words, the essence of marketing is the bringing together products possessing want satisfying capabilities with markets made up of potential customers having particular funds.

A product may be defined as a bundle of utilities consisting of various product features and accompanying services. The bundle of utilities or the physical and pyschological satisfactions that the buyer receives is provided by the seller when he sells a particular combination of product features and associated services. Customer does not buy merely the physical and chemical attributes of a product. He is really buying want satisfaction. He will buy a product which will offer him expected satisfaction. Thus brand, package, label, price, status of manufacturer and distributor and services offered to the customer constitute a part and parcel of a product. It should be noted that what a buyer buys is mixture not of goods and services, but rather of expected physical and psychological satisfactions. Therefore, the term 'product' should not mean the physical product itself but the total product including brand, package, label, price, status of manufacturer and distributor and services offered to the customer in addition to the physical goods.

According to Philip Kotler, "A product is anything that can be offered to a market for attention, acquisition, use of consumption; it includes physical objects, services, personalities, place, organisations and ideas." A product has many other dimensions besides its physical appearance. In fact, product like an onion with several layers and each of the layers contributes to the total product image. Philip Kotler is of the opinion that a product has three layers or dimensions which must be distinguished. As shown in Fig., these dimensions are: *(a)* core product, *(b)* formal product, and *(c)* augmented product.

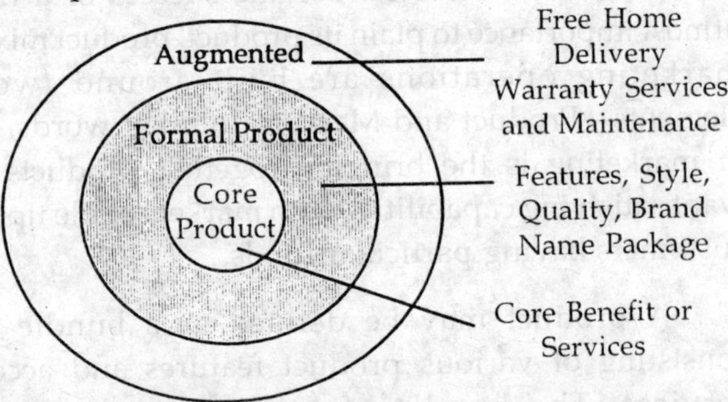

Fig. Dimensions of a Product

A. **Core Product.** It is the fundamental dimension of a product as it represents of bundle of benefits to its prospective buyer. The core product answers the question: "What is the buyer really buying?" For instance, a woman buying a washing machine is buying comfort and not a mere collection of drum, beater and nuts and bolts for their own sake; and a woman buying a lipstick is buying hope and not a set of chemical and physical attributes for their own sake. The basic job of a market is to sell the core benefits.

B. **Formal Product.** It is the larger packaging of a core product. It is what the target market recognises as the tangible offer. For isntance, washing machines, lipsticks, motor cars, televisions, etc., having the following attributes; *(a)* features, *(b)* style, *(c)* a level of quality, *(d)* a brand name, and *(e)* packaging. Services ahve also got features which are generally intangible. Thus, services like auto repair, electricity supply, management consultancy, psyhological counselling and medical advice are all products.

C. **Augmented Product.** It is a broader conception of the product. It represents the totality of benefits that a person may receive or experience in getting the formal product. The augmented product of a T.V. distributor is not only T.V., but also delivery, free installation, warranty, and service and maintenance. This dimension of the product is very important for a firm operating in a competitive market. The firm that develops the right augmented product will be able to attract more customers and servive in the competitive market.

KINDS OF PRODUCT

Product or goods can be classifed into two broad categories depending upon the use for which they are meant. These categories are: *(I)* consumers' goods and *(II)* industrial goods:

I. Consumers' Goods

Consumers' goods are meant for final consumption by the ultimate consumers. Bread, butter, TV sets, cosmetics and garments are all consumer goods. On the other hand industrial goods are meant for use in the commercial production of other goods or in connection with carrying out some business activities. Machine tools, iron-ore, and electronic computers are all industrial goods. It should be noted that all goods cannot be classifed exclusively as consumers' goods or indusrial goods. For example, typing paper is used for both personal and business correspondence and therefore is both a consumers' and an industrial goods. The distinction between consumers and industrial goods is necessary in order to understand the behaviour of their purchasers. The purchasers of industrial goods have an altogether different approach as compared to the purchasers of consumers' goods.

Consumers' goods can be further classified into convenience goods shopping goods, and speciality goods. a brief description of these is given below:

(i) **Convenience Goods.** These include items which the consumers buy frequently, immedaitely, and with minimum shopping efforts. Cold drinks, cigarettes, magazines and newspapers, drugs and most grocery items are the examples of convenience goods. These goods are non-durables *i.e.,* they are consumed or used up rapidily. At the time of buying these goods, the habit of the consumer dominates his behaviour. He does not take much item in marking the buying decision.

(ii) **Shopping Goods.** These include items which consumers select and buy after making comparisions on such criteria as suitablity, quality, price and style. In case of a shopping goods, a substantial number of consumers habitually make shopping comparisons before they take a buying decision. Furniture items, dress materials, shoes, and how should appliances are the examples of shopping goods. A shopping goods is durable and is used up slowly. The consumer has to compare different stores offerings and devote considerable time and effort to take the buying decision.

(iii) **Speciality Goods.** As the name implies, the consumers have to make a special purchasing effort to purchase speciality goods. Items in this category must possess unique features or have a number of brand names or both. Fancy goods, stamps and coins for collectors and prestige brands of men's suits may be termed as speciality goods. The consumers are already aware of the product or brand they want and they are willing to make a special purchasing effort to find the outlet handling it. Thus, in case of speciality goods, the consumers do not compare the desired sepciality goods with others. But they may take considerable time in deciding to start the special search required because goods are often in the luxury price class.

II. Industrial Goods

Industrial goods are those meant for use in making other products or for rendering a service in the operation of a business organisation. For a comprehensive analysis, industrial goods may be classified on the basis of use (instead of buying habits as in case of consumers goods) into five categories, namely, raw materials, fabricating parts and materials, installations, accessory equipment and operative supplies. A brief description of these are given below:

(i) **Raw Materials.** Raw materials are those industrial goods which will become part of another physical product and which have received no processing at all than that necessary for economy or protection in physical handling. Raw materials may be divided into natural products: Minerals, land, and products of the forests and the seas: and agricultural products: Wheat, cotton, tobacco, fruits, live-stocks and animal products such as eggs and raw milk. Raw materials are usually graded for standardised quality.

(ii) **Fabricating Materials and Parts.** These are partial or complete items which become part of the final product. They have already been processed to some exent. Fabircating materials undergo further processing, *e.g.*, pig iron going into steel, yarn being woven into cloth, leather being shaped into shoes, and flour becoming a part of cake or bread. Fabricating parts are assembled with no further change in form *e.g.*, spark plugs in an automobile, barrel of a rifle and buttons on a coat.

(iii) **Accessory Equipment.** Accessory equipment includes industrial goods usually less expensive and having shorter life than installations. They are required for the manufacture of final product though they do not form part of the finished products, *e.g.*, portable drills, hand tools, work-lift trucks, etc. these items are highly standardised.

(iv) **Installations.** Installations are long-life and expensive major equipment of an industrial user. These are necessary for further production of goods, but they do not form part of those products, *e.g.*, heavy machinery, diesel engines, trucks, factory sites and production lines.

(v) **Operating Supplies.** Operating supplies are short-lived and low priced items usually purchased with a minimum of effort. They are the 'convenience goods' of industries. They do not have a signficant impact on the long run profitability of an organisation. Supplies include floor wax, lubricating oils, heating fuel and office stationary like pins, pens, pencils, papers, etc. Operating supplies do not become a part of finished product.

Distinction between Industrial Goods and Consumer Goods

Industrial goods and consumer goods are two broad divisions of manufactured goods. But they show latent differences which are evident from the following definitions given by the American Marketing Association.

"Consumer goods are destined for use by ultimate consumers or households and in such forms that they can be used without commercial processing." Against this industrial goods are defined as "those goods which are destined to be sold primarily for use in producing other goods or rendering severice as contrasted with goods destined to be sold primarily to be ultimate consumer." These definitions *prima facie* bring out two differences. Firstly industrial goods are not meant for consumption, so their buyers are different from the buyers of consumer goods. Secondly, further processing is required in the case of industrial goods before they can be finally consumed..

In the industrial products the customer is well informed and know the relative merits of a particular product, alternative sources of supply and also the various competitive products available.

But this classification is not an air-tight compartment. An industrial product may serve the two markets simultaneously. For example, a typewriter may be used in industrial concern and it may also be used for personal purpose. In the later case it is pure consumer product.

Differences in the Marketing of Industrial and Consumer Goods

However the marketing remains 'the same, yet there are important differences in marketing the industrial product and marketing consumer products. The prime difference in marketing of those goods is nature of their demand. The demand of consumer goods is 'original' while that of industrial goods is 'derived'. The industry is to supply the goods according to the wants of actual consumers or users. It means that the demand of industrial product is derived from the demand of consumer products in which the industrial products may play an important part in making.

Again the knowledge and sophistication of customers varies according to whether the goods are industrial goods or consumer goods. The industrial buyer is well informed of the relative merits and demerits of the alternative success of supply of various competitive products. Moreover the number of customers of industrial product is small as compared to the number of consumers of consumer products. Therefore, in marketing industrial products, greater emphasis is placed on personal selling through salesmen whereas in marketing the consumer products, emphasis is laid on mass marketing and hence most of the selling has to be one through advertising.

PRODUCT LINE

Product line refers to a group of products that are closely related because they satisfy a class of needs, are used together, are sold to the same customer groups, are marketed through the same type of outlets, or fall within given price changes in product line or product item naturally changes the product mix and vice versa. The following are instances where the product mix is altered. (Product mix consists of all the different product lines a firm offers.)

(a) Product Modification. It is the process by which the existing products are modified to suit the changing demand on account of fashion changes. Such a decision is required at a time when the product is in the maturity stage of the product life cycle. Product modificaton may be defined and deliberate alteration in the physical attributes of product or its packaging.

(b) Product Elimination. There are some products which cannot be improved or modified to suit the market needs.

Here, the profitable alternative would be to withdraw the product. The process of withdrawal is technically known as 'product elimination'.

(c) **Product Line Modification.** Product line is altered or modifed through the following methods:

(i) ***Product Line Contraction.*** This is also known as "Contraction of Product Mix." It is a method by which a fat and long product line is thinned out. It is also termed as 'Simplification'. The decision to reduce the product items might be due to the purposeful act of the management to suspend the production of unprofitable products. Marketing problems also compel the manufacturers to withdraw certain items.

Product line contraction is a major decision from the point of view of management. "Many sick or marginal products never die; they are allowed to continue in the company's product mix until they fade away." These products will, in course of time, eat away the profits earned by the other products. The decision to give away a product often results from changes in the market. Market saturation makes a product unprofitable. Products also may be abandoned, even though still profitable, if the management feels that the same resources could yield a higher profit from other products. Thus, the process of avoiding or stopping the production of a particular product is called simplification. It is also termed as Product Line Contraction. From this viewpoint it is opposite of diversification. In spite of the advantages, most managements are shy and do not accept "Product pruning" programmes. R.S. Alexander categorically states, "But putting products to death—or letting them die—is a drab business and often engenders much of the sadness of a final parting with old and tried friend." The reasons for this are partly logical and partly sentimental.

(ii) ***Product Line Expansion.*** It is just the opposite of the above and is referred to diversification. To utilise the marketing opportnities a firm may have to expand breadth and depth of its product line. The expansion of the product line is undertaken by increasing the lines and/or items of products. New lines may be related or unrelated to the present products. For example, manufacturers of radio sets may start producing television sets and tape-records.

Diversification, by definition, means that something new will be added. It may be new products, new markets, new technologies or even a new company. Generally, it means adding a new product (not various qualities of the same product) to the existing product line or mix. For example, if a fan manufacturing company starts producing sewing machines, it is a case of diversification. It does not mean that the new product should be complementary or an allied product to the existing one. It may be a product which may be entirely distinct and different from the existing products. The term is applicable not only to production but also to selling. For instance, if a wholesaler dealing in engineering goods starts selling simultaneously confectionary items, it is also a case of diversification. Some of the reasons for such a change are:

(1) There is a technological development in the process of production,

(2) New markets are to be created,

(3) There is a constant threat for the existing product due to abrupt changes in fashion,

(4) The advantage of the reputation of the company's name and its existing products to be spread to other products,

(5) The spare capacity of the factory is to be fully utilised.

Diversification is profitable only in the large companies which are "multimarket and multiproduct". Further, such companies must have financial resources supported by a well-organised management. Diversification of products, to a very large extent, is capable of preventing recessionary trends entering the industry. The usual way in which diversification is brought about is by means of mergers like one company acquiring another.

Hindustan Machine Tools offers a good example in this regard. Started as a company manufacturing various machine tools (lathes, drillling machines, etc.), it moved into the field of watch-making. Their diversification process continues and their latest entry is in the field of manufacturing printing presses and electric bulbs.

(iii) **Changing Models or Styles of Existing Product.** Continuous changes in fashion, desires and needs of the consumers compel the management to review the existing products and their style.

For example, some time ago, a cigarette manufacturing company used to sell two varieties of cigarettes. One variety was popular in South India while the other dominated the North Indian markets. The company withdrew one variety and tried to popularise another. Quite contrary to this, another cigarette manufacturing company, that had only a medium variety, introduced other varieties in the market. This kind of problems arise mainly because of the fundamental fact that 'different individuals have different tastes'.

(iv) **Quality Variations.** In contrast to the above, under certain circumstances a manufactuer is forced to produce differing qualities of a particular product. Even if the quality of the product is good, a single quality may not be enough to retain the market. For example, manufacturers of pens invariably market pens of different varieties with varying quality at different prices.

In the matter of quality, the manufacturers of consumer goods particularly speciality goods and convenience goods, face the problem of changing the quality often to suit the market.

PRODUCT MIX

In the modern age a producer produces a number of products so that the needs of maximum number of consumers may be satisfied, maximum sales may be made and maximum profits may be earned. As the needs, wants, tastes and likings of all the consumers are different, they can not be satisfied with a single product, therefore, different product of different characteristics are offered to different consumers so that the enterprise may capture a goods share in the market. All the product being produced by an enterprise are known as Product Mix. Thus, product mix is the composite of all the products offered for sale by a business and industrial enterprise. It is necessary to understand the meaning of the term product item and product line before coming to the definition of the term product mix.

Product item means a specific product of certain specifications, such as—Lux Soap, Colgate Toothpaste, Facit Typewriter, H. M. T. Watch, Rath Vanaspati, Televista Televiosion and Bajaj Chetak Scooter.

A product line is a group of different product items, closely related with each other. All the products of a product line are clsoely related with each other either because they satisfy a class of needs, or used together, or are sold to the same group of customers, or are sold through the same channel of distribution, or are within same pricing range. Toothpaste. Watch, T.V., Scooter, Typewriter are the examples of a product line. Here, it is appropriate to note that a particular brand of a poduct is a product item and all the brands of the same product are included in product line.

Product Mix is the composite of all the products offered for sale by a business or industrial enterprise. The term 'Product Mix has been defined by American Marketing Association as, "Product Mix is the composite of products offered for sale by a firm or a business unit." For example if an enterprise manufactures or deals with different varieties of Soap. Oil, Toothpastes, Toothbrush, etc., the group of all these product is called 'Product Mix'.

On the basis of above discussion, it can be concluded that a single product item is called as a product item. All the product items of the same group are collectively known as a Product Line and all the product lines manufactured or distributed by an enterprise are collectively known as 'Product Mix'.

FACTORS AFFECTING THE PRODUCT MIX

Following are the factors which affect the Product Mix of an enterprise:

(1) Changes in Market Demand. Purchasing power of consumer's habits, tastes, needs and wants of consumers; attitudes and preferences of consumers keep on changing from time to time. Every such change results in the change in the demand of a product. A business or industrial enterprise has to make necessary changes in its product mix in accordance with the changes in demand. For example, an increase in the income of consumers increases their purchasing power. As a result of which, the demand for inferior goods falls and the demand for superior goods increases. Keeping this change in mind, producers have to change their production. They have to decrease the production of inferior goods and increase the production of superior goods.

(2) Production Capacity. The enterprise has also to change its product mix from time to time so that the best possible results may be achieved from its resources. Such change also become necessary to improve the quality of production. For example, the product mix may be enhanced by starting the production of a by-product with the use of wastes and scraps.

(3) Marketing Capacity. Sometimes, the changes in product mix of an enterprise may be necessary to get the maximum results of marketing efforts of the enterprise. For example, if a product is not getting desired response from the market, the decision may be taken to step the production of such a product and the resources of the enterprise may be diverted to produce a new product.

(4) Competitive Policies and Strategies. An enterprise has to keep a close eye upon the marketing policies and strategies of its competitors and should make necessary changes in its marketing policies and strategies. For example, if the competitors have made any change in packing or size or colour or price etc. of their products, relevant changes should also be made in the product of the enterprise.

(5) Earn Maximum Profits. Ultimate objects of every business and industrial enterprise is to earn the maximum possible profits. Product mix of the enterprise requires to be changed for this purpose also. For example, the production of less profitable product may be stopped and the production of more profitable products may be increased.

(6) Financial Resources. Finance is the blood of all the activities of an enterprise. Availability of financial resources also necessitates some changes in the products mix of an enterprise. For example, if a particular product is continuously going into a loss, the decision may be taken to change such product. Similarly, if the financial resources of an enterprise are not adequate to carry on production of all the products, the decision may be taken to curtail a product item.

(7) Image of Producer. Sometimes, product mix of the enterprise is changed to improve the image of the producer. For example, a decision may be taken to produce the products only of high quality.

BRAND

The American Marketing Association has defined a brand as a name, term, symbole or design or a combination of them which is intended to identify the goods and services of one seller or groups of sellers and to differentiate them from those of competitors'. A trade mark is a brand that has been given legal protection thus ensuring its use exclusively by one seller. 'Trade mark' is thus a legal term.

We are living in an age of brands. Whether in industrial goods or consumer goods, there is a proliferation of brands. Fifteen years ago in India, there were hardly 4 to 5 brands of tooth pastes. Today we have more than a dozen brands. Similarly, among soaps, one had to choose from a handful of brands. Today we have a big assortment of brands, and brand competition has development as a feature of the Indian marketing scene.

In an age of brands, the brand name is quite often the major selling tools, and the most important component of the total product offering.

Giving brand names to products facilitate an effective promotional campaign. Advertising an undifferented or unbrantiaded product becomes a difficult task. A brand name facilitates advertising and functions as a demand stimulant.

The intensive brand promotion undertaken by the marketers of various products have made consumers extremely brand conscious. These days no one asks for just tooth paste. He or she asks specifically for Binaca Fluoride, Signal, Colgate or Forhans. No woman asks for just bathing soap, she may insists on a particular brand. A man who wants a steel cupboard may straight away go in for a Godrej without thinking twice about several other brands available. The brand image developed by sales promotional measures creates different degrees of brand loyalty among consumers. The significance of the brand name on the total sales appeal is evident from the fact that several goods products have failed in the market solely due to wrong brand appeal.

In India, a brand receives such legal protection under the Trade and Merchandise Marks Act, 1958 after it fulfills the following conditions as laid down under Sections 11 and 12 of this Act:

1. It is not similar to any existing trade mark.
2. It is otherwise not entitled to protection in court.
3. It does not hurt the religious sentiments or feelings of any class or section of the citizens.
4. It does not comprise or contain scandalous or obscene matter.
5. It is not contrary to any law for the time being in force.
6. It is not likely to deceive or cause confusion.

When a brand mark is registered and legalised it becomes a trade mark. Thus registered brands are Trade Marks. In that sense all trade marks are brands but all brands are not trade marks. Trade marks is defined as a "brand or part of a brand that is given legal protection because it is capable of exclusive appropriation." – (Glossary of Marketing Terms – AMA). Thus, the trade mark is essentially a legal term protecting the manufacturer's right to use the brand name or trade mark.

BRAND CLASSIFICATION

Brands may be classified into the following three kinds:

(i) **Manufacturer's Brand.** A brand which is owned by a manufacturer and/or registered as a trade mark under the manufacturer's name is referred to as manufacturer's brand.

(ii) **Distributor's or Private Brand.** A brand which is owned by a distributor and/or registered under a distributor's name is referred to as a distributor's or private brand. It is private because the manufacturer is not identified or the product is not recognised because of him. The manufacturer simply manufactures the product and brands it as per specifications of the distributor.

(iii) **Mixed Brands.** A company may opt for both its own and its distributors' brands in respect of its products. It may sell some products in its own brand name and the rest may be sold to dealers under their own brand names.

Both manufacturer's and distributor's brands may be further divided on the basis of persons and region.

Products may carry an individual brand name for each product item as, for example, Hindustan Lever's Surf detergent power and Lux toilet soap or Government Soap Factory, Bangalore's point detergent powder. Products may also carry the family name of the manufacturer as for example, Tata's trucks, Modi's Continental truck Tyre or Mafetlal's Cotton Fabrics. The family name may blanket all products or there may be separate family names for different products.

Sometimes products may carry just the company's name or the company's name coupled with product's own generic name as, for example, Colgate Palmolive & Co's., Colgate Tooth Paste or Lakme Lipstick or Face Cream.

Geographical coverage of a product is still another way of classifying brands. A brand is referred to as a national brand when the product is to be identified throughout the country by only one brand. For example, Hindustan Lever's Dalda brand of Vanaspati ghee is a national brand. But when a product is identified by different brands in different regions of the country, these brands are referred to as regional brands.

ADVANTAGES AND LIMITATION OF BRANDING

It is obvious from the definition of brand that its major function is to create an identification of product so that it is easily recognised and distinguished from the competitive offerings. A brand endows a number of advantages and limitations on both consumers and marketers. Some of these are described here:

Consumers' Advantages and Limitations

Advantages

(a) It is easier to lodge complaints and claims against marketers when a branded product fails to live up to its proclaimed value satisfaction. Thus, it gives to consumers both trade and legal protection against unscrupulous trade practices.

(b) There is a considerable saving of time and energy in shopping for goods because a brand render product identification much easier. The money value of this saving is significant in the industrial buying.

(c) Certain brands provide status and prestige to consumers which endow them a somewhat conspicuous pyschological satisfaction otherwise not normally available.

(d) When a product is distinguishable by its brand, consumer has an assurance of quality and consistency in the product attributes being offered.

Limitations

(a) Popularity of brands render them out of the common man's reach because they command a premium price.

(b) Consumers are often confused in product selection on account of the plethora of brands offered in the market. The confusion is confounded when all the brands carry an assurance of similar value satisfaction.

(c) Brand loyalty helps save time and energy in product selection but it discourages the consumer from trying out other new brands which may possibly be more satisfying.

Marketer's Advantages and Limitations

Advantages

(a) Brand loyalty ensures repeat and replacement purchases and considerably helps the marketers in overcoming competitive pressure.

(b) Brand as a peripheral product attribute also has significant communication value. It assists advertising and sales promotion in building up demand for product (s).

(c) Brand builds up an unique reputation for its owner which facilitates new product introduction in terms of easy and immediate recognition and favourable consumer disposition.

(d) It discourages price competition because every product item has a distinctive image and is considered an exclusive offering. It ensures marketer's independence in pricing decisions.

(e) Brand reputation ensures some kind of market control in as much as it serves as an antidote to possible retailer hostility (when their margins are reduced).

Limitations

(a) Brand imposes responsibility for maintaining consistent quality and delivering proclaimed value satisfactions. In case of failures, marketer cannot escape identification owning to brand recognition.

(b) Some products by their very nature do not lend themselves to branding. For examples, nails, rivets, pins, fruits and vegetables (unless canned.)

(c) Building up brand recognition and loyalty are very expensive. Small business cannot afford it. Thus, it helps promote market monopolies.

BRAND STRATEGIES

A company may choose any one or a combination of the above referred to classes of brands and formulate its own brand strategy. Usually, the following strategy options are available to a company:

1. **Multi-brand Product Strategy.** It refers to the practice of offering more than one brand in a product category. For example, Hindustan Lever offers Lux and Pears in its toilet soap category and Bata Shoe Company offers Ambassador and Exclusive brands of shoes in men's wear category.

2. **Single-brand Product Strategy.** it refers to the use of a single brand name for all the products sold by a

company whether the brand name is that of a family, compnay or an individual. For example, the 'Erasmic' brand is put on shaving blades, shaving cream and after shave lotions manufactured by Hindustan Lever Ltd.

3. **Mixed Brand Strategy.** In this strategy, a manufacturer offers his products to consumers in his own as well as as distributor's brand names. For example, a manufacturer sells detergent washing powder both under its owns as well as its distributors' brands.

4. **Distributior's or Private Brand Strategy.** A manufacturer may opt to introduce his products under a distributor's brand name. For example, in the Indian cotton textile industry it is a common practice for dealers, usually whole-salers, to prescribe their own brand names while booking orders. Sahakari Bhandar (Super Bazar) of Bombay has been selling toilet soap, talcum powder, detergents, etc. under its own brand name Aparna.

5. **Trading-up and Trading-down Strategy.** When marketers known for marketing low-priced products introduce products with high price and presumably of higher quality, it is known as trading-up. Conversely, when marketers, introduce cheaper products than their original links, it is regarded as trading-down. When this kind of strategy is adopted has to be blended with adequate brand differentiation. Marketers, therefore, use different brands for products traded-up and traded-down so as not to alienate the current clientele.

METHODS OF DETERMINING BRAND

Some important methods of determining a brand are as follows:

(1) **On the Name of Manufacturer.** Some of the manufacturers use their own name as the brand for their products. Main reason for selecting the name of brand on the name of manufacturer is the goodwill and popularity of manufacturer. For example—all the products of Tata, Bata, Modi, Dalmia, Philips, Bajaj, Mafatlal, S. Kumar, J.K., etc., are named after the name of their manufacturers.

(2) **Special Name.** Some of the manufacturers select a special name for their products. For example—The scooters manufactured by Scooters (India) Limited are named as Vijay Super and the fans and Sewing Machines manufactured by Jai Engineering Works Limited are named as Usha.

(3) **Special Mark.** Some of the manufacturers do not give a name to their products. They select a mark for their products. For example—Rath Ghee, Khazoor Ghee, Do Tote mark Pan Masala, etc.

BRAND POLICIES AND STRATEGIES

Brand policies and strategies can be divided into three parts—*(A)* Brand Policies and Strategies adopted by Manufacturers, *(B)* Brand Policies and Strategies adopted by Middlemen, and *(C)* Other Brand Policies and Strategies. Details in this regard are given below:

(A) Brand Policies and Strategies Adopted by Manufacturers

It includes the following brand policies and strategies:

(1) Marketing Under the Own Brand of Manufacturer. Under this brand policy and strategy, a manufacturer sells all his products under the brand name of his own. There are various policies under this category and a manufacturer can select any of these policies. Main policies of this category are

as under – *(i)* Individual brand; *(ii)* Product line brand; *(iii)* Family brand; *(iv)* Local brand; *(v)* Provincial brand or State brand; *(vi)* Regional brand; *(vii)* National brand; *(viii)* International brand; *(ix)* Fighting brand, and *(x)* Competitive brand.

Main advantages of this brand policy and strategy are – *(i)* It increases the goodwill of manufacturer. *(ii)* It facilitates in the implementation of advertisement and sales promotion programmes of the enterprise. *(iii)* It helps in bringing stability in the prices of products of the enterprise. *(iv)* It helps in controlling the marketing activities of the enterprise. *(v)* It helps in adopting a suitable policy regarding product mix of the enterprise.

Main disadvantages of this brand policy and strategy is that middlemen do not find any existence of their own.

(2) Marketing under the Brand of Middlemen. Under this policy and strategy of brand, a manufacturer does not use any brand for his products. The manufacturer sells his products to the middlemen without any brand. Under this situation, the middlemen are free to use any brand for their products.

Main advantages of adopting this policy are – *(i)* The manufacturer has no need to concentrate upon the marketing of products. *(ii)* The manufacturer can invest his resources in the best possible manner to produce the best quality of the goods at most reasonable costs.

Disadvantages of this brand policy are – *(i)* The manufacturer has to depend upon the marketing policy and efficiency of middlemen. *(ii)* The middlemen may create unhealthy competition among the manufacturers because if they get products from any of these manufacturers at cheap rate, they stop to sell the products of earlier manufacturer, *(iii)* If the middlemen are not efficient enough or they do not take appropriate interest in marketing the products of an enterprise, the enterprise may have to face a very critical situation.

(B) Brand Policies and Strategies Adopted by Middlemen

It includes the following brand policies and strategies:

(1) Use of the Brand of Manufacturer Only. Under this brand policy and strategy, the middlemen sell all the products of a manufacturer under the brand name of the manufacturer. They do not use any independent brand name for the products.

Main advantages of this policy are: *(i)* Middlemen have not to make special efforts for selling the products. *(ii)* The middlemen get full advantage of the goodwill of manufacturer. *(iii)* It increases the sales of the middlemen.

Main disadvantages of this policy is that middlemen do not find any existence of their own.

(2) Joint Use of the Brand of Manufacturer and the Brand of Middlemen. As is evident from the heading, under this policy, the products of two brand names are marketed – the products of the brand of manufacturer and the products of the brand of middlemen.

Main advantages of this policy are – *(i)* Middlemen feel that they have their own existence. *(ii)* It increases the sales of the product very high because of the use of brands of both the manufacturer and middlemen. *(iii)* The middlemen get full advantage of goodwill of manufacturers and their own goodwill. *(iv)* The middlemen feel assured that they do not depend upon the manufacturers.

Main disadvantages of this policy is that this policy is not appreciated by the manufacturers because they feel that the middlemen will concentrate upon the sale of the products of their own brand and will not pay due attention towards the sales of their brand.

(C) Other Brand Policies and Strategies

Other brand policies and strategies may be as under:

(1) **Multiple Brand Policy.** Under this brand policy and strategy a business and industrial enterprise uses different brands for its different products.

(2) **Product Line Brand Policy.** Under this brand policy the enterprise uses a single brand for all the product items of a product line. Brands for all the product lines of the enterprise are different.

PACKAGING

While formulating packaging policies and strategies, it is important for marketers to develop a packaging concept around which these are to be formulated. A packaging concept is a description of product package and the functions it is supposed to perform in respect of that particular product. The conceptualisation of package involves determining package functions and developing an appropriate mix of these functions so as to attain product objective. For example, in case of Zodiac neckties and hand-kerchieves package visibility was defined as the basic packaging concept and therefore, rigid plastic package was developed.

Classification of Packaging

(1) **Family Packaging.** The products of a particular manufacturer when packed in an identical way is known as family packaging. The shape, colour, size etc. of packaging will be similar for all his products. Family brands are made meaningful by using family packaging, also. In such cases packaging methods, material used for packaging the appearance etc. will be one and the same for all the products of a manufacturer.

(2) **Re-use Packaging.** Packaging that could be used for some other purposes by the consumers after the packed goods have been consumed is known as re-use packaging.

This aspect increases the sales value of the product considerably.

(3) Multiple Packaging. It is the practice of placing several units in one container. This helps to introduce new products and increase the sales.

The various aspects of packaging are now treated as a mangement activity.

The following are the problems encountered in packaging:

(a) Cost of packaging

(b) Appearnace

(c) Kinds of designs

(d) Convenience

(e) Re-use purpose

Inspite of its various advantages, packaging has been subjected to criticism. One among them is that it adds cost. To some extent this complaint holds goods. It is true that packaging expenses definitely increase the price. But the benefits derived are sufficient to compensate the increase in cost. For example some medicines which we buy are to consumed at once. Their preservation is very important. Only a good package can render this service. So long as the product is capable of absorbing the packaging cost proportionately this criticism cannot be accepted.

In considering some of the more sophisticated uses of packaging the protective aspects of packaging should not be disregarded. Attention is therefore drawn to the following hazards against which packaging should provide a defence:

1. Insect Attack, *e.g.* months in clothing.

2. Mould, *e.g.* in canned foods, paints.

3. Flavour loss or change.

4. **Chemical change,** *e.g.* mental corrosion, coffee rancidity.

5. **Moisture Gain and Loss.** Many products have an optimum moisture content, *e.g.* cement, ceramic paints, frozen foods.

6. **Contamination by Dust or Dirt.** Clothing, food and fine machinery are obvious examples of products liable to damage in this way.

7. **Pilferage.** Loss through pilferage can be quite high-especially if there are many handling points.

8. **Product Loss.** Liquids and powders are highly susceptible to loss, *e.g.* powder leakage, liquid evaporation.

9. **Damage by Mechanical Handling.** Most damage occurs in the handling process and, the more frequently product are handled in the distribution process, the greater is the need for protection. One of the advantages of the liner rain and other container transport development is that they will result in less damage through handling. Damaged goods have to be replaced and are likely to cause loss and inconvenience to seller and purchases. Often slightly damaged products may not be returned, but may inhibit repeat purchase.

GROWTH AND IMPORTANCE OF PACKAGING

The growth of self-service stores and the importance of gaining distribution, shelf space and display have made packaging decisions in the field of consumer goods a highly important area of decision in regard to product policy and planning. Even in the marketing of industrial goods packaging is taking on increasing significance and extending beyond the obvious necessity of providing for production, transportation and storage.

The demand for packaging has led to an enormous increase in the range of packaging equipment and materials available. There have been spectacular increase in the use flexible packaging involving special papers, plastics and aluminium foil. New printing methods have been developed, *e.g.* flexography, by which process it is possible relatively inexpensively to reproduce photographs or artwork in a wide range of colours on a wide range of materials.

Packaging design is influenced by the cultural, social and political environment. In the USA, for example, the house wife buys approximately 90% of her weekly purchases from supermarkets and self-service shops in one day. In the UK the percentage of food purchase from self-service outlets is much lower and there is still a great deal of daily shopping. In Latin countries pre-packed foods are rather slow in sales growth. Attitudes to colour differ; white is symbolic of mourning in many far Eastern countries as opposed to purple in Latin countries.

A package should be designed to perform many functions:

(i) Provide Protection. At any stage in the distribution process and ulimately in the home or factory of the user or consumer (*e.g.* against product damage, contamination, evaporation, chemical change, pilferage): For example, surface treatment of packaging avoids deterioration of appearance after transit and/or storage.

(ii) Offer Convenience. This covers handling, storage and opening of packages at all stages of distribution, and frequently in eventual use.

(a) Convenience of Storage in Warehouse, Shop and House. In designing the package there must be a

consideration of the economics of stocking large quantities of bulky, slow-moving low unit proit-margin products, and the difficulties of stacking certain carton shapes.

(b) Convenience in Use. There must be a consideration of the development of new materials and functional designs—acrosol containers, vacuum cans for vegetables, flip-top cigarette packets. New packaging ideas may lead to new products or product formulation, *e.g.* hair sprays, cheese spreads. Safety features should also be considered, as in the design of easy-opening cans eliminating the possibility of cuts and finger nail damage.

(iii) Reduce Transport Costs. This is achieved by the use of lightweight yet adequately strong materials, especially important when goods have to be transported by air.

(iv) Provide Opportunities for Re-use. The package may be deliberately designed so that it can be used for the storage of other items once the original product is consumed, *e.g.* plastic and aluminium containers. On the other hand, some packages are designed so that refills may be bought. The design may be so differentiated that only a refills of the same product can be used in the original container.

(v) Create a Favourable Product Image. The package has frequently to represent the product symbolically—to convey its buying advantages. The packaging "image" will be reinfored if there is a close tie-in with advertising and promotion.

(vi) Establish Product Differences. The package is often the major way in which narrowly differentiated products are distinguished. The difference may be in the art design, the shape or the materials used. A package can be used to convey an impression of quality differences. Gift packs are a good example of extending the range through packaging.

(vii) Establish Corporate Identity. Some companies aim at promoting individual products in their own right. Others deliberately aim at creating a company rather than product loyality, *e.g.* Heinz baby foods.

(viii) Gain Display at Retail Level. The package must be easy to arrange on shelves or racks and at the same time should attack the potential customer. Developments in print techniques. *e.g.* flexography, combined with newer packaging materials, *e.g.* poltingthylene film, have significance in this connection.

As an important peripheral attribute of product, a package has the following functions to perform:

I. Utilitarian Function. Package performs a utilitarian function by retaining and enhancing the product value of consumers in the following ways:

(a) Package protects products from deterioration, spilling, spoilage and evaporation during its transit from manufacturer to consumer.

(b) It enhances product use convenience by keeping it clean and undisturbed.

(c) It helps easy brand identification.

(d) It makes product handling easier and safe on the retail store shelves.

II. Profit Function. Package also performs a profit function in the following two ways:

(a) Consumers assigning relatively higher value to package are usually prepared to pay higher price for this product attribute. As a result, higher contribution to profit flows from package.

(b) Effective package cuts costs of handing and transportation and protects product from damage, thereby, saving a company from cuts in profits.

III. Communication Function. Package performs a commnication function by becoming an important adjunct to the components of the communication-mix, namely, advertising and sales promotion. It performs this function in the following ways:

1. It promotes product at the point of purchase and triggers impulse buying.
2. Package repeats the selling message imprinted on it before consumers when it is repeatedly handled during a series of uses. This encourages repeat and replacement purchases.
3. A change in product package design and message considerably facilitates implementation of product brand repositioning strategy of a company.
4. Package features communicate product message and motivate consumers product message and motive consumers to buy.
5. It makes product identification and differentiation both easy and effective. In a competitive market when differences in the tangible product attributes are not conspicuous, it is the package whose unique presentation makes products look different from the competing brands.

Packaging Policies and Strategies

Every producer adopts a certain policy and strategy. There may be different types of packaging policies and strategies and a producer has to select any one of these policies and strategies. Use of a particular policy depends upon the needs, requirements and circumstances of the producer. Some of the important packaging policies and strategies are as under:

(1) **Transit Packaging.** Every product has to be delivered to its real consumers. Delivery of a product from

producer to consumer is the process involving many activities. One of these activities is the transportation of product from the place of producer to the place of consumers. Product must be packed in the manner that it may reach to the consumers in its original condition. Such packing of product is called transit packaging. Thus, transit packaging is that from of packaging which is meant to keep a product safe in the process of physical distribution. It is also known as distribution packaging. The materials, generally used for transit packaging are the drums, wooden containers tins, sacks of jute or hard board etc. Main stress in this type of packaging is upon the safety of product.

(2) **Consumer Packaging.** The packaging in which a product is finally delivered to its consumers, is known as consumer packaging. Material used for consumer packaging may be—a bottle of glass, a bottle of plastic, a jar, a tin, a box of plastic, a box of hard board, a box of iron, polythene bags, etc. Main stress in consumer packaging is upon the attraction of packaging. Packaging must attract the attention of consumers and it may be convenient for consumers to handle.

(3) **Product Line Packaging or Family Packaging.** When a producer uses identical packagings for all the product items of a product line, it is called product line packaging or family packaging. This type of packaging is widely used by the producers of consumer goods and generally by the producers producing a large number of product items in a particular product line. The best example of family packaging is the packaging of shoes, Canvas Shoes, Chappals, Hawai Chappls mainly by the producers of a repute such as—Bata, Relaxo, BSC, CSC, Sona, Liberty, etc.

Main advantage of this type of packaging is easy identification of the products. It helps in getting the Brand loyalty of conumers.

(4) **Re-use Packaging.** The form of packaging in which the packages can be re-used after consuming the product, is called re-use packaging. For example—Containers of Ghee, Oil, Biscuits, Toffees, Sweets, Coffee, Medicines, etc. These packages are either of tin or plastic or glass or hard board etc. This type of packaging is very useful from the point of view of consumers because it makes the packaging easy and convenient to handle and empty packages can be re-used for some other purposes.

(5) **Multiple Packaging.** Multiple packaging is the packaging in which many products of different types are packed in a single packaging. This type of packaging is widely used by retailers because it saves their time, money and energy. Various products of different nature may be packed in a single package such as—readymade garments, towels, pen, pencils, rubber etc.

Packaging Decision

A decision taken in respect of packaging of a product, is known as packaging decision. When a producer wants to take a decision in respect of packaging of a product, he has four main points for considerations to take the decision. These considerations are as follows:

(1) **Package Design.** The very first decision taken by a producer in regard to packaging of a product, is to decide the design of packaging. Decision of design of packaging includes following five decisions: *(i)* Which type of material will be used for packaging? *(ii)* What will be the design of packaging? *(iii)* What colours will be used on packaging? *(iv)* What will be

the matter printed on packaging? *(v)* What will be the brand name and trade mark on packaging? In addition to the decision on above questions, the design of packaging is determined keeping in view the convenience of consumers and middlemen. The design of packaging must be such that it may facilitate the activities of storage, transportation, and distribution. Other factors affecting the decision of design of packaging are—nature of product, cost of packaging, size of packaging, legal restrictions, advertisement, etc.

(2) **Package Cost.** While taking any decision on packaging of a product, the cost of package plays an important role. The package must be selected only after considering the cost of package and its effect on the price of product.

(3) **Package Size.** Very important decision in respect of packaging is to decide the size of packaging. The size of packaging differs from product to product, producer to producer and time to time. In additicn to it, a single product is offered by a single producer to the consumers at a single time in different sizes of packaging. The size of package depends upon the nature of product and the quantity generally purchased by cosnumers. As different consumers buy a product in different sizes, it is advisable that the product must be packed in the packages of different sizes.

(4) **Package Test.** When a package is decided for a product, the efforts are made to test it so that it may be assured that the package will meet the requirements of consumers. There may be four types of test for this purpose:

(i) Technical Test. Technical test is the test carried out with the purpose of testing whether the

package design is proper or not for the safety of product?

(ii) *Middlemen Test.* This test is carried out with the purpose of testing the suitability of package from the point of view of middlemen.

(iii) *Consumer Test.* Consumer test of package aims at testing the package with a view whether it will be liked by the consumers or not?

(iv) *Appealing Test.* This test, tests the package whether it looks attrative or not? If a package is approved in all the four tests, it is finally decided and if a test fails at any stage, it is disapproved.

Product Labelling

Packages and their lables should give buyers accurate and up-to-date information as to the contents and necessary guidance regarding the use of the product. Packaging process completes only after giving the proper label to it. It means, the labelling is an integral part of the packaging. A label may be any thing – a piece of paper, printed statement, imprinted metal, leather – which is either a part of a package or attached to it.

Packaging, branding and labelling go together and constitute an integral part of product planning and development. Label give the proper information about the contents and use of the product. Labelling is also an important marketing decision for legal reason as well. For example, consumer interest in food labelling has increased as an aging and health-conscious population tries to toxic substances, fats and sodium. The Food & Drug Adminstration and the Consumer Product Safety Commission can require that certain products be labelled or marked with warnings, instructions, ingredients, certification and manufacturer's identification. Informed customers are essential for the efficient functioning of the free market economy. Labelling must recognise the consumer's right to be informed and so must incorporate the necessary information from the customer point of view.

Apart from the statutory information, the label should provide:

- Picture of the product
- Colour, size and appearance of the product
- Direction for use of the product
- Brand name
- Date of manufacturer and expiry date
- Name of manufacturer
- Statutory warning, if any

PURPOSES OF LABELLING

(i) A label describes the product specialities which make the product a quick-mover. Without label, it is very difficult to judge the contents inside the package.

(ii) It helps in avoiding the unwanted confusion among the competitive products availabe in the market. A small spelling mistake in case of drugs and chemicals may prove fatal to the users.

(iii) It gives sufficient information about the product to the user.

(iv) It is a strong sales total that encourages self-service operations.

PRODUCT LIFE CYCLE

The concept of product life cycle indicates that sooner or later all products die and that if management wishes to sustain its revenues, it must replace the declining products with the new ones. The product life cycle concept also indicates what can be expected in the market for a new product at various stages. Thus, the concept of product life cycle can be used as a forecasting tool. It can alter management that its new product will inevitably face saturation and decline, and the host of problems these stages pose. The product life cycle concept is also a useful framework for describing the typical evolution of marketing strategy over the product life cycle. This will help in taking sound marketing decisions at different stages of the product life cycle.

Like a human being, a product has also a certain length of life. Again, like a human being, a product has also to pass through certain identifiable stages in its life. As the life of a human being can be divided into six stages – Infant, Childhood, Youth, Adult, Old and Death, in the same manner life of a product can also be divided into six parts – *(1)* Introduction, *(2)* Growth, *(3)* Maturity, *(4)* Saturation, *(5)* Decline, and *(6)* Obsolescence. These six stages are collectively known as the Life-cycle of a product. The team Life-cycle of a product has been defined by many eminent authors. Some of the important definitions are as under:

> *Philip Kotler,* "The product life-cycle is a attempt to recognise distinct stages in the sales history of the product."

> *Arch Patton,* "The life-cycle of a product has many points of similarity with the human life-cycle; the product is born, grown lustily, attains dynamic maturity then enters its declining year."

> *Willian J. Stanton,* "From its birth to death, a product exists in different stages and in different competitive environment. Its adjustment to these environment determines to a great degree just successful its life will be.

Analytical study of the above definitions, indicates that different stages in the length of the life through which a product has to pass, are known as its life-cycle. The life of a product begins with its introduction into the market. Then the product enters into a period during which its market grows rapidly. After this, the product reaches maturity and then the stage of saturation comes. After the stage of saturation, the market of the product starts to decline and finally the life of product comes to an end.

It is important to note in this reference that the length of life-cycle differs from product to product. The Life-cycle of some products is very short such as fashionable ready-made garments. On the other band, some are the products whose life-cycle goes on upto a long period such as machine. It is also important to note that some of the products come out of the market even before passing through all the stages of their life-cycle in the same manner as some persons die in childhood or at young age.

VARIOUS STAGES OF THE LIFE-CYCLE OF A PRODUCT

A product passes through six different stages in its life-cycle. These stages can be explained with the help of following diagram:

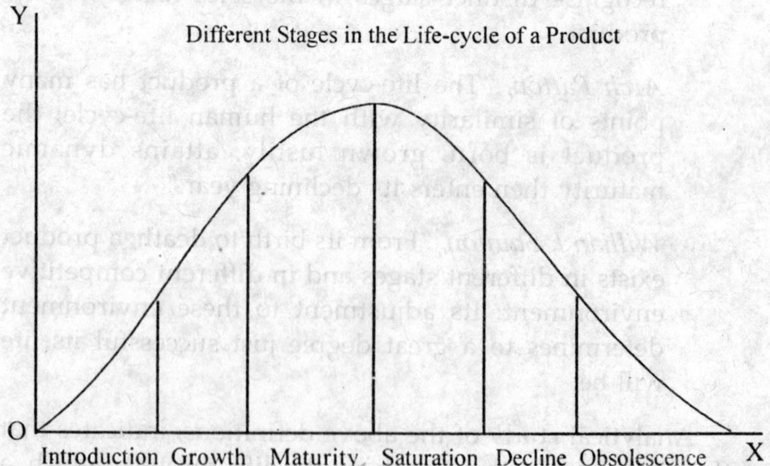

These stages of the life-cycle of a product can be explained as under:

(1) **Introduction.** This is the very first stage of the life-cycle of a product. At this stage, the product is introduced into the market. The product is made known to its potential consumers throught various programmes of advertisement. The quality, characteristics and utilities of the product are widely publicised in the market. At this stage, heavy expenditure is spent on the programmes of advertisement and sales promotion. As the consumers do not know about the uses of product, the sales of a product remains very low at this stage. As the product is introduced at very competitive price, the amount of profits remains very low or rather negligible at this stage. Some of the products fail to capture market at this very stage.

To get success at this stage of product, it becomes necessary that effective advertising and promotion programmes must be prepared and implemented so that uses and characteristics of the product may be convinced to the consumers. The system of physical distribution must also be very sound.

(2) **Growth.** This is the second stage of life-cycle of a product. Under this stage, the product gains priority and recognition among the consumers. Consumers like the brand of product and as a result of which the sales of the product increase very rapidly. Increase in sales result in the productions at large-scale and the promotion at large-scale brings many internal and external economies to the enterprise. Consequently, the cost of production comes down and the profits of the enterprise go up. Increase in profits attracts new competitors to enter into market.

In order to maintain the stage of growth for a long time, the marketer must concentrate upon programmes of advertisement and sales promotion. New and alternative uses of product must be widely communicated to the consumers. New market segments for the product must be discovered and the system of physical distribution must be made very sound. A close study of the reactions of the consumers must also be made so that necessary changes may be made in the product.

(3) **Maturity.** At this stage, a product captures significant place in the market. The customers like and prefer the product. Total volume of sales goes on increasing but the rate of increase in the volume of sales declines. The reason of such declines is the entrance of some new competitors into the market. At this stage, the expenditure of the enterprise on advertising and sales promotion increases so that the deamnd of product may be maintained. At the same time, the price of product should be reducted due to the increase in competition. Consequently, the rate of profits of the enterprise declines.

This stage of product is a challenge to the marketer which must be faced with strong determination and concrete efforts. The marketer must change his marketing strategies, policies and programmes keeping in view the changing circumstances of the market. He must have a close eye upon the policies and strategies of his competitors.

(4) **Saturation.** Saturation is the stage in the life-cycle of a product when total sales of the product are at the maximum possible level. The sales of the product become stagnant at this stage. This stage continues till substitutes of the product enter into the market. The production goes on increasing and the

competitors try to capture the market. The costs of advertisement and sales promotion increase and consequently the profits of the enterprise decrease.

At this stage of product, the marketer must try to develop new and alternative uses of the product. Necessary developments and modifications must also be introduced so that some new consumers may start to use it.

(5) **Decline.** Decline is the stage of a product when the sales of the product start to decline. Substitute products capture the market and the popularity of old product goes on declining. The consumers prefer substitute products. This is the stage when there is a great fall in the total sales of the product and profits of the enterprise become almost nil.

At this stage, the marketer must try to find out whether there is any possibility of selling his product or not. If he finds that the possibilities of selling his product are nil, he should decide to stop the production of the product and to divert the resources of the enterprise for the production of some new products. If he finds that the possibilities of selling his product are still alive, he must go ahead to explore such possibilities and necessary changes must be made in the product according to the tastes, habits and likings of consumers.

(6) **Obsolescence.** This is the stage of death for a product. The demand of the product is almost nil and there is no effect of advertisement and sales promotion measures of the enterprise on consumers. New substitutes capture the market and the old product is practically out of the market. This is the stage when the enterprise suffers a loss and the possibilities of creating any demand for the product are almost nil.

At this state, it is advisable that the marketer should stop the production of this product and think of starting the product of some new products.

IMPORTANCE OF PRODUCT LIFE CYCLE

The concept of product life cycle is very important from marketing point of view of a producer or a marketer. The main utilities of the concept are:

1. **Life of a Product is Limited.** According to the concept the life of a product is always limited. The product will die out over a period of time irrespective of the fact, that the product had made tremendous progress during the past. Knowing this fact, management always try to improve its existing product or to develop a new product.

2. **Estimation of Profits.** The quantum and rate of profits increases or decreases with the quantum of turnover. An introductory stage, profits are negligible, then they go up and after some time they begin to fall and gradually they move to nil. Thus, the management can well predict the firm's profits in different stages of the life-cycle of the product.

3. **Marketing Programme.** Different policies, procedures, and strategies are followed in the different stage of the life cycle of a product. So, management can prepare the marketing programmes accordingly and may get success.

FACTORS AFFECTING THE LIFE-CYCLE OF A PRODUCT

There are many factors affecting life-cycle of a product. The statement of Joel Dean is very important in this regard. He said, "The length of the product life-cycle is governed by the rate of technical change, the rate of market acceptance and the case of competitive entry." Some of the important factors affecting life-cycle of a product are discussed hereunder:

(1) **Rate of Technical Changes.** Life-cycle of a product depends upon the rate of technical changes taking place in the country. If technical changes take place in the country at a very high rate, the life-cycle of the products in that country will be very limited because new and improved products take place of the old products. On the other hand, if the rate of technical changes in a country is not so high, the life-cycle of the products in that country may be longer. For example, rate of technical changes in India is lower when compared with that of the other developed countries. As a result of it, the life-cycle of products in our country is higher than that of the developed countries.

(2) **Rate of Market Acceptance.** The length of life-cycle of products in a country depends upon the rate of market acceptance in the country also. If the customers of a country accepts a new product very fast, the life-cycle of products in such country will be very limited because the customers who have accepted a product so fast, can accept another product on next day and the product may stand out of the market. On the other hand, if the customers of a country accept a product gradually, the life-cycle of products in such country may be quite long. For example, the rate of market acceptance in our country is very low and therefore, the life-cycle of most of the products in out country is quite long.

(3) **Ease of Competitive Entry**. The success or failure of a product in the market depends to a large extent upon the situation of competition in the market. If the competitors can enter into a market very easily, the life-cycle of the product will be very short because

the competitors can make the products out. On the contrary, if the competitors cannot enter into a market so easily, the life-cycle of products in such market can be fairly long.

(4) **Risk Bearing Capacity.** The enterprises having more risk bearing capacity can keep their products standing in the market for a long period because they can face all the challenges of market effectively. On the other hand, the enterprises having less risk bearing capacity are unable in facing the challenges of the market, life-cycle of their products is curtailed to short.

(5) **Economic and Managerial Forces.** Economic and managerial forces of an enterprise also determine the success of the enterprise in the market to a great extent. If an enterprise enjoys sound economic and managerial forces, the life-cycle of the product of such enterprise can be longer than that of the products of an enterprise suffering from weak economic and managerial forces.

(6) **Protection by Patent.** If the patent of a product is get registered, the life-cycle of the product can be fairly long, and if the patent of a product is not get registered, the life-cycle of the product is cut short.

NEW PRODUCT DEVELOPMENT

Product planning and development is an important function of the marketing department of any concern following consumer orientation. It includes a number of decisions, namely, what to manufacture or buy, how to have its packaging, how to fix its price and how to sell it. In case of a manufacturing organisation, the production department, will develop and produce products on the advice of the marketing department because it is the marketing department which knows better the requirements of the customers. In case of a purely trading organisation, the purchase department will purchase these products as are suggested by the marketing department. The work of product planning and development will be performed by the marketing department itself.

Whatever may be the nature of operations of a concern, product planning and development is necessary for its survival and growth in the long-run. Every product has a life cycle and it becomes obsolete after the completion of its life cycle. Therefore, it is essential to develop new products and alter or improve the existing ones.

On the most common product planning problem relates to the addition of new products to the existing product line. Addition of new products involves generation of new product ideas, securing of various possibilities, economic analysis, product development, product testing, test marketing and developing markets. Another important problem of product planning is modification or elimination of existing products. The need for continuous modification of the product is great because society's needs are always changing, and different products must be forthcoming to fulfill them. All products have certain deficiencies for they are the result of a great many compromises. The perfect product has yet to be made. Research makes possible the reduction of these deficiencies resulting in improved products.

STAGES IN PRODUCT DEVELOPMENT

Product development does not just happen, it has to be planned. Dynamic firms plan their innovations for five to ten years in advance. They have a definite idea of exactly what product developments they want and what new product they will need to cater to the demands of their customers. Experience has proved that those firms which are most successful in developing marketable products are the ones which have formally recognised the function of planning product development. The function of planning and developing new products involves the following phases:

(i) **Generation of New Product Ideas.** The product planners must visualise new product ideas. Ideas may be contributed by professional designers, scientists, customers, sales force, dealers, competitors, etc. Ideas may also come from brain-storming sessions of management. It may be noted that the source of ideas is not so important as the firm's system for stimulating new ideas and then acknowledging them and reviewing them promptly.

(ii) **Detailed Study of New Product Ideas.** The ideas generated at the first sage are examined to eliminate those which have no potential or which are no capable of making any significant contribution to the marketing objectives. The ideas should be screened properly because any idea passing this stage would cost the firm both money and time.

Sources of New Product Ideas

Ideas for new products can come from any sources. *e.g.*:

(a) from research and development personnel;

(b) from markeing personnel;

(c) from associated companies in other countries;

(d) from customers;

(e) from outside technological or scientific discoveries;

(f) from employee suggestions;

(g) from brainstorming sessions of executives;

(h) from competitors;

(i) from knowledge or government needs;

(j) from individual executives;

(k) from a study of unused patents.

(iii) **Commercial Feasibility.** The product planners evaluate the 'extent and importance of identified markets' needs and appraise the exent to which present products fulfill them. They evaluate new ideas in the light of the company's capability with respect to scientific knowledge, technological skills and financial resources. Only the most feasible and profitable ideas are picked up for further detailed investigation. Marketing research is critical during this phase since it can reveal the changing behaviour of buyers, strategies of competitors and availability of new technological ideas.

(iv) **Product Development.** This phase relates to actual development of the new product based on the product data evaluation system. A programme is made for the proper development of the product. First of all precise description of the features of the proposed product should be studied. After this, selected consumers may be called upon to offer their comments on the proposed product. Decisions regarding branding, packaging, labelling, etc., are also made during this phase. When the product takes a tangible form, consumer test can be done. Consumer testing will provide the ground for final selection of the product for mass production and distribution.

(v) **Testing Market.** Test marketing is necessary to find out viability of marketing programme for large-scale distribution. Before the product is widely distributed, it is tried in a selected market. Customers' relation may be noted and product may be improved further, if necessary.

(vi) **Commercialisation.** After the test marketing gives green signal for the introduction of the product in the national market, the firm may proceed to finalise all features of the product. The marketing deaprtment will launch a full fledged production promotion campaign for mass distribution. Distribution channels will be chosen to make available the product wherever it is demanded. After this, the life cycle of the product will start.

Each of the above stages becomes progressively more expensive in terms of money and scarce manpower. But once the produce idea passes through these stages and careful analysis has been done at each stage, the chances of product failure will be reduced considerably.

SOURCES OF NEW PRODUCT IDEAS

The new product-development process starts with the search for ideas. The search should not be casual. Top management should define the products and markets to emphasize. It should state the new-product objective, whether it is high cash flow, market-share domination, or some other objective. It should state how much effort should be devoted to development breakthrough products, modifying existing products, and copying competitors' products

New product ideas can come from many sources customers, competitors, employees, channel members, and top management.

1. **The Marketing Concept holds that Customers'** needs and wants are the logical place to start in the search for new-product ideas. Hippel has shown that the highest percentage of ideas for new industrial products originate with customers. Technical companies can earn a great deal by studying a special set of their customers, the lead users, namely, those

customers who make the most advanced use of the company's product and who recognize needed improvements ahead of other customers. Companies can identify customers' needs and wants through customer surveys, projective tests, focused group discussion, and suggestion and complaint letters from customers. Many of the best ideas come from asking customers to describe their problems with current products.

2. **Companies Also Rely on their Scientists,** engineers, designers, and other employees for new-product ideas. Successful companies have established a company culture that encourages every employee to seek new ideas for improving the company's production, products, and services. Toyota claims that its employees submit two million ideas annually, about 35 suggestions per employee, and over 85% of them are implemented. Kodak and some American firms give monetary and recognition awards to their employees who submit the best ideas during the year.

3. **Companies can Find Good Ideas by Examining their Competitors'** products and services. They can learn from distributors, suppliers, and sales representatives what competitors are doing. They can find out what customers like and dislike in their competitors' new products. They can buy their competitors' products, take them apart, and build better ones. Their competitive strategy is one of product imitation and improvement rather than product innovation. The Japanese are masters of this strategy, in that they have licensed or copied many Western products and found ways to improve them.

4. **Company Sales Representatives and Middlemen are a Particularly Good Sources of New-product Ideas.** They have first hand exposure to customers' needs and complaints. They often learn first of competitive developments. An increasing number of companies train and reward their sales representatives, distributors, and dealers for finding new ideas. For example: Bill Keefer, chairman of Warner Electric Brake and Clutch requires his salesforce to list on each monthly call report the three best product ideas they heard on customer visits. He reads these ideas each month and pens notes to his engineers, manufacturing executives, and so on, to follow up the better ideas.
5. **Top Management can be Another Major Source of New Product Ideas.** Some company leaders, like Edwin H.Lard former CEO of Polaroid, take personal responsibility for technogical innovation in their companies. This is not always constructive, as when a top executive pushes through a pet idea without throughly researching market size or interest. When Land pushed forward his Polavision project (instantly developed movies), it ended as a major product failure, because the market became more interested in video-tapes as a way to film action.

IDEA-GENERATING TECHNIQUES

Really good ideas come out of inspiration, perspiration, and techniques. A number of "creativity" techniques can help individuals and groups generate better ideas.

1. **Attribute Listing.** This technique calls for listing the major attributes of an existing product and then modifying each attribute in the search for an improved product. Consider a screwdriver. Its attributes : a round, steel shank, a wooden handle,

manually operated and torque provided by twisting action. Now a group considers ways to improve product performance or appeal. The round shank could be made hexagonal so that a wrench could be applied to increase the torque; eletric power could replace manual power; the torque could be produced by pushing.

2. **Morphological Analysis.** This method calls for identifying the structural dimensions of a problem and examining the relationships among them. Suppose the problem is that of "getting something from one place to another via a powered vehicle."

3. **Forced Relationship.** Here several objects are considered in relation to each other. An office-equipment manufacturer wanted to design a new desk for executives. Several objects were listed a desk, television set, clock, computer, copying machine, bookcase, and so on. The result was a fully electronic desk with a console resembling that found in an airplane cockpit.

4. **Synectics.** William J.J. Gordon felt that Osborn's brainstorming session produced solutions too quickly, before a sufficient number of perspectives had been developed. Gordon decided to define the problem so broadly that the group would have no inkling of the specific problem.

5. **Need/Problem Identification.** The preceding creatively techniques do not require consumer input to generate ideas. Nee/problem identification, on the other hand, starts with consumers. Consumers are asked about needs, problems, and ideas. For example, they can be asked about their problems in using a particular product of product category.

6. **Brainstorming**. Group creativity can be stimulated through brainstorming techniques developed by Alex Osborn. The usual brainstorming group consists of six to ten people. The problem should be specific. The sessions should last about an hour. The chairman starts with, "Remember, we want as many ideas as possible—the wilder the better—and remember, no evaluation." The ideas start flowing, one idea sparks another, and within an hour over a hundred or more new ideas may find their way into the type recorder. For the conference to be maximally effective.

PRODUCT MARKET STRATEGIES

A major product strategy input relates to the degree, if any, of change in the basic characteristics of the product that may seem desirable at a particular time. These alternatives range from no change to an entirely new product, and the impact of each depends upon the degree of other marketing change taking place at the same time. It shows nine different combinations of the product market strategies that a company might consider using to improve its profitability. Notice that each product strategy is associated with some market strategy and that each has important implications for the other:

1. **No Product Change—No Market Change**. This is the least complex product-market strategy. There are two main versions : simplifying the product's design and altering the amount of integration in the product's manufacturing materials instead of buying them. Both seek to improve profitability mainly through cost reduction, and both involve selling essentially the same product to the same market.

2. **No Product Change—Improved Market**. This strategy aims to improve the product's market and profitability by increasing sales to present markets.

This process of remerchandising, in other words, leaes basic features of the physical product unchanged but changes the accompanying services.

3. **No Product Change—New Market.** This product-market strategy is especially significant for companies with products already in, or about to enter, the market maturity stage of the life cycle. During this stage, industry sales tend to reach a plateau and then gradually fall off. But some companies explore the possibility of rejuvenating the product's sales and profit growth rates through finding new markets. In searching for new market segments for a product approaching saturation in its present market, management should consider both possible new users and new uses.

4. **Product Change—No Market Change.** The three versions of this strategy are product line simplification and product discontinuance, new models (really new or improved products), and planned obsolescene (designing a new modification that makes the consumer want to replace the old model, such as an annual model change). Strategies involving product line simplification and product discontinuance envision profit increases through cost reductions. Those involving either new models or planned obsolescence seek profit increases through growth in sales volume.

5. **Produt Change—Improved Market.** The two main types of the strategy are product customization (tailoring product specifications very closely to buyer needs), and product systems (combining a series of separated operations into a system as in the automatic washing machine). Both aim to improve profitability through increasing sales volume.

6. **Product Change—New Market.** This strategy seeks increased profitability through additional sales volume generated by changing certain features of the product and selling it to a new market segment, so companies often must change certain product features to match them better with the individualized needs of new target market segments. Trading up and trading down are the main forms of this strategy.

7. **New Product—Improved Market.** This strategy aims to increase profitability through adding sales volume gained from new products sold to the same market segments. Often the new products are extensions of the present product line, for example, the ready-to-eat cereal added to a line of regular cereals or the addition of new flavours to an old product line, as was done by Ovaltine. Sometimes the new product are members of related product lines sold to the same market segments as present products, for example, the pet food added by a marketer of breakfast cereals.

8. **New Product—No Market Change.** This strategy seeks increased profitability through selling a new product to the same market segment, the new product replacing an older product sold for the same general purpose. Thus, product replacement strategy aims at retaining the level of sales now coming from a particular market segment where an older product's sales are being endangered by competitor's new products serving the same uses. Examples of new products that replaced old ones are numerous. A few of them are automobiles, which replaced carriages, diesel carriages, diesel locomotives, which replaced steam locomotives, jet planes, which replaced piston-driven aircraft, the transistor, which replaced the vacuum tube, and the

ballpoint pen, which largely replaced the fountain pen. For companies having products in the market maturity stage, new products should be waiting in the wings, ready for market introduction at the proper time.

9. **New Product – New Market.** This strategy to increase profitability through greater sales volumes obtained from selling new products in new markets. Thus, it involves product mix diversification – selling unrelated product lines to entirely different markets. Companies adopt this strategy for reasons such as an unexpected research breakthrough or discoveries of profitable opportunities to develop products for new markets.

VARIOUS STEPS TAKEN IN PRODUCT DEVELOPMENT PROCESS

The experience of many firms shows that the process of developing a new product contains of six steps that can be fairly well described as follows:

(1) **Exploration.** This is the search stage in which ideas for new products are sought. In this stage of product development, careful attention is paid to developing products that meet company objective. The explanation for a new product may be done through *(a)* consumer's requests, *(b)* letters to produces, *(c)* competitive products, *(d)* market research, *(e)* capacities of plant *(f)* policies of state and *(g)* objectives of customers etc.

(2) **Screening.** Screening cosists of a preliminary evaluation to determine whether the ideas has possibilities and should be further pursued, or should be dropped. In this phase, questions such as the following should be asked about product:

(a) What is the approximate market for new product?

(b) Can this product be sold by the existing sales forces, agents or dealers?

(c) Are any serious difficulties foreseen in producing?

(d) Are there any important patterns, licensing agreements, or other legal restrictions which affect the manufacture of product?

(e) Will there be any serious difficulty in obtaining raw material etc.

(f) How much money will be needed for the production and distribution of this item?

(g) Can financing be obtained and at a reasonable cost?

(h) What is the estimated cost of production, selling price, and gross margin?

(3) **Specification.** If the proposed product passes the screening test, it is expanded into a realistic recommendation. In this step, a more through analysis is made of the marketability of the product, the features that consumers may desire, and competitor's probable actions. Finally a scheduled and budged are established for prototypes or models.

(4) **Development.** This step consists of transforming an idea for a product, into an actuality. Prototypes of the new product are built so that they can be shown and demonstrated.

(5) **Testing.** This is a critical stage where the worth of the original product idea and the judgement about its feasibility are proved or disproved. Sample

product are market tested, and user reactions are analyzed. When a final agreement is reached on the exact specifications for the product, the design is "forzen", that is no additional design changes are made. The product is then ready to be produced.

(6) **Commercialisation.** This is the final step in the series and is the one with which we are most familiar. Commercialization consists of all the actions involved in fullscale production of the product, advertising and selling the product, and pledging that the company with its resources will stand behind and guarantee the new product.

FACTORS RESPONSIBLE FOR THE FAILURE OF A NEW PRODUCT

The development of a new product is always not successful. There may be following reasons responsible for the failure of product:

(i) **Weakness in Distribution.** The distribution of the product is one of the major marketing problems. It is this marketing function, which enables the product to reach the proper markets at proper time and at a proper price. Distribution management is considered to be one of the important ones where management decisions requires farsightedness and vision.

(ii) **Insufficient Marketing Effort.** It is wrong to assume that a manufacturer just ends his efforts the moment a product is ready for sale. Advertising and proper promotional activities also form a part of his job to make the product known to consumers. Proper selection of the channels of distribution and the methods of physical distribution also help in proper and efficient marketing of products.

(iii) **Inadequate Sales Force.** Selling is done by personal or impersonal methods. Impersonal methods include advertisement and similar promotional activities. Personal methods, on the other hand, are more intimate and more efficient promotional activities should be backed by adequate sales forces to introduce the product properly in the market. If salesmen are not trained or do not possess salesmen qualities, the product will not succeed.

(iv) **Competition.** Severe competition leads products to struggle hard in the market. There are various methods to overcome severe competitions including price cuts (mark down prices) and various kinds of discounts etc. Consumer products are most affected by severe competition. However, it should be noted that it is not the low prices alone that will help a product to compete and succeed in the market. Basically offering high quality products excelling the existing ones is the basic determinant in deciding the success of a product in the market. There is a wide spread recognition that it is ultimately the quality of a product which will enable the product to withstand competition.

(v) **Poor Timing.** The fundamental principle to be followed in product planning is to find out the exact time at which the product is to be introduced in the market. Usually when and how are the two questions a manufacturer is often finding difficult to answer. A close analysis of the market conditions and consumer behaviour and attitudes is essential to find an answer to the two problems.

(vi) **Higher Costs.** Higher final costs than anticipated at the time of product planning is another reason for product failure. It might be partly due to wrong pricing policies adopted by the firm. The cost estimates also often go wrong when the products are finally introduced into the market.

(vii) **Product Defect.** This arises out of technical flaws in the process of production. This is a fundamental reason for product failure. Low quality of products, poor design or packing may lead to product failure. This can be done away by the proper product testing.

(viii) **Indequate Market Analysis.** Biased information or improper analysis of the market will yield only wrong data. Acting on such data leads to product failure.

All these problems could be solved by the timely action of the management. Blain Cooke opines that today three products or more of new products fail. According to him, "the new products which fail are not in literal marketing sense products at all – they are merely interesting but worthless artifacts of the product process".

CONSUMER ADOPTION PROCESS

Once a product is introduced in the market, the major challenge rests with the marketing function. The product so introduced is to be 'adopted' *i.e.,* purchased and diffused *i.e.,* percolated through out the markets. Any new idea or brand catches on through a gradual process which starts with some adopting it easily and other doing so only after the so-called 'opinion' leaders' have satisfied themselves and set and example. The faster it happens the better it is for the firm. Addition is the decision of an individual to use the product; while diffusion is the collective spread of individual adoption decisions the rough out a market. Thus, adoption process is concerned with the individual whereas the diffusion process is concerned with the aggregate behavior.

The fundamental reason for studying the diffusion and adoption process is the increase in the level of understanding of how? when? and why? new products are accepted or rejected. Naturally a more comprehensive understanding of this rocess will enhance the success of future new product introductions.

Stages in Consumer Adoption Process

The adoption process is belived to follow a five stage sequential process beginning with actual awareness of a product's existence and ending with adoption or comitment to the product. From the point in time when an individual first hears of an innovation to the point in time when adoption occurs has been recognised as consisting of five logical stage names awareness – interest – evaluation – trial and adoption.

1. **Awareness Stage.** Here the individual is exposed to the innovation but lacks complete information about it. That is, the individual is aware of the innovation but is not yet motivated to seek further information. He knows of product existence.

2. **Interest Stage.** The individual becomes interested in the new idea and seeks additional information about it. The innovation is favoured in a general way but is not yet judged in terms of its utility to a specific situation. He seeks further information.

3. **Evaluation Stage.** The individual applies his mental faculty to the innovation to compare present and anticipated situation and then decides to whether or not try it. It is to do with careful weighing as to whether or not to try it.

4. **Trial Stage.** The individual uses the innovation on a small-scale in order to determine its utility in his own situation. That is, he tries it once or twice to confirm its utility.

5. **Adoption Stage.** The individual decides to continue the full use of the innovation. That is the purchases and repurchases.

It is worth emphasizing here that any innovation may be rejected at any stage of adoption process. Even rejection can take place after adoption which is called as discontinuance. Further, a consumer may move through several of these stages simultaneously as it happens in case of impulse buying.

However, understanding of the sequence of these stages of adoption and types of communication most effective in each stage will enable the firm to develop a promotional campaign consistent with behaviour of consumer particularly in case of a firm attempting to market a new product, Initially more mass media should be employed to relay product awareness and information on product utility. As time assess, the appeal should be moulder to include more personal appeal, as consumer is keen on evaluating, trying and adopting the new product. The strategy employed, of course, must give some consideration to the nature of the new product. The new product characteristics affect the adoption process. Factors such as the relative advantage, compatability, complexity, divisibility and communicability, normally determine the ease with which consumers accept a new product.

Adopter Categories

Companies are finally interested in the level and rate of diffusion because, the ultimate level of diffusion is a limit on the total sales of the company, while the rate of diffusion affects how quickly the company covers its costs and begins to make a profit. The notion of diffusion suggests that some people adopt a new product well before others. That is, people vary in they degree of innovativeness. One means of classifying people according to their innvativeness is based on the normal distribution curve as developed by Mr. E Rogers and Mr. Shoemaker in 1971. Using the mean and standard deviations, it is possible to categories the adopters into five main classes as given in the figure on next page. These are; innovators—early adoptors— early majority—late majority and laggards.

1. **Innovators.** These represent the first 2.5 per cent of the total adoptors. They are young risk runners, better educated, more cosmopolitan, but less integrated with local groups. They are the forerunners and important to the victory of new product so introduced.

2. **Early Adoptors.** These represent the next 13.5 per cent of the total adoptors. These adopt in the per groups act as taste-makers or opinion leaders in their local group. These are wealthier and better educated and have greater technical knowledge of the innovation. As they are integrated with the community they exert influence. Others turn to them for their advice the moment they come in contact with these persons.

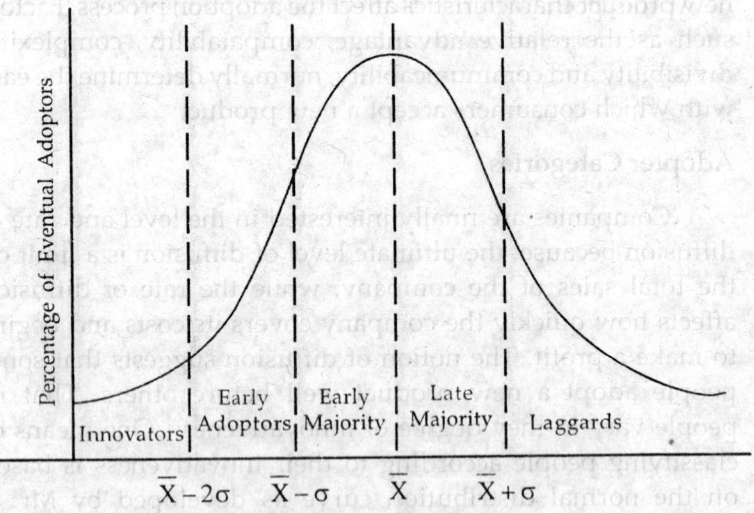

Fig. Consumer adoptor categories

3. **Early Majority.** This group accounts for the next 34 per cent of the total adoptors. These are average people in terms of income, education, age and occupations. These tend to be more cautious before adopting normally waiting until its benefit and other features have been clearly demonstrated well before adoption.

4. **Late Majority.** This group represents the next 34 per cent of the total adoptors. These are more conservative, less educated and older with limited purchasing power. The reason for their adoption is that majority of the people have adopted or the product is within their purchasing power now.

5. **Laggards.** This last chunk accounts for remaining 16 per cent of the total adoptors. This group considers adopting as the last resort as there is no alternative. The features of this group are not available because, very less is known about this group.

At this point of discussion it is worth emphasizing that these five categories are 'ideal types'. It may be difficult to identify individuals with these exact specifications in actual practice.

❑

10

Secrets of Sales Performance

In the channel of communication and information between the marketplace and upper management, field sales managers are the first and closest representative of management. In that capacity, they first screen and evaluate information and alert upper management to what they perceive as useful and important. They then transmit and implement company policy and procedure downward to the sales force. These same field managers are expected to make certain decisions and solve local problems, thereby relieving upper management from implementation issues associated with tactical-level problem solving. With sales districts treated as profit centres, sales managers become directly concerned with generating sales and profits for the firm. Their success or lack of it directly affects the income statement and balance sheet of their firm. They are the point of the sword implementing firm strategy and tactics in the day-to-day contact with customers and competitors. Moreover, how they manage the reps in implementing policy and strategy will seriously affect not only the current but the future success of the firm in the marketplace.

Surveys of top executives consistently conclude that sales and marketing experience is essential for securing a trip to the executive suite, although not necessarily to the CEO chair. Why has sales and marketing experience proved so important in many firms?

The sales rep to manager to middle and upper management progression of an individual performs a number of important functions for the firm. Typically, when a person is hired as a sales rep he or she eventually receives some territorial assignment. Successful reps who exhibit managerial skills may then be promoted into a management position. In many firms these managers are provided so much latitude that they in effect become president of a small company, with revenue, cost, and personnel responsibilities. This accountability enables a manager to demonstrate any executive talent, or lack of it, in running that small business. If field sales managers are successful, they may be promoted into upper sales management, where they will have extended revenue, cost, personnel, and asset-management responsibility. The natural promotion process with gradual enlargement of the person's responsibilities is partly a test of executive talent. Thus the sales districts become a proving ground where the firm can identify and test the competency of potential middle and upper-management executives.

The position of sales manager in one firm may require a different emphasis on job related responsibilities than a job with the same title but in a different firm, even in the same industry. One expert suggests that 80 per cent of a sales manager's field time should be spent with the top one-third of the sales force. Also indicates that there are a number of activities that often complement and support that mission. Thus each area of responsibility can be broken down into even more detailed activities.

Manager of the Sales Force

The field sales manager, must perform the same managerial functions of planning, organizing, leading, and controlling as any other manager. The proper execution of these functions results in higher performance levels for both the manager and the reps in the sales force. Since managers are usually evaluated on the basis of how well their district performs, a manager's success, for the most part, depends on the success of the reps. Correspondingly, the reps depend on the manager to help and support them in their territories as well as represent their interests to upper management. For other sales managers and reps to be successful, they must operate as a team. The sales manager-sales rep relationship is probably the clearest organizational example of shared responsibility for success or failure.

Administrative

Field sales managers have reported that they spend on average about 24 per cent of their time on administrative tasks. For many managers those tasks include managing a field office. The field office will certainly include clerical help and may, in a large field office, include a varietyof other areas ranging from computer systems management to traffic and warehousing. Administrative responsibilities force the manager to attend to such duties as record keeping, report writing, and administrative supervision of staff people. These duties are important. For example, staff people are usually critical to the success of a field office and the sales force they support. Their morale and sense of identification with the reps in the field and their customers can be the difference between a successful and a not-so-successful sales district.

The daily operation of the sale force also generates administrative activities in the form of reports, sales rep evaluations, customer problem definitions and resolutions, and a host of other bureaucratic and functional duties. Completing these routin matters promptly and efficiently contributes to the smooth and successful operation of a district.

The manager's marketing responsibilities and activities also depend on the company and the industry. In consumer products firms selling package goods, such as Campbell Soup, Ralston Purina, and Kellogg, the manager and the rep develop extensive marketing campaigns for their customers. In other situations the manager's marketing duties are limited to information collection and sales forecasting.

In many firms the sales force is perceived both as a spontaneous source of information and as a way to collect information. Although numerous studies have clearly indicated that sales reps are neither proficient nor interested in these tasks, sales managers must see to it that they are carried out.

In many companies sales managers also have some forecasting responsibility, particularly as part of the marketing planning and budgeting process. The level of sophistication expected of the sales manager depends on the circumstances. If the manager's estimates are used to confirm research forecasts or as general guidelines for marketing policy, then constructing a forecast at the sales manager level would probably require only the mahager's "best estimates" of future sales and costs. If, ho,wever, very specific decisions such as production scheduling, quota setting or, inventory management are at stake, then very precise, numerical forecasts would be expected. In this case the manager would probably develop the necessary sales, market share and cost-oriented forecasts using experiential as well as statistically based forecasting techniques augmented by microcomputer forecasting packages.

Personal Selling

Field sales managers in some firms and industries often retain some personal selling responsibilities. There are several reasons for this. First, if commissions are a large part of a rep's income, retaining certain protected "house accounts" for a manager may be the only way to encourage reps to accept promotion to sales manager. Having personal accounts may also benefit management in that the sales manager will have direct communication with customers. Furthermore, it is not unusual for large customers to "insist" that they be temporarily or permanently serviced by a member of management. Managers report that on average they allocate 17 per cent of their time to face-to-face selling and 12 per cent to phone-selling activities.

Financial

Each sales rep represents thousands of dollars in investment in training and customer relations. Each rep also represents annual costs in salary, benefits, and other support costs that must be managed. The resulting profit center can represent a sizable proportion of the company's annual performance. Moreover, many managers are held directly responsible for the size and turnover of company inventory in their districts. Other companies may require a manager to monitor the size and distribution of accounts receivable in their district.

The sales manager may also be asked to perform specific financial activities such as sales forecasting and analysis, customer financial analysis, forecasting, and control of cost data. Many sales managers have direct budget responsibilities including travel and entertainment cost tracking. Less frequently, depending on the industry and company, sales managers may be required to make decisions or provide input on corporate capital expenditures in their districts.

Relationships

The sales manager exists as a position and as a person within an organizational structure. Sales manager has specific formal authority and responsibility boundaries that are defined in superior-subordinate patterns. There are also informal structures that follow patterns of communication. Thus as a person the sales manager maintains a communication network that extends weblike inside as well as outside the firm.

External Relationships

A sales manager will develop and maintain business relationships that extend beyond the formal organizational structure. These area normal part of the job and may involve almost any number of temporary and/or permanent relationships with individuals and organizations external to the firm. These relationships may be grouped into five categories:

1. Suppliers such as trucking firms, placement services at colleges and universities, and equipment vendors.

2. Customers who distribute and/or consume the company's products. For the most part this relationship is maintained as a part of the sales rep's call pattern.

3. Professional organizations such as The Sales and Marketing Executives provide membership, education, and contacts with fellow sales managers.

4. Competitors are otten well known to one another. Ethically and legally managers must be cautious about these relationships. Companies are increasingly concerned about any competitive contacts even at relatively "low" levels in the organization.

5. General business community organizations provide the sales manager with contacts and company representation for businesspeople at all levels of the local community.

Although the final two sets of relationships are voluntary, many firms actively encourage their managers to participate in them.

Knowing and understanding these relationships enables the sales manager to solve many problems that could not be solved by going through routine organizational channels. One sales manager with a large industrial equipment firm described the process he had to go through to solve one of his problems.

The change from sales rep to sales manager usually involves more than just a change in title and a broadening of responsibility. Five important categories of differences between selling and managing can be identified: primary responsibility, working relationships, role, company administrative responsibility, and managerial perspective.

Primary Responsibility

The rep's primary responsibility is to develop accounts and increase sales in these territory. The sales rep's perspective is limited to his or her territory and the products sold. He or she is not responsible for other people except for the development of long term customer relations. Managers also must make the numbers, but they have additional longer-range responsibilities such as developing their sales people into better reps and managers.

Company Administrative Responsibility

Although the rep is responsible solely for a territory, the manager is part of management and must be concerned with other levels in the organization. The sales rep focuses solely on accounts and tries to build account loyalty, while the manager tries to build company loyalty.

Managerial Perspective

The sales rep's activities are geared toward a single selling-related goal. The rep must be impatient to achieve goals and never give up trying to sell an account. The sales rep may, at times, be able to successfully bend some of the rules in order to achieve sales goals. The scope of the manager's goals and activities is much broader, covering multiple territories and company-level issues. A manager must be concerned with what is best for the company. What is the payoff next year as well as this year? Sales managers must learn to recognize when the efforts invested in a person or a project are not worth the payoff. Finally, because the manager is a direct agent of the company, he or she must adhere more closely to management rules and guidelines.

The move to the sales manager position by a rep requires a substantial change in perspective. Moreover, the promotion often requires a geographic move that may impose additional personal and professional strain. The successful move from selling to managing truly requires an exceptional change in role and perspective on the part of the new manager.

The process of sales manager selection may be divided into three stages: determining the relevant promotion criteria, identifying possible candidates and measuring them against those criteria, and consulting with executives who normally participate in the selection process.

Determining Promotion Criteria

A field sales manager is a first-line supervisor. Some general qualities define the characteristics a successful first-line. supervisor should possess: a desire to be a manager, intelligence, analytical ability, the ability to communicate, and integrity. Even though there have been very few analytical studies that have attempted to identify the characteristics of the best field sales managers, two approaches may be used. The first focuses on identifying traits and behaviours of ideal managers, while the second employs a broader "profile" approach.

Traits and Behaviour. The management literature consistently suggests that because leadership is the difference between effective and ineffective management, the ability to lead should be one of the criteria used to select managers. In spite of this admonition, some 200 senior sales executives who ranked the importance for forty four promotion criteria used in their companies to select field sales managers did not identify traditional leadership traits as either number one or two in importance. Rather, they reflected sales rep performance behaviours and other behaviours, such as persistence, or personal characteristics, such as creativity. As Table indicates, it is not until the third factor, ideal manager traits, that leader/manager dimensions are considered important.

The universal application of the first two criteria to select a manager will produce a good managerial choice only if the person's performance as a sales rep is significantly related to the person's performance as a manager. If, however, extraordinary sales success as a sales rep is not a good predictor of managerial success, then using sales related promotion criteria will hinder selection of the best managers. In a related study, these same researchers found that there was almost no differenece between small and large companies in their use of these promotion criteria.

Using Profiles. Some experts in sales management suggest that the best way to select a top-quality field sales manager is to take a two-step approach. The first step is to group sales reps into one of the four personality classes listed in Table. The second step is to select a manager only from those sales reps in groups 1-3. It is their contention that sales reps from group 1 will need very little training those from groups 2 and 3 will need very specialized and individual training programmes and those from group 4 should rarely if ever be selected for promotion to management.

Promotion to Sales Manager

Factor	*Name*	*Description*
	1	*2*
1	Sales performance	Sales volume, net profit, percent of quota achieved
2	Sales rep traits	Creativity, judgment persuasiveness, persistence
3	Ideal manager traits	Integrity, dependability, intelligence
4	Biographical	Marital state, physical appearance, parents' occupations

	1	*2*
5	Political power	Worked with successful manager, length of service, mentor
6	Managerial orientation	Time management ability, regard for authority and company policy, desire to be promoted
7	Education	College degree, advanced degree
8	Other	Home life, civic mindedness, willingness to relocate

Identifying Managerial Candidates

As much as possible, the firm's formal promotion criteria should be well known to the sales force. Thus when a position is available the candidate pool is more easily identifiable. Many firms, however do not have a promotion-from-within policy and will select a field sales manager from outside the firm. A common reason offered by executives for doing this is that the current salespeople do not have the qualifications necessary to become good managers.

Larger companies and companies with developed product lines can build and maintain a formal process of identification and preparation of current sales force members. for a managerial position. For example, one research study found that larger, better-performing corporations were more likely to promote from within, while lower technology firms and those firms with less policy standardization had a lower incidence of insider promotion.

Four Basic Types if Salespeople

Type	*Characteristics*
1. Consultative	Career-oriented Academically inclined Self-confident Thinks independently Image and status conscious Patient Not impulsive Team-oriented
2. Relationship	Strong work ethic Independent Patient Self-sufficient Cooperative Conservative values Strong and rigid value system
3. Closing	Extroverted Optimistic Highly competitive Positive thinker High energy Strongly developed work ethic Self-confident Conveys enthusiasm when "on"
4. Display	Low career aspirations Enjoys company of others Impulsive Loses interest easily High energy Work tends to revolve around home life or other outside activities

The promotion directly from rep to manager can entail substantial strain. To ease the strain and maximize learning and effectiveness, some organizations first promote the new manager into a small district and then" into larger districts as he or she exhibits success and "promotability." The strain of the transition can also be reduced by sending the new manager to training sessions that prepare him or her for the promotion. For example, larger organizations such as Xerox, IBM, and Procter & Gamble promote reps into assistant manager positions. Georgia-Pacific, for example, has an assistant branch manager position in its organization. It identifies sales reps with management potential and assigns them to work with its best current managers. At Gillette a person may spend up to two years as assistant district manager before getting a promotion to district manager.

Other firms prefer to promote reps into staff positions such as sales training manager before appointing them to a manager position. Where the selling activities and selling success do not provide sufficient preparation for a managerial position, assignments to staff positions can provide the person with the opportunity to develop those necessary skills.

Payoffs and Problems

Sales supervisors reported salaries in 1989 of approximately $62,000. This represents an increase in base salary of some 12 per cent over the past three years, with future increases pegged at 9 per cent plus an increasing amount of incentive pay." These salary figures do not reflect bonuses and commissions and are averages computed across a wide variety of firms and industries.

Promotion to sales manager is not necessarily a fairy tale in which everyone lives happily ever after. Sales managers can experience substantial-job-related tension that reduces job satisfaction. Moreover, this tension has been found to negatively affect satisfaction with the manager's supervisors and customers as well as with company policy in general. Managers, like reps, apparently also suffer from role-related problems. Role ambiguity appears to be specifically related to the job itself, supervision, and fellow workers, along with company policies. Although role stress can be reduced by a better organizational definition of job responsibilities, it also appears that higher levels of self-esteem can reduce role stress and ultimately increase job satisfaction.

Women as Sales Managers

The time will come when it is no special concern whether the sales manager is a male or a female. When women entered the sales force in large numbers in the late 1970s and remained to develop careers, the natural progression to sales manager was inevitable. What have been their experiences? How have the people they manage related?

A general study of men and women as organizational leaders found no differences in the leadership styles of men and women. But a research study that compared sales rep's perceptions of the leadership styles of male and female sales managers found that sex-role stereotyping was prevalent among both male and female sales reps. Female managers were perceived by the respondents as being less effective than their male counterparts using the same leadership style. That study recommended that companies provide special training for new female sales managers in developing a credible leadership style.

Selecting the right salesperson to promote to field sales manager will never be a perfect process. In some companies the requirements for being the best field manager are considerably different from those for being the best field sales rep. Before a company can hope to do a better job of manager selection and training, executives must understand the differences between the responsibilities and activities necessary to be a good manager and a good sales rep.

Arnie Tommazato's career path with Halen Industries had been typical. He had been a field sales manager for five years, promoted to a staff job as a training manager for two years, followed by a move to a district manager position for six more years, and, for the past two months, as. a regional manager. Now the national sales manager position was vacant, but his general management inexperience prevented him from being considered for it. The job was attractive not only for the high salary, fringes, and options, but also because it had substantial prestige and potential for advancement. The two previous national sales managers had finished their careers with the company on the board of directors after stints as CEO. Arnie was going to enjoy watching the other five regional managers vie for that promotion.

The road up from field sales manager to general sales management may require several stops along the way. These stops sometimes include appointments away from direct sales management. Moreover, there will be competitors for each promotion, not all of them from within the company! What is different about general sales management? What should be the nature and character of the training and development provided to field sales managers so they can perform their current positions more effectively and prepare them for higher positions?

As a sales rep is promoted up through fiel sales manager to a general sales management position, responsibilities and activities gradually shift from predominantly line to primarily staff. For example, men and women in executive sales-management positions have indicated that their two most important responsibilities are staff related planning and organizing. They listed their most important activities as forecasting, programme development, and setting objectives and strategies.

The promotion upward through the position of field sales manager into executive sales management requires the selection of the type of person who is able to adapt and successfully make the transition to an executive staff mentality.

Promotion to these levels can produce annual base salaries over $500,000. To reap those financial and personal rewards, however, a person must be willing and able to make the sacrifices and the geographic and organizational moves necessary to attain this level.

Corporate Task

Should a firm be especially concerned with its field sales managers and their development? Is there anything special about field sales managers that warrants singling them out for special attention? The answer to both of these questions is an unqualified "yes!"

This special attention is justified for two reasons: First, because so many executives receive their initial training and development through sales, a company's future depends on their receiving the correct preparation. Second, the research evidence is clear that sales reps promoted to field sales manager often adopt the style and techniques of their former manager. Thus each sales manager imprints subordinates and passes on a good or bad legacy of managerial style to those sales reps he or she managed. Thus it is doubly important that the field sales manager's development be thorough and positive.

An additional reason for devoting time and effort to field sales manager training and preparation is that good field sales management can directly and dramatically improve sales force productivity. That is, good sales management can increase a district's sales performance and/or reduce selling costs without increasing selling expenses. Thus corporate bottom-line profit can be materially enhanced without an additional commitment of resources.

Those to be promoted from field sales manager to the next level must have first mastered the field-level job. Since this is a necessary but not sufficient condition for promotion, they must also demonstrate the capacity to successfully perform the responsibilities at the next level. Thus the first corporate task is to determine what constitutes high. performance at the field sales manager level, how that performance can be equitably assessed, and how a manager can be helped to reach those levels. The second task is to provide those managers who want it with the proper training and experience to develop their skills for possible promotion to a higher position in the company.

What is an Effective Sales Manager

A company must first defme what constitutes effective performance on important sales management job-related dimensions before it can decide which field sales manager to promote to the next level. State Farm has defined its evaluation areas clearly:

State Farm's sales managers, working through the company's network of agencies, are coaches in the strictest sense. Although they themselves normally come up from the ranks of salespeople, they no longer sell. "We did some research on what the managers were doing and what we wanted them to do," Donald W.J. Frischmann says. "As a result, we have defined five management performance criteria: *(1)* recruiting, *(2)* training, *(3)* agent-manager relations, *(4)* sales leadership, and *(5)* business management.

State Farm has achieved some success using these five areas as a basis for evaluating the performance of its sales manager. However, answering the more general question, what is an effective sales manager? requires that management address the issue of performance—what is it and how can it be measured at a managerial level?

A direct study of sales managers had them evaluate themselves and then compared the characteristics of the high versus the low self-rated managers. The study found that highest rated managers had the lowest job tension, were less likely to manipulate sales reps, were much more people oriented, and were more likely to use their expertise and ability to reward in managing the sales force. Unfortunately there have been almost no published research findings on how managers are or should be evaluated by their companies.

Some obvious evaluation criteria can be used. An effective field sales manager is more than someone who simply meets monetary sales and profit goals. For some firms, particularly smaller ones, achievement of sales and profit goals may be the only criterion because the firm's continued existence depends on the sales manager's annual achievement. In other firms, however, effective performance may be judged on dimensions such as district administration, personnel development, and sales force management and leadership.

Sales and Profit

A district's sales and profit performance is the sum of the sales and profit performance of the individual sales reps and the manager in that district in that evaluation period. Any sales rep seeking a promotion to a managerial position must realize that, as a manager, he or she will be held accountable by middle and upper sales management for the sales volume of the sales people reporting to him or her. Ultimately managers must make the numbers as the district level as they had to as reps at the territorial level. The performance of the manager's district is compared against predetermined company quotas or that district as well as against the performance of other districts.

All field sales managers can expect to be evaluated first on how well their district meets sales quotas. This is understandable since sales managers are first-level line supervisors with direct sales responsibility. More recently, with more sophisticated analytical tools and data-collection procedures, field sales managers are—increasingly being evaluated on their performance relative to district profit and/or return on on investment goals.

Hard quantitative criteria can and are used in this evaluation. A manager's evaluation and fitness for promotion are often determined by the answers to questions like the following:

(a) What percent of quota was achieved on what products by the district?

(b) How many of the reporting sales reps made quota?

(c) What happened to costs in the district?

(c) Did he/she come in over/under budget on expenses and still make sales and profit objectives?

(d) What was the district's profit and return on investment?

Building the Sales Team

One of the sales manager's responsibilities is to develop a loyal and productive sales force. This includes, as one company describes it, "the improvement of the quality of the sales force through judicious hiring and development, and termination where necessary." Thus the sales manager may also be evaluated on how well he or she recruits, selects, and trains new people. Recruiting, selecting, and training activities important to building and developing an efficient and effective sales force are covered in Part Three.

The objectives in this area as well as the criteria used to judge performance can be extremely difficult to quantify. This difficulty can result because other departments in the organization often assist with the process, making it difficult to assess responsibility, and because some recruits may not develop into outstanding reps or managers for several years. Thus, performance evaluation on this criterion is in part judged by the sales manager's superior. In the vast majority of cases this judgment will be exercised by a person who has experienced the same successes and failures as a field manager. Even though this will probably be a knowledgeable and understanding evaluation, determining the evaluation criteria is not easy. This list suggest some criteria that might be used:

(a) The number of sales reps successfully promoted from a manager's district to field sales manager and/or other positions in the company. This seems simple enough, but what about the influence of the previous managers or company training programmes? Or what about those reps who have left and become successful at other firms? Moreover, it can take a long time to find out whether a promoted sales rep is successful in a new position.

(b) Low turnover in the sales force. Low turnover could indicate good management and satisfied sales reps. However, turnover is also a function of personal situations, company support, and the reps' alternatives. High turnover does not always indicate bad management. it could also reflect low satisfaction with the company or the fact that the field sales manager is so successful in preparing the reps that the competition is hiring them away.

(c) No complaints are received by management from sales reps. The assumption is that the manager is functioning appropriately if there are no formal grievances, and in the vast majority of cases this is probably true. A company could install elaborate grievance procedures that circumvent the field sales manager or conduct frequent satisfaction surveys. The least obtrusive approach is to monitor turnover and exit interviews for any indications that a manager is having problems.

Leadership and Managing the Sales Team

A field sales manager's ability to communicate and lead the sales force at the district level is an indicator of future performance at higher levels in the organization. Some useful criteria for manager evaluation along this dimension include the following:

(a) **The Level of Commitment by the Sales Reps to the Company and the Manager.** Do they follow the manager willingly? Are the sales reps following company strategy and meeting their objectives?

(b) **The Peiformance Level of the Sales Force.** What evidence is their that the reps understand company goals? Do they make the sacrifices necessary to achieve them?

(c) **The Extent of Customer Satisfaction with the Sales force in the Manager's District.** If sales reps' morale is high and they are making extra efforts, then customer coverage and satisfaction should reflect this.

To a large extent the skills of leadership and communicatjon will be reflected in the field sales manager's performance in the day-to-day management of the district. Part Four explores how these skills may be applied to specific issues and activities in sales force motivation, compensation, and evaluation. Effectively applying good leadership and communication skills usually results in higher-quality performance by managers in their daily operations. Eventually this will result in higher performance levels against district goals. Specific examples of such criteria include the quality and consistency of their performance in such specific managerial activities as the following:

(a) Recommending raises that are fair, thoughtful, and related to a rep's performance.

(b) Working with problem reps and turning them into productive members of the sales force.

(c) Handling termination of reps as fairly and equitably as possible.

(d) Managing customer relations. Are the customers in the district satisfied? Have their problems been quickly and easily resolved?

(e) Maintaining sales rep morale, involvement, and commitment.

Trade-offs Across Promotion Criteria

Executives cannot expect all sales managers to exhibit both outstanding interpersonal and analytical skills. Rather, a successful manager will have achieved some minimal level of competence in each skill, particularly the interpersonal ones. Beyond that minimal level, each sales manager's personal characteristics will compel him or her to master one or more skills. A skill mastery in one area often compensates for weaknesses in other skill areas. This is particularly true of some analytical skills, which, at higher management levels, may be delegated to staff specialists.

❐

11
Retailer and Wholesaler Promotion Process

RETAILERS

The word 'Retail' is derived from a French word with the prefix re and the verb tailer meaning "to cut again". Evidently, retail trade is one that cuts off smaller portions from large lumps of goods. It is a process through which goods are transported to final consumer. In other words, retailing consists of the activities involved in selling directly to the ultimate consumer for personal, non-business use. It embraces the direct-to-customer sales activities of the producer, whether through his own stores by house-to-house canvassing or by mail order business." It is immaterial who does the selling, but to be classified as retailing selling activities must be direct to the ultimate consumer. While most retailing is done through retail stores, it may be done by any institution. Manufacturers engage in retailing when they make direct-to-consumer sales of their products through their own stores (as Bata and Corona Shoe Companies., D.C.M. stores, Mafatlals and Bombay Dyeing) by door-to-door canvass, or mail order or even on telephone. Even a wholesaler engages in retailing when he sells directly to an ultimate consumer, although his main business may still be wholesaling.

A retailer is a merchant, or occasionally an agent, or a business enterprise, whose main business is selling directly to ultimate consumers for non-business use. He performs many marketing activities such as buying, selling, grading, risk taking, and developing information about customers' wants. They are marketers and customers of producers and wholesalers. A retailer may sell infrequently to industrial users, but these are wholsale transactions, not retail sales. If over one half of the amount of volume of business comes from sales to ultimate consumers, *i.e.*, sales at retail, he is classed as a retailer. Retailing occurs in all marketing channels for consumer products.

IMPORTANCE OF RETAILING

The retailer is an intermediary in the marketing channel because he is both marketer and customer, who sells to the last man to consume. He is a specialist who maintains contact with the consumer and the producer; and is an important connecting link in a gigantic mechanism of marketing. Though producers may sell directly to consumers such method of distributing goods to ultimate user is inconvenient, expensive and time consuming as compared to the job performed by a specialist in the line. Therefore, frequently the manufacturers depend on the retailers to sell their products to the ultimate consumers. The retailer, who is able to provide appropriate amenities without an excessive advance in prices of goods is rewarded by larger or more loyal patronage.

The general service which a retailer provides are:

(1) The retailer anticipates the wants of the consumers and then supplies them the right kind of goods at a reasonable price. His job is to make the consumers' buying as easy and convenient as possible, *i.e.*, he acts as a consumers' agent.

(2) He performs the service of bulk-breaking, *i.e.*, dividing large quantities into small units, such as individual cans, bottles, boxes, wrappers, packages, appropriate for consumer use.

(3) He also assumes risks by guaranteeing the goods he sells to the consumers.

(4) He also offers free delivery of goods, credit on open accounts, free alteration, liberal exchange facilities, instructions in the use of goods, revolving credit plans, and long term instalment programmes.

(5) He offers a large assortment of merchandise of suitable size, colour, design, style and seasonal items-ranging from domestic utensils, household requisites to speciality goods.

(6) He creates time and place utility by storing the products in off season and by transporting these goods to the places where they can be readily available as and when needed by the consumer.

(7) He adds to the convenience and case of consumer purchasing by offering convenient shopping locations, market informations, personal salesmen, and other services as free parking privileges, children's nurseries, cooking and sewing classes, style shows, unformed doormen, lessons on product use and a multitude of other facilities may be offered and found sufficiently desired to result in increased patronage.

(8) He acts as a specialist in selling. He offers physical facilities and man-power so that producers and wholesalers can meet the consumers at their doors.

(9) He helps the producers in distributing their products by using advertising display and personal selling.

(10) He provides useful inforamtion to the producers about the like and dislikes of the consumers, their wants and needs and their buying behaviour.

(11) The level of retail sales is one of the most useful barometers of the nation's economic health. *e.g.*, when sales of cycles pick up, sales of steel and components also increase, as does employment and

thus increasing purchasing power. But when sale godown, manufactuers cut back production, unemployment increases, and retail sales also goes down.

Facilitating Services

In order to carry out functions involving transfer of ownership and physical supply effectively, retailers perform a number of facilitating functions, *i.e.,* functions relating to standardisation and grading, financing risk taking and market information.

A retailer of fresh fruits and vegetables has to standardise and grade these to make these acceptable to customers. They establish standards, inspect goods they receive, and sort them in various classifications. Quite often they purchase in large quantities and then divide them and repack them before selling when the retailers sells goods on credit he performs financing function. From the moment he sells and collects the last penny from the customer, when goods are sold on credit, he is said to be performing a financing function.

Another function performed by retailers is that of risk taking. During the entire time a retailer holds title to particular goods, he must inevitably bear a wide variety of risks. Not only the goods may be destroyed through fire or flood, but also there is often the danger of theft, deterioration, or spoilage. Furthermore, such merchants are also faced with the threat that consumers will not accept their product or will purchase them only at unprofitable prices. He also undertakes risk in handling of fashion goods and other items for which consumer demand varies greatly from time to time.

Since the retailer knows about the wishes of his customers the price, quality and the kind of merchandise available in the market as well as the existing and anticipate style trends, he keeps in stock the goods usually required by customers.

CLASSIFICATION OF RETAILERS

Retailers may be classified in more than one way such as on the following basis:

1. **Size.** That is according to their sales volumes during a particular period, say a year. Retailing may be both a small scale and a large scale operation; and it may be integrated and non-integrated.

2. **Geographic Location.** The stores classified according to these criteria tell about consumer buying habits. The retailers may be found in rural trading centre, large cities, outlying suburbs, or along the main streets of a town.

3. **Product-line handled.** That is according to the goods dealt with. They may be classified: *(a)* General merchandise stores (such as department stores, dry goods stores, variety stores, and general stores) dealing in furniture, home furnishings, appliances, household goods, groceries, drugs, convenience goods and shopping goods; *(b)* single-line stores, dealing in assorted group of products (such as grocery stores, furniture stores, medical stores, building material stores, hardware stores, sporting goods stores, cloth stores and book stores); they may also carry two related lines, such as men's and women's clothing; *(c)* Limited-line or speciality stores, which carry a limited variety of products such as shopping or convenience goods—apparel, shoes, gifts and decorative accessories selling stores.

4. **Form of Ownership.** On this basis we have independent stores and corporate chain stores; less important are leased department, company stores, consumer co-operatives, etc.

5. **Method of Operation.** On this basis retailers may be of two types; *(a)* full-service retailers, where the sale

is generally made at the counter, especially of high-fashion goods or where a salesman's demonstration, explanation or fitting is needed. Such retailers are super markets, and discount retailers *(b)* non-store retailing, where buyers and sellers meet and transact their business at the buyer's home or at some other non-store location, known as door-to-door or house-to-house selling. Major forms of non store retailing are mail order selling, automatic vending and personal selling on a door-to-door basis.

ESSENTIAL REQUIREMENTS OF RETAILERS

The essential requirements of a retailer are:

(1) **Selection of Goods.** Retailers are more in touch with the consumers as compared to the wholesalers, and therefore, it is necessary for the retailers to be more careful in judging the future needs of the market. Sometimes such stocks are maintained the use of which has already become obsolete. The retailers must be up-to-date in their selection of the goods to be stocked by them. More heavy stock would not attract customers, but a moderate customer to their well-equipped shops. The 'dead stock' is the bug-bear of business and that unsold and unsaleable stock has brought ruin to many business men should never be overlooked.

(2) **Knowledge of Merchandise.** Individuality has so much developed amongst the masses that a great variety of goods has considerably increased and is still increasing. The retailer should, therefore, be more up-to-date in this respect and must have a practical knowledge of the merchandise which will satisfy this new demand. His work is, thus, more complicated and he should take enough care while appointing salesmen, selecting shop assistants, etc.,

who would be called upon to deal with the customers.

(3) **Bying and Selling.** The success of a retail business is more dependent on the buying of merchandise in the right market, at the right price, and at the right time. Such retailers who are new in the line, are sometimes heard to say to their customers that they cannot sell at the price charged by some other shopkeepers on account of their buying the goods at a higher price, without taking into consideration the fact that this is of no concern to their customers who will not consent to pay a higher price for their article merely for its being purchased at a dearer market. Retailers must compete in price and quality and should charge their customers at a definite rate of profit which ought to be the lowest possible in the circumstances and which should not be more than what is charged by others.

(4) **Cash and Credit Purchases.** A good many retailers at important trade centres buy beyond the capacity of their capital and become inextricably entangled in debt to their creditor, wholesalers, who naturally sell for price which is more than normal because they grant credit. The retailer, therefore, finds himself in a helpless position when he is called upon to compete with those who purchase for cash. Buying on credit may, of course, be allowed to a limited extent but over-buying should always be avoided and retailers should not trade too much beyond the limits of their available capital. Financial consideration, as a rule, should dictate the maximum stock that can be safely kept. On the other hand, a well-selected variety of stock should always be held by a retail shop unless it is a multiple shop, as loss is frequently suffered on account of inadequate stock,

for this means not only lost sales but loss of customers, who being disappointed to have their wants supplied transfer their purchases elsewhere.

(5) **Price, Quality and Cypher System.** Higgling and hesitancy should be avoided and a competitive fixed price should always be asked for with uprightness. The price charged ought to be such that the customers will not generally be in a position to purchase the same article in the market at a cheaper price. The competitive price and quality of the goods sold are two most important factors which are the keynotes of success in business and their supreme necessity cannot be too much exaggerated. Retailers should know that it is better to have a quick turnover of stock at a lower margin of profit.

(6) **Display of Goods.** Sometimes goods are so disorderly arranged that the goods required, though available on the spot, cannot be produced on the requisition by the consumer. The goods should, therefore, be not only properly arranged but should also be properly displayed to draw the attention of the customers. Window dressing which costs little but is very effective in retail trade as it makes an emotional appeal to the shopping public at the start, frequently results in solid business. "In the newer window-dressing," said Mr. George Edger, "the three cardinal principles are: *(i)* to show reasonable thing, *(ii)* to show it as simply as possible, and *(iii)* to show it so that the eye can determine every detail put into the window. In such window-dressing instead of crowding the window, the trade aims at a display which represents the prevailing note of the season."

(7) **Situation.** Locality of the shop is a great factor to attract customers. The best locality is the place where

there already exist other shops of the same nature, because for shopping purposes customers generally visit the place where a market for their requirements has grown up and where they can select the articles of their need from more than one shop. While opening shops this essential matter of selection of site in a desirable locality should not be overlooked. No particular place can be pointed out for the retailer to reach his goal. Success can be achieved by combining the various qualifications essential for a businessman with other necessary factors. Personal aptitude, knowledge, enthusiasm and apprenticeship, combined with the possession of saleable goods and adequate stock generally make for success.

Mr. Nystrom has summed up the chief requirements of the retailers thus:

In order to attract customers retailers should have:

(i) accessibility to consumers;

(ii) a satisfactory trading place;

(iii) suitable stocks of merchandise offering an opportunity for cosnumer choice;

(iv) service offered and rendered to customers;

(v) personal relation of store employees towards customers including not only promptness of attention but also courtesy, interest, friendliness and honesty;

(vi) reasonable price;

(vii) window display and counter display (which are the most effective forms of advertising);

(viii) sales promotion including all methods and devices for giving the public information about the goods and services offered;

(ix) the demand of customers should be aroused by means of suitable advertising so that they may be persuaded to pay a visit to the shop;

(x) trained salesmen who are the backbone of the success of the retail house;

(xi) staff employed should be polite, courteous and attentive to customers; and

(xii) clearance sales, which are usually organised at the end of a season to attract customers in large numbers.

WHOLESALER

Physical distribution of goods and services produced or dealt in by all enterprises is an important function of marketing management. It includes all the activities to be performed by an enterprise in the process of distributing goods and services from the place of production to the place of consumption. Thre are various channels of distribution for a product. An important channel commonly used, particularly for the distribution of consumers goods, is under:

Manufacturer→Wholesalers→Retailers→Consumers

Wholesaler is an important chain of the channel of distribution because it is an agent between a manufacturer and retailers. A wholesaler purchases the goods from manufacturer in bulk quantity and re-sells it to retailers in small quantity. The term 'Wholesaler' has been defined as under:

Mason & Rath, "A person or firm that buys merchandise and re-sells it either to retailers for subsequent re-sale to the consumer or to business firm for industrial and business use is called a wholesaler."

Marris E. Hurley, "Wholesalers and marketing middlemen who occupy position midway between retailer and the producer or manufacturer."

American Marketing Association, "Wholesalers sell to other merchants and or industrial, institutional and commerical users but they do not sell in significant amounts to ultimate consumers."

On the basis of above definition, it can be concluded that a wholesaler is the first link in the chain of middlemen. A wholesaler purchases goods from manufacturers and sells to the retailers. He buys goods in large quantities and sells them to retailers in small quantities for re-sale to the industrial and commerical consumers. He does not sell the goods directly to the consumers. A wholesaler may be a sole trader, or a partnership firm or a company.

Characteristics of Wholesalers

Some of the important characteristics of wholesalers are as under:

1. A wholesaler buys the goods direct from the manufacturer.
2. A wholesaler purchases the goods generally in large quantities.
3. A wholesaler purchases the goods generally for cash.
4. Wholesalers have a team of agents who help them in selling the products to the retailers. Wholesalers provide the goods to the retailers generally at their trading places.
5. Wholesalers sometimes make grading of the goods under their own name or brand.
6. Wholesalers generally deal in a single product or limited products (generally in the products of a single product line.)

7. Wholesalers generally deals in the products of a single manufacturer as some limited manufacturers.
8. Wholesalers maintain warehouses and godowns at different places in the city or in different cities of the country.
9. The location of godown or office and display of goods is not of much importance to the wholesalers.

CLASSIFICATION OF WHOLESALER

Wholesalers can broadly be classified on the following basis – *(I)* On the basis of functions, *(II)* On the basis of areas served, *(III)* On the basis of services rendered. The deatils in this regard are as follows:

(I) Classification of Wholesalers on the Basis of Functions

On the basis of functions, wholesalers can be divided into three parts as follows:

(1) Manufacturer Wholesalers. Manufacturer Wholesalers are the persons engaged in manufacturing activities as well as in distribution activities. The manufacturers who sell their goods to the retails are known as manufacturer wholesalers. They may also make large-scale purchasing from other manufacturers so that the demand of retailers may be met. Main object to act as a manufacturer wholesaler is to play double role in marketing. It increases their profits.

(2) Retailer Wholesalers. Retailer wholesalers are the wholesalers who purchase goods directly from manufacturers, and sell them to the consumers. Thus, the manufacturers who retail their goods direct to the consumers through their own shops, are also called retailer wholesalers. In this manner, retailer wholesalers also play double role in marketing. It

also helps them in minimising the costs, and increasing the sales and profits.

(3) *Pure Wholesalers.* Pure wholesalers are the wholesalers who carry the business of purchasing and selling the goods in large quantities only. Such wholesalers do not enagage themselves in the activities of production or retailing. Such wholesalers maintain their warehouses or godowns in different parts of the city or in different cities of the country. They collect goods from different manufacturers and supply these goods to the retailers. Such wholesalers are known as Distributors also.

Pure wholesalers can be further divided into three parts as follows:

(i) *Mill Supply Wholesalers.* Mill supply wholesalers are the wholesalers, who supply goods to the mills or manufacturers. Such wholesalers deal in raw-material, capital goods, equipments and other supplies. They purchase these materials and equipments from a large number of manufacturers in large quantities and supply to the industrial users. Such wholesalers generally sell their goods throughout a state or country through their agents.

(ii) *Single Line Wholesalers.* Single line wholesalers are the wholesalers who deal in a particular product line only. They purchase and sell different product items from different manufacturers of their line. In this manner, they maintain large varieties of goods of their line and sell them to the retailers.

(iii) *Complete Line Wholesalers.* Complete line wholesalers are the wholesalers who deal in complete line of goods required by a particular industry or a trade. Such wholesalers concentrate upon the needs and requirements of a particular trade only and they deal in all the necessities of such trade. For example, hospital supply wholesalers can supply all the requirements of hospitals.

(II) Classfication of Wholesalers on the Basis of Area Served

On the basis of area served, wholesalers can be divided into three parts as follows:

(1) Local Wholesalers. Local wholesalers are the wholesalers who purchase goods from a number of manufacturers and re-sell these goods in a particular area or city only. Such wholesalers generally deal in the goods according to the requirements of retailers of their area. As these wholesalers are very close to the retailers, retailers feel it very convenient to purchase their requirements from such wholesalers.

(2) Regional Wholesalers. Regional wholesalers are the wholesalers who purchase goods in large quantities from different manufacturers and sell them to the retailers of a particular region. This region may be a state or some particular districts of state or a particular district. This type of wholesalers is very common these days.

(3) National Wholesalers. National wholesalers are the wholesalers, who purchase goods from different manu-facturers and distribute these goods to the retailers all over the country. Such wholesalers supply goods to the local or regional wholesalers also.

(III) Classification of Wholesalers on the Basis of Services Rendered

On the basis of services rendered, wholesalers can be divided into five parts as follows:

(1) ***Jobbers.*** Jobbers are the wholesalers who purchase goods from different manufacturers and store these goods in their own godowns and sell them to the retailers. These wholesalers perform the activities of purchasing and selling only. They do not engage themselves in production activities. Such wholesalers are also known as Pure Wholesalers.

(2) ***Processors.*** Processors are the wholesalers who purchase goods from different manufacturers for grading and processing. They classify the goods into different grades and sell these goods according to their grades, generally in small packets. Sometimes, they sell these goods under their own brand name.

(3) ***Industrial Distributions.*** Such wholesalers act as wholesalers or distributors for a single manufacturers. These wholesalers collect goods from a single manufacturer only and sell these goods to the retailers in their authorised area.

(4) ***Exporters.*** Such wholesalers purchase goods from different manufacturers of their country and sell these goods in foreign countries. They may sell these goods in the same from or after processing.

(5) ***Importers.*** Such wholesalers purchase goods from foreign manufacturers and sell these goods to the manufacturers or wholesalers or retailers of their country. These wholesalers may sell the goods in the same form or after processing.

FUNCTION OF WHOLESALER

Wholesalers occupy a predominant position in the channels of distribution. This is more so in a widespread economy, where the wholesaling function is of vital importance. They assemble merchandise from many sources, warehouse it, and regroup the goods for convenient buying by retailers. Most modern wholesale merchants provide information and advisory services to retailers, and they are often in a position to provide local market information to manufacturers as well. Their most important service, of course, is that of making it possible for the manufacturer to sell to thosands of small retailers to whom the merchandise cannot be sold direct from the factory. This is more so because of their lack of resources and storage space to purchase in large quantities to make such direct purchase economically feasible. On the basis of functions they perform, wholesalers could be grouped as follows:

1. **Limited Function Wholesalers.** They are basically merchant wholesalers but do not provide full services, and often provide only the minimum services among the limited functions.

2. **General Merchandise Wholesalers.** Such a wholesaler never restricts the varieties of products to be handled. He may even handle unrelated product lines. For eample, a wholesaler may stock food items together with hardware. These kinds of middlemen are fast disappearing from the city areas since all fields are gradually getting specialised.

3. **General Line Wholsalers.** Contrary to the above kinds of wholesalers, they deal in closely related items, for example, a wholesaler dealing in various types of cosmetics.

   In industrial goods marketing, these wholesalers are known as "industrial distributors." This kind of wholesalers is found in hardware and automobile spare parts business.

4. **Speciality Wholsalers.** As the name suggests this kind of wholesalers has introduced specialisation in the wholsale trade. Such a wholasaler deals only in

one merchandise. But within that limited line he might offer the whole range and also specialise in concentrating of the products of a single or a special group of manufacturers. This will enable him to get all support from manuacturers including the sales promotional supports.

5. **Functional Wholesalers.** This kind of wholsalers actually falls under the category of Agent middlemen. They do not take title to merchandise nor do they see the goods they sell. Their main function is to facilitate selling, although there are some buying functional middlemen. They are classified into:

   (a) *Brokers.* This group operates to bring the buyer and the seller together. Brokers are especially important in the food, textile, real estate and in secondhand machinery markets. Primarily, brokers sell information—information of products available for sale or purchase.

   (b) *Drop-shipment Wholesalers.* Though by nature they are also wholesalers, they do not handle the good they sell. They simply collect orders from retailers and pass them on the manufacturers who deliver the goods direct to the retailers. Such wholesalers are found in industrial marketing. They perform most of the wholesaling functions, with the exception of storage and handling.

   (c) *Commission Merchants.* They are mostly found in the agricultural marketing field and handle the selling function for large numbers of producers. Like the broker, a commission merchant finds markets for the products. But unlike the broker, he generally handles the goods he sells but does not own them. Consequent on the emergency of co-operative marketing in the agricultural sector in recent years, the importance of these merchants has declined.

(d) *Manufacturers' Agents.* These agents work for several non-competing manufacturers and act as sales representatives for them in a territory. Their man job is to call on and sell to wholesalers and industrial buyers. As a rule, the manufacturer's agent does not handle goods. He sends the orders to the manufacturer, who, in turn, delivers the products direct to buyers.

(e) *Selling Agents.* Like the manufacturers' agents, selling agents sell for the manufacturers but usually handle the entire output of such manufacturers. They take over the entire marketing job for a commission. The selling agent is prominent in the texitle and drugs and pharmaceutical industries, where many small producers have to sell products fast and at the lowest possible cost.

(f) *Converters.* They operate both as manufacturers and wholsalers. But their production operation would be simple, concentrating more on selling. This is found in textile industry, where the raw cotton is bought and after dyeing, printing, etc., finished cloth is sold. These kinds of wholesalers are rarely found in India.

(g) *Assemblers.* Their specialisation is in the agricultural field. Some are agent middlemen and some are merchant middlemen, and in most cases they combine both the types. Their main job is assembling goods from various places.

SERVICES OF WHOLESALERS

Whoesalers are vital link between manufacturers and retailers. They purchase the goods from different manufacturers and sell these goods to the retailers. Thus, wholesalers render very important services both to the manufacturers and retailers. Some of the important services rendered by manufacturers are divided into three parts: *(I)* Services to the manufacturers, *(II)* Services to the retailers. *(III)* Service to the consumers. The details in this regard are as follows:

(I) Services to the Manufacturers

The wholesalers render following services to the manufacturers:

(1) **Facilities of Distribution.** Wholesalers take over the liability of manufacturers to distribute the goods produced by them. Thus, they relieve manufacturers from this liability.

(2) **Helpful in Concetrating upon Production.** As most of the liabilities of manufacturers are taken over by wholesalers, manufacturers can concetrate upon production. They have not to bother about distribution.

(3) **Helpful in Large-scale Producton.** Wholesalers help in increasing the sales of goods. They purchase the goods from manufacturers in large quantities. It enables the manufacturers to produce at large-scale. Large-sale production help the manufacturers in reducing the cost of production considerably.

(4) **Helpful in Expanding the Market.** Wholesalers distribute the goods produced by the manufacturers in different segments of the market. They try to sell

these goods in new market also. It is the wholesaler who makes the goods produced by a manufacturer available in all parts of the country. Thus wholesalers help in expanding the market for products.

(5) **Benefit of Advertisement.** Generally, the wholesalers advertise on their own expenses. It helps manufacturers in increasing the sales of their products, it re-doubles the effect of advertisement.

(6) **Helpful in Standardisation and Grading.** Some of the wholesalers sort out the products into different grades. These grades are developed on the basis of common characteristics or quality or nature of products. It helps manufacturers to adopt the policy of standardisation and grading.

(7) **Helpful in Price Determination.** As wholealers are in close touch with the retailers they can be of great help in determining the price of products.

(8) **Facility of Raw-materials.** Wholesalers provide the facility of raw-materials also to the manufacturers. Different type of raw-materials are collected by wholesalers from different manufacturers and sold to the manufacturers of consumer goods.

(9) **Financial Help.** Wholesalers provide financial help also to the manufacturers because they purchase goods in large quantities and generally on cash payment. Some wholesalers make advance payment also while placing their orders.

(10) **Facility of Storage.** Wholesalers take over the liability of manufacturers of storing goods also. They store the goods manufactured by manufacturers in their own godowns and thus, the manufacturers are relieved from the liability of storing the products.

(II) Services to the Retailers

Wholesalers provide some very important and useful services to the retailers. These services may be explained as under:

(1) **Financial Assistance.** Financial resources of retailers are generally limited. Wholesalers provide valuable financial assistance to them by selling the goods to them on credit. It helps the retailers in maintaining rotation of their working capital.

(2) **Benefit of Advertisement.** Wholesalers generally advertise for the products dealt with by them. Such advertisement is very helpful to the retailers because they get direct benefit from it. It increases their sales and profits.

(3) **Valuable Consultation.** Wholesalers advise retailers on their marketing problems for time to time. Advice of wholesalers is very useful for the retailers in solving their marketing problems and in increasing their sales.

(4) **Helpful in Making Selection.** A wholesaler generally maintains large variety of a product. It helps retailers in making the selection of variety.

(5) **Helpful in Purchasing the Goods According to Needs.** As the goods are purchased by wholesalers in large quantities and sold to the retailers in small quantities, the retailers get the facility of purchasing the goods in the quantity of their need.

(6) **Stability in Prices.** Wholesalers purchase the goods in large quantities and sell them to the retailers in small quantities. Thus, the risk of fluctuations in price is borne by the wholesalers themselves. This helps retailers in stabilising their prices.

(7) **Facility of Packaging.** The goods are packed generally by the wholesalers. They pack the goods in different sizes according to the specifications suggested by retailers. It helps retailers in selling these goods to the consumers in different size or quantities.

(8) **Facilitiy of Sorting, Grading and Standardisation.** The activities of sorting, grading and standardisaton are performed by the wholesalers. It relieves the retailers from this liability.

(9) **Facility of Transportation.** Generally,the wholesalers provide goods to the retailers at their shops. It relieves the retailers from the liability of transportation.

(10) **Benefits of Specialisation.** Generally, the wholesalers deal with the product of a particular product line or a particular producer. It this manner, the wholesalers are generally the specialists of their line. Retailers get the advantage of their ability, efficiency and experience.

(III) Services to the Consumers

Though the wholesalers are not in direct touch with the consumers, yet they offer some valuable services to the consumers. Some of the services provided by wholesalers to the consumer are as under:

(i) Wholesalers provide neccessary information to the consumers about new products introduced in the market. They do so by their advertisement programmes.

(ii) Wholesalers distribute the goods to the retailers according to the needs, wants and requirements of consumers.

(iii) Wholesalers maintain large variety of a product. Therefore, the wholesalers help in increasing the variety to be maintained by retailers and thus, the consumers get full range of a product.

(iv) Wholesalers undertake market research also. This is also beneficial to the consumers.

(v) Wholesalers maintain equilibrium in the demand and supply of products.

(vi) Wholesalers help in stabilising the prices of products in the market.

(vii) Wholesalers help the manufacturers in production. It provides the goods to the consumers at most reasonable prices.

❐

12

Strategic Issues in Promotional Strategies

Direct marketing is a form of marketing in which an organization seeks to generate a direct and measurable response to advertising which offers goods or services or information about them. Direct marketing includes not only the creation and distribution of advertising but also all the other activities involved in receiving, processing, recording, analyzing, and following up on the responses to advertising. The advertising may be communicated by mail, broadcast, telephone, or print or may involve combinations of these media. The response may be an order, inquiry or contribution and may be transmitted by mail, phone, or other electronic means.

A response directly to the advertising. Unlike the package goods advertiser or the institutional advertiser, direct marketers try to do more than create awareness of and recognition for a company, product or brand. The objective of the direct marketer is to get a response, which may be in the form of an inquiry or an order. It may come in by mail telephone, or other electronic means but it occurs in direct response to the promotional message. This does not mean that creating awareness and recognition is unimportant. Even direct marketers benefit from the buildup of marketplace awareness that occurs when many promotions have been sent out over a period of time. The emphasis on getting a response simply means that the advertising must be of a special type.

It must contain enough information, must be sufficiently persuasive, and must make the type of offer that will motivate readers to inquire for further information or actually place an order. The chapters in this book that deal with the proposition and with copy and art fully explain the special advertising and promotion techniques used by direct marketers.

The psychology of direct marketing is somewhat special. It tends to blend aspects of personal selling with elements of advertising. The seller actually takes the initiative in presenting specially selected goods directly to the prospect and urges an immediate response. This is quite different from the more passive display of retail merchandise in stores in which the customer must decide to go shopping before response can occur.

A Data Base of Information About the Respondents. When a response comes in, the direct marketer must fill the order or send out the requested literature. But that is only the beginning of the total marketing process. Direct marketer make special efforts to capture information about respondents and about the order, contribution, or inquiry received. Identification information about the respondent captured in a data base permits the direct marketer to contact the respondent again with additional offers. In addition, information about the response permits the direct marketer to make the most appropriate new offers to past respondents. By also capturing the dates of past activity, the direct marketer can classify previous respondents in the data base according to the recency and frequency of prior activity. Since recent and frequent respondents tend to reply to additional offers at a higher rate than other names in the data base, the direct marketers can improve overall response and profitability by selecting only the best candidates for future offers.

Implicit in the concept of building a data base of information is the related direct marketing principle of segmentation. Segmentation refers to the ability to break down a customer file or somebody else's mailing list into segments according to demographic characteristics, psychographic characteristics, or previous response characteristics. The ability to segment gives the direct marketer the option to promote' to certain customer classifications and not to others or to promote more frequently to some classifications and less frequently to others. The end purpose of the data base is to permit very selective marketing which results in higher response rates and higher profitability.

Tested and Measurable Advertising. In many cases, the direct marketer can measure the actual response to individual cells of promotion by putting a unique code number of the response piece in a direct mail package, putting a coupon in a magazine and, etc. As keyed responses come in the direct marketer can measure the response in magazine A versus magazine B, the response in January versus February, the response to list A versus list B, etc. This means that over the long run, the direct marketer can develop some reasonably scientific information about which media, offers, ads, seasons, and parts of the customer file pull the better rates of response and which pull the less good rates.

In addition to reading the results of overall promotions, the direct marketer also can fashion some very precise split tests. A-B split tests can be done within mailing lists or periodicals to determine how the marketplace actually reacts to different offers, formats, prices, etc. This kind of testing is much more precise and factual than opinion research that only elicits the attitudes of people regarding different advertising approaches. The direct marketer's general objective is to test advertising in small quantities first in order to determine what works best and to use the results of those tests as a basis for investing larger amounts of promotion dollars as profitably as possible later. Performing live market tests and measuring results are a way of life for the professional direct marketer.

Promotion Economics. The direct marketer allocates a far larger proportion of the sales dollar to promotion than manufacturers or most sellers of packaged goods. The term "promotion" here refers to the total cost of creating, producing, and distributing advertising which will generate responses. It is not unusual for a direct marketer to spend 15 to 25 per cent or more of net sales on promotion. While this may seem like an extraordinary amount, remember that the direct marketer usually does not pay commissions to sales people or give discounts to retailers. Not surprisingly, the direct marketer focuses a lot of attention on the promotion expense line in the profit and loss statement. Not only is it large. It directly reflects the level of response rates achieved and the resulting profitability of individual campaigns. There are a wide variety of direct marketing methods, and there are many different applications in both the consumer sector and in the business-to-business sector.

The major strategic factors that affect the nature of a direct marketing promotion are selecting the product establishing the promotion objective, choosing media, determining which selling system to use, deciding on the level of promotion intensity, and arranging for a fulfillment system.

Product Selection. It is becoming increasingly the case that direct marketing-methods can be used to sell, or at least assist in the sale of all kinds of goods and services. Price level once was considered a barrier, but today $9500 necklaces are sold by mail, $50,000 investment-grade diamonds are sold through news letters and used computers are sold over the telephone. A price barrier may be at the low end because in a low-priced item, there may not be sufficient margin to allow for normal levels of promotion and fulfillment expense. It also used to be said that a successful direct marketing item had to be unique or at least unusual and preferably not available at retail. Yet within the past year, over 500,000

American families have purchased a collection of 2101 simple hardware store items assembled in a cabinet containing twenty-five plastic drawers for $21,95. The packaging is unusual, but the items themselves are anything but. It also has been said that it is better if the item is discretionary in nature and that basic commodities cannot be sold through mail order. While it is true that it would be almost impossible selling ruled pads, pencils, copier paper, doormats, etc., through catalogs and by telephone marketing. Again, the old "rules" seem less applicable than they may have been in this the past.

But a few of the old rules still apply today. First, if an item is going to be sold through direct marketing means, it must be something that can be described in words and pictures. There must be enough gross margin to pay for the typical cost of doing business through a direct marketing channel. Remember, however, that it is not essential that the final sale be completed exclusively through direct marketing methods. Direct marketing can be used simply to generate inquiries which may be followed up by personal selling efforts. This widens the scope of possible products and services even further. In the final analysis, a product or group of products must be of interest to a definable group of people who can be reached efficiently through an established direct marketing medium. The medium is the market, and the product is the fulfillment of a need or want.

Promotion Objective. Before commencing the development of a campaign, the direct marketer must decide whether the objective is to generate orders or to generate, qualify, and convert leads. There is a major difference between these two direct marketing approaches which will have a great effect on the nature and format of the promotion. Direct marketing methods also can be used simply to maintain communications with a target audience. A typical example of this would be keeping in contact with customers between sales calls. That type of communications contact' is not considered as a primary promotien objective in the context of this chapter.

Media Selection. The media that are available to the direct marketer are:

Mail

Print

Telephone

Broadcast

The selection of media appropriate for an offer depends on a number of different factors including the degree of audience selectivity, required, the amount of space needed to present the offer, the need to "show" the product, and how high a promotion cost per thousands the marketer can afford in relation to probable response rates.

The Selling System. There are six major methods of selling by direct marketing. The conditions under which each method is most frequently used are described below.

One-Shot. This is an offer to sell an item in a single transaction. When the prospect buys and shipment is made, the transaction is complete, though there may be extended payments. This method of selling generally is used for items that are relatively easy to understand or services that do not require demonstration or personal sales efforts. It is possible to sell low-to nigh-ticket items in this manner.

Two-Step. First, there is an ofter to supply additional information about a product or service, such as literature, a catalog, or a personal visit. Then efforts are made to qualify the inquiries and convert them to sales. This method of selling frequently involves combinations of print, mail, telephone, and personal sales calls. It is used most frequently in connection with complex and highticket items which require extended consideration, personalized information, or a demonstration. This method may also be used simply to build a mailing list of names to whom a catalog may be sent.

Catalog. This is an offer of an assortment of merchandise from which the prospect may select one or more items. The catalog may remain in force for months and sometimes for more than a year. The customer frequently keeps a copy for future use. This method of selling is applicable when there is a relatively broad assortment of items to be offered to a target audience. In the consumer sector such items are frequently of a discretionary nature, while in the industrial product area. A catalog is most analogous in concept to a retail store which displays a variety of merchandise and invites customers to make selections.

Subscription. This is an offer of ongoing service, usually for a specified period; it generally is paid for in advance. It is used most frequently in magazine selling.

Club. This is an offer of ongoing product shipments under an automatic shipment plan or a negative option plan. Payment is made on receipt of merchandise, and the customer may have to complete a minimum commitment before cancelling. While this selling system most frequently applies to books and records, offers of service such as insurance and special telephone features are conceptually similar to club operations.

Continuity. This is an offer of a specified series of items to be shipped at regular intervals over a period of time. Usually the customer may cancel at any point, and payment is made in installments. Again, the most common application of this method is found in the publishing business. The selection of the appropriate selling system depends on the nature of the product, the amount of product items available, the selling price of the item, and the complexity of the information that must be presented before a purchase decision can be made. Another important factor is the psychological question of human inertia. Subscription, club and continuity plans rely to a certain degree on the fact that some customers will continue to accept shipments for some time after they have ceased to be truly interested in the product or service they are receiving. It sometimes may require an extensive period of testing to determine whether a company can more profitably sell a product through oneshot or two-step marketing. Within that area of testing, it may take quite a few subtests to determine how to convert the maximum percentage of leads.

Promotion Intensity. The direct marketer thinks not only of the product that is being presented to the target audience but also of the total offer or proposition that is being made. The offer or proposition consists of:

(a) The product or service

(b) The price

(c) The payment terms

(d) Commitment

(e) The guarantee

(f) Promotional enhancements.

It is not unusual for companies first entering the world of direct marketing to struggle with the question of promotion intensity, because they may be faced with a new tone and style of advertising. Companies that are accustomed to merchandise awards or contests for their sales people sometimes shy away from even the thought of a sweepstakes addressed directly to their customers. Usually the concern expressed relates to questions of company image. Obviously, every company can choose to have whatever marketing image it feels is best. Some companies, however may find that the image that they created before direct marketing somewhat impedes the development of truly exciting direct marketing offers and promotions.

Like most other thing in direct marketing the question of image and its effect on response rates can be subjected to extensive testing. Test results then can be used to define the value of different levels of promotion intensity and the impact of predetermined company image on response rates. The final decision regarding the type of promotion most suitable for the company then can be made on the basis of factual test information.

Fulfillment System. As indicated in the definition at the beginning of this chapter, direct marketing includes not only the generation of responses but also the fulfillment of orders, inquiries, etc. The fulfillment system, which includes order processing, inventory control, customer service, etc., is as important a marketing consideration as the offer and the agvertising package. This is so because the customer's satisfaction will be a direct result of how the order is handled. The finest products and the greatest advertising will be of no value in the long run if the customers whose names appear in the data base have had their orders mishandled or delayed. Unhappy customers will not want to respond to the next promotion. Before any direct marketing promotion is started, the company should be sure that it is prepared to:

(a) Respond promptly to requests for information

(b) Fill orders promptly

(c) Make adjustments and corrections courteously when problems occur

(d) Handle routine billing and customer service efficiently and courteously

If the company is unable to handle this back-end part of its business, it should delay the implementation of any front-end promotions. Not all firms using direct marketing today are 100 per cent mail order. Increasingly, companies are entering the field from other areas of marketing retailing, direct selling, or manufacturing. For these companies, adapting the traditional approaches of the total direct marketer may be particularly difficult. Such a company already has ancther established way of doing business. It looks at advertising and promotion differently from the direct marketer.

THE SALES PERSONNEL

Salesmen may have considerable knowledge and selling skills, but being people first and producers second, they need security, acceptance, recognition, encouragement, and sometimes a kick in the pants. They produce because they have a desire to work with and for their leaders, a confidence in their ability to do the work, a belief that management will help them, and a faith in their superiors that will carry them through inevitable disappointments and discouragements. These inner resources, without which no salesman can succeed, are fostered largely by the sales manager and his staff. It is the sales manager who equips salesmen for success. The manager who thinks and acts in terms of what the can do for his salespeople normally finds that he more he gives, the more he gets. The new salesman can be compared to a market opportunity that is ready to be tapped and cultivated.

The sales recruit has been influenced by parents, teachers, and former employers. Management has not hired him because he has the knowledge, skills, experience, and desire to be successful on his own, but because it is confident of its ability to convert a newcomer with appropriate "can-do" and "will-do" characteristics into an effective producer for his new company. The initial step in this conversion programme is sales training—the process of imparting knowledge, developing skills, and shaping attitudes and work habits for the purpose of maximizing the sales person's effectiveness.

The new salesman reports to work with stars in his eyes. He has been wooed by the recruiter. He has survived the successive hurdles of the selection process. He may have been wined and dined and given every attention during the hiring sequence. The recruit feels wanted, valued, and enthusiastic. At this point, many sales managers are guilty of a glaring error. They ignore the newcomer, shifting their attention to other functions, such as putting out "fires," hiring other people, doing paper-work. A relocated employee may be left on his own to locate a new residence, find a school for his children, initiate family social contacts, meet his fellow workers, and generally establish himself and, his, family in a new and possibly strange community.

Often the indoctrination process is limited to getting the new salesman souped-up enough to get out and knock on doors. You convince him there's nothing to it. Here's the presentation and there are the prospects. All you do is go out and show the product to the prospects and the money comes rolling in.

Strangely, the foregoing procedure frequently follows a meticulous recruiting and selection sequence. The new sales recruit may be lonely, uncertain of what he is getting into, a bit frightened, may be even desperate. He may be down on his luck or discouraged. The Horatio Alger dream may not be coming true. Perhaps he has experienced the taste of failure. Perhaps a new sales position is his gamble that it can be different and he is experiencing the feeling of a man putting his few remaining chips on this turn of the wheel. He needs to be encouraged and to feel a strong, sure, helping hand.

Indoctrination should build understanding and convictions that will last, not wear off the way a quick shot in the arm does. Indoctrination is a necessary preliminary functions, separate from training. Plunging headlong into training frequently results in instant terminations.

Indoctr,ination should be a positive process-welcoming the recruit to his new work environment, introducing him to fellow workers, informing him of job details and company philosophies, policies, and expectations, and generally preparing the recruit for his subsequent training and his subsequent life with the new company.

Many salesmen trend to resist training, especially if they are not convinced of its value to them. The trainee must respect the company, its products, its selling methods, and its policies toward solving customers' problems. Above all, the recruit must be convinced of his sales manager's willingness and ability to tell him, show him, and teach him how to be productive. Trainees need more than a warm and friendly leader. Research has shown that nice guys often make bum bosses. The power-driven manager has been found to be the most successful sales manager because of his basic desire to influence and lead others by creating a good climate. His subordinates have both a sense of responsibility and a clear knowledge of the organization. They adhere to the work rules, not because they are hit over the head, but because they become loyal to the institution.

The power-driven manager will quickly convince the recruit that the RMA and solid work habits will develop the salesman's ability to manage himself, which is a prerequisite for managing prospects and closing sales. Such a manager will do what he requires his salesmen to do. His attitude will be "Let's go into the field together; when it rains on you, it will rain on me." He will demonstrate that classroom-taught selling methods work in the field" Numerous cases have been cited where a sales trainee is trained in the classroom to use a given sales technique but when he is field-trained, the trainer uses an entirely different method. For example, the trainee is taught to use a semi-automated sales presentation but his field trainer uses a completely different, unstructured form during the initial field training.

A salesperson comes to his firm with a certain level of education, experience, and knowledge. However, there is always a gap between what the trainee already knows and what he needs to know. The size of this gap depends on whether the recruit is new to his present firm, new to the product he will sell, or new to the occupation of selling. The sales trainee must first be made aware of his own role with respect to both prospective buyers and his own organization. He must clearly understand the functions he is to perform and the environment in which he is to perform them. Knowledge needs will vary widely with the type of sales position. Usually, where the salesperson's primary function is in-store or route selling, the required knowledge is quite simple and can be' obtained by reading descriptive literature and manuals, attending brief classroom sessions, and observing an experienced salesperson. The knowledge-gathering process may be considerably more complex and time consuming for many other sales-force members. For example, the aspiring salesperson in life insurance or real estate may be required to take in-house or outside courses, do considerable studying at home, or use programmed learning materials in order to prepare for license-granting examinations. Industrial selling will often require extensive exposure to formalized training media including audiovisual materials, literature, lectures, case histories and field trips. Because trainees have had different levels of preparation, some firms will divide the training programme into segments so that a trainee can attend only the session which he requires. In general, the salesperson must acquire knowledge about four broad areas of the company; its offerings, its environment, its history and policies, and its operations and procedures.

It should be reassuring to even the most inexperienced sales-person that he knows'more about the product than any prospect he will ever encounter. Thus, he should be intimately familiar with every feature of every product he sells and with how it is designed and manufactured. In addition, he must be aware of why the product incorporates these features and of what benefits the features give to the ultimate purchaser. He must be prepared to discuss limitations in usage as well as causes and frequency of failures.

The salesman should be familiar with his competitors, their relative sales and profit volume, and their methods of operation. He must understand the advantages and disadvantages of his competitors' products, prices, and selling programmes, as compared with his own. Moreover, he must be aware of the extent to which competitive offering are being accepted by the marketplace. He should be able to determine customer needs and whether or not these needs are currently being satisfied. He should understand the dynamic influences in the general environment, including changing life styles, social pressures, technological advances, regulatory activities, and business trends, as they affect present and emerging new markets.

The salesman should understand why his company uses its current channel structure and distribution methods. He should understand and be able to support his company; policies concerning returns, allowances, billings, cancellations, and markup-granting policies. He must also know the company's history, philosophy, objectives, and standing in the trade. He must be aware of policies concerning personnel and compensation. He should be familiar with the background of the firm's executives.

The salesperson should be able to discuss his company's plan of organization and the relationship of the sales function to other functional areas. He should be particularly familiar with the areas of the company which closely support the selling operation. He should have a through understanding of the company's sales-control techniques and systems, including the format and need for call reports, sales meetings and clinics, quota systems, and profit-sharing plans. He should be well versed in the principles behind the company's selling techniques as they apply to stimulating purchases, solving customer problems, and upholding the highest standards of ethical selling practice. After a sales trainee has obtained the required knowledge, he must acquire the necessary skills to use that knowledge effectively and productively. In contrast to the acquisition of knowledge, developing skills require practice, either in front of prospects or under conditions that closely simulate such situations.

The mastery of selling, not unlike the mastery of gold, require continuous practice of the fundamental techniques, under the watchful eye of the sales manager, the selling pro. However, the golfer including the weekend duffer, views golf as a pleasurable recreational activity, an opportunity to enjoy himself with his friends, an athletic function which has no major impact on his financial resources or family happiness. Thus, he can enjoy the game despite his inability to developing golfing skills.

In broad terms, the successful sales trainee must learn to apply the principles of the company's selling techniques. Applied to the basic promotional functions introduced, he must learn how to find prospects, call on them, stimulate desire for possession, close orders, and retain customers. He must develop an instinct in selling situations for perceiving and diagnosing prospects' problems and needs, for probing and finding clues which will enable him to uncover latent desires, and for providing a desirable remedy at the right moment. Especially vital in developing communications skills is learning how to listen, absorb, and react when prospects, managers, and peers are expressing their needs. Salesmen must learn how to plan and use their time systematically and how to analyze their successes and failures so that each experience serves as a building block for future selfconfidence and success.

The trainer must foster instinctiveness in communication by compelling the trainee to actually perform selling activities. Reading, hearing, and thinking, as previously indicated, are not enough. Skill training calls for more than telling the new person what to do and how to do it. It calls for showing and teaching him how, and then reviewing and critically analyzing the trainee's performance. Skills can be developed in the training classroom through role playing, relevant sales case work, analysis of salesmen's call reports, business games, and other methods. A unique skill-development methods was devised. by the Seminar Film Company, which customizes "film that talk back" for larger firms. This method employs movies showing typical company prospects in various situations, and calls for instinctive sales responses. For example, the movie might show a protective receptionist being approached by a salesman and saying, "Yes, may I help you?" immediately a vanishing white line appears on the screen and the sales trainee must learn to respond before the line disappears. After the trainee. has delivered his response, the receptionist might say, "I don't believe Mr. Big will have time to see you today."

Despite the helpfulness of simulated situations, true interaction with prospects can only take place in the field. Ideally, as the trainee observes the field trainer in action, he will be convinced that what .he was taught really works. The trainee observes the field trainer's selling plan, prospecting, setting of appointments, approaches in business offices and at residential doors, sales presentations, closes, use of rebuttals—all the consecutive detailed steps of selling under live conditions. The astute trainer will confer with the trainee after each call or series of calls to answer questions, to associate what happened with material covered in classroom training session, to highlight critical incidents that took place during the call, to explicitly recall the reason for the success or failure of the call, and to allow the trainee to take notes where needed.

After field observation by the trainee has shown him how, the trainee does it himself while the field trainer observes. Often the trainer and trainee will alternate in making calls and also have "curbstone conferences" between calls. The trainer can use a prepared checklist to quickly locate a trainee's weak points.

The alternate-calling system is particularly useful when the trainer uses his own presentation to demonstrate the method of correcting weaknesses in the trainee's presentation. The trainee's next presentation should include the improvements that have been recommended by the trainer. Any system that requires a sales manager or experienced salesman to observe the trainee is costly since the trainer's personal production will normally be reduced.

Moreover, a trainee is often reluctant to perform in front of experienced salesmen or managers for fear he may do poorly and be subjected to considerable negative criticism. Therefore, if the curbstone conference or end-of-the-day critique is to be welcome by and constructive to the trainee, the trainer must focus on showing, the newcomer how to improve his strengths rather than on emphasizing his weaknesses. Many firms will compensate trainees by paying them full or partial commissions on sales made by the trainer. These earnings are deserved when the trainee has been active in setting up prospects for the trainer.

The primary objective of field observation is to demonstrate the application of company selling techniques and methods. If preliminary field observation is to be used at all, it should be in addition to not instead of, the field sessions that follow inside training. Obviously the costs of additional field training and the risk of confusing the unprepared newcomer are related to the nature of the specific selling task.

Sales training is a planning process in that it establishes the specific courses and methods of action that management desires the new salesman to follow. Supervision involves directing and controlling the activities of the salesperson to be sure he does not wander too far from the prescribed course of action. Any plan must be subject to a certain amount of standardization and the people who implement the plan must be disciplined to some degree. Properly applied, standardization and discipline are more for the benefit of the salesman than for his managers and company. Standardization prescribes a tracks for' the salesman to run on while discipline keeps him on the track.

Many salespeople are narcissistic exhibitionists at heart, and are never happier than when in front of prospects making a pitch. They love to be the center of attention and find that an audience aspires them to surprising heights of artistry. Yet, it has been found that even better salespeople do not have the raw creativity to develop original selling techniques.

It was indicated earlier that sales presentations with high amounts of company input were perceived by sales executives as most effective in facilitating the training of sales-force members. Yet the memorized presentation was rated as least effective. Despite the apparent ease of training a person to plug in a projector of flip the pages of an easel, flip chart, or read-off binder, this training procedure is not completely without challenge. The trainee must still be taught to gain an audience, neutralize, and prime the prospect for a captive session.

Sales trainees often find it difficult to memorize lengthy presentations. Therefore, training consists of pounding the material into the salesman's brain by use of repetitive drills and role-playing sessions. This process demands much of the trainer's time, patience, and energy. Moreover, salespeople often resent being servile to considerable structure in terms of what to say and how to say it. Yet, salesmen are best compared to actors who must be fed their lines. They may be articulate, but they are not necessary good extemporaneous speakers. For example, when they are thrown off stride by some incident or interruption, many salesmen tend to return to the beginning of a sales presentation section. A number of training procedures can develop skills in extemporaneous speaking, delivering lines, and reading with feeling, enthusiasm, and sparkle. One trainer holds impromptus speaking sessions where trainees are required to deliver spur-of-the-moment three minute speeches on such far-out subjects as baby carriages; grandfather clocks, and mirrors. In another organization trainees are drilled in reading brief arbitrarily selected newspaper articles aloud in a sparkling and scintillating way.

Even the veteran salesman often has difficulty in coping with a new objection or new form of sales resistance. When salesmen get together at sales meetings, conventions, social events, or over a cup of coffee, they exchange ideas or phrases which have worked in the past. The newcomer has not had these opportunities and is concerned with his ability to handle objections such as 'I'am happy with my present supplier" or "how to I know it will sell" or "the price is too high "or "I've used up my open-to-buy."

As mentioned earlier, many firms prepare a booklet of standard rebuttals and verbal-proof stories which respond to recurrent objections. Classroom drill sessions help the trainee build a reservoir of answers to meet nearly every contingency. Some trainers recommend ways that the salesman can use his rebuttal folder in the presence of the prospective customer in case of memory lapse.

It would seem that the new salesman would be delighted to be guided by a structured, proven selling plan that has been designed by specialists, This is quite true during the early training stages. But the person in selling is often quite impatient. If the company selling plan does not result in instant results, the greenest recruit may not hesitate to figure out a better way. This amateurish reconstruction is, more often than not, so illconceived and remote from the company plan that the product could not be given away much less sold. Even the intelligent trainee who experiences early successes by using his learned routine with few modifications is likely to try to improve the system. This person may want to do his own thinking and use his own knowledge. He absorbs the company method, evaluates it, masters it, and then comes to his own conclusions.

In larger organizations, the sales-training function may be a team effort. Home office personnel may design the programme, the district manager may supervise the training programme, staff instructors may conduct classroom sessions, while experienced salesmen, unit field managers, branch managers, or the district manager himself may conduct the field-training activities. When the inside training programme is divided into discrete sessions or courses, outside training specialists or consultants may be called upon to conduct various segments. For example, several sales consulting firms are specialists in lead-getting or telephone selling, or servicing department stores.

In smaller firms and in the local operations of some larger firms, a single sales manager may personally perform all the training functions listed in the first paragraph of this section. In considering such a possibility, one reopens the argument of whether the sales managers should be actively involved in personal selling and field-related activities. In some companies, trainees are sent to universities or special school for part of their training.

Occasionally sales trainees join other newly hired people in indoctrination sessions conducted by the firm's personnel department. The lineup of training personnel will depend on the size and the unique demands of a given firm. One useful guideline is to delegate the field training to the same individual who will later be responsible for supervising the trainee. This is particularly effective when the supervising manager receives permanent overrides on the trainee's production. Money is a major motivating force for convincing field managers to develop skilful trainees.

Some training programmes can be completed in a few hours; others last for two or more years. If the trainee is salaried, it will be tc the firm's advantage to prepare him as quickly as possible for field productivity so as to avoid undue delays in generating a profit on the firm's investment in training and compensation costs. New salesmen who are compensated on a commission basis, are anxious to go out in the field as soon as possible. If there is neither money nor the promise of a paycheck in time to pay the grocery bill, the new salesman may be persuaded to search the want ads for a salaried job.

The speed of training a given individual will receive depends on the number and complexity of the knowledge, skill, and attitude requirements, the number of trainees being trained simultaneously, the availability of trainers, whether training is done individually or in classes, where the training takes place, the steps in the training process, the design of the training programme, the teaching ability of the trainers, and the learning capacity of the trainees. When replacement trainees are readily recruitable, trainers may have limited patience with trainees who catch on slowly. When one speaks of the speed of training, the question arises as to when a new salesman is no longer considered to be a trainee. However, one approach suggests that the salesperson moves through a salesman's career cycle (SCC) consisting of the four stages of preparation, development, maturity, and decline. This model suggests that the preparation stages is concluded when the salesman competes his initial training and is permitted to call on prospects without being accompanied by a field manager. To determine whether a given sales trainee should be advanced to the development phase, management might require an affirmative answer to each of the following questions:

1. Is he aware of his specific job requirements?
2. Does he have favourable attitudes toward the learning process?
3. Does he perceive direct and purposive relationships between customer needs, company goals, and his own behaviour?
4. Has he developed the skills to put his knowledge into action?
5. Has he developed an understanding of personal interaction and the barriers to making it successful?
6. Does he appear willing and able to acquire new capacities?

In practice, field training takes place in the prospects office and residences, on curbstones, in restaurants, and enroute to and from sales calls. In large firms, inside training may either be decentralized, and allocated to local district or branch offices, or centralized in the company's home office. Decentralization has a number of advantages in that the trainee is trained by the same people who will ultimately supervise him and benefit from his productivity on a regular basis. Moreover, he will be indoctrinated in the same regional environment that he will have to "live with" when he advances to the development stage of his career cycle.

The disadvantage is that training personnel in the local office may be part-time trainers who may not offer the trainee the required intense attention because of other managerial demands such as administrative duties, hiring, supervision, and personal selling. In a centralized framework, a full-time staff of teachers is usually available. Indeed, there are advantages, from a learning viewpoint, in being removed from the distractions and temptations of one's daily 'routine. Yet there is little doubt that centralized training is costly in terms of financing trainees' travel and hotel expenses and supporting large scale training facilities and personnel.

In a number of firms part of the initial training takes place at national or regional headquarters and part in a local setting. Normally, the visit to central headquarters will come first. Promising recruits are introduced to members of top management, taken on a detailed tour of the central office, and provided with a basic introduction to company policies and philosophies and fundamental selling techniques. The detailed nitty-gritty skill-development exercises take place in the local office, where they can be reinforced by training in the field.

In a somewhat narrower context, supervision has been looked upon as a process whereby sales managers influence salespeople in much the same way as salesmen influence prospective customers. In this sense, the purpose of the supervisory relationship is to guide the behaviour of sales-force members in a direction that is compatible with the goals of the firm. One weakness of this approach is that the employee is seen as a passive object being manipulated to carry out mandates of others rather than as an active seeker of goals. This is analogous to a seller who fails to reconcile his own interests with those of the prospective customer. Therefore, this chapter treats supervision as a one-on-one technique to guide and motivate the individual salesman and to provide him or her with continued help in planning activities, utilizing time and efforts more effectively, and developing the instinctive skills to deal with unique situations. Effective supervisions improves the salesman's can do and will do characteristics, with emphasis upon the latter.

Ideally, the salesmen's initiative should come from within. Management's job is to help salespeople develop their self-motivation, realize their growth potential, increase their capacity for assuming responsibility, and achieve a readiness to direct behaviour toward the goals of the organization: Yet, it has been found that even in an ideal organization climate, many salesmen when left to their own devices do only the minimum which they believe will be acceptable. Even money the well-known silent supervisor, will not inspire all salespeople. It is the sales manager who determines what his salesmen will accomplisht.

Supervision takes place in the field and is oriented to the salesman's daily activities in front of prospects. Supervising sales-force members is aimed toward *(1)* improving the salesman's morale; *(2)* uncovering selling deficiencies; *(3)* providing additional training; *(4)* enforcing company needs; and *(5)* stimulating improved performance. An examination of these aims reinforces the notion, that supervision involves directing and controlling the activities of the salesperson to be sure he does not wander too far from the plan of action that was prescribed in the training programme. The larger portion that was prescribed in the supervisory activities required to achieve these aims.

There is little doubt that one-on-one supervision of sales personnel is a neglected function in many organizations. Five reasons are offered for this neglect: it's not needed, it's too 'costly, too time consuming; too difficult, and resented by salesmen. There is tendency on the part of some sales managers to dichotomize salesforce members into two groups—those who have it and those who don't. the first group consists of the selfstarters who require little supervision; the second group is made up of the helpless and hopeless weak sisters who could not make the grade even with supervision twenty-, four hours a day.

Most salespeople are in the development phase of the salesman's career cycle (SCC) and may be required to make many sacrifices, work long and possibly odd working hours, and sustain numerous refusals and substantial chastisement. They have the capacity to learn and the willingness to endure negative situations, but they have a periodic need of tender care by management. One cannot dispute the fact that it is costly and time consuming to supervise the individual salesman. The reader is surely aware that the field sales manager wears many hats. He is frequently engaged in administrative functions and in recruiting, training, and acquiring personal sales. He often writes the house organ, conducts local sales meetings, and designs and administers contests. In terms of profitability, he often questions the wisdom of working in the field with a salesman or paying a field supervisor to perform this function.

Sales-force members are frequently so scattered geographically that it is difficult for the supervisor to spend much time with each subordinate. In addition, due to the unpredictability of human beings, every demand upon the supervisor is unique. The active field supervisor may spend time with a different salesman each day. Each salesperson may face a different problem and react in a different way. The supervisor is under pressure to uncover the deficiencies and recommend an instant solution. He has a new audience every day, somewhat like the baseball star who is expected by every new group of spectators to hit a home run. Often, it is the salesmen who need help the most that are least receptive to supervision. They are convinced that the supervisor is there to appraise, evaluate, spy, and criticize rather than to assist. They become salesmen to enjoy freedom from close supervision and control. They may employ questionable selling techniques which they do not want management to discover.

For every salesperson who is helpless and hopeless, there are many who can be developed into outstanding performers if their weaknesses are spotted and corrected in time. This is particularly true of inexperienced salesmen who have yet to accustom themselves to the rejections and disapointments that are a part of selling. In the absence of proper supervision, they may resort to flight tactics, fight tactics, or other "coping devices." Outward manifes ations of emotional flight by the salesperson can be recognized in behaviour such as the following:

1. He avoids prospecting for new customers.
2. He avoids contact with difficult customers.
3. Instead of asking for orders, he develops a sizeable group of people who want to think it over, thus creating a list of imaginary future buyers.
4. He is willing to spend considerable time in waiting rooms or driving in his car in order to avoid customer contact.
5. His apathy towards prospects turns to sympathy.

Under stress conditions the salesman may become so nervous that he may remove himself from the field and resort to such coping devices as sleep, drugs, alcohol sex, golf, movies, and so on. In contrast to those who attempt to escape from the tensions of the sales job, there are those who display fight reactions. For example, a salesperson may behave as follows:

1. He finds fault with his company and with its products, promotional methods, prices, service, methods, etc.
2. He complains to and about sales supervisors, exaggerating and falsifying to strengthen his attack.
3. He may display hostility in dealing with customers or prospects.
4. He may speak against the company when dealing with customers or prospects, criticizing products, services, prices, methods, management, and policies.

5. He may not get along with people and this may result in disputes, violence, and dismissal.

When the salesperson's work assignments provoke intolerable anxieties in him, it may be the result of the inherent disappointments ot selling, described earlier by the selling penddulum. There are also more specific reasons. The salespersons may have been assigned to duties beneath his capabilities, with resultant routinization and boredom.

On the other hand, he may have been placed in a job that is dearly over his head, in terms of his ability to function and to engage in the required personal relationships. For example, a salesman may be quite successful when he is supplied with qualified prospects by his employer, but he may find it difficult to create leads by his own efforts, that is, by telephone solicitation, cold canvassing, and other creative prospecting methods. The company may fail to provide a strong, compatible supervisor. Instead, the latter may be weak, incompetent, vindictive, punitive, unreliable, and/or autheritarian. Management may fail to structure and define the salesman's duties, goals, responsibilities, and scope of authority.

The salesperson may be placed in a work environment where he is not accepted, either covertly or overtly, and where his past history or present inadequacies may be sources of rejection or conflict. Even when the salesperson is not subjected to open attack, he can be deprived by the in-group of support, membership, and acceptance and can become, in essence, an outcast. In addition, salesmen fear slumps, layoffs, and discharges when the general outlook for the health of a company or an industry is not favourable. Low morale is fostered by the absence of a shoulder to lean on someone in the firm to answer the salesman's job-related questions and also help in solving his personal problems.

Many grievances or concerns ot the salesman are fancied, but even these call for coaching and counselling by sales manager. Coaching is a teaching technique for imparting facts and methods, or ways to accomplish a task. The personality of the salesperson is not affected. Coaching involves instructional aid while the salesman is performing or immediately following performance of the task. Counselling is called for when a salesperson's personal feelings become involved and when his attitudes come into play.

Consider the case of the salesman who complains of a sales slump that has persisted for two weeks. Such a salesman requires understanding and support by his sales manager. The manager should listen carefully to the salesman's account of his experiences and encourage the salesman to disclose why he feels the slump has occurred. The manager should not attempt to judge the salesman or to offer unsolicited advice. The aim of counseling is to render the salesperson independent so that he will be able to solve similar future problems by himself. Thus, the competent sales counsellor will help the salesman to help himself. Presume that in this case the sales supervisor uncovers no serious flaws in the salesman's work habits or sales techniques. He should seek to build confidence in his subordinate by showing him that the slump is the result of nothing more than the "law of averages" in action.

The important thing to remember is that the "head" on the coin does not become upset when "tails" comes up ten times in a row. Similarly, you have little to worry about when you run into a negative streak. Think of yourself as a coin that accepts nos as well as yeses in a sequence that is impossible to predict. As shown in the above example, counseling may be the ideal solution for an imagined sales problem. Often, however, the concern is quite real and the salesman has truly developed certain bad habits or weaknesses that must be spotted and corrected.

Many sales managers are of the mistaken impression that coaching in the field means that the sales manager should pick up a sales kit and take the slumping salesman out on a few calls to show him how easy it is to make a sale. This may prove that the firm's product can be sold, but it will not prove that the salesman can sell it. Therefore, it must be repeated that it is insufficient to just tell or show the salesperson how to do it. He must be taught how, and this calls for the supervisor to alternate calls with the salesperson and observe him until he masters the techniques bring taught. Only then will the supervision process bring about self-development.

Despite the acknowledge importance and effectiveness of field supervision, it is quite costly in terms of demands upon the sales manager's time and energy. Moreover, selling deficiencies can often be uncovered in the office with equal effectiveness. In fact, there are certain continuous inside methods of supervision that may be more effective than field supervision, which is necessarily occasional. One such technique is the proper use of activity reports or call reports. Unfortunately, the literature has stressed the use of these reports for evaluation and for assisting management rather than as tools for uncovering the salesman's deficiencies and improving his performance.

This author prefers to call them activity reports rather than call reports since the report, properly designed, develops more data when it includes all the activities and not just the results of sales calls on prospects or customers. This need is properly emphasized when one remembers that selling is more than what happens in front of the prospect. Consider the following sample report of the past week's activities prepared by a salesman who obtains all his prospects by use of the telephone:

Number of the telephone calls 110

Number of telephone contacts with prospects 73

Number of appointments made by telephone 26

Number of sales presentations completed 4

Number of sales 1

The salesman earned only $90 in weekly commissions even though his sales conversion rate, one sale in four presentations, was approximately equivalent to the company average. The problems is that only four sales presentations were delivered despite twenty-six appointments. There are two possible explanations for this performance: either the salesman did not bother to keep most of his appointments or the appointments were so poorly set up that the prospects were unwilling to keep them. A detailed review of each appointment would covered, counselling may be called for. Otherwise, coaching in the technique of making solid appointments by telephone may be required. In either case, there is little need for the sales manager to accompany the salesman on field calls, at least until the results of the present counselling and coaching have been studies. The salesman's activity report and its subsequent analysis may pinpoint the need for improving the salesman's sales presentation or his closing techniques. He may require additional training in technical aspects of the product, in preparing proposals, or in analyzing customer requirements. He may be referred to various books or technical manuals, asked to reread material published by the company, enrolled in company refresher programmes. Some firms supply sales-force members with programmed learning materials to be studied or played at home. In all cases, a plan of action must be developed to offer direction to the salesman. An important part of this plan is the follow-up procedure, which akes sure that the additional training results in improved performance.

Supervision is much more than altruistically serving the needs of sales-force members. This and the previous chapter have focused on improving the company's selling effectiveness by developing a thorough knowledge of the salesman's needs and behaviour. However, the achievement of company goals is the sought-after reward for the skilful development of happy salespeople. In most cases, the company plan requires that the salesman be disciplined to do the company job the company way. The salesman's needs must necessarily be servile to those of the company. Accordingly, management is often willing to tolerate such negative situations as high turnover of sales people, low sales-force morale, and numerous customer complaints if such conditions are required for the achievement of company objectives. Happy salesmen and a low turnover rate are of little comfort to a company in distress. The pattern of supervision should be adjusted to the needs of the firm. Frequently, salesmen's priorities must be reordered to generate a prescribed product or customer mix. Management may compel salesmen to concentrate on slower-moving items in the product line or to focus on larger rather than smaller customers. Sometimes salesmen are required to submit detailed expense accounts or the company places a limit on travel and entertainment expenses.

The company might also impose certain credit restrictions or adjust its minimum down-payment requirements, advertising allowances, or billing terms. These techniques can be considered to be "automatic supervisors" in that they control the salesman's actions and exert constant pressure on him to conform to the overall sales plan set forth by management. It may also be in the company's best interest to control the content of the sales message to prevent inaccurate or unethical statements by sales-force members. The memorized or otherwise structured sales presentation is a highly effective method of accomplishing this objective. This type of sales message also assists the sales supervisor in trouble shooting the poor producer. Many firms that depend on standardized or canned sales presentations argue, that supervision boils down to seeing that the salesman does not deviate form"the standard pitch".

The demands of consumerism have persuaded may sales managers to step up the intensity of monitoring the sales calls of new of questionable salespeople. A number of firms, especially those who sell directly to consumers, have initiated a posts ale system of verifying the sales transaction with the new customer for the purpose of uncovering misunderstandings, complaints, or buyer's remorse. The order is not processed until all customer grievances have been settled. One firm, which sought to control sales misrepresentations and irregularities, supplied salesmen under surveillance with the names of bogus prospects in whose premises tape recorders has been planted. The latter plan was costly in that those who assisted in the detective work were well compensated for their cooperation. It was, however quite effective since several unethical salespeople were caught red-handed and either were reprimanded or terminated.

Some readers may question the need for this section in the chapter on supervision. They may say, "If the salesman's morale is improved, if his selling deficiencies are uncovered, if the appropriate additional training has been provided, and if the company needs have been stressed, improved performance by the salesman will be an automatic result. Perhaps the salesman shouldn't have been hired in the first place. Perhaps he was oversold in the job interview, accepted the job as a temporary stopgap, recognized early that the job did not suit him, and is floundering because he never did have his heart in it. Perhaps the salesman was inadequately trained for his particular job assignment.

On the other hand presume that the selection and training functions were performed properly. The salesperson may still flounder or fail for two major reasons: *(1)* incompatibility with management, and *(2)* a lack of positive and constructive leadership. Personality conflicts are often difficult to resolve. Extreme sensitivity, as well as a strong sense of self-righteousness, often lead to incompatibility and friction. Early exposure and a frank discussion of differences are usually quite helpful. But what is meant by that intangible something called "leadership"? Of the thousands of definitions that have been advanced" over time, the most meaningful one is a sales management context is "that ingredient of personality which causes people to follow."

Burton Bigelow once described the sales manager's leadership as "a priceless ingredient that turns the effort of ordinary salespeople into extraordinary results." These ordinary people are characterized by similar attitudes and motives which the sales supervisor must understand and know how to deal with. According to Bigelow, mediocre people prefer to avoid making decisions;

- are lukewarm and uncertain in their enthusiasm;
- lack faith in themselves and have little native confidence in others'
- are afraid of responsibility and inhospitable to any suggestion that they accept it'
- are undecided as to where they are going-even as to where they want to go.

If one is mindful of the old Chinese proverb which says "knowledge, like water, takes the form of the vessel into which it's poured," one will no doubt argue that the sales leader who can transform mediocre people into productive producers is a rare genius. Alexander Hamilton rejected the notion that the expert leader is a genius when he observed: Men give me credit for some genius. All the genius I have lies sin this When I have a subject in hand, I study it profoundly. Day and night is before me. I explore it in all its bearings. My mind becomes pervaded with it. Then the effort which I have made is what people are pleased to call the fruit of genius. It is instead the fruit of labour and thought. Sales leadership is the process of shaping a human being, molding him, as if he were clay, into what the leader wants him to be, until he is capable of performing as the leader wishes him to perform. Fortunately, what a sales leader does is considerably more tangible than what a leader is. Past experience and current practice indicate a number of guidelines, of varyipg degrees of importance, for the effective leadership of sales personnel:

1. Keep salesmen excited.
2. Exp ct enough-not too little-not too much.
3. Establish clear-cut objectives.
4. Set up a step-by-step programme to reach sales subjectives.
5. Plan ahead for yourself and your sales force.
6. Sell the programme enthusiastically.
7. Coach salespeople in the how as well as the what.
8. Sell the sales force on the importance of the job.
9. Continually inspect and promptly correct.
10. Challenge the fighters-bolster the timed.
11. Tell salespeople how they stand.
12. Use the power of incentives.
13. Be the boss through thick and thin.
14. Set the pace.
15. Bestow praise when earned.
16. Encourage and assist salespeople, one at a time.
17. Display wisdom, fairness, and human understanding.

The above list was succinctly summarized at Willy Loman's funeral in the play "Death of a Salesman". The job of the sales manager is to help the salesman to keep the smile and the shoe-shine, to avoid the earthquake, to keep the spots off his hat, to make the salesman dream the right dreams, and then help to make these dreams come true. "Many salesman can outsell me but none can outtry me." This statement, made by a salesman of construction equipment, is a tribute both to the man who made it and to his supervisors who provided the spark that started the motivational process within him. Such an attitude is indicative of collaboration and interdependence between the salesperson and management through the development of mutual target setting. How does such mutuality come about? One way of promoting greater sales efficiency, raising salesforce morale, and blending the goals of the organization and the individual so that the achievement is mutual is management by objectives (MBO). This process features management's use of input from the salesman in every phase of the selling job.

Conversely, management often has much to gain by granting the employee equal time to inject his intimate knowledge of the marketplace into the discussion. In MBO, criteria are agreed upon for the appraisal of sales results. This opens the door for supervision because the sales manager can focus his supervisory efforts on areas where the salesman is failing to meet mutual objectives. In turn the sales-force member will expect and receive help in the form of advice, reprimands, retraining, etc., when needed.

Deviations from the planned selling results provide automatic feedback which, in turn, serves as meaningful input for the planning of future goals, strategies, methods of appraisal, and rewards for both parties. The give-and-take exchange between management and the sales-force member becomes more fruitful and acceptable to the salesman when at least a portion of the input from management is objective and based on hard data. For example, one author describes the computer-based system used by an industrial marketing firm to help the salesman use field time more effectively.

In this system, the salesman feeds the computer data on each of his accounts, such as number of calls made in the current three-month period, number of expected calls in the upcoming quarter, average time per call, expected annual sales, expected sales for each account, and the sales adjustment factor based on the account's impact on profitability due to purchased product or commissions.

In essence, the MBO approach compels the sales manager to study each salesperson and customize the goal-setting and supervision package to satisfy ea h employee's unique set of needs and, expectations. Instead, management may discover that the sales force can be subdivided into a few group of employees who have common needs and goals.

This alternative method of "sales-force segmentations" calls for applying different motivation, communication, administrative, goal-setting, and supervisory principles to each group in order to achieve maximum performance from each. Mossien and Fram suggest several bases for sales-force segmentation. First, salesmen can be segmented by job title so that a person would be classified as a trainee, salesman, senior salesman, or master salesman, depending upon his level of productivity. Hi segmentation by financial recognition, some salespeople would be on salary plans, others on commission programmes, and still others on mixed plans. Commission and bonus rates and salary levels would be geared to the needs and productivity of each group. Other bases for segmentation are by peripheral benefits and personal recognition. For example, company cars would be available to certain groups and not to others and there would be separate sales contests, award incentives, national sales meetings, and, retraining sessions.

Segmentation by communication differences is based on the belief that it is inappropriate to address the top professional in the same manner as one addresses the neophyte. Accordingly, it not far-fetched to consider the preparation of separate house organs, newsletters, and local sales clinics for each of the sales-force segments. The underlying value of this motivating method is that it provides a system by which career salespeople can grow in status, financial remuneration, and level of communication with management. The differing needs and motivational requirements of various salesforce members are recognized without the need for the extensive customization that is demanded in the MBO process.

One authority has stated that education may be one of the greatest forces for motivating sales-force members. No salesman will ever live long enough to learn all he needs to know about selling through his personal experiences alone. That's why salesmen read books, watch other salesmen, and exchange ideas by participating in meeting and seminars. Knowledge drives out fear. The absence of fear creates confidence. Confidence is based on understanding which must be assiduously cultivated if it is to bear good fruit.

Teaching salesmen is quite different from teaching students in the college classroom. The, key to this difference is the subject's readiness to learn. Often the bright college student will not learn because the material is not meaningful to him and the instructor has done little to make it meaningful. Only a grade is at stake. The sales supervisor or trainer is more fortunate than the professor in that he is in the position of being able to make all of his material meaningful to his salesmen. Most salesmen are ready to learn. They are totally involved. The best way to motivate a customer to place reorders is to sell him a product that prodnces favourable results. Similarly, the best way to motivate a salesman to learn is to offer him instruction and guidance that is convertible into productive sales results.

Every salesman must be handled differently. The "can't" salesman needs a boot. The "won't" salesman needs a needle. The wounded salesman needs a bandaid. Finally, the producing salesman needs a blue ribbon which may prevent him from becoming ill at a later date. The diagnosis or troubleshooting process can take place in the office, in, the car, on the curbstone, on the golf course, in the lunchroom, or any place that the salesman and his supervisor can meet on a one-on-one basis. A useful troubleshooting tool is the checklist or a "why I didn't get the order" form. The checklist should consist of a lengthy list of items covering every facet of the selling programme, from prospecting to closing. The checklist is a sequential inventory of techniques or characteristics which are necessarily possessed by the "ideal" salesman.

By periodically discussing and observing the items on the list, the supervisor is in a position to note a salesman's points of strength and weakness relative to a given selling situation or over a period of time. The salesperson may also use the checklist as a self-improvement tool by evaluating his own strong and weak points. Too often selling errors are not permanently corrected by the sales supervisor. One sales researcher suggests the use of "dialogue analysis" as a method of reorienting experienced salesmen. In this approach, transcriptions of conversations between salesman and prospects are analyzed. The dialogues recreate real situations involving communications between people. These conversations are analyzed for proper use or misuse of techniques, ideas, concepts, and strategies in selling. Although the best method of collecting dialogues is by use of concealed tape recorders, some managers, salesmen, and prospects may find this method objectionable and even unethical. An imperfect but useful alternative is dialogue material contributed by salesmen or sales managers as a result of their recall of selling experiences.

❐

13

Substantive Findings in Trade Dealings

Promotional campaigns can be specifically aimed at competitor's weaknesses, and with much greater effectiveness if an industry consists of only a few firms. A fifth justification for sales promotion revolves around the perceived high risk the customer associates with committing resources in the purchase of a product. Although there is little evidence that sales promotion can change attitudes, there is evidence that most consumers see individual sales promotional schemes as quite distinct phenomena from the products with which such schemes are associated. That is to say, brand image is affected neither positively nor negatively by the value of a scheme to the buyer. It is simply an extra inducement to buy its function is to change behaviour by providing a stimulus to buy.

Risk felt by potential customers is most likely to be present in the buying situation when:

1. The Product is New and Untried.

Sales promotional remedy—sampling, de-monstration, trial run, guarantee of benefit, free trips for customer to visit the factory or other users.

2. Benefits will not be Felt or Completed for Some Time.

Sales promotional remedy—delayed invoicing, premium offers, linked services.

3. The product on its own is not quite perceived to be adequate value-for-money.

Sales promotional remedy—premium offers, couponing, collection schemes, and contests.

4. The Buyer is Afraid that new Products will be Launched thus Rendering the One Bought Obsolete before it is Fully Depreciated.

Sales Promotional Remedy—leasing agreement with discounts for trading-up, guaranteed buy-back arrangements.

5. The product will not be compatible with the buyer's consumption system.

Sales Promotional Remedy—tailor-made package deal, training facilities, container premiums.

The final advantage in sales promotion is the existence of a large number of marginal customers. Marginal customers are those buyers who are almost at the point of purchase but not quite. Every other element of the proposition put to them has been assembled and still the deal has not quite been completed, just an extra push will do it. Sales promotion schemes provide a last-minute and Specific inducement that is possible to introduce without disturbing any other element of the deal. To summarize,

Price Deals. Price deals are simply a short-term reduction in the price of a product, either nationally or, more usually, locally, in order to stimulate demand that for some reason has fallen off. A scheme like this might include refunds on new products, cents-off coupons, or some type of combination.

If a price offer is going to succeed, the first and most obvious factor to be looked at is the normal brand buying motives of the consumer. The consumer must buy based primarily on price alone for price offer to be effective in inducing a brand switch. Research indicates that if the consumer buys for any other major reason, dropping the price temporarily will make little difference to sales.

Price discount or cents-off deals are probably the oldest type of sales promotion within this category. A price discount is usually apparent only at the point of sale. It is marked on the package and is not usually advertised. Although with evidence in inducing buyers to switch brands, one does find more and more promotions being advertised, particularly in the FMC6 business. A price offer alone is of little practical use in attracting customers who have never used the product before. They will want to know far more about it than the mere fact that there is three cents off, as the original price and value to them were unknown anyway, Moreover, a price offer does not make existing customers buy more often, but they may buy in larger quantities.

This brings us to another main conclusion about the type of product that a price offer is used to sell. It is not just a product bought often by the same customer and with an elastic demand curve. It is also a product that most people use anyway, and at a certain usage rate that sales promotion cannot affect. Since the offer is usually marked on the package, this type of promotion relies on adequate display for its effectiveness, this accounts for the importance attached to it in self-service stores of all kinds, which rely on massed display.

Here is one final, but important point before leaving the subject of price offers. Market researchers and others have frequently found that consumers, when other guides are lacking, take price as an indicator of quality. If one is unable to test a new, unfamiliar, complex, seldom-bought brand of product, it is impossible to learn whether it is worth the money. All one has to fall back on is a rather vague conception of what the price should be, the salesperson's argument, and the price being asked. "The higher the price, the better the quality must be", the potential buyer thinks. "I mean; after all, a high price must reflect high costs; and high costs mean that the quality of the materials and workmanship must be good – don't they?" situation like this, to offer a promotional price reduction is to inject an element of disturbance into the buyer's' set of information. It looks incongruous; almost as if a lowered price says something different from all the other consistent elements of the marketing mix. The buyer may, therefore, reject the proposition, thinking that the offer is inappropriate and possibly that a corner has been cut somewhere or the pack is a specially small one.

Coupon offers may be the fastest growing area of sales promotion. Coupons are certificates that are placed in consumers' hands through door-to-door distribution or through direct mail; they can be part of a newspaper or magazine ad; they are in some packages, and on some packages. They can be in any amount ranging from two cents to a dollar or more. Most manufacturer's coupons are coded so that sorting and processing are easier.

Nevertheless, many retailers are less than enthusiastic about redeeming coupons. For one thing, the selling process is slowed down. TIme is required in sorting, handling, and counting. Then, the retailer must wait to be reimbursed. Certainly whether the handling allowance allowed by the manufacturer to the retailer is adequate is still debatable.

Contests. Contests remain one of the most popular types of consumer promotions. Because, of the increasing need of people to get "something for nothing" contests have grown dramatically during the 1980s and 1990s. Although much of this popularity is due to advent of satellite television.

Because of certain legal factors, advertisers for many years employed contests of skill-eliminating the element of chance and thus removing the lottery stigma. The familiar 25-words-or-less contest and many other devices of the sort were common for years.

There are many criticisms levelled at the use of contests. Most notably, critics are concerned with the many costs associated with designing an effective contest. Selecting appropriate prizes is a particularly difficult problem. The prize must be attractive to the consumer, yet it must not overshadow the basic product sold by the sponsor. Often the relative attractiveness of cash, merchandise, or travel is a function of the particular market segment targeted. The media strategy employed to communicate the contest may also be complex and costly. Retailers may often be part of this process and may resent their participation. There are also critics who suggest that contests generate more ill will than goodwill. Losers may become opinion leaders against the company, particularly in light of the scandals associated with contests in the past. This brings up another criticism. Great care must be taken to meet the letter of the law in designing contests. For example, all prizes must be awarded. A final criticism concerns the effectiveness of contests. It is. difficult to know what level of sales increase is generated by the contest.

The arguments in favour of contests are also convincing. The primary argument in their favour is that contests generate mass interest and excitement-entries number in the millions-as well as a real enthusiasm among customers and employees. It also provides something new for the company to advertise. After several months of creating me-too messages or desperately looking for a unique point to make, advertising people can let a contest take the burden off of them for a while. Contest copy tends to write itself as long as it is supported by lots of enthusiasm and excitement in the background. Contests appeal to the consumer's desire to play, to compete, to win, to get something for nothing. The impact tends to be quite positive.

Rebates. Rebates first became popular in the mid 1970s and have remained popular. Simply stated, a rebate is a refund of a fixed amount of money for a certain period of time. Cash rebates remain a viable sales promotion technique to build shopping traffic and to move certain products.

Premium Offers. Although there are numerous definitions of what a premium is, suffice it to say that a premium is a tangible reward received for performing a particular act, usually purchasing a product. The premium can be considered something extra which makes the purchase of the product more appealing. The premium may be free, if not, the amount the consumer must pay is well below market price. Premiums may be used to attract customers to a particular store, to buy a par cular product, or to stimulate the purchase of larger amounts of a product. Thus, getting an extra amount of product is a premium, as is the jar with Nescafe, a free dispouser with Fem liquid soap.

Direct premiums are incentives that provide Immediate consumer action and give on-the-spot action in return. There is no confusion about money, mailing, clipping, chance, packaging, saving things, or tearing off box tops. Best of all, there is no waiting. Several generations ago direct premiums included small gifts from a storekeeper, free prints, books, or even the baker's dozen. By definition, a direct premium is usually considered to be one given free with the purchase at the time of the purchase.

Direct premiums are strong today in many fields—food, financial institutions, toiletries, publishing, apparel, office supplies, and even the oil business edible. The standout newcomer of the 1990s is the fast-food restaurant business. In the FMC6 business, always a big direct premium user in the past, the separate direct premium gave way to a boom of factory-packs.

Four basic variations exist that qualify as direct premiums.

1. Incentives given separately at the time of a product purchase the truly direct premium.

2. In-packs-inserted into the product package at the factory as a plus to the consumer.

3. Container premiums – which reverse the idea of the in-pack, putting the product inside the premium tead or *vice versa.*

4. On-packs-another form of factory-pack that rides outside the package, firmly affixed to it by a paper or plastic band, sleeve, or other device.

The mail premium is considered a self-liquidator as enough is charged for the premium that it pays for itself. The last three variations were not widely used until recently. Then, they came as a sort of reaction from the overuse of self-liquidators, when many users sought a compromise between the cumbersome separate premium and the slow self-liquidator.

Three other versions of the direct premium are: traffic-builders, door-openers, and referral premiums. Traffic-builder is a title given to many forms of promotion that hold out hope of bringing people into retail stores-under many guises from supermarket continuity promotions to loss leaders. But the true traffic-builder premium is none of these – it is, simply, an incentive to bring a prospect to one's place of business.

Where the traffic-builder tries to get doors opened from the outside, what we call a door-opener aims at having them opened from the inside by consumers in their homes or business people in their offices. By far the most obvious user of door-openers is the direct-selling field, in which door-opening favours are a staple device to get consumers' attention. Their use is a subtle foot-in-the-door on house-to-house canvassing and sometimes a clincher in telephoning for an appointment. In addition, door-openers serve similar purposes in many other industries-wherever the ultimate sales effort must be made in the prospect's home or office.

The final category of premiums is based on referrals provided by the receiver. Many people believe that the best advertising is a satisfied customer. The use-the-user plan, as it used to be called, helps sellers in many fields to get sales leads from satisfied customers and to reward the present users with a premium for their assistance.

In its simplest form, the plan works this way. You have sold your product to Mrs. Consumer. She likes it. You ask her for the names of one or more friends who have seen the product and might be prospects to buy.

You offer her an attractive incentive if any of the friends or neighbours buys. There are four basic variations.

1. Major appliance dealers' salespeople may go into the customer's home, get names, and follow through in person with the prospects.
2. Many credit card organizations and other membership organizations offer several different premiums to those who bring in their friends.
3. Party-plan operators, who repay hostesses with incentives, also use them to book new parties. That is, the hostess whose guest agrees to hold a party of her own is usually rewarded with a premium in addition to those earned by sales at her party.
4. Direct sellers may ask customers for permission to use their names with friends and neighbours.

Consumer Sampling. One of the keys to success for many marketers is getting the physical product or service into the hands of the consumer. In some cases, particularly if the products is new or is not a market leader, an effective strategy is to give the product to the consumer, either free or for a small fee. Because of the extremely high costs of sampling consumers in this manner, great care must be taken in employing this technique.

A primary criteria in using sampling when you have a product that virtually sells itself. That is, the product must possess benefits or features that are easily discerned by the consumer. Another factor to consider is whether to provide the product free or to include a nominal charge. There are arguments for and against both. Obviously, giving the product away guarantees that the target market you wish to reach is sampled. On the other hand, this guarantee does not include a certainty that the product will actually be used. Many such products are not normal size, and the consumer has little remorse in discarding it or putting it away for future use. In addition, some consumers view products that cost nothing as being woith that amount. However, the nominal fee helps defray the costs of this promotional technique. Any charge, of course, works against the basic idea of sampling and may help defeat the sampling operation.

There are several ways of distributing the samples to the consumers. The most popular is through the mail. However, the tremendous increase in postage costs, combined with packaging and bundling requirements makes this method increasingly less attractive. An alternative is to use organizations that specialize in door to-door distribution. This approach is particularly attractive with bulky items or in areas where reputable distribution organizations exist. This approach can also allow for a selective sampling technique, in that certain neighbourhoods, dwellings, and even people can be selected, Also, these firms can vary their service from simply hanging a product on every doorknob to actually delivering the product.

Another distribution method is in conjunction with advertising. This may involve a coupon that the consumer can mail in for the product or an address that is mentioned in the body of an advertisement. A similar message may also be included within radio and television messages. The cost of this approach may be quite high given the high cost of advertising space and the low response rate.

Products can also be sampled directly through the retailers. This simply involves either setting up a display unit near the product that allows easy access to that product or hiring a person who physically distributes the product to consumers as they pass by. This technique helps build goodwill for the retailer and is effective in reaching the right consumers. On the other hand, retailers often resent the inconvenience and require high payments in order to cooperate. This technique might also create conflict with other brands sold by the retailer.

The final form of distribution deals with specialty types of sampling. For instance, several companies specialize in packing a group of samples together and delivering the package to a homogeneous consumer group such as newlyweds, new parents, students, or tourists. Such packages may be delivered at hospitals, hotels, or student centres. There has been particular interest recently in the college freshman. Evidence exists' which shows that many important long-term product decisions are made during the seventeen to nineteen year old time period. Consequently, incoming freshmen are given packages of products or coupons that can be redeemed for products.

The arguments supporting sampling as a viable sales promotion device are numerous. Most notably, since it is more and more difficult for marketers to get consumers to take notice of their products, sampling appears to assist in this difficult problem. Also, samples can be distributed in conjunction with other elements of the promotional mix, greatly improving the impact of the overall strategy. The job of the salesperson is made easier when the product is actually in the hands of the consumer. As a matter of fact, sampling may be the primary reason why a retailer would select one manufacturer's product over another.

The criticisms of sampling are also real. There is serious concern over whether sampling costs are excessive when the overall results are considered. Part of this problem relates to the fact that measuring sampling effectiveness is difficult. Perhaps the most serious criticism relates to the inability of the marketer to ascertain whether the product is all propriate for sampling. Also, a product must be unique or of exceptional quality in order to convince the consumer to actually go out and purchase it.

Packaging. It is clear that in the case of many products that average consumer has a low level of product and brand awareness. In these cases, combined with the increased popularity of self-service marketing, the product package becomes the primary selling device. Clearly, this importance is substantiated by the fact that companies spend nearly $ 50 billion a year on the development, design, and manufacturing of packages.

In respect to the definition given to sales promotion earlier, packaging is really a quasi-form of sales promotion. That is, in a very general sense, the package is an immediate incentive in addition to the base product offered to the consumer. Although it may not be separated, from the base product and, consequently, is the product, it never the less has enough characteristics common to the techniques discussed thus far to be classified as sales promotion. Since the inception of modern packaging in the early 1900s, packaging has had two primary purposes. The first is to simply protect the product. The technology in this area has been phenomenal. Packaging exists now that has dramatically extended product shelf life, as well as keeping the product inside safe from damage. In some instances the package protects the consumer from the product. The functional aspect of the package also includes the needs of the reseller. Packages should be easy to box, move, and stack on the retailers shelves.

The second primary purpose of packaging is its ability to promote. In this regard, packaging can perform several promotional roles. It can attract the customers' attention and encourage them to examine the product. Through verbal and non-verbal symbols, the package can inform potential buyers about the product's content, features, uses, advantages, and hazards. A firm can create desirable images and associations by using certain colours, designs, shapes, and textures in packages. Many cosmetics manufacturers, for example, create impressions of richness, luxury, and exclusiveness by using packages of certain colours and shapes. A package may perform a promotional function also when it is designed to be safer or more convenient to use, if such characteristics help stimulate demand.

Regardless of the specific objectives to be achieved by a package, the marketer must be constantly cognizant of the impact that a package may have in promoting the product. For instance, changing the package may have a devastating effect on sales. Attempting to sell a male related product in a package that appears too feminine, may not only lose sales but may also cause the product to be shelved in the wrong part of the store. A package should reflect the positioning strategy of the firm in all ways, from the colour, to the directions, to the style of lettering.

Although not nearly as extensive as consumer sales promotions, promotional efforts directed at the employees of the company have became an important element of the overall marketing programme. Just as there is a need to motivate the consumer to purchase the product, there is an equal need to motivate employees to work harder, to be positive opinion leaders about the company, and to purchase the product. The same high level of satisfaction that is desired in a customer is also desired in employees. Many of the programmes designed to motivate employees' are the responsibility of management primarily the personnel department. This is particularly true with plant-based employees. For example, placing a suggestion box in a plant is a common method reported to make the employees feel as though they are part of the decision-making process. Although this strategy was initiated by personnel, the publicity introducing it, the awards given for good suggestions, and so on, may be the input of the promotional manager. Thus, you are forewarned that in the case of some of these motivational techniques, several areas of management may be involved. Promotions are directed at two groups of employees-plant-based and salespeople. Although this classification clearly does not include all possible employees, it does reflect a huge majority.

Plant-based Employees. Plant-based employees include all employees that are not directly responsible for making sales. It includes peons, office workers, assembly line workers, middle managers, top managers, and so on. It is with this group in particular that many of the motivational programmes are more management inspired and directed. Also, most of these programmes tend to be highly customized to the needs of the company or employee.

Perhaps the most common programme of this type might be titled the orientation or indoctrination programme. It is usually provided to blue collar employees and to employees at the managerial level who are new in the job market. This programme can range from a short speech by someone in the personnel department to a slide presentation, to a full-scale multimedia programme. Regardless of the sophistication of the programme, the content tends to be the same: history of the firm, description of products and distribution net-works, company rules and policies, and reasons for being proud to work for that particular company.

Although there are no measures as to the effectiveness of these programmes, management assumes that providing this information can only help. Another type of programme aimed at plant based employees includes a whole series of efforts that put the employee in contact with the product in some advantageous manner. The most common of these is the company store. Although this inay not actually involve a real store, the crux of the incentive is to allow employees to purchase company products at a greatly reduced price. In the case of companies with a great many sub-idiaries, this could mean a substantial savings for the employee.

For General Motors employees or those working for Airstream it would equate to several hundred dollars off on the purchase of their next automobile or travel trailer. Another programme under this heading is to use employees as part of the product testing process. In some cases, this may even include advertising, packaging, and pricing. For example, many razor blade manufacturers encourage their male employees to shave at the plant every morning with some version of their product. Texas Instruments has market tested many of their learning aids products with the children of employees.

Another whole set of programmes directed at plant-based employees, as well as salespeople, fall under the heading of *fringe benefits*. This includes hospitalization, life insurance, profit sharing, bonus systems, stock options, free uniforms, and free parking just to name a few. Although these programmes tend to fall under the auspices of the personnel department, the promotion department can assist in designing material to present and explain the programmes to employees. The support of many employees has been lost because they misunderstood the benefits they thought they were to receive. The final set of programmes might be labelled as company image or institutional promotion efforts. Research has shown that it is important for employees to be proud of the company for which they work.

Salespeople. Sales promotion activities directed at the sales force is classified in two ways. The first set of activities deals with programmes that better prepare salespeople to do their jobs. This includes sales manuals, training programmes, and sale presentations as well as supportive materials such as films, slides, and other visual aids. The second set of activities are concerned with promotional efforts or incentives that will motivate salespeople to work harder. The types of incentives employed has greatly expanded during the last decade.

Training, the first set of activities, tends to be closely related to the job of the sales manager and will be covered in greater detail in the chapter on personal selling. However, in some firms, the sales promotion staff actually has the responsibility of training and equipping the sales force. They are often involved in designing the actual presentation employed by the sales force. This might include the sales manual, product catalogues, visual aids, photographs, and other materials. Of course, depending on the needs and orientation of the company, the sales promotion staff might be involved in the small part of this effort or not at all.

Probably one of the most common and popular activities under this heading is the sales meeting. These meetings can take place at the local level or internationally, although national meetings are the norm. Depending upon the company and its objectives, the meeting will be some combination of business and pleasure. Often-times, local and regional meetings will be very business-oriented and the national meetings will be primarily educational and social. Although the social elements are important and can be an effective form of motivation, the training and educational elements tend to be more meaningful.

Another part of the training-related process developed for the sales force is supportive materials. This tends to be illustrative materials that either provide information to the salesperson or materials that can be used directly in the sales presentation. Typically the sales manual is the most useful to the salesperson because it contains elements of both product information and the sales presentation. In the case of technical companies with extensive product lines the sales manual might be several books. It usually contains product descriptions, prices, manufacturing processes, delivery times, product applications, and suggested sales techniques to name but a few.

The sales manual is as important to the salesperson as a playbook is to a professional football player. Because much of the information is confidential and the salesperson may make extensive notes within it, it is guarded closely. Often, the sales promotion staff has a large part in the design of this manual. Sales portfolios and product models are devices that are used in conjunction with the sales presentation. The portfolio can take many forms: a flip chart, a ring binder, slides, photographs, transparencies, and so on. It is coordinated with the verbal presentation to illustrate and highlight certain parts of the presentation. The models serve the same purpose, depending upon the need.

Some products demonstrate very well others do not. A prototype or scale model might work well for small equipment, but look like a ridiculous toy for a three-story overhead crane. In the latter case slides or a movie might be substituted, or even more common, the prospect would be taken to where the product is installed and operating. Here again, sales promotion expertise is employed to develop and design the appropriate materials. There are also materials that the sales force receives on a somewhat regular basis. One such example is the house organ. Also known as the company newsletter, newspaper, or magazine, its purpose is to relay company programmes, policies, new products, meetings, awards, and retirements to the personnel.

Larger companies may also develop special bulletins developed just for the sales force. Such bulletins may highlight certain products, meetings, or people. In any case, these types of communications can be helpful in making the salesperson feel informed and in creating higher morale and motivation for the entire sales force. Developing incentive programmes for the sales force is very much the domain of the sales promotion department. Sales incentives have been the fastest growing segment of the incentive field for many years and now also represent the largest single segment. It is not difficult to understand the popularity of this device for improving sales performance. The sales force of any company represents a more or less captive audience-measurable and capable of being reached most readily. This is the most, direct point at which one can apply stimulus to add profitable volume.

Although the prizes or awards given to a salesperson as part of the incentive programme are very important, they are only a part of the incentive programme. There are several other considerations in this process. The first step is to determine the objectives of the incentive programme. The overall objective of any incentive programme, whatever its specific orientation to sales goals, is to get a little more sales effort from everyone in the organization. To do this, the incentives must obviously be keyed to each participant's individual past performance and present potential. This suggests, of fourse, the setting of quotas as a basis for awarding incentives, and a majority of sates incentive campaigns do indeed base awards on quotas. In fact, the success of the wisdom and equity of quotas may very well determine the success of the entire programme. While specific objectives are as individual as the sales manager's name, common objectives are to:

(a) introduce a product to a new distribution area,

(b) reduce selling costs,

(c) improve working habits,

(d) offset competitive promotions, and

(e) increase total sales volume.

Another value of defining objectives lies in the fact that it forces a closer examination of just how the incentive campaign is going to arrive at the objective. This is the second step in the process—to communicate clearly to members of the sales force precisely what they are expected to achieve and how they are to achieve it. This begins by specifying the basis of awards. Four broad methods are used to provide award credits to salespeople.

(1) A fixed number of awards are given to the top producers in terms of total volume.

(2) Awards are tied to unit sales on an absolute basis.

(3) A fixed number of awards are given to those performing best in relation to their individual quota.

(4) A quota is set individually for each salesperson, and awards are based on the percentage of quota performance.

A third step in designing an incentive programme is deciding just which members of the sales force should participate. In some cases, all salespeople may be the obvious answer. But if there are several categories of sales people, divided by product line, by type of account, or In some other manner, it may be appropriate to limit the campaign to one or two groups or to provide different goals and rules for different classes of sales personnel. The fourth step involves several time decisions. Three time factors are important: the specific break time of the promotion, the duration of the campaign, and the planning lead time allowed to prepare for the push.

The promotion break date has to be dictated by marketing decisions. For example, if the sales incentive programme backs a trade or consumer promotion or if a new product is being introduced, these factors will determine when the campaign begins. How long to run the programme is influenced by the user's product distribution, type of salespeople, program objective, and the executives' experience or feeling as to what works best for their particular organization.

Initially, the decision begins with a choice between offering travel, merchandise, or a combination of the two. Travel has come to be the glamour incentive award in recent years, and users will probably wish to consider it if they are planning a relatively long-term promotion with a budget that can be tailored to offer trips to a fair number of winners at the top-with merchandise awards for lower qualifiers. In looking at specific types of merchandise utilized in sales incentive programmes, there are no particular rules except the obvious ones of fitting types of items to the people involved and of matching budget allocations. But it may be useful to see what merchandise is selected by large numbers of salespeople when they are given free choice from a catalogue of thousands of items. Besides merchandise and travel, there are two other forms of prizes used-cash and honour awards.

Cash has several drawbacks associated with it. It has motivational power to the same degree as the salary or commission income of the salesperson, but no special stimulus or recognition value. There are also practical arguments against cash awards. First, cash will buy from a third to twice as much when put into merchandise form. Also, awards offered to salespeople are usually in a class the recipients look on as luxuries. Thus, these awards are special, while the cash may not be. However, during economic down times, cash awards may gain in appeal.

The sixth and final step in developing a sales incentive programme is selecting a theme. Confronted with an important objective, a realistic quota, workable rules and attractive awards, one would think that the average salesperson would be ready to work their tail off for the ABC Corporation. However, it doesn't work that way. The salespeople may know all the right answers as to what they should do and how; they may have a clear view of their own self-interest in the programme, and they may still just stand there. They have to be sold, and sold hard, at every step throughout the campaign. Their imaginations have to be sparked and their enthusiasm fixed up. All the things a sales manager and promotion manager do to promote a campaign stem from one or more words that are called a theme.

The theme of a sales incentive programme is much the same as any other theme, except it may appear a bit more outlandish in some cases. A theme of some sort is necessary to provide a frame for the whole picture of the incentive programme, to give unity to the promotional materials, and to add a little extra fun. Popular themes have been related to games or sports company honour club, to name but a few.

Everybody knows what a middleman or dealer is, but it's hard to find agreement on how to move this person to desired action. A dealer, to generalize a bit, is someone with a very hard head full of gross margin figures, with a store full of absolutely, priceless shelf space, and with very little imagination when it comes to merchandising a manufacturer's product. While the stereotype may be somewhat overdrawn, it is still basically true that in most fields the state of dealer relationships is a source of major frustration. The retailer's perfectly good arithmetic tells him to get the best dollar movement out of every square foot. The manufacturer is certain he has an appealing formula, if the dealer will only push it. Bringing the two points of view closer together is partially the responsibility of sales promotion. There are a great many promotional devices available to the manufacturer that hopefully will convince or motivate middlemen to engage in certain activities. The appropriate devices to employ depend on a myriad of factors such as type of middleman, services offered, product distributed, price structure, margins, competition, and so on. These promotional devices include:

Point-of-purchase displays,

Contests,

Trade shows,

Sales meetings.

Push money,

Dealer Loaders,

and Trade Deals.

Point-of-purchase Displays. Point-of-purchase (POP) displays are provided free by the manufacturer to the retailer in order to promote a particular brand or group of products. The forms POP displays take is really a function of the industry but can include special racks, display cartons, banners, signs, price cards, and mechanical product dispensers.

In an industry such as the grocery field where a consumer spends about three-tenths of a second viewing a particular product, anything that can give a product greater visibility is valuable. This is even more important when evidence suggests that a large percentage of the consumers' choices are actually made in the retail store. And since most retailing is totally or partially self-service, displays playa big role in the decision-making process. However, it is one thing for manufacturers to know POP dIsplays are good for them, but quite another to convince retailers that they will benefit as well. Unfortunately, this is not always accomplished, as judged by a recent estimate that as much as 25 per cent of the free point of purchase material is never used by retailers. Probably the most effective incentive for a middleman to use a POP is for the manufacturer to take great care in planning and designing every detail of the display. If a retailer is willing to use your display there must be a high probability that it will generate greater sales. for the retailer. It is important that the theme shown on the POP material is coordinated with the theme used in advertisements and by salespeople. In addition, the display should be designed with the physical elements of the retailer in mind. Since shelf space is at such a premium, the display should not waste it.

Many of the most successful supermarket displays are end-of-the aisle structures that take up no shelf space. The display should also be well-designed. Structurally, it should be constructed of quality materials so that it is sturdy, will not fall apart, and can be easily assembled and un-assembled. Aesthetically, the display should use colours, pictures, and shapes that are attractive and that harmonize with the general theme of the store. Finally, one of the most successful ways of promoting POP materials is through a professional, well-planned presentation. In the case of Proctor and Gamble, this involves many hours of preparation which would include supportive statistics, examples of the POP, a discussion of the promotional strategy, and good selling techniques.

Contests. As was the case in motivating salespeople, contests can also be developed to motivate middlemen. Thus, much of the criteria described earlier applies equally as well with channel members. The prizes tend to be the same, and there is often a need to customize the programme for the particular reseller group one is trying to motivate. Typically, the prize is awarded to the organization or person who exceeds quota by the largest percentage. Great care is necessary in designing contests. Although there is a need to involve as many people as possible in a contest, the rewards offered may be so stimulating that the possible winners might engage in activities that are detrimental to their companies. Retail salesclerks have been known to push the product of the contest company to the total exclusion of competing brands. These practices can cause serious conflict between channel members. Also, the length and quality of contests need to be carefully governed.

Contests are only effective if they take place periodically. This notion of "something special" should also be displayed in the manner in which the contest is promoted and organized and in which the prizes are awarded. Contests can provide short-term benefits and can help improve the relationship between the manufacturer and other middlemen if conducted properly.

Trade Shows. Thousands of manufacturers of consumer and industrial products display their wares at trade shows. For many types of businesses, trade shows provide the major opportunity to actually write orders for their products. For others, it allows them to demonstrate their products, provide information, answer questions, and to be compared directly with their competitors.

In turn, trade shows allow manufacturers to gather a great deal of information about their competition. Since all the companies are attempting to provide a clear picture of their own products to potential customers, this same information is available to competitors. Consequently, quality, features, prices, and technology can be easily compared. The motivation al aspects of trade shows cannot be underestimated. The booths are usually staffed by the manufacturer's top salespeople. The trade show brings these salespeople into direct contact with top executives representing various middle agents. The salesperson can meet these people, introduce the product, demonstrate it, fleld questions, gather information, and stablish future contacts.

The social aspect of trade shows is also important. The atmosphere tends to be relaxed. A great many free products are distributed. Parties are sponsored by most manufacturers. Unfortunately, this element of trade shows can get out of hand, and sales are garnished by the company that spends the most money on the most outrageous party. Although the trade show is quite a bit less formal than the normal selling situation, it does not mean that any less care should go into its planning. Companies spend more than $7 billion annually on trade shows, and the success for the entire year may hinge on however a company performs at the trade shows. For many companies, all their planning efforts and much of their marketing budget and efforts are directed at the trade show.

Sales Meetings. Somewhat related to trade meetings, but not nearly as elaborate, are sales meetings sponsored by manufacturers or wholesalers. Usually, these meetings are conducted at the regional level and are directed by sales managers and their field force. In some instances, a major marketing officer from corporate headquarters may direct the proceedings. The purposes for these meetings are quite varied. Often times, they occur just prior to the buying season and are used to motivate middle agents, to explain various aspects of the product or the promotional campaign, or simply to answer questions.

Besides annual or semi-annual meetings, there are also periodic meetings that may be called for a whole set of additional reasons. A common set of reasons revolve around the need to stimulate through contests or facts and figures, to discuss problems, and to announce new products. Sales training is also a ma:or part of these meetings. However, a company must be careful anytime it takes employees away from their job. In many cases, special incentives must be offered just to guarantee attendance.

Push Money. Although the term push money as acquired a negative, almost Illegal interpretation, it is a common technique used by many manufacturers. It simply means that for a given period of time, a manufacturer will pay a dealer a monetary bonus for every unit of product sold. For example, a manufacturer of refrigerators might pay a Rs. 500 bonus for model A, Rs. 200 for model B, and Rs. 1000 for model C, between May 1 and September 1. At the end of that period, the dealer would send in evidence of these sales to the manufacturer and would receive a cheque in a few days. As is the case in most of marketing, there are certain situations in which push money is more effective. Undoubtedly it works much better when the dealer has an inherent responsibility for the sale of the product.

Products that have to be demonstrated, explained, or have a high unit cost would be best. This strategy also requires the complete cooperation of the retailer. If retailers feel that push money would be bad for morale or would cause a disproportionate emphasis on a particular brand; they will more than likely to its use. There are also some ethical issues related to push money that have not yet been resolved.

Dealer Loaders. A dealer loader is a premium that is given to a retailer by a manufacturer for buying a certain amount of product. Although there are several possible combinations, two types of dealer loaders are most common. The first is labelled *buying loaders* and are typically gifts given for buying a certain order size. The second is called *display loaders* which in essence is a display that is given to the retailer after it has been taken apart. For instance, Philips may have a display containing several types of appliances as part of a special programe. When the programme is over, the retailer would receive all the appliances if he had purchased the specific order size.

Both strategies can be successful in the right situation. Buying loaders are most often used as a door opener in order to get shelf space in a new retail outlet, or when an exceptionally large amount of product must be sold. Display loaders are used in conjunction with special promotions when it is important to get the point-of-purchase display into the store. The underlying motivation for both is to move large amounts of product in a shorr-period of time.

Trade Deals. Trade deals incorporate a whole series of strategies that have one common theme to encourage middlemen to give your product special promotional effort that it would not normally receive. These promotional efforts can take the form of special displays, larger than usual amounts being purchased, superior store location, or just greater promotional effort. In return, retailers received special allowances, discounts, goods, or cash.

The money spent on trade deals is substantial, and in many industries, such as groceries, it is a fundamental way of doing business. As such, trade deals ate expected in many businesses and may provide the primary incentive in receiving retail support. In addition, these programmes are flexible and can be changed from day-to-day or even more frequently if necessary. The largest problem is making sure that everyone in the organization is aware of these frequent changes. There are many examples of companies that created bad will or lost customers' because not all the parties processing the sales order were aware of these changes. Finally, trade deals can be combined with other promotional strategies that provide an irresistible package for a particular middleman.

The negative aspects of trade deals are also quite real. The most serious has already been alluded to earlier. In many industries, trade deals are expected, and a manufacturer who did not offer such incentives would be doomed to failure. Obviously, these deals can get out of hand quite easily. In some situations, where the retailer may dominate the channel, manufacturers may be played against one another until some have reduced their profit levels to an untenable point. There are also the problems of retailers either not passing the discount on to the consumer or not meeting their end of the agreement. In the former instance, the programme developed by the manufacturer may revolve around a lower price. If the retailer does not cooperate, the manufacturer is put into a dis-advantageous position. The latter problem exists be use it is so difficult to monitor the many retail outlets involved in the promotion. Even if retailers are suspected of pocketing allowance money, there is a great risk in confronting them with the fact.

The Count and Recount. Technique is one approach used as part of the buying allowance. This is the offer of a certain amount of money for each unit of product moved out of a wholesaler's or retailer's warehouse during a specified time period. The title comes from the fact that the local sales representative will take a count of merchandise on hand at the beginning of the period and a final recount at the end of the time period. Thanks to the computer, this counting process can be greatly simplified.

A buy-back allowance is another type of buying allowance. This allowance immediately follows another type of trade deal and offers a specified amount of money for new purchases of the product based upon the quantity of purchases made on the first deal. For example, Proctor Gamble might offer Rs 50 off the price a case of Pentre Shampoo on a count recount deal between July 1 through July 31 and then offer Rs 40 case on a buy-back allowance from August 1 through August 31. The amount allowed on the buy-back cannot excceed the amount bought on the count-recount deal.

The final type of buying allowance is referred to as free goods allowance. This is the offer of a certain amount of product to wholesalers or retailers at no cost but based upon the buying of a stated amount of the same or another product of the manufacturer the middle agent is given free merchandise instead of money. Simply illustrated, a manufacturer might offer a retailer one free case of merhandise for every twenty purchased.

The second category of trad deals relates to advertising and display allowances. An advertising allowance is a common technique employed primarily in the consumer products area. In this situation, the manufacturer pays the wholesaler or retailer a certain amount of money for advertising the manufacturer's product. The money can only used to purchase advertising, although policing this process may prove difficult. Many manufacturer's will require some evidence of performance in order to assure themselves of proper behaviour. Nevertheless, middlemen may view this as a type of personal bonus and engage in devious behaviour such as billing the manufacturer at the much higher national rate rather than the local rate. Several types of criteria can be used to determine the amount of the allowance, from a flat dollar amount to a percentage of gross purchases during a specified time period.

Another form of display or advertising allowance is a dealer listing. In this instance, a manufacturer may be announcing a new product or running a special promotion.

As part of a regional or national campaign the manufacturer will provide space on the advertisement to list all the retailers at which the product may be purchased. This technique not only generates traffic for the retailer but also makes the retailer feel like he is receiving a direct benefit by the manufacturer. There is also a certain prestige involved when a local retailer has his name associated with a national advertisement.

While all of us are familiar with the tools of sales promotion since we constantly use them and are exposed to them, most of us, even marketing professionals, are hardly aware that they are sales promotion devices.

While, in a way, it might seem that sales promotion sprang forth full-grown: like Athena from the head of Zeus in reality it had been there all along, maturing and blossoming without anyone's realizing it. So, as we have seen, now sales promotion is bigger than advertising and is growing by leaps and bounds. What, then, is sales promotion? Perhaps the best way to begin answering this question is to give some examples that are readily recognizable to the consumer. The introduction to Part I provided a few examples of sales promotions employed by some of the nation's airlines. Following are a number of others that might be more familiar.

Other forms of sales promotion include company-sponsored sports event: athletic equipment furnished by the manufacturers gratis to famous sports figures: customized articles of clothing hearing a company trademark, to be worn by salespeople and other personnel; free merchandise, such as clothes, automobiles, and other "props" given to TV programmes in return for a mention in the credits; and merchandise supplied to TV game shown to be used as prizes. Still other types of sales promotion are exhibits, displays, and demonstrations.

Numerous and varied as these' examples of sales promotion are, they represent only a part of the picture. They are just some of the promotions employed by manufacturers and retailers to motivate consumers to buy, including techniques for getting them to try a new product, bringing them into the store, inducing them to keep coming back, and fostering goodwill. Manufacturers' also use sales promotion techniques designed to stimulate retailers, wholesalers, and their own sales personnel to sell.

Sampling is only one of a number of elements that make up what is called the sales promotion mix. These will be covered in greater detail later in this chapter and in other parts of the book. However, in delving into the background of sales promotion, we shall discuss a few promotions that have documented histories as well as some of relatively more recent ancestry. It can be reasonably assumed that premiums, or a primitive form of them, became a part of life long before history began to be recorded. Premiums probably came into existence at approximately the same point; in time when samples first emerged upon the scene.

The first weapon maker to discover that the customer was more likely to purchase a stone knife from him than from his competitor, because he offered a free arrowhead along with his merchandise, had found the secret of motivation by means of premiums. So much for conjecture, however. More tangible evidence, in the form of written documentation, of the vestiges of premium usage during a later period has been found.

Detailed studies of the documents have uncovered facts concerning the merchandising practices of the ancient Greeks and Romans. In Athens, long before the Christian era, purchasers of idols of Zeus, Atlas, Hermes, or other Greek gods received incense, lamps, and drinking cups as free gifts or premiums from the merchants. Other Greek businessmen gave bracelets and jewellery to customers who purchased garments priced above a set minimum. The practice was continued in ancient Rome, where evidence has been discovered indicating that cosmetics dealers gave their customers relatively expensive gold trinkets that reputedly possessed love powers.

The premium, an inducemnt to buy, is such a natural merchandising device that indications of its use have also been found in an ancient civilization that thrived in China for thousands of years before the birth of Christ.

The practice continued and was brought to the new world, where it flourished. One common example was storekeepers' informal custom of giving children candy or a few gumdrops when they accompanied their parents to the general store. Lollipops were, and still are, given by barbers to children to induce them to have their hair cut or to stop them from crying in the barber's chair. Adults, on the other hand, were lured by the unique inducement known as the "baker's dozen." The customer paid for twelve rolls and received an additional one free. All other things being equal, you can bet your bottom dollar that most customers bought from the baker who offered the thirteen rolls than from the one who sold the standard dozen. Present-day variants of this type of promotion include offering two extra packs of cigarettes or a lighter with each carton, adding a free bar of soap to a package of three, and including a few extra ounces of fruit juice in a can at no additional cost to the customer: In the old days the word premium wasn't even used.

Among the advantages accruing to companies that use coupon plans is the brand loyalty of their customers. Coupon collectors rarely change brands. A natural outgrowth of the coupon plan was the trading stamp. The stamps issued by trading stamp companies allowed the customer a little more freedom of choice than cigarette coupons and the trading stamps produced by individual retailers. With the hitter two the consumer is locked in to a particular brand of cigarettes or a specific retail store. However, trading stamps that are issued by Independent stamp manufacturers and are sold to a variety of retail stores allow consumers to obtain their trading stamps from a number of different outlets. Trade shows are another form of sales promotion, but not a consumer type, and are a very positive means of displaying merchandise to dealers and distributors. These shows have their roots in ancient times.

The early existence of trade shows is well documented in a number of passages in the Old Testament. The Book of Esther describes how, for a period of six months. Ahasuerus, King of Persia, "showed the riches of his glorious kingdom," much as the late Shah of Iran, his recent successor, did in a magnificent display at Persepolis, Iran, in 1971. Since Tyre had been established well over 2000 years before the time of the Hebrew prophet who wrote about it, it can be reasonably assumed that trade shows have been around for a long long time.

Archaeologists have discovered even more tangible evidence relating to the early beginnings of point-of-purchase advertising, yet another type of sales promotion. The ancient Roman city of Prompeii, located in southern Italy near Naples, was a flourishing port and a vacation resort for the wealthy. Without warning, one day in the year 79, it was literally buried alive under tons of cinders, ash, and lava by a sudden volcanic eruption of Vesuvius Nearly seventeen centuries later, in 1748, archaeologists rediscovered the city. It was so remarkably preserved by the volcanic ash and cinders that furniture and other household items remained practically in their original state, and point-of-purchase advertising, outdoor advertising, and signs were intact and easily read.

Specially advertising is of much more recent vintage than sampling, premiums, and trade shows, although we can be reasonably sure that some facets of this form of promotion had their roots in antiquity, as well. The first use of advertising specialities in relatively modern times has been traced back to Auburn, New York, and the year 1845. At that time and in that place an insurance salesman attached his business announcements to calendars that he gave away to both existing customers and potential ones. Since that time, speciality advertising has come to include ballpoint pens, key rings, coffee mugs, new kinds of calendars, and scores of other useful, relatively inexpensive items that carry a printed advertising message and are given freely, with no obligation on the part of the recipient. Sometimes the advertising speciality is related to the donor's business. By their very nature, road maps given by oil companies and recipe booklets distributed by food manufacturers and processors encourage the recipient to use more of the product being promoted by the manufacturer.

To establish the relationship between sales promotion and marketing, we can say that sales promotion is a component of the latter, once removed. However, to make a family analogy, we might say that sales promotion is a grandchild of marketing. In this respect, a family tree provides an excellent graphic display. Broken down to its principal elements, marketing has four major sub-divisions that make up the marketing mix. To simplify the study of the discipline, they have been called the "four P's: product, place, price, and promotion. Each of these may be likened to a son or daughter in the marketing family and can be depicted as the major limbs of the tree. So when we examine the elements of promotion which are advertising, personal selling, publicity, and sales promotion we are looking at the branches or twigs on the limb: the next generation of marketing, known in the trade as the promotion mix and also as the tools of selling.

Advertising

The most glamorous elements of the promotion mix are contained in advertising. It is readily known to us through the miss media, which it employs to deliver its message. We see it on TV, in our newspaper is and magazines, on outdoor billboaras, and in trains, buses, and taxicabs. And we receive it in our mail and hear it on our radios. Although there are others, these, in essence, are the principal media through which advertising informs us and/or attempts to persuade us to do something. Usually we are being asked to buy something, whether it be a product, a service, or an idea.

Advertising is, in fact, the most important means of announcing sales promotions. By definition: Advertising is a tool of marketing for communication of ideas and information about goods or services to a group; it employ paid space or time in the media or uses another communication vehicle to carry its message; and it openly identifies the advertiser and his relationship to the sales efforts.

Personal Selling. While advertising is impersonal and directs its message to a mass market, personal selling, as the term implies, usually involves one salesperson and one customer. However, a number of salespeople can make a presentation to a group representing one company that is a potential buyer, or even to a group of individual buyers representing more than one company. Personal selling is present at each marketing level, ranging from the salesperson at the local hole in wall store through wholesalers salespeople and manufacturers' sales forces who sell to wholesalers, large retail chains, and other manufacturers.

The presentation of a product, service, or idea by a salesman in direct contact with his prospect. It covers all types of salesmanship, including telephone selling, and [illegible] middlemen, and the [illegible] consumer.

Publicity

This element of the promotion mix is in reality an important part of public relations. Public relations has always been considered a tool of management, which calls upon it to interpret and to announce corporate positions and policy as well as to handle consumer, community, employee, and stockholder relations, among other things. While public relations still retains its former management functions, two of its components, publicity and press agentry, play an important role in marketing and in the promotion mix. Publicity, alpng with advertising, makes known the birth of new products or services and of improvements to them. It accomplishes this end through press releases or news stories sent to the various news and trade media, press conferences, and other media events, and press agentry calls attention to them by other methods. Along with advertising, publicity is a means of bringing sales promotions to the attention of the public.

Sales Promotion. Essentially, the job of sales promotion, the subject of this book is exactly what the term implies the promotion of sales. However, advertising, publicity, and personal selling also promote sales. The definition provided by the American Marketing Association leaves to sales promotion those activities not covered by the other three areas of the promotion mix, as well as various non-recurring selling efforts that are not ordinarily considered part of marketing;. The following is a consolidation of the best definitions of sales promotion, together with some contributions from the author.

Sales promotion consists of all the marketing and promotion activities, other than advertising, personal selling, and publicity, that motivate and encourage the consumer to purchase, by means of such inducements as premiums, advertising specialities; samples, cents-off coupons, sweepstakes, contests, games, trading stamps, refunds, rebates, exhibits, displays, and demonstrations. It is employed, as well, to motivate retailers', wholesalers', and manufacturers' sales forces to sell, through the use of such incentives as awards or prizes, direct payments and allowances, cooperative advertising, and trade shows.

Roger A. Strang of the University of Southern California, differs with the traditional definitions of sales promotion. He correctly points out that all of them suggest that sales promotion "is a catch-all for all those marketing activities which do not fall neatly into advertising, personal selling or publicity. This he believes to be wholly inadequate. The definition he offers is certainly less complicated: "Sales promotions are short-term incentives to encourage purchase or sale of a product or service."

The difference between promotion and sales promotion. By this time it should be perfectly clear that although they are related and the terms are similar, there is a significant difference between promotion and sales promotion. As it has been explained, sales promotion is a part or subdivision of promotion. Promotion encompasses all the tools of selling, including sales promotion, and is itself a component of marketing. It is responsible for moving the demand curve upward and to the right by utilizing some or all of the elements of the promotion mix-advertising, personal selling, and publicity, along with sales promotion.

Some claim that point-of-purchase advertising belongs in the category of advertising rather than sales promotion or that trade shows are a part of advertising or personal selling, rather than a part of sales promotion. Others may contend that exhibits and displays, along with the sponsorship of sports and special events, are more closely related to publicity or publics relations. Still others hold that direct-mail advertising comes under the aegis of sales promotion rather than advertising. It might also be argued that travel incentives are a form of premium or prize—a service premium. And so it may well be. However, premiums, prizes, and travel incentives still remain under the broad banner of sales promotion.

❐